The Neuropsychology of Schizophrenia

edited by
Anthony S. David
*King's College Hospital
and the Institute of Psychiatry, London*

John C. Cutting
*Honorary Senior Lecturer,
Institute of Psychiatry, London*

LAWRENCE ERLBAUM ASSOCIATES, PUBLISHERS
Hove (UK)   Hillsdale (USA)

Lawrence Erlbaum Associates Ltd., Publishers
27 Palmeira Mansions
Church Road
Hove
East Sussex, BN3 2FA
U.K.

British Library Cataloguing in Publication Data
Neuropsychology of Schizophrenia. –
    (Brain Damage, Behaviour & Cognition
    Series, ISSN 0967-9944)
    I. David, Anthony S.   II. Cutting, John
    III. Series
    616.85

    ISBN 0–86377–303–6 (Hbk)

Typeset by DP Photosetting, Aylesbury, Bucks
Printed and bound by BPCC Wheatons, Exeter

Contents

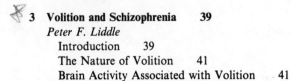

List of Contributors

Richard Bentall, Department of Clinical Psychology, Liverpool University, PO Box 147 Liverpool, L69 3BX, U.K.

Monte S. Buchsbaum, Department of Psychiatry, Mount Sinai School of Medicine, New York, New York 10029, U.S.A.

John C. Cutting, Institute of Psychiatry, De Crespigny Park, Denmark Hill, London SE5.

Anthony S. David, Department of Psychological Medicine, King's College Hospital and Institute of Psychiatry, London, SE5 9RS, U.K.

Michael E. Dawson, Department of Psychology, University of Southern California, Los Angeles, California 90089, U.S.A.

Karel W. de Pauw, Department of Psychiatry, Doncaster Royal Infirmary, Armthorpe Road, Doncaster, DN2 5LT, U.K.

Gillian Dunkley, West Dorset Psychology Services, 10 Cornwall Road, Dorchester, DT1 1RT, U.K.

Terry Early, Department of Psychiatry and Behavioral Sciences, Mail Route D-28, University of Texas Medical Branch, 301 University Avenue, Galveston, TX 77555-0428, U.S.A.

Hadyn Ellis, School of Psychology, University of Wales College of Cardiff, PO Box 901, Cardiff, CF1 3YG, U.K.

Kirsten Fleming, National Institute of Mental Health Neuroscience Center at St Elizabeth's, 2799 Martin Luther King Jr Avenue, Washington D.C. 20032, U.S.A.

Simon Fleminger, Academic Department of Psychiatry, London Hospital Medical College, Turner Street, London, EC1 2AD, U.K.

Chris Frith, MRC Cyclotron Unit, Hammersmith Hospital, DuCane Road, London, W12 0HS and Psychology Department, University College, Bedford Way, London, WC1H 0AT, U.K.

James M. Gold, National Institute of Mental Health Neuroscience Center at St Elizabeth's, 2799 Martin Luther King Jr Avenue, Washington D.C. 20032, U.S.A.

Terry Goldberg, National Institute of Mental Health Neuroscience Centre at St Elizabeth's Hospital, Washington D.C. 20032, U.S.A.

Michael Green, UCLA Research Center, Box 6022, Camarillo, California 93011, U.S.A.

Christian Guth, Wagner–Jauregg–Krankenhaus, Linz, Austria.

John W. Haller, Department of Psychiatry, Washington University School of Medicine, 4940 Audubon Avenue, St Louis, Missouri 63110, U.S.A.

David Hemsley, Department of Psychology, Institute of Psychiatry, London, SE5 8AF, U.K.

John R. Hodges, Addenbrookes' Hospital, Hills Road, Cambridge, CB2 2QQ, U.K.

Ralph Hoffman, Department of Psychiatry, Yale Psychiatric Institute, Yale University School of Medicine, New Haven, Connecticut 06520, U.S.A.

Peter Jones, Department of Psychological Medicine, Institute of Psychiatry, Denmark Hill, London, SE5 8AF, U.K.

Shôn Lewis, Academic Department of Psychiatry, Charing Cross & Westminster Medical School, Fulham Palace Rd, London, W6 8AF, U.K.

Peter Liddle, Royal Postgraduate Medical School, Hammersmith Hospital, Du Cane Road, London W12 0HS, U.K.

Peter McKenna, Fulbourn Hospital, Cambridge, CB1 5EF, U.K.

Ann M. Mortimer, Charing Cross Hospital Medical School and St Bernard's Hospital, Ealing, Middlesex, UB1 3EU, U.K.

Robin Murray, Department of Psychological Medicine, Institute of Psychiatry, Denmark Hill, London, SE5 8AF, U.K.

Hazel E. Nelson, Horton Hospital, Long Grove Road, Epsom, Surrey, KT19 8PZ, U.K.

Keith H. Nuechterlein, Neuropsychiatric Institute, University of California, 300 UCLA Medical Plaza, Los Angeles, California 90024, U.S.A.

Christos Pantelis, The Mental Health Research Institute & Royal Park Hospital, Private Bag 3, Parkville, Victoria 3052, Australia.

Michael I. Posner, Department of Psychiatry, Washington University School of Medicine, 4940 Audubon Avenue, St Louis, Missouri 63110, U.S.A.

Marc Raichle, Department of Psychiatry, Washington University School of Medicine, 4940 Audubon Avenue, St Louis, Missouri 63110, U.S.A.

Jill Rapaport, Department of Psychiatry, Yale University School of Medicine, New Haven, Connecticut 06520, U.S.A.

Daniel Rogers, Burden Neurological Hospital, Stoke Lane, Stapleton, Bristol, BS16 1QT, U.K.

Peter Slade, Department of Clinical Psychology, Liverpool University, PO box 147, Liverpool, L69 3BX, U.K.

Elaine Walker, Department of Psychology, Emory University, Atlanta, Georgia 30322, U.S.A.

Brain Damage, Behaviour and Cognition
Developments in Clinical Neuropsychology

Series Editors
Chris Code, University of Sydney, Australia
Dave Müller, Suffolk College of Higher and Further Education, U.K.

Published titles

Cognitive Rehabilitation Using Microcomputers
Veronica A. Bradley, John L. Welch and Clive E. Skilbeck

The Characteristics of Aphasia
Chris Code (Ed.)

The Neuropsychology of Schizophrenia
Anthony S. David and John C. Cutting (Eds)

Neuropsychology and the Dementias
Siobhan Hart and James M. Semple

Acquired Neurological Speech/Language Disorders in Childhood
Bruce E. Murdoch (Ed.)

Neuropsychology of the Amnesic Syndrome
Alan J. Parkin and Nicholas R.C. Leng

Clinical and Neuropsychological Aspects of Closed Head Injury
John T.E. Richardson

Unilateral Neglect: Clinical and Experimental Studies
Ian H. Robertson and J.C. Marshall (Eds)

Acquired Apraxia of Speech in Aphasic Adults
Paula A. Square (Ed.)

Cognitive Rehabilitation in Perspective
Rodger Wood and Ian Fussey (Eds)

Forthcoming title

Clinical Neuropsychology of Alcoholism
Robert G. Knight and Barry E. Longmore

Series Preface

From being an area primarily on the periphery of mainstream behavioural and cognitive science, neuropsychology has developed in recent years into an area of central concern for a range of disciplines. We are witnessing not only a revolution in the way in which brain–behaviour–cognition relationships are viewed, but a widening of interest concerning developments in neuropsychology on the part of a range of workers in a variety of fields, Major advances in brain-imaging techniques and the cognitive modelling of the impairments following brain damage promise a wider understanding of the nature of the representation of cognition and behaviour in the damaged and undamaged brain.

Neuropsychology is now centrally important for those working with brain-damaged people, but the very rate of expansion in the area makes it difficult to keep up with findings from current research. The aim of the *Brain Damage, Behaviour and Cognition* series is to publish a wide range of books which present comprehensive and up-to-date overviews of current developments in specific areas of interest.

These books will be of particular interest to those working with the brain-damaged. It is the editors' intention that undergraduates, postgraduates, clinicians and researchers in psychology, speech pathology and medicine will find this series a useful source of information on important current developments. The authors and editors of the books in this series are experts in their respective fields, working at the forefront of contemporary reseearch. They have produced texts which are accessible and scholarly. We thank them for their contribution and their hard work in fulfilling the aims of the series.

CC and DJM
Sydney, Australia and Ipswich, UK
Series Editors

Conference speakers and discussants **Back Row**, left to right: E. Walker, E. Taylor, T. Shallice, T. Goldberg, H. Ellis, P. Garety, J. Gray, D. Hemsley, S. Fleminger, H. Nelson, T. Early, C. Pantelis, M. Green, K. Nuechterlein, P. Slade. **Front Row**, left to right: R. Bentall, C. Frith, P. Liddle, R. Hoffman, J. Cutting, A. David, D. Rogers, S. Lewis.

Foreword

Early in 1991, we had the idea for a book on the neuropsychology of schizophrenia, for which there seemed to be an obvious need. The trouble with such ideas is knowing whether they are shared by colleagues and peers. We decided that the best way to test this was to organise an international symposium on the topic at the Institute of Psychiatry in London. This took place on the 10th and 11th October of that year. The response from invited speakers was extremely encouraging, as was the meeting's attendance. The book was the natural next step. However, books of conference proceedings litter the shelves of libraries and offices, standing in testament to wasted human endeavour, not to mention wasted natural resources. We were determined that this should not be just "the book of the conference"; the publishers agreed. To ensure this, contributors were chosen because of their eminence in the field as well as for their skill as communicators. Their brief was wide, in that we asked for detailed reviews, empirical data, and theoretical speculation, all in the same chapter! The symposium served to focus the minds of the contributors into producing early drafts, which were precirculated and later mulled over in the light of discussions during and after the symposium. Eventually, completed chapters emerged, which we believe cover the breadth and depth of this exciting hybrid discipline. We trust their efforts were worthwhile.

The meeting and hence this book would not have been possible without the generous support of The Wellcome Trust. Lundbeck Pharmaceuticals and Sandoz (UK) also provided sponsorship, for which we are grateful.

Finally we thank the staff of the Institute of Psychiatry, in particular Mrs Lee Wilding for her administrative help.

ASD and JC
October 1992

1

The Neuropsychology of Schizophrenia—Introduction and Overview

Anthony S. David
Department of Psychological Medicine, King's College Hospital and the Institute of Psychiatry, London.

John C. Cutting
Institute of Psychiatry, London

The idea that there is a "neuropsychology of schizophrenia" is of relatively recent origin. Indeed, the term "neuropsychology" itself only dates back three or four decades. The concept to which it refers, however, is far from new.

The thrust of Kraepelin's and most of his *fin de siècle* German contemporaries' research into schizophrenia was towards elucidating the biological basis of the condition, which included questions such as whether particular parts of the brain were damaged more than others. The spate of higher-order neurological deficits uncovered in the last half of the nineteenth century—aphasia, agnosia, apraxia, alexia, etc.—led many psychiatrists to suppose that schizophrenia, like these other conditions, would turn out to have a specific link with some damaged brain site, e.g. Broca's aphasia with a lesion in the left second and third frontal gyri. A minority of more neurologically-orientated physicians (e.g. Wernicke and Kleist) did, in fact, develop just such a detailed system (without any real neurobiological evidence, however). Kraepelin, although committed to this approach, was rigorous enough to realise that he could not as yet justify such schemes.

Bleuler's incorporation of Freud's and Jung's psychodynamic explanations of psychiatric phenomena paved the way for a multitude of non-neuropsychological approaches—psychodynamic, social, existential, behavioural, and cognitive models—which persisted as the mainstream of thinking for over 70 years. All these merely adopted some current

1

psychological model of mind (or non-mind in the case of behavioural) and schizophrenia was slotted into these in the most plausible way possible.

As late as the early 1980s, when one of us was contemplating a book on the matter, the title *Neuropsychology of Schizophrenia* was suggested to a publisher, who was enthusiastic about the title as anything to do with the brain was becoming a selling-point in the United States. By the time the literature had been reviewed, however, it was clear that, apart from Kraepelin's, Wernicke's, and Kleist's modest beginnings, there was no corpus of work on the neuropsychology of schizophrenia, and the name was changed to *The Psychology of Schizophrenia* (Cutting, 1985). Ten years on, the situation is radically different. All the chapters in this book reflect this to a greater or lesser degree. Even those contributors who are still promoting what are essentially "preneuropsychological era" models, feel obliged to give their views some neuropsychological relevance.

Is there a common definition of the neuropsychology of schizophrenia? As already mentioned, neuropsychology *per se* is a new term, although its origin may have had psychiatric connections. Perhaps the first use of the word was in 1913, when Sir William Osler spoke at the opening of the Henry Phipps Psychiatric Clinic of the Johns Hopkins Hospital, Baltimore (Bruce, 1985). This was just 2 years after Bleuler's description of *The Schizophrenias* (Bleuler, 1911–1950). The second landmark was the appointment of Karl Lashley as Research Professor of Neuropsychology at Harvard in 1937. However, Donald Hebb's book, *The Organisation of Behaviour: a Neuropsychological Theory*, published in 1949, finally established neuropsychology on the intellectual map. Coming more up to date, the first journal devoted to the topic was launched in 1963—*Neuropsychologia*, edited by Henry Hécaen.

One way to avoid the arbitrariness of definitions is to look at current usage. Unfortunately this takes us even further from consensus. A recent target article in the journal *Behavioural and Brain Sciences* by Gray et al. (1991) carried the same title of this book, and Hemsley (Chapter 6) summarises many of the underlying theoretical points made in that article. For Gray and colleagues, neuropsychology is any study of behaviour in relation to the hardware of the brain (see also Robbins, 1990). In this case the brain refers to any brain, including that of the rat. The "neuro" prefix comes in because of experimental manipulation of that organ, either through lesioning or pharmacological agents. The limitations and advantages of inferences about human behaviour derived from animal work have been much debated over the years. Clearly they have an important place in providing the foundation to human neuropsychological theories.

Another usage is the application of psychometric tests derived from studies on populations with known brain lesions, to psychiatric patients. This is perhaps the most traditional form of psychiatric neuropsychology

(David, 1989). It can be subdivided into the use of broad test batteries, which show patterns of deficits in, for example, visual–spatial or linguistic skills, which in turn may be interpreted in terms of right and left hemisphere problems (e.g. Flor-Henry & Gruzelier, 1983; see also Liddle, Chapter 3), and the use of more specific, custom-built tests intended to examine in detail a single psychological function or brain area, e.g. the use of the Tower of London and Wisconsin Card Sort test (WCST) (Shallice et al., 1991), or chimeric faces, a right posterior hemisphere test, (David & Cutting, 1990; see also Ellis and de Pauw, Chapter 18; Pantelis and Nelson, Chapter 13; Cutting, Chapter 14). This approach is, in essence, argument by analogy; the analogy may hold at a number of levels. For instance, at the behavioural level, the apathy and amotivation of the frontal-lobe-patient may resemble that of the chronic schizophrenic, as well as at the neuropsychological level, when there may be frequent perseverative errors on the WCST in both patient groups. Dunkley and Rogers (Chapter 11) go as far as to say that dementia praecox is as much a dementia as that of the Alzheimer type.

There is no reason why the neuropsychologist should be wedded to psychiatric nosology and indeed this may lead research into blind alleys. O'Carroll (1992) in a recent review showed how neuropsychology could act at different clinical levels from the diagnostic, e.g. schizophrenia (Dunkley and Rogers, Chapter 11; Pantelis and Nelson, Chapter 13), through the syndromic or subsyndromic, e.g. positive syndrome (Hemsley, Chapter 6), negative syndrome (Frith, Chapter 9), the "reality distortion" of Liddle (Chapter 3) to the symptom level, e.g. delusions (Bentall, Chapter 19), delusional misidentification (Ellis and de Pauw, Chapter 19), and hallucinations (Slade, Chapter 15; David, Chapter 17).

Fortunately, advances in neuroscience and neuroimaging have allowed these analogies, particularly with respect to brain localisation, to be tested. The structure of the brain region of interest may be examined with the detailed morphometry of the psychoneuropathologist or through CT and magnetic resonance brain imaging. Similarly, functional imaging utilising metabolism or cerebral blood flow (Early et al., Chapter 2; Liddle, Chapter 3) may serve not only to test the pattern of activation at rest or in response to a cognitive challenge (Weinberger et al., 1986; see also Nuechterlein et al., Chapter 4; Fleming et al., Chapter 12), but also the assumptions about the regional specificity of the test in question, based on patient data and crude clinicopathological correlations, which often turn out to be spurious. Also, the power of pharmacological agents to modify and produce abnormal psychological phenomena requires localisation in terms of neurotransmitter sites as well as functionally specific anatomical regions (Early et al., Chapter 2).

Early and colleagues report two separate findings in non-medicated schizophrenics: (1) an increase in blood flow (relative to the rest of the brain) in a subcortical region on the left; and (2) a tendency to ignore stimuli presented in the right visual field. Although this is in support of some lateralized deficit—neurobiological and psychological—in schizophrenia, it is somewhat idiosyncratic. The neurobiological finding is in line with several studies showing left hemisphere overactivity and right hemisphere under-activity in the condition. The psychological finding is curious, however, because visual neglect in subjects with focal lateralised brain damage is virtually always restricted to the *left* visual field, unless there is anomalous lateralisation of the search control mechanism. Moreover, right hemisphere damage also impairs search in the right visual field more than does left hemisphere damage in that (right) field.

Liddle (Chapter 3) reports different patterns of blood flow in different subtypes of schizophrenia. Patients with predominantly poverty of speech, flat affect, and decreased spontaneous movement exhibited reduced left-sided dorsolateral frontal perfusion. Patients with predominantly thought disorder and inappropriate affect exhibited decreased right-sided ventral frontal perfusion. One patient with catatonia resembled the former group.

It is not surprising that different symptom clusters in schizophrenia are associated with different blood flow patterns. Different mental activities provoke different blood flow patterns in normals, of course. Liddle's results, however, are intriguing because they go some way towards mapping the cerebral dysfunction in different subtypes, though whether they reflect an end-stage cerebral dysfunction or some primary problem is not clear. The patients were all medicated.

As mentioned earlier, neuropsychology owes its distinctiveness from the rest of psychology by virtue of its reference to the brain. However, this has led to an obsession with brain localisation. While the location of schizophrenic disturbances to a cortical area would be a valuable achievement, the story would not end there. In fact this would provide but one link in a complete neuropsychology of schizophrenia chain, which would stretch from neural ultrastructure and chemical transmission to the most abstract of phenomenal experiences. Neuropsychology can justifiably regard as its legitimate domain the intervening steps between the abstract levels of representation—hallucinations, delusions, etc. and "pure" psychological phenomena, e.g. memory and attention. No direct reference may be made to the brain provided two underlying assumptions are held, namely, that these psychological processes may become distorted by dysfunction at a lower level—in the brain—and that schizophrenia is the manifestation of just such a distortion. In other words, cognitive psychology may be applied usefully to the study of schizophrenia but some reference to the biological underpinnings to cognition must be made eventually (Fleminger, Chapter 20; Bentall, Chapter 19; Slade, Chapter 15). This is the chief difference between the work done in the 1980s and earlier work.

Much of the earlier endeavour may be described as "preneuropsychological" only insofar as neural bases for such phenomena as described by Green and Nuechterlein (Chapter 5) have yet to be elucidated fully. Green and Nuechterlein report abnormalities in processing visual information in schizophrenia, measured by a technique known as "backward masking", in which two stimuli are presented for recognition, at different interstimulus intervals, with the purpose of evaluating the potency of the "sensory register" or "icon"; manics were equally impaired. This study illustrates the typical "preneuropsychology of schizophrenia methodology" amongst psychological studies on schizophrenia, and is included as an excellent example of its kind. Green and Nuechterlein attempt a bold integration of their findings (personal communication). They suggest that the interruption of information from a target involves the interaction of transient and sustained visual channels, which do not appear to interact before the level of the primary visual cortical area. The deficit observed may be an example of a general sensory gating deficit, which involves the failure to attenuate the second of two paired stimuli (in this case the mask). Gating is believed to involve mesolimbic dopamine pathways in the brain.

McKenna and colleagues (Chapter 10) adopt the traditional approach to the psychology of schizophrenia: examining one mental function—memory—and comparing its potency in schizophrenics and normals. What gives this chapter a neuropsychological slant is the choice of memory, as this is conventionally regarded as relatively intact in schizophrenics, but impaired if brain damage is present. McKenna et al. find gross memory deficits in their schizophrenics, especially in the realm of semantic memory. This has less in common with the everyday concept of memory but refers to a store of knowledge about the world. McKenna et al. speculate that access to this store may be unreliable, giving rise not only to deficit but also to "productive" symptoms such as illogicality and delusions. This has some resemblance to Cutting's theory regarding impaired real-world knowledge and schizophrenia. Cutting (Chapter 14) puts forward a strong case for this to be the result of right hemisphere dysfunction, having first outlined the ground rules for such an inference (see also Cutting, 1990).

Fleming et al. (Chapter 12) propose that the memory deficit in schizophrenia is a result of some higher-order control-mechanism disorder, which is itself a consequence of frontal lobe dysfunction. This chapter conforms to the newer neuropsychological approach of trying to relate some psychological deficit in schizophrenia to a comparable psychological deficit in subjects with known brain disease. It is theoretical, but draws on data from such diverse sources as twin studies and cerebral blood flow conducted at the United States' National Institute of Mental Health.

Pantelis and Nelson (Chapter 13) set out to examine theoretical formulations, such as those of Fleming et al., by administering recognised frontal lobe tests to schizophrenics. The authors find evidence for frontal lobe dysfunction in schizophrenia but extend this anatomical localisation to subcortical connections. The "frontal lobe hypothesis" of schizophrenia is fashionable at the moment and, although not all neurobiological procedures confirm it, certainly has to be taken seriously on the evidence of results such as these.

In the case of Frith's work on the theory of mind (Chapter 9), there has been very little time to examine brain–cognition relationships in detail. Frith approaches the problem of the psychological deficit in schizophrenia from two relatively novel angles. The first relies on new findings on the nature of cognitive development in infants. The second incorporates the tendency in experimental psychological research to talk in terms of metapsychological entities, i.e. to go beyond the base mental functions (attention, perception, memory, etc.) and examine how the person's whole mind tackles complex problems, including how it monitors and evaluates its own activity. The chapter is a theoretical discussion of how different levels of metapsychological development/maldevelopment might give rise to specific schizophrenic symptoms. The discussion does have a strong neuropsychological element, in that putative abnormalities in schizophrenia are related to functions of various parts of the brain (see also Frith & Done, 1988). In any event, psychological "facts", be they metapsychological or whatever, will remain so in spite of advances in the neurosciences. In this sense they are not reducible (Churchland, 1988). Nevertheless, the two-way flow of information between neurological and psychological sciences, whose interface is neuropsychology, can only serve to illuminate the study of schizophrenia and other enigmas. Exemplifying this is the work contained in Nuechterlein et al.'s chapter (Chapter 4). Nuechterlein and co-workers studied PET scans and EEG coherence, during an attention task—the continuous performance test—known to be sensitive to right hemisphere activity, and found impairment in schizophrenia. These results are consistent with other neurobiological and psychological studies implicating right hemisphere dysfunction in schizophrenia, although prefrontal areas may also be implicated.

One study which is in some way an exception is that by Bentall (Chapter 19), who presents a coherent account of the nature and cognitive underpinnings of paranoid delusions. What is distinctive about this chapter is that it underplays the role of brain dysfunction or even abnormal perceptual experiences. Instead, Bentall portrays delusions as extensions of normal beliefs and this is backed up by experimental evidence from patients. Like Fleminger's chapter (Chapter 20), Bentall's is complementary to the entirely brain-based accounts contained elsewhere in this book.

This discussion leads on to another hybrid label: cognitive neuropsychology. This is a new branch of psychology as well as a very old one (see Ellis &

Young, 1988; McCarthy & Warrington, 1990). Here the aim of study is to elucidate the cognitive subcomponents of psychological processes. The existence of these subcomponents or abstract "modules" (Fodor, 1983), is inferred from their absence in cases of focal brain damage or disease. The study of patients with cerebral lesions is therefore only a means to an end. Can this approach be tailored to psychiatric disorders? Ellis and de Pauw (Chapter 18) provide a rationale concerning the origin of Capgras syndrome, one form of delusional misidentification, and David (Chapter 17) outlines the sort of models of normal cognition that might become distorted to produce key psychological symptoms such as auditory hallucinations. Ellis and de Pauw provide us with a comprehensive and critical review, finally espousing what the authors refer to as cognitive neuropsychiatry. It is predicted that such an approach may be seen more often in the future (David, 1993).

The levels of explanation and investigation, as well as the parallels between the traditional subject matter of neuropsychology and that of psychopathology, are shown in Table 1.1. The example of a cerebrovascular accident affecting the left hemisphere is compared with schizophrenia.

Neuropsychology is not only defined by its subject matter, or indeed by its aims. It has as its hallmark a methodology, part statistical technique, part theory, and part experimental strategy. This is the dissociation of function or, more distinct still, the double dissociation of function (Teuber, 1955). This may be applied to a single case or to a series. It describes a pattern of results in which one task is impaired, usually markedly so, in relation to another or, in the case of a double dissociation, there are at least two subjects, one of whom has a dissociation of function in one direction and the other has it in the other direction. This notion has been analysed in detail and refined (Shallice, 1988) but remains a potent force behind neuropsychological research. Dissociations, be they single or double, are rarely described overtly in schizophrenia research yet as leading commentators

TABLE 1.1
The Levels of Explanation for Neurological and Psychological Disorders

	Aetiology	Pathology	Brain localisation	Clinical syndrome	Phenomenology	Cognition
Neurology	Genetic Smoking HBP, etc.	Ischaemia/ infarction	e.g. left hemisphere	"Stroke"	Aphasia Alexia	e.g. optic aphasia Phonological dyslexia
Psychiatry	Genes ?virus ?Obstetric complications ?Toxins	?Dystrophy/ atrophy ?Receptor overactivity	?Temporal lobes ?Frontal lobes	Schizophrenia or psychosis	Hallucination Delusion Amotivation	?Inner speech ?Reasoning ?Planning

argued some two decades ago, much research founders on this issue. Chapman and Chapman (1973) described what has become known as the "differential deficit problem" in such research. They argued that what may be taken for a dissociation may in fact be an artifact of a failure of the two tasks in question to be matched accurately on such factors as reliability and, especially, difficulty. As schizophrenics are liable to do badly on most tasks for a variety of theoretically trivial reasons, the experimenter must convince the sceptic that the bad performance is specific to a particular task, justified and predicted *a priori*. The sceptic will be persuaded only by a clear demonstration of adequate or good performance on a well-matched control task, or better still, if performance is superior on the control task, in relation to a comparison group, a version of the double dissociation (see Hemsley, Chapter 6).

Hemsley reports a study using a classic behavioural technique derived from animal research. The technique is known as "latent inhibition" and tests a subject's ability to inhibit a conditioned response to two stimuli. Schizophrenics were less likely than normals to be influenced by the earlier conditioning, and achieved an association between one of the stimuli and a new stimulus *more readily*. Hemsley argues that this behaviour, i.e. being less influenced by previous associations between events in a subject's current behaviour, is a core problem in schizophrenia and explains most of the complex features of the condition. Although this is not primarily a neuropsychological approach, the search for dissociations is. Hemsley also invokes some speculation concerning the involvement of the left hemisphere in the task he employs.

Encompassed in this book are some novel approaches to the study of schizophrenia; these include research from a neurodevelopmental framework. The observation that disturbances in cognitive and motor function may precede the onset of schizophrenia has given much impetus to new theories concerning both aetiology and pathogenesis (Jones et al., Chapter 8; Walker, Chapter 7). Walker relies on one of the harder pieces of evidence for pinpointing the neuropsychological substrate of schizophrenia— lateralised motor pathology in children who subsequently become schizophrenic. She also uses one of the most innovative and direct techniques of all the contributors here. She obtained "home movies" of the children of families in whom one child subsequently became schizophrenic. Comparing developmental abnormalities in the schizo- phrenic-to-be child with its normal-to-be sibling the most striking difference was an increased incidence of left-body side abnormalities, i.e. emanating from right hemisphere dysfunction. This study is outstanding, for its ingenuity and for its combining neuropsychological and developmental research principles.

Jones and colleagues examined the intelligence quotients of subjects who eventually become schizophrenic, comparing these with those eventually developing affective disorder. The preschizophrenic subjects had lower intelligence quotients than the preaffectives. They concluded that this represented an earlier onset of the condition in schizophrenia as opposed to affective psychosis. Jones and colleagues take overall intellectual performance as evidence of brain ability, and note deficits in schizophrenia vis-à-vis controls, especially males, the gender prone to "developmental" disorders.

These apparent continuities and discontinuities between childhood and adult psychopathology force a third question on to the neuropsychological research agenda. Not only must we find out what happened to the brain and where, but also when. The temporal dimension does not end with the onset of the disorder. Whether or not the lesion or lesions responsible for schizophrenia are static, the clinical state appears to change with time (Dunkley and Rogers, Chapter 11; Pantelis and Nelson, Chapter 13). Dunkley and Rogers examine the Kraepelinian notion that schizophrenics do indeed have a dementia, not explained by the social understimulation endemic in a psychiatric hospital, nor by the cognitive side-effects of physical treatment. They show, conclusively, that this is the case. These authors argue that there is some pervasive neuropsychological deficit in schizophrenia, providing a nice link between what the originator of the concept of schizophrenia (Kraepelin) believed and the current tendency to look back to Kraepelin and ignore the social psychiatric movement (1930s–70s) in between. Nuechterlein and colleagues (Chapter 4) are interested in neuropsychological accounts of schizophrenia, both as a state and trait. Their approach is complementary to Dunkley and Rogers' in that it capitalises on variations in course, relapses and remissions, in the quest for vulnerability markers. Such vulnerability spans cognition, functional relatedness of brain regions, an index of which is E.E.G. coherence, and focal defects in metabolic activity revealed on P.E.T. images.

The beginnings of other approaches derived from cybernetics are to be found in the computational models referred to by Ellis and de Pauw (Chapter 19) and David (Chapter 17), and Fleminger's proposal for the action of top down processes in delusion formation (Chapter 20). Fleminger presents a schematic model of delusions, which says as much about the factors that maintain delusions as generate them. Though primarily non-neuropsychological, it deserves a place here because of a willingness to view both neurobiological abnormalities and extreme cognitive bias as important contributing variables.

Hoffman and Rapaport (Chapter 16) explore two general explanations of the nature of schizophrenic auditory hallucinations. Are they an effect of incompetent perception of ambient speech? or are they the by product of a subject's own internal subvocalisations? They conclude in favour of the latter explanation, basing their argument on some intriguing experiments.

Slade (Chapter 15) also puts forward an explanation of the nature of hallucinations. The essence of this is that they are the result of an interaction between the four factors: (1) stress; (2) predisposition; (3) current environmental stimulation; and (4) mood. The argument is theoretical and represents one of the most typical preneuropsychological models of schizophrenia, namely a multifactorial explanation. Although not in any direct sense neuropsychological, Slade's proposal is pertinent to neuropsychological formulations themselves, as it highlights non-brain factors, which any pure neuropsychologist should consider. Slade's pioneering use of the single case methodology in his early formulations has a distinctly contemporary ring. The neuropsychological element in these two chapters is small but is complemented by David's comprehensive review. After reviewing critically the neurological literature on auditory hallucinations of all types, David narrows in on the neuropsychology of inner speech and attempts to illustrate how disturbances of this mechanism may give rise to typical psychotic experiences. Despite their different theoretical orientations, all of these authors writing about hallucinations, emphasise inner speech as the critical element, which any study of schizophrenic patients' "voices" must address.

Hoffman and Rapaport (Chapter 16) also allude to computer simulations and network models of cognition, which we predict will become a major focus over the next decade. As for our earlier justification for using the "neuro" prefix, which permitted reference (implicit and explicit) to the brains of both humans and animals, we may have to bend the rules even further to include silicon chip-supported artificial brains.

The chapters that follow all examine the general issue of the psychology of schizophrenia. The neuropsychological component is examined from the standpoint of brain imagery, neuropsychological test results, phenomenology, neurodevelopment, and electrophysiological studies. The theoretical stance of different authors varies considerably, but we hope that the "neuropsychology of schizophrenia theme" can be traced in all the chapters, if not in a direct reference then in the formulation of some complementary psychological proposal as yet partially or yet-to-be assimilated.

REFERENCES

Bleuler, E. (1950). *Dementia praecox or the group of schizophrenias* (J. Zinkin, Trans.). International Universities Press: New York. (Original work published 1911.)

Bruce, D. (1985). On the origin of the term "neuropsychology". *Neuropsychologia, 23,* 813–814.

Chapman, L.J., & Chapman, J.P. (1973). Problems of measurement of cognitive deficit. *Psychological Bulletin, 79,* 380–385.

Churchland, P.S. (1988). Reduction and the neurobiological basis of consciousness. In A.J. Marcel, & E. Bisiach. (Eds.), *Consciousness in contemporary science.* Oxford University Press: Oxford.

Cutting, J. (1985). *The psychology of schizophrenia.* Edinburgh: Churchill Livingstone.

Cutting, J. (1990). *The right cerebral hemisphere and psychiatric disorders.* Oxford: Oxford University Press.

David, A.S. (1989). The neuropsychology of the functional psychoses. *Current Opinion in Psychiatry*, 2, 84–8.

David, A.S. (1993). Cognitive neuropsychiatry? *Psychological Medicine*, 23, 1–5.

David, A.S., & Cutting, J.C. (1990). Affect, affective disorder and schizophrenia: A neuropsychological investigation of right hemisphere function. *British Journal of Psychiatry*, 156, 491–5.

Ellis, A., & Young, A.W. (1988). *Human cognitive neuropsychology.* Hove: Lawrence Erlbaum Associates Ltd.

Flor-Henry, P., & Gruzelier, J. (Eds.). (1983). *Laterality and psychopathology.* Elsevier, Amsterdam.

Fodor, J.A. (1983). *The modularity of mind.* MIT Press: Cambridge, MA.

Frith, C.D., & Done, D.J. (1988). Towards a neuropsychology of schizophrenia. *British Journal of Psychiatry*, 153, 437–443.

Gray, J.A., Feldon, J., Rawlins, J.N.P., Hemsley, D.R., & Smith, A.D. (1991). The neuropsychology of schizophrenia. *Behavioral and Brain Sciences*, 14, 1–84.

McCarthy, R.A., & Warrington, E.K. (1990). *Cognitive neuropsychology: A clinical introduction.* Academic Press: London.

O'Carroll, R. (1992). Neuropsychology of psychosis. *Current Opinion in Psychiatry*, 5, 38–44.

Robbins, T.W. (1990). The case for frontostriatal dysfunction in schizophrenia. *Schizophrenia Bulletin*, 16, 391–402.

Shallice, T. (1988). *From neuropsychology to mental structure.* Cambridge University Press: Cambridge.

Shallice, T., Burgess, P.W., & Frith, C.D. (1991). Can the neuropsychological case-study approach be applied to schizophrenia? *Psychological Medicine*, 21, 661–673.

Teuber, H.L. (1955). Physiological psychology. *Annual Review of Psychology*, 9, 267–296.

Weinberger, D.R., Berman, K.F., & Zec, R.F. (1986). Physiological dysfunction of dorsolateral prefrontal cortex in schizophrenia. I. Regional cerebral blood flow evidence. *Archives of General Psychiatry*, 43, 114–124.

NEUROIMAGING AND NEUROPSYCHOLOGY

2 The Left Striato-pallidal Hyperactivity Model of Schizophrenia

Terrence S. Early, John W. Haller, Michael I. Posner,
and Marc Raichle
Washington University School of Medicine, St Louis, U.S.A.

Positron emission tomography (PET) was used to demonstrate an abnormally high ratio of region-to-whole brain blood flow (CBF) in the left globus pallidus of neuroleptic-naive patients. This finding has been replicated in PET image averaging studies and in a separate cohort of schizophrenic patients and controls. Schizophrenic patients also demonstrate abnormal orienting to right visual hemispace, consistent with an abnormality of the left hemisphere. Both of these findings could be due to reduced dopaminergic modulation of the left ventral striatum, resulting in striato-pallidal hyperactivity and hemineglect. Schizophrenic patients are thought to be similar to patients with hemiparkinsonism involving the left striatum, with the difference that only non-motor parts of the striatum are involved. Neuroleptic medications may work by restoring symmetry to striatal function.

INTRODUCTION

Positron emission tomography (PET) was used to demonstrate an abnormally high ratio of region-to-whole brain blood flow (CBF) in the left globus pallidus of neuroleptic-naive patients (Early et al., 1987). This finding has been replicated in PET image averaging studies and in a separate cohort of schizophrenic patients and controls. Schizophrenic patients also demonstrate abnormal orienting to right visual hemispace, consistent with an abnormality of the left hemisphere (Posner, et al., 1988). Both of these findings could be due to reduced dopaminergic modulation of the left ventral striatum, resulting in striatopallidal hyperactivity and hemineglect (Early et al., 1989a,b). Schizophrenic patients are thought to be similar to patients with hemiparkinsonism involving the left striatum, with the

15

difference that only non-motor parts of the striatum are involved. Many authors believe that neuroleptic medications may work by restoring symmetry to striatal function (Bracha, 1987; Gruzelier & Hammond, 1979; Jeruss & Taylor, 1982; Tan & Gurgen, 1986).

PET STUDIES OF NEUROLEPTIC-NAIVE SCHIZOPHRENIC PATIENTS

Positron emission tomography (PET) can provide a three-dimensional image of physiological measurements such as blood flow, oxygen metabolism, and glucose metabolism. These measurements are indices of brain function in that they reflect the activity and number of nerve terminals in a region of brain tissue. PET has been used in several studies of regional brain activity in schizophrenic patients. Most studies of previously medicated patients have shown a reduction in relative frontal flow or metabolism that has been termed "hypofrontality". Schizophrenic patients also have certain similarities to patients with frontal lobe injury in terms of symptoms and performance on neuropsychological tests. However, hypofrontality is generally not reported in studies of neuroleptic-naive patients. The reason for this discrepancy is unclear. It is possible that conventional periods of medication withdrawal are not sufficient to eliminate the effects of neuroleptic medication. Alternatively, medication withdrawal may select for patients with more prominent negative symptoms of the sort that have been associated with hypofrontality since the earliest studies (Ingvar, 1974).

Because of these concerns, never-medicated patients were studied with PET to eliminate the possibility of effects of antipsychotic medication. In addition, a method of anatomical localization was used that permitted objective, accurate, and reliable localization of small regions of the brain, such as the globus pallidus (Fox et al., 1985). Most *in vivo* studies of metabolism have not reported values for the globus pallidus because of the difficulty in localizing this structure. Finally, the probability of type I (false-positive) error due to multiple comparisons was decreased by replicating the findings of the exploratory study with a separate sample of patients. In the first phase of this study, regional cerebral blood flow (rCBF) was measured in five patients with schizophrenia and ten normal control subjects. An exploratory analysis of 17 bilateral regions indicated an abnormally high ratio of left globus pallidus to whole brain blood flow in the patient sample. In the replication study, rCBF was measured in five additional never-medicated patients and ten additional control subjects. Only the globus pallidus and frontal regions were analysed. This analysis confirmed the finding of an abnormally high ratio of left globus pallidus to whole brain blood flow (Fig. 2.1).

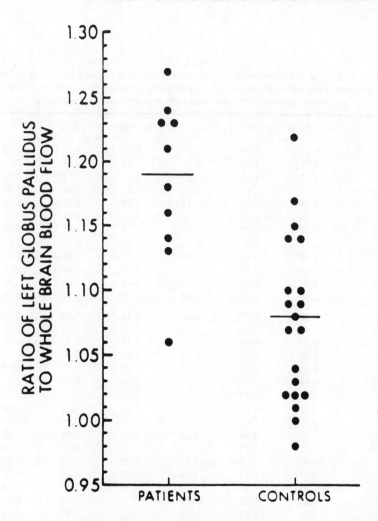

FIG. 2.1   The ratio of left globus pallidus/whole brain blood flow in ten never-medicated patients with schizophrenia and 20 normal control subjects. The mean for each group is indicated by a horizontal line.

In keeping with other studies of neuroleptic-naive patients, no evidence for reduced frontal flow (hypofrontality) was found. A power analysis indicated that patients were unlikely to have any significant degree of hypofrontality in the regions examined. There is a trend towards increased rCBF in patients for two anterior cingulate regions (P < 0.06, two-tailed Student's t-test). Data concerning rCBF in the globus pallidus, dorsolateral prefrontal cortex, and anterior cingulate gyrus are presented in Table 2.1.

TABLE 2.1
Relative (region to mean regional) blood flow for frontal regions in ten neuroleptic-naive schizophrenic patients and 20 controls in the eyes closed resting state. There is no evidence for relative hypofrontality in the schizophrenic patients

Subject	DLPFC-R	DLPFC-L	ACNG1-R	ACNG1-L	ACNG2-L	ACNG2-R
PT 1	0.99	0.99	1.25	1.31	1.15	1.23
PT 2	0.72	1.02	0.88	0.98	0.85	0.96
PT 3	1.06	1.09	1.20	1.08	1.13	0.96
PT 4	0.86	0.92	1.33	1.23	1.09	0.96
PT 5	0.85	0.98	1.14	1.25	0.82	1.01
PT 6	0.78	0.76	1.19	1.16	0.94	0.97
PT 7	0.96	0.99	1.23	1.01	1.18	0.98
PT 8	0.74	0.86	1.01	1.02	0.88	0.88
PT 9	0.89	0.88	1.19	1.23	1.06	1.10
PT 10	0.85	0.67	1.20	1.10	0.89	0.76
Mean	0.87	0.92	1.16	1.14	1.00	0.98
SD	0.10	0.12	0.12	0.09	0.12	0.08
NL 1	0.95	0.97	1.21	1.16	0.92	0.92
NL 2	0.96	0.93	1.30	1.23	0.92	0.78
NL 3	0.94	0.98	1.32	1.14	0.78	0.78
NL 4	0.82	0.94	1.19	1.17	1.00	0.95
NL 5	0.83	0.97	0.97	1.08	0.89	0.98
NL 6	0.98	0.96	1.15	1.08	0.79	0.85
NL 7	0.92	0.90	1.07	0.96	1.04	0.93
NL 8	0.95	0.97	1.12	1.06	0.73	0.80
NL 9	0.82	0.66	1.00	0.79	0.94	0.76
NL 10	1.03	1.04	1.16	1.09	0.58	0.77
NL 11	0.85	0.70	1.13	1.12	0.94	0.90
NL 12	0.85	0.82	1.17	1.09	0.87	0.83
NL 13	0.68	0.72	1.05	1.05	1.16	1.14
NL 14	0.82	0.99	1.26	1.10	0.69	0.84
NL 15	0.85	0.86	1.16	1.23	0.90	0.90
NL 16	0.90	0.93	1.27	1.16	0.86	0.87
NL 17	0.87	0.92	1.21	1.22	1.12	1.12
NL 18	1.05	0.96	1.15	1.12	0.77	0.75
NL 19	0.79	0.88	1.19	1.17	0.84	0.86
NL 20	0.98	0.98	1.08	1.15	1.05	1.08
Mean	0.89	0.90	1.16	1.11	0.89	0.89
SD	0.09	0.10	0.09	0.10	0.14	0.11

DLPFC-R, right dorsolateral prefrontal cortex; DLPFC-L, left dorsolateral prefrontal cortex; ACNG1-R, right anterior cingulate gyrus area 1; ACNG1-L, left anterior cingulate gyrus area 1; ACNG2-R, right anterior cingulate gyrus area 2; ACNG2-L, left anterior cingulate gyrus area 2; PT, patient; NL, normal control; SD, standard deviation.

A Between-group Image Comparison Technique: The *t*-Image

In our laboratory, PET image averaging techniques have been used to demonstrate blood flow (rCBF) changes associated with cognitive activation. Subjects are studied in rest and activation conditions, the two scans are subtracted, and the difference image is reconstructed in a standard stereotactic space. Averaging multiple standardized rCBF difference images enhances the ability to detect rCBF changes associated with activation. A variation of this program has been developed for comparing two independent groups of subjects rather than the same group in a rest and activation state. This method, which creates a "*t*-image", uses intragroup averaging and intergroup subtraction of images, corrected for regional variance.

The *t*-image is created by first reconstructing individual PET images into standardized stereotactic space. This involves conversion of primary tomographic images to anatomically standardized three dimensional images using stereotactic anatomical localization and interslice interpolation. A 49-slice three-dimensional image with 2 mm cubic voxels is generated. Each voxel of the image is located by its distance in three directions (x, y, z) from the centre of a line defined by the anterior and posterior commissures (AC–PC midpoint).

For each group, individual images are averaged voxel-by-voxel into a single mean rCBF image. In addition, the within-group variability is calculated for each voxel from these data. Comparison images are generated for experimental versus control group averaged images by computing a Student's *t* for all voxels: The resulting *t*-image represents the regional differences between the two groups corrected for the local variances. No statistical probabilities are assigned to the calculated *t*-values because of the large number of comparisons represented in each image.

A *t*-image created from the PET scan data of ten neuroleptic-naive schizophrenic patients and 20 normal controls illustrates the left globus pallidus abnormality (Fig. 2.2). The location and shape of this region is appropriate for the section of ventral pallidum innervated by the limbic striatum. The left globus pallidus has the highest *t*-value for any increase in rCBF in patients relative to controls.

Additional regions of high activity, such as the left temporal and insular cortex may be abnormal as well, but must be replicated in a separate group.

Studies now in progress are examining the replicability of the globus pallidus finding and other abnormalities suggested by the *t*-image. Preliminary results are that the finding of increased relative left globus pallidus activity is replicable.

For a new group of ten neuroleptic-naive patients and 20 controls, left globus pallidus is elevated on the left (mean = 1.15 versus 1.09, $P = 0.014$)

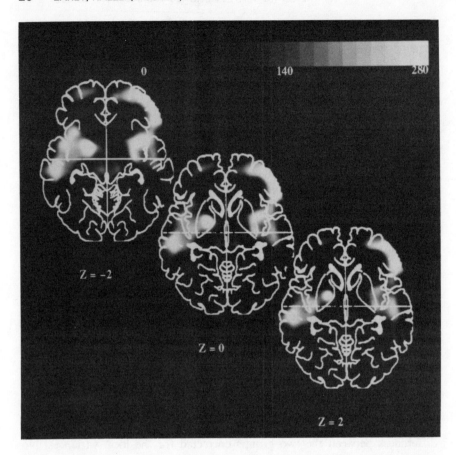

FIG. 2.2   *t*-image comparing ten neuroleptic-naive schizophrenic patients to 20 controls. The image demonstrates the increase in left globus pallidus blood flow in schizophrenic patients. Possible increases in left temporal and right frontal regions are also suggested by the *t*-image.

but not on the right (mean = 1.13 versus 1.10, *P* = 0.19, by 2-tailed Student's *t*-test).

WHY THE GLOBUS PALLIDUS?

> The pallidum ... [is] ... an activating center for locomotion and for turning attention, as though fascinated, towards an object or event appearing from the contralateral side. (Hassler, 1978)

All regions of the cortex project to striatum (Pycock & Phillipson, 1984) and from there to the globus pallidus. If the striatum is envisioned as a funnel, the globus pallidus is the tip. Consequently, lesions in remote areas of the brain are likely to alter neuronal activity in the globus pallidus. For example, lesions of the dopaminergic system, hippocampus, or frontal cortex are associated with altered neuronal activity in the globus pallidus (Gray et al., 1991; Hosokawa et al., 1985; Wooten & Collins, 1983).

The globus pallidus hyperactivity probably reflects increased neuronal activity of projections to the left globus pallidus. Cerebral blood flow (CBF) and glucose metabolism (CMGlu) in a region of brain tissue are thought to reflect metabolism in the terminal fields, rather than in the cell bodies of neurons within the region (Schwartz et al., 1979; Raichle, 1987). Thus, regional metabolism reflects the firing rate of (inhibitory or excitatory) neurons projecting to that region.

Major projections to the globus pallidus include the striatum and subthalamic nucleus. The striatum can be subdivided into dorsal striatum (caudate and putamen) and ventral striatum (nucleus accumbens and olfactory tubercle). Different regions of the cortex project to different regions of the striatum. Alexander et al. (1986, 1990) have emphasised separate functional loops for cognitive and sensorimotor brain systems involving regions of the cortex, striatum, pallidum, and thalamus. Thus, the putamen receives projections from sensorimotor cortex and has a greater role in motor programming. The caudate nucleus receives projections from regions such as the dorsolateral prefrontal cortex (DLPFC) and has a greater role in cognitive activities associated with the DLPFC. Lesions of the caudate nucleus produce deficits on delayed alternation tasks similar to those seen with lesions of the DLPFC. Finally, the ventral striatum is associated with reward, motivation, and drive. Regions that project to the ventral striatum also are implicated in these aspects of behaviour.

The ventral striatum receives input from limbic cortical regions including anterior cingulate gyrus, insula, entorhinal cortex, hippocampus, and amygdala (Heimer et al., 1985; Nauta, 1989). Projections from the ventral striatum are directed to the ventral pallidum. The ventral pallidum in turn projects to the mediodorsal nucleus of the thalamus, substantia nigra–pars compacta (SN–PC), ventral tegmental area (VTA), lateral habenular nucleus, and amygdala (Nauta, 1989; Nauta & Domesick, 1984). Projections from the mediodorsal nucleus of the thalamus return to anterior cingulate cortex (Alexander et al., 1990). The anterior cingulate loop and associated regions is illustrated in Fig. 2.3. The motor loop and cognitive loop are included for comparison.

Dopaminergic input to the striatum originates in the substantia nigra–ventral tegmental area complex (SN–VTA) and projects to all regions of the striatum (Pycock & Phillipson, 1984). It is thought that the dopaminergic input has a modulatory rather than information carrying role. Nigrostriatal neurons are generally thought to have an inhibitory effect on striatopallidal neurons.

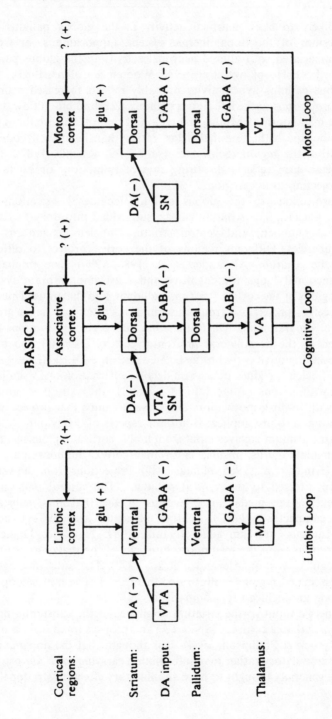

FIG. 2.3   Schematic diagram of corticostriatopallidothalamic circuitry. DA, dopamine; GABA, gamma amino butyric acid; glu, glutamate; SN, substantia nigra; SN–PC, substantia nigra–pars compacta; VA, ventral anterior nucleus; VL, ventrolateral nucleus; VTA, ventral tegmental area; VTA-SN, ventral tegmental area and substantia nigra.

The mesolimbic dopaminergic system has long been implicated in the pathogenesis of schizophrenia (Crow & Johnstone, 1987). The observation of globus pallidus hyperactivity is compatible with an abnormality of the left mesolimbic dopaminergic system. However, these results are not compatible with prevailing notions of excessive dopaminergic activity in the mesolimbic system in schizophrenia, as a lesion of dopaminergic neurons will produce hyperactivity of the left globus pallidus.

A lesion of the substantia nigra or ventral tegmental area results in increased metabolism in the globus pallidus on the lesioned side (Brown & Wolfson, 1982; Kelly et al., 1982; Kolzlowski & Marshall, 1980; Trugman & Wooten, 1986; Wooten & Collins, 1981, 1983). A selective lesion of the dopaminergic projections to the basal ganglia disinhibits the GABAergic projection to the globus pallidus. The increased firing of this projection is reflected in increased metabolic activity in the terminal fields in the pallidum. Reduced dopaminergic modulation of the dorsal striatum in hemiparkinsonism results in impaired motor function and enhanced metabolic activity in the globus pallidus. In an analogous manner, reduced dopaminergic modulation of the left ventral striatum could result in the PET findings and asymmetric impairment of attention in schizophrenics. This impaired modulation could be caused by the death or sustained functional inhibition of dopaminergic neurons projecting to the striatum due to some other lesion.

An example of the latter would be increased dopaminergic input to the left amygdala, as has been reported in a replicated neuropathological study of schizophrenic patients (Reynolds, 1983, 1987). Dopaminergic stimulation of the amygdala inhibits dopamine turnover in the nucleus accumbens (Louilot et al., 1985) which could result in a functional lesion of this projection.

Kindling the amygdala with ferric chloride injection (Csernansky et al., 1985) results in ipsilateral striatal dopaminergic receptor supersensitivity and a contralateral turning bias following the administration of apomorphine (also seen following 6-hydroxydopamine (6-OHDA) lesions). Electrical kindling produces effects on turning behaviour consistent with damage to the ipsilateral dopaminergic striatal input (Mintz et al., 1987). This suggests a way that epilepsy might come to be associated with psychosis (see also Gray et al., 1991).

Thus, a variety of abnormalities could result in striatopallidal hyperactivity and an asymmetric impairment of attention. PET studies of neuroleptic-naive patients do not support an abnormality of frontal cortex at the onset of the illness. "Frontal" type behavioural deficits could be due to dysfunction at the level of the basal ganglia. Striatopallidal hyperactivity secondary to abnormalities of the amygdala or hippocampus is a particularly intriguing possibility. Abnormalities that produce psychosis are proposed to do so through left striatopallidal hyperactivity and associated dysfunction of regions dependent on the left ventral striatum.

Evidence for an asymmetric (left hemispheric) impairment of attention is presented in the next section. Following this, animal studies are reviewed to clarify the link between dopamine, striatopallidal hyperactivity and attention.

ATTENTION STUDY

A separate group of patients was studied with a task that measures the ability to direct attention within the visual field (Fig. 2.4).

Patients were slow to respond to targets in the right visual field following an invalid cue in the left visual field. Valid cues preceding targets in the left or right field resulted in no asymmetry of response time. If not cued, schizophrenics were much slower to respond to stimuli on the right. In fact, *all* patients were slower to respond to a right visual field target following a left visual field cue than in the opposite situation. This impaired ability to orient to right hemispace is similar to that seen in patients with hemineglect due to a stroke. As each subject served as their own control in the comparison of right-side to left-side performance, the finding could not be accounted for by any general deficiency in understanding instructions or lack of motivation.

Evidence for subtle right-sided hemineglect in schizophrenic patients is available from a number of other studies. Results of the visual orienting study have been replicated by Potkin et al. (1989), who also found that patients had fewer eye fixations in right hemispace when scanning a visual form. The number of fixations in left visual hemispace were normal.

Torrey (1980) found evidence for right-sided neglect in schizophrenic patients using the face–hand test and a test for graphesthesia. Manshreck and Ames (1984) replicated the observation of poorer right hand performance on graphesthesia and also demonstrated right hand impairments on tests of stereognosis that correlated with measures of thought disorder. Mild right-sided neglect may potentially explain a great deal of the literature on left hemispheric cognitive dysfunction in schizophrenia.

Schizophrenic patients also demonstrate a form of motor behaviour similar to the turning behaviour seen in animals with motor hemineglect. A rotometer was used to measure turning preferences in human subjects. Hemiparkinsonian patients were found to turn in the expected direction; toward the side of the damaged striatum (Bracha et al., 1987). When applied to drug-free schizophrenic patients, all patients showed a turning preference to the left (Bracha, 1987). This was in contrast to the normals, who on the whole turned as frequently to either side. While the authors suggested that their finding was likely to reflect overactivity of dopaminergic projections to

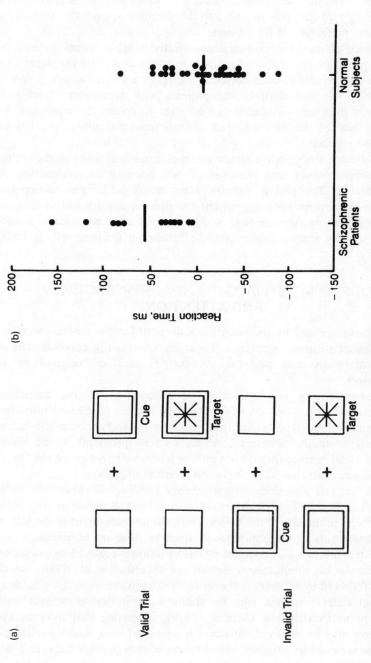

FIG. 2.4 (a) Schematic diagram of the covert visual orienting task. The cue is brightening of one of the boxes, which directs attention to that side. The cue-to-target interval is too short for eye movements to occur. Subjects respond by pressing a button as rapidly as possible following the occurrence of the target (a star). The task measures the ability to direct attention within each visual hemifield. (b) The scattergram demonstrates impaired ability to orient to right hemispace following an invalid cue on the left in the schizophrenic patients.

the right striatum, we suggest that it could reflect underactivity of dopaminergic projections to the left. Medication apparently normalises the turning preference in the patients.

Increased leftward turning was demonstrated in schizophrenic patients in another paradigm that required patients to swivel in a chair 180 degrees to collect a coin reinforcer after detecting a target on a video screen (Lyon & Satz, 1991). Normal controls and patients with depression or schizoid personality disorder consistently turned right to collect the reinforcer. In contrast, nine of the 34 medicated schizophrenic patients turned left to collect the reinforcer.

In summary, this selective review omits discussion of many studies using more complex tasks that demonstrate left hemispheric dysfunction in schizophrenia. The globus pallidus abnormality and right hemispatial orienting impairment both suggest left hemispheric dysfunction. A form of left hemispheric dysfunction that could account for the behavioural results is suggested by studies concerning the functional anatomy of the basal ganglia.

DOPAMINE, STRIATO-PALLIDAL HYPERACTIVITY, AND ATTENTION

Alterations of behaviour and attention also result from unilateral lesions of dopaminergic neurons in animals. These lesions result in combinations of motor, attention, and postural asymmetries that are referred to as hemineglect.

Motor responses to destruction or stimulation of the ascending dopaminergic projections involve intentional neglect (decreased initiation of contralateral movements), contralateral slowing, and abnormalities in the patterning of motor behaviour. Animals circle ipsilateral to the lesion (Pycock, 1980) because they do not initiate motor activity toward the "bad" side of space contralateral to the lesion (Carli et al., 1985).

These animals also demonstrate sensory hemineglect (Marshall, 1979; Marshall & Gotthelf, 1979; Marshall et al., 1980; Schallert et al., 1983) contralateral to the side of the lesion. Thus, the animals orient to the side of space that inputs to the non-lesioned striatum. Sensory hemineglect seen immediately following a unilateral 6-OHDA lesion is replaced by extinction only with double simultaneous stimulation (Marshall et al., 1980), which may be followed by recovery if the lesion is not too extensive. Like turning, this contralateral neglect can be changed to ipsilateral neglect with apomorphine (Marshall & Gotthelf, 1979), suggesting that receptor up-regulation may be involved. Bilateral lesions lead to a severe avolitional state characterised by akinesia, aphagia, and adipsia (Ross & Stewart, 1981; White, 1986).

A permanent deficit of attention can also be demonstrated in unilaterally lesioned rodents (Schallert & Hall, 1988). Rats do not disengage attention from an ongoing oral behaviour (such as eating) to respond to vigorous stimulation contralateral to the lesion. At the time of the eating bout, they display normal responsiveness to stimulation of the bad side. The disengage deficit has not been localised but is also produced by selective dopaminergic lesions of the median forebrain bundle. It can be dissociated from the motor hemineglect component because it is present in some rats who have recovered completely from the hemineglect, and it is apparently not due to extinction.

A final component of the rotating rodent model is the development of dopamine receptor supersensitivity. Severing dopaminergic input results in the development of dopamine receptor supersensitivity on the side of the lesion (Heikkila et al., 1981). This may account for the recovery experienced by some animals following the lesion and can be seen as an adaptive response that compensates for the reduction in dopaminergic input. Supersensitivity results in different rotational responses to direct and indirect dopaminergic agonists (Pycock, 1980; Wooten & Collins, 1981, 1983). The direct dopaminergic agonist apomorphine causes circling contraversive to the lesion; the rats have greater dopaminergic stimulation on the lesioned side due to the receptor supersensitivity and consequently orient towards the contralateral space. The indirect agonist amphetamine, which depends on endogenous stores of dopamine, causes the opposite imbalance and ipsiversive circling.

Summary

To summarise, schizophrenic patients have many features in common with animals subject to left-sided lesions of the ascending dopaminergic projections:

1. Increased metabolism in the ipsilateral globus pallidus (Early et al., 1987; Wooten & Collins, 1981).
2. A multifaceted hemineglect syndrome, which includes:
    (a) motor hemineglect, indicated by a tendency to turn to the left (Bracha et al., 1987; Lyon & Satz, 1991; Pycock & Marsden, 1978);
    (b) right-sided sensory neglect (Manshreck & Ames, 1984; Marshall et al., 1980; Schallert & Hall, 1988; Torrey, 1980);
    (c) impaired ability to shift attention to the right following an invalid cue on the left (Posner et al., 1988; Ross & Stewart, 1981).
3. (Possible) dopamine receptor supersensitivity on the side of the lesion (Farde et al., 1987; Heikkila et al., 1981).

LATERALISED EFFECTS OF NEUROLEPTICS

Dopamine turnover in the two nigrostriatal pathways is reciprocally regulated such that electrical or pharmacological stimulation of one side causes inhibition of the other (Glowinowski et al., 1984). This reciprocal regulation of dopamine turnover may be important for interhemispheric interaction and also suggests a potential mechanism of action for antipsychotic medications compatible with the model outlined here. Antipsychotics may work by reducing the postulated abnormal asymmetry in striatal dopaminergic input.

There is data to suggest that antipsychotic medications do have a lateralised effect. Serafetinedes (1973) found that neuroleptic treatment is associated with a shift in EEG voltage to the left. Treatment is also associated with lateralised alterations in visual evoked potentials (Myslobodsky et al., 1983) and a reversal in the asymmetry of the Hoffman reflex (Tan & Gurgen, 1986) (an electromyographic measure). Unmedicated patients have poorer performance on tasks presented to right hemispace, such as letter cancellation tests and form sorting tasks. Treatment reverses the side of deficit (Tomer, 1989; Tomer & Flor-Henry, 1989). All of these findings are consistent with neuroleptic-induced inhibition of the right hemisphere.

A study of the effects of acute treatment with haloperidol on lateralised dopamine turnover suggests that neuroleptics have lateralised effects (Jerussi & Taylor, 1982). Normal rats were tested for circling behaviour and were found to have higher levels of DOPAC (a dopamine metabolite) in the striatum ipsilateral to the direction of rotation. Rats treated acutely with haloperidol demonstrated the reverse asymmetry in striatal DOPAC levels.

POSITIVE SYMPTOMS

In clinical neurology, positive symptoms are thought of as release phenomena due to loss of a system that *inhibits* a particular behaviour. Thus, such symptoms as hyperreflexia and spasticity are positive symptoms due to release of lower reflexes from tonic inhibition by the corticospinal tract. In schizophrenia, positive symptoms include thought disorder, hallucinations, delusions, and abnormalities of cognitive processing such as ideas of control. Attention has long been thought to inhibit as well as facilitate processing and an impairment of systems of attention might be associated with a release of positive symptoms. We would associate the positive symptoms with an asymmetric loss of dopaminergic modulation of the left ventral striatum.

Thought derailment is one of the positive symptoms of schizophrenia. Andreason (1979) defines detailment as "A pattern of spontaneous speech in which the ideas slip off the track onto another that is clearly but obliquely related, or onto one that is completely unrelated". With derailment, the *linear*, goal-directed nature of speech is disrupted by frequent divergence from the semantically meaningful (if idiosyncratic) goal. In the process of starting the thought there is a slippage off topic that may be only partial, in which case the next thought fragment seems somewhat related, or it may be complete. Meaning is lost from speech because the main topic cannot be referred to constantly.

These deficits of language and thought suggest a failure to exercise a selective control over the semantic relations of words. This possibility was explored in a neuropsychological test that required subjects to select and act upon either a word or a non-linguistic symbol.

The subject is required to press one of two keys as quickly as possible according to directions indicated by either an arrow pointing left or right or the word left or right presented visually on the centre of a cathode ray tube. On pure trials only an arrow or a word is presented. On mixed trials both are presented and the irrelevant one may either agree or disagree with the instructed direction. Normals are equally fast with arrow or word and show mutual interference between the two. Patients with lesions of the left cerebral hemisphere are faster with the arrow than the word stimulus, and receive much more interference of the arrow on the word than the reverse (Posner et al., 1988). Patients with lesions of the right cerebral hemisphere are faster with the word stimulus and receive more interference of a conflicting word on the arrow than the reverse. Schizophrenic patients show the pattern of deficits found in patients with left hemisphere lesions (Fig. 2.5). They are very slow and make many errors with the word stimulus, particularly when it has to compete with an arrow in the opposite direction. Following neuroleptic treatment, the patients tend to show more normal performance with the word stimulus.

Errors of word recognition seen in schizophrenic patients may be due to reduced access of the word to left hemisphere mechanisms that code its meaning. Alternatively the inability to respond quickly to words may reflect impairment in the ability of the person to attend selectively to the word meaning. While these are both complex functions, our tests involve only a single word on each trial and thus indicate that the deficit does not depend upon higher level emotional, syntactic mechanisms or upon sustained attention. The deficit can be demonstrated with a single verbal instruction. Moreover, the clear effect of neuroleptics in improving word processing as well as the high educational attainments of the patients indicate that the word deficit is not due to impaired reading ability.

PET imaging of cerebral blood flow by Petersen et al. (1988) has recently been used to identify neural systems associated with semantic processing of single words. These studies suggest that the semantic processing of individual visual and auditory words activate an area of the left

(a)

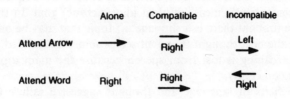

(b)

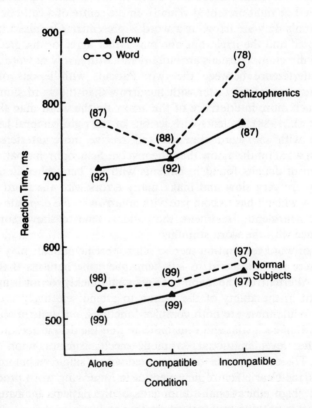

FIG. 2.5   (a) Display used for the arrow–word conflict task. Subjects are asked to attend to the arrow on half of the trials and to the word on half of the trials. (b) Schizophrenic patients perform in a manner similar to individuals with diffuse damage to the left hemisphere in that they are slower in responding to the word cue when it occurs alone or conflicts with the direction indicated by the arrow cue.

dorsolateral prefrontal cortex (DLPFC). Weinberger et al. (1986) have shown bilaterally increased rCBF in this region in normal subjects during the Wisconsin card sorting task, a neuropsychological task performed poorly by patients with DLPFC lesions. Schizophrenic patients are impaired on this task and do not show increased blood flow to the DLPFC, a finding that is shared by patients with Parkinson's disease (Weinberger, 1986).

Single cell recording in the DLPFC of non-human primates has identified this area with representation of information when the information is not physically present (Wurtz et al., 1980). Tests of delayed alternation are impaired by selective dopaminergic lesions of the prefrontal cortex (Brozowski, et al., 1979) or VTA (Simon et al., 1980). The ability to direct behaviour on the basis of self-generated (as opposed to perceived) representations demonstrated in these studies in primates is compatible with a role in semantic processing in humans.

A second area of the brain that is active during processing of word stimuli, and in non-linguistic active processing tasks, lies on the midline of the cerebral hemispheres and includes the anterior cingulate gyrus (area 24) and the supplementary motor cortex (medial area 6). The anterior cingulate has long been implicated in attention and lesions in this area can result in hemineglect or an avolitional state known as akinetic mutism (Fisher, 1983). The midline system is closely connected to the basal ganglia and receives input from the nucleus accumbens (via the mediodorsal nucleus of the thalamus) and from the dorsolateral prefrontal cortex.

The dorsolateral prefrontal cortex and the midline areas are closely interconnected anatomically. The PET data indicates that these regions function together in processing the semantics of visual words. Thus, we suggest that lesions of the striatum may act upon the midline system to reduce the ability of the schizophrenic subject to select semantic information. Studies of schizophrenic patients in semantic tasks (Done & Frith, 1984) have often been used to argue that schizophrenics show normal activation of semantics but cannot select the appropriate information nor inhibit inappropriate activations. The functions of semantic selection and inhibition have long been assigned to attention based upon studies of normal persons processing word stimuli (Neely, 1977; Posner et al., 1988). An anatomical model of a deficit in midline systems due to inappropriate activation from the basal ganglia provides a basis for observations on language abnormalities and other positive symptoms in schizophrenic patients.

Apart from the formal thought disorder, typical symptoms of schizophrenia include auditory hallucinations, ideas of control, thought insertion, and thought withdrawal. These symptoms may be considered to be due to the perception of internally generated speech and cognitive processing is perceived as being alien or not self-directed. Frith and Done (1988) have emphasised the need to account for these symptoms in anatomical models of schizophrenia. They distinguish between "stimulus intentions" (thoughts generated by external stimuli) and "willed intentions" (internally generated thoughts) associated in the motor domain with the arcuate premotor area and supplementary motor area, respectively. They postulate that schizophrenic patients have an impairment in the corollary discharge that would normally inform an organism that a given stimulus intention was self-generated. Our model differs in that we conceive of a separate centre for the generation of intentional cognitive action programmes. One way to attempt to understand these symptoms is by analogy to intentional motor behaviour. The supplementary motor area (SMA) and subjacent anterior cingulate gyrus have been associated with intentional motor (Goldberg, 1985) and cognitive (Fisher, 1983) activity.

A particularly striking aspect of the involvement of the SMA in intentional activity is provided by case reports of the "alien hand phenomenon" of the right hand following infarctions of the left SMA (Goldberg et al., 1981). The patients found their right hands engaging in autonomous motor activity that was not intended consciously. This phenomenon has also been reported in split-brain patients, where far more than the alien hand phenomenon has been demonstrated. Following commissurotomy the left and right hemispheres of split brain patients express different beliefs, emotional reactions, and preferences (Gazzaniga, 1985). These patients demonstrate that it is possible for a brain to have two separate generators of intentional cognitive activity. In these patients the left hemisphere controls language and motor activity. The differing intentions of the right hemisphere are usually uncovered only with careful testing. The corpus callosum may have an inhibitory role on homologous cortical regions of the right hemisphere, which may be important for the experience of mental and behavioural unity.

The functions of midline frontal regions (SMA and anterior cingulate cortex) are expressed through projections to the striatum (Goldberg, 1985) and are dependent on striatal dopaminergic input (Jurgens, 1984; Ross & Stewart, 1981). Deficient dopaminergic input to non-motor parts of the left striatum would be expected to impair these functions, perhaps by interfering with a normal pattern of left hemispheric dominance for these command functions. This impairment of dominance could result in a release of function by homologous regions of the right hemisphere, leading to partial control of processing by the right, and the generation of autonomous cognitive programmes that interfere with those generated by the left.

NEGATIVE SYMPTOMS

An example of a negative symptom in clinical neurology is the paralysis directly due to the impaired function of the corticospinal tract. In schizophrenia, symptoms such as apathy, alogia, affective flattening, autism, and poverty of the amount and content of speech are considered negative symptoms. These symptoms are similar to the abulia or akinetic mutism seen with SMA or ACG legions (Fisher, 1983) or with lesions of ascending dopaminergic projections to these regions (Ross & Stewart, 1981). Decreased as well as conflicting volitional cognitive activity might be accounted for by our model. Akinetic mutism is an extreme avolitional state that is sometimes mistakenly diagnosed as catatonia. Spontaneous, self-generated actions and speech are severely reduced and externally driven behaviour in the form of echolalia and echopraxia are enhanced. Akinesia of a lesser degree may be seen in Parkinson's disease or neuroleptic treatment.

Negative symptoms could in fact be due to a dopamine deficiency, as has been suggested by Crow and Johnstone (1987). This is compatible with reports of beneficial effects of dopaminergic agonists on these symptoms (Costall & Naylor, 1986) and progression of negative symptoms with age. One might suggest that negative symptoms would be associated with a more bilateral reduction in dopaminergic modulation of the striatum that represents a progression beyond unstable hemispheric dominance.

ACKNOWLEDGEMENTS

This research was supported by the McDonnell Center for Studies in Higher Brain Function, the National Institutes of Health Grant HL13851 from the National Heart, Lung, and Blood Institute, Health and Human Service; the National Alliance for Research on Schizophrenia, and Depression Grant; "1989 NARSAD Young Investigator Award Recipient"; National Institute of Mental Health Grant MH48196, Department of Health and Human Sciences.

REFERENCES

Alexander, G.E., DeLong, M.R., & Strick, P.L. (1986). Parallel organization of functionally segregated circuits linking basal ganglia and cortex. *Annual Review of Neuroscience, 9*, 357–381.

Alexander, G.E., Crutcher, M.D., & DeLong, M.R. (1990). Basal ganglia-thalamocortical circuits: Parallel substrates for motor, oculomotor, "prefrontal" and "limbic" functions. *Progress in Brain Research, 85*, 119–146.

Andreason, N.C. (1979). Thought, language, and communication disorders. *Archives of General Psychiatry, 36*, 1315–1321.

Bracha, H.S. (1987). Asymmetric rotational (circling) behavior, a dopamine asymmetry: Preliminary findings in unmedicated and never-medicated schizophrenic patients. *Biological Psychiatry, 22*, 995–1003.

Bracha, H.S., Shultz, C., Glick, S.D., & Kleinman, J.E. (1987). Spontaneous asymmetric circling behavior in hemi-Parkinsonism: A human equivalent of the lesioned-circling rodent behavior. *Life Science, 40*, 1127–1130.

Brown, L.L., & Wolfson, L.I. (1983). A dopamine-sensitive striatal efferent system mapped with (^{14}C)-deoxyglucose in the rat. *Brain Research, 261*, 213–229.

Brozowski, T.J., Brown, R.M., Rosvold, H.E., & Goldman, P.S. (1979). Cognitive deficit caused by regional depletion of dopamine in prefrontal cortex of rhesus monkey. *Science, 205*, 929–932.

34   EARLY, HALLER, POSNER, RAICHLE

Carli, M., Evendon, J.L., & Robbins, T.W. (1985). Depletion of unilateral dopamine impairs initiation of contralateral actions and not sensory attention. *Nature, 313,* 679–682.

Costall, B., Naylor, R.J. (1986). Neurotransmitter hypothesis of schizophrenia. In P.B. Bradley, S.R. Hirsch (Eds.), *The psychopharmacology and treatment of schizophrenia* (p. 135). Oxford: Oxford Medical Publications.

Crow, T.J., & Johnstone, E.C. (1987). Schizophrenia: Nature of the disease process and its biological correlates. In F. Plum (Ed.), *Handbook of physiology—the nervous system* (Vol. 5, part 2, chapter 21). Bethesda, MD: American Physiological Society.

Csernansky, J.G., Csernansky, C.A., Bonnett, K.A., & Hollister, L.E. (1985). Dopaminergic supersensitivity follows ferric chloride-indiced limbic seizures. *Biological Psychiatry, 20,* 723–733.

Done, J.D., & Frith, C.D. (1984). The effect of context during word perception in schizophrenic patients. *Brain and Language, 23,* 318–336.

Early, T.S., Reiman, E.M., Raichle, M.E., & Spitznagel, E.L. (1987). Left globus pallidus abnormality in never-medicated patients with schizophrenia. *Proceedings of the National Academy of Sciences, U.S.A., 84,* 561–563.

Early, T.S., Posner, M.I., Reiman, E.M., & Raichle, M.E. (1989a). Hyperactivity of the left striato-pallidal projection. Part I: Lower level theory. *Psychiatric Developments, 2,* 85–108.

Early, T.S., Posner, M.I., Reiman, E.M., & Raichle, M.E. (1989b). Left striato-pallidal hyperactivity in Schizophrenia. Part II: Phenomenology and thought disorder. *Psychiatric Developments, 2,* 109–121.

Farde, L., Weisel, F.A., Hall, H., Halldin, C., Stone-Elander, S., & Sedvall, G. (1987). No D2 receptor increase in PET study of schizophrenia [Letter]. *Archives of General Psychiatry, 44,* 671.

Fisher, C.M. (1983). Honored guest presentation: Abulia minor vs. agitated behavior. In *Clinical Neurosurgery,* vol. 31, chapter 2. Baltimore, Maryland: Williams & Wilkins.

Fox, P.T., Perlmutter, J.S., & Raichle, M.E. (1985). A stereotactic method of anatomical localization for positron emission tomography. *Journal of Computer Assisted Tomography, 9,* 141–153.

Frith, C.D., & Done, D.J. (1988). Towards a neuropsychology of schizophrenia. *British Journal of Psychiatry, 153,* 437–443.

Gazzaniga, M.S. (1985). *The social brain.* New York, NY: Basic Books Inc.

Glowinowski, J., Besson, M.J., & Cheramy, A. (1984). Role of the thalamus in the bilateral regulation of dopaminergic and GABAergic neurons in the basal ganglia. In *Functions of the basal ganglia* (pp. 150–163). CIBA Foundation Symposium 107. London: Pitman Publishers.

Goldberg, G. (1985). Supplementary motor area structure and functions: Review and hypothesis. *Behavioral and Brain Sciences, 8,* 567–616.

Goldberg, G., Meyer, N.H., & Toglia, J.Y. (1981). Medial frontal cortex infarction and the alien hand sign. *Archives of Neurology, 38,* 683–686.

Gray, J.A., Feldon, J., Rawlins, J.N.P., Hemsley, D.R., & Smith, A.D. (1991). The neuropsychology of schizophrenia. *Behavioral and Brain Sciences, 14,* 1–84.

Gruzelier, J., & Hammond, N. (1979). The effect of CPZ upon psychophysiological, endocrine, and information processing measures in schizophrenia. *Journal of Psychiatric Research, 14,* 167–182.

Hassler, R. (1978). Striatal control of locomotion, Intentional actions and of integrating and perceptive activity. *Journal of Neurological Science, 36,* 187–224.

Heikkila, R.E., Shapiro, B.S., & Duvoisin, R.C. (1981). The relationship between loss of dopamine nerve terminals, striatal (^{3}H) spiroperidol binding and rotational behavior in unilaterally 6-hydroxydopamine-lesioned rats. *Brain Research, 211,* 285–292.

Heimer, L., Alheid, G.F., & Zabortsky, L. (1985). Basal ganglia. In *The rat nervous system* (pp. 37–86). Australia: Academic Press.

Hosokawa, S., Motohiro, K., Aiko, Y., & Shima, F. (1985). Altered local cerebral glucose utilization by unilateral frontal cortical ablations in rats. *Brain Research, 343,* 8–15.

Ingvar, D.H. (1974). Distribution of cerebral activity in chronic schizophrenia. *Lancet, ii,* 1484–1486.

Jerussi, T.P., & Taylor, C.A. (1982). Bilateral asymmetry in striatal dopamine metabolism: Implications for pharmacotherapy of schizophrenia. *Brain Research, 246,* 71–75.

Jurgens, U. (1984). The efferent and afferent connections of the supplementary motor area. *Brain Research, 300,* 1984.

Kelly, P., Graham, D.I., & McCulloch, J. (1982). Specific alterations in local cerebral glucose utilization following striatal lesions. *Brain Research, 233,* 157–172.

Kozlowski, M.R., & Marshall, J.F. (1980). Plasticity of (^{14}C)2-deoxy-D-glucose incorporation into neostriatum and related structures in response to dopamine neuron damage and apomorphine replacement. *Brain Research, 7,* 167–183.

Louilot, A., Simon, H. Taghzouti, K., & LeMoal, M. (1985). Modulation of dopaminergic activity in the nucleus accumbens following facilitation or blockade of the dopaminergic transmission in the amygdala: A study by *in vivo* differential pulse voltammetry. *Brain Research, 346,* 141–145.

Lyon, N., & Satz, P. (1991). Left turning (swivel) in mediciated chronic schizophrenic patients. *Schizophrenia Research, 4,* 53–58.

Manshreck, T.C., & Ames, D. (1984). Neurologic features and psychopathology in schizophrenic disorders. *Biological Psychiatry, 19,* 703–719.

Marshall, J.F. (1979). Somatosensory inattention after dopamine-depleting intracerebral 6-OHDA injections: Spontaneous recovery and pharmacological control. *Brain Research, 177,* 311–324.

Marshall, J.F., & Gotthelf, T. (1979). Sensory inattention in rats with 6-hydroxydopamine-induced degeneration of ascending dopaminergic neurons: Apomorphine-induced reversal of deficits. *Experimental Neurology, 65,* 398–411.

Marshall, J.F., Berrios, N., & Sawyer, S. (1980) Neostriatal dopamine and sensory inattention. *Journal of Comparative Physiology, 94,* 833–846.

Mintz, M., Tomer, R., Houpt, S., & Herberg, L.J. (1987). Amygdala kindling modifies interhemispheric dopaminergic asymmetry. *Experimental Neurology, 96,* 137–144.

Myslobodsky, M.S., Mintz, M., & Tomer, R. (1983). Neuroleptic effects and the site of abnormality of schizophrenia. In: *Hemisyndromes: Psychology, neurology, psychiatry* (pp. 347–388). New York, NY: Academic Press.

Nauta, W.J.H. (1989). Reciprocal links of the corpus striatum with the cerebral cortex and limbic system: A common substrate for movement and thought? In J. Mueller (Ed.). *Neurology and psychiatry: A meeting of minds* (pp. 43–63). Basel: Karger.

Nauta, W.J.H., & Domesick, V. (1984). Afferent and efferent relationships of the basal ganglia. *Function of the Basal Ganglia.* CIBA Foundation Symposium 107. London: Pitman Press.

Neely, J.H. (1977). Semantic priming and retrieval from lexical memory: Roles of inhibitionless spreading activation and limited-capacity attention. *Journal of Experimental Psychology: General, 106,* 226–254.

Petersen, S.E. Fox., P.T., Posner, M.I., Mintun, M., & Raichle, M.E. (1988). Positron emission tomographic studies of the cortical anatomy of single word processing. *Nature, 331,* 585–589.

Posner, M.I., Early, T.S., Reiman, E.R., Pardo, P.J., & Dhawan, M. (1988). Asymmetries in hemispheric control of attention in schizophrenia. *Archives of General Psychiatry, 45,* 814–821.

Potkin, S.G., J.M., Urbanchek, M. Carreon, D., & Bravo, G. (1989). Right visual field deficits in reaction time after invalid cues in chronic and never-medicated schizophrenics compared to normal controls. *Biological Psychiatry, 25*, 74–79.

Pycock, C.J. (1980). Turning behavior in animals. *Neuroscience, 5*, 461–514.

Pycock, C.J., & Marsden, C.D. (1978). The rotating rodent: A two component system? *European Journal of Pharmacology, 47*, 167–175.

Pycock, C.J., & Phillipson, O.T. (1984). A neuroanatomical and neuropharmacological analysis of basal ganglia output. In L.L. Iverson, S.D. Iversen, & S.H. Snyder (Eds.). *Handbook of psychopharmacology*. (Vol. 18, pp. 191–227). New York: Plenum Press.

Raichle, M. (1987). Circulatory and metabolic correlates of brain function in normal humans. *Handbook of physiology—the nervous system V*, (chapter 16, pp. 643–674). Baltimore, Maryland: Williams & Wilkins.

Reynolds, G.P. (1983). Increased concentrations and lateral asymmetry of amygdala dopamine in schizophrenia. *Nature, 305*, 527–529.

Reynolds, G.P. (1987). Post- mortem neurochemical studies in human postmortem brain tissue. In H. Hafner, W.F. Gattaz, W. Janzarik (Eds.). *Search for the Causes of Schizophrenia* (pp. 236–240). Heidelberg: Springer.

Ross, E.D., & Stewart, R.M. (1981). Akinetic mutism from hypothalamic damage: Successful treatment with dopamine agonists. *Neurology, 31*, 1435–1439.

Schallert, T., & Hall, S. (1988). "Disengage" sensorimotor deficit following apparent recovery from unilateral dopamine depletion. *Behavioral Brain Research, 30*, 15–24.

Schallert, T., Upchurch, M., Wilcox, R.E., & Vaughn, D.M. (1983). Posture-independent sensorimotor analysis of inter-hemispheric receptor asymmetries in neostriatum. *Pharmacology Biochemistry and Behavior, 18*, 753–759.

Schwartz, W.J., Smith, C.B., Davidsen, L., Savaki, H., Sojoloff, L., Mata, M., Fink, D., & Gainer, H. (1979). Metabolic mapping of functional activity in the hypothalamo-neurohypophysial system of the rat. *Science, 205*, 723–725.

Serafetinedes, E.A. (1973). Voltage laterality in the EEG of psychiatric patients. *Diseases of the Nervous System, 34*, 190–191.

Simon, H., Scatton, B., & LeMoal, M. (1980). Dopaminergic A10 neurones are involved in cognitive functions. *Nature, 286*, 150–151.

Tan, U., & Gurgen, F. (1986). Modulation of spinal motor asymmetry by neuroleptic medication in schizophrenic patients. *Journal of Neuroscience, 30*, 165–172.

Tomer, R. (1989). Asymmetrical effects of neuroleptics on psychotic patients' performance of a tactile discrimination task. *Journal of Nervous and Mental Diseases, 177*, 699–700.

Tomer, R., & Flor-Henry, P. (1989). Neuroleptics reverse attention asymmetries in schizophrenic patients. *Biological Psychiatry, 25*, 852–860.

Torrey, E.F. (1980). Neurological abnormalities in schizophrenic patients. *Biological Psychiatry, 15*, 381–388.

Trugman, J.M., & Wooten, G.F. (1986). The effects of L-DOPA on regional cerebral glucose utilization in rats with unilateral lesions of the substantia nigra. *Brain Research, 379*, 264–274.

Weinberger, D.R. (1986). Prefrontal cortex physiological activation: Effect of L-DOPA in Parkinson's disease. *Neurology (Suppl. 1) 36*, 170.

Weinberger, D.R., Berman, K.F., & Zec, R.F. (1986). Physiologic dysfunction of dorsolateral prefrontal cortex in schizophrenia. *Archives of General Psychiatry, 43*, 114–124.

White, N.M. (1986). Control of sensorimotor function by dopaminergic nigrostriatal neurons: Influence on eating and drinking. *Neuroscience and Biobehaviour Review, 10*, 15–36.

Wooten, G.F., & Collins, R.C. (1983). Effects of dopaminergic stimulation on functional brain metabolism in rats with unilateral substantia nigra lesions. *Brain Research, 263*, 267–275.

Wooten, G.f., & Collins, R.C. (1981). Metabolic effects of unilateral lesion of the substantia nigra. *Journal of Neuroscience, 1(3)*, 285–291.

Wurtz, R.H. Goldberg, E., & Robinson, D.L. (1980). Behavioral modulation of visual response in the monkey: Stimulus selection for attention and movement. *Progress in Psychiatry, Biology, and Physiological Psychology*, *9*, 43–83.

3

Volition and Schizophrenia

Peter F. Liddle
Senior Lecturer In Psychological Medicine, Royal Post Graduate Medical School, Hammersmith Hospital, London.

Schizophrenic patients can perform most routine mental activities in a satisfactory manner when circumstances provide sufficient external guidance. However, difficulties in initiation and organisation of activity become apparent when circumstances do not adequately constrain responses; that is, when the activity might be described as arising from the patient's own volition. Using positron emission tomography (PET) it is possible to delineate the brain regions involved in the performance of voluntary acts. Studies of normal individuals demonstrate that the prefrontal cortex is implicated in the initiation of simple motor acts and in the generation of verbal responses. In schizophrenic patients who have impaired ability to initiate activity, there is underactivity of dorsolateral prefrontal cortex at the site which is active in normal individuals performing self-directed activity. Patients with difficulties in the organisation of activity have underactivity of the orbital prefrontal cortex and overactivity at a site in the right anterior cingulate which is implicated in the suppression of inappropriate responses. Furthermore, there is substantial evidence that dopamine plays a role in the modulation of voluntary activity. However, the effect of dopamine appears to be determined by a complex interplay of internal and external circumstances. These observations suggest that adequate treatment demands more than the simple titration of the dose of dopaminergic agents.

INTRODUCTION

If we are to make sense of schizophrenia and assemble a clear picture from its protean clinical manifestations and its association with diverse and subtle brain abnormalities, we must start with a reasonably clear picture of what features are central to the concept of schizophrenia. The foundation of our

39

current concept is Kraepelin's amalgamation of hebephrenia, catatonia, and dementia paranoides into a single illness. The central feature that linked these conditions was "a weakening of those emotional activities which permanently form the mainspring of volition" (Kraepelin, 1919). In a later essay, Kraepelin described the characteristic feature of schizophrenia as "that destruction of conscious volition ... which is manifest as loss of energy and drive, in disjointed volitional behaviour" (Kraepelin, 1974/1920).

Progress depended not only on a reasonably clear picture of the cardinal features of the illness, but also on the ability to diagnose the condition reliably. Volitional impairment is difficult to assess at interview because its manifestations are least evident in a structured setting. It is manifest in daily life, but performance in daily life is influenced not only by volition but also by a variety of other factors. A clinical feature that is this difficult to assess is scarcely a suitable basis for reliable diagnosis. In contrast, delusions and hallucinations provided a relatively direct and reliable indication of seriously disturbed mental function characteristic of schizophrenia, and hence have assumed a cardinal place in the diagnosis of schizophrenia (e.g. American Psychiatric Association, 1980). Consequently, the view of the essential character of schizophrenia shifted from emphasis on volitional impairment to emphasis on delusions and hallucinations.

However, the relative success of dopamine blocking drugs in alleviating delusions and hallucinations served to emphasise the fact that many patients remained seriously disabled even after the resolution of their delusions and hallucinations. This turned the focus of attention back to the question of what aspect of the illness is principally responsible for the impaired occupational and social function of schizophrenic patients.

Nearly 20 years ago, Strauss et al. (1974) reintroduced the terminology of positive and negative symptoms into psychiatry to provide a framework for relating schizophrenic symptoms to performance in daily life. Positive symptoms reflect an excess of brain processes; negative symptoms entail the diminution of normal brain processes. In general, negative symptoms have a more devastating impact on long-term adjustment. Subsequently, Crow (1980) employed the distinction between positive and negative symptoms in his proposal that there are two major types of pathological process in schizophrenia. He proposed that negative symptoms are associated with structural damage to the brain and predict poor outcome.

Crow favoured a restricted view of which symptoms should be designated as negative symptoms. He placed a major emphasis on two abnormalities that could be assessed at interview, namely poverty of speech and flattened affect. However, such a narrow focus excluded the disjointed volitional behaviour, described by Kraepelin, which can have such a devastating effect on occupational and social function. Andreasen (1982) introduced a broader concept of negative symptoms that included poverty of speech, flat affect, avolition, anhedonia, and attentional impairment. However, her scale for assessing negative symptoms did not address the question of direct assessment of avolition. Instead, she proposed that avolition should be measured by measuring performance in daily life. This was unsatisfactory because of the variety of factors that influence the activities of daily living.

If we are to identify, and eventually to treat, the weakened and disrupted volition that can have such a devastating impact on the lives of schizophrenic patients, we need to re-examine the nature of volition.

THE NATURE OF VOLITION

There is a sense in which volition is essentially a subjective experience: the experience of freely choosing to act. However, when describing the volitional impairment characteristic of schizophrenia, Kraepelin was concerned with observable features of behaviour. He described the characteristic features of schizophrenia as loss of drive and rudderless behaviour, which showed no evidence of planning (Kraepelin, 1974/1920). We require a working definition of voluntary activity that makes it amenable to scientific investigation. For our purpose, we will regard an act as voluntary insofar as its performance is not dictated by external circumstances. Voluntary acts are self-initiated and follow a path that is planned by the individual.

BRAIN ACTIVITY ASSOCIATED WITH VOLITION

Using positron emission tomography (PET) it is possible to delineate the brain regions involved in the performance of voluntary acts. PET can be used to provide a series of tomographic images of regional cerebral blood flow (rCBF) during the performance of a variety of different activities. rCBF is an index of local brain activity. By establishing the differences in patterns of brain activation between activities that differ in the degree to which the response is dictated by external circumstances, it is possible to identify brain regions that become active when the task involves self-direction.

For example, it is possible to compare the pattern of brain activation while the subject carries out a word generation task, in which they generate and articulate words in a given category, with the pattern of activation during a word shadowing task in which the subject articulates words that are produced by the experimenter. Both tasks involve the articulation of words. The major difference between the two tasks is the fact that in the word generation task the subject initiates a self-directed search through their store of words to identify words within the category. Studies of normal individuals reveal that the principal difference between regional rCBF during word generation and that during word shadowing is an increase of rCBF in the left dorsolateral prefrontal cortex (Frith et al., 1991).

Similarly, the pattern of brain activation during the self-directed selection of a simple motor action can be determined by measuring rCBF while the subject flexes and extends either the index or middle finger of the right hand in response to a touch by the experimenter, under conditions that differ in the extent to which the subject can choose which finger to move. In the constrained condition, the subject moves whichever finger is touched by the experimenter. In the self-directed condition, the subject chooses which finger to move whenever the experimenter touches either finger. The major difference in rCBF between the constrained and self-directed conditions is increased rCBF bilaterally in the dorsolateral prefrontal cortex during the self-directed condition (Frith et al., 1991).

Thus, in normal individuals, self-direction of both a verbal task and a simple motor task is associated with activation of the dorsolateral prefrontal cortex, indicating that self-direction of activities of various types involves activation of this region of prefrontal cortex.

During voluntary activity, it is necessary not only to initiate a particular programme of action, but also to inhibit the intrusion of alternative courses of action. Fuster (1989) has argued, on the basis of studies in monkeys, that the orbital (ventral) prefrontal cortex plays a major role in the suppression of inappropriate responses. This is consistent with the evidence that patients with injury to orbital prefrontal cortex are prone to behave in an inappropriate manner (Blumer & Benson, 1975).

So far, there have been no PET studies designed in a way that could be expected to highlight the brain regions concerned with the suppression of inappropriate courses of action during self-directed activity. However, a study by Pardo and colleagues at Washington University (Pardo et al., 1990) of brain regions activated during the Stroop task addresses a closely related issue. In the Stroop task, the individual is presented with the names of colours printed in ink of a colour that differs from the colour name (e.g. the word "red" printed in green ink), and is asked to specify the colour of the ink. Correct performance requires suppression of the conflicting tendency to respond to the colour name. Pardo and colleagues found that the site of greatest increase in rCBF during the performance of the Stroop task compared with a baseline condition in which colour of ink was congruent with colour name, was located in the right anterior cingulate cortex.

VOLITIONAL DISORDERS IN SCHIZOPHRENIA

Kraepelin (1920) described both loss of volition and disjointed volition as characteristic of schizophrenia. My own studies (Liddle, 1984, 1987; Liddle & Barnes, 1990) suggest that these two features of volitional impairment reflect different aspects of the schizophrenic disease process. In a study of the relationships between schizophrenic symptoms, I found that schizophrenic symptoms segregated into three distinguishable syndromes: (1) psychomotor poverty (poverty of speech, flat affect, decreased spontaneous movement); (2) disorganisation (disorders of the form of thought, inappropriate affect); and (3) reality distortion (delusions and hallucinations). This segregation of schizophrenic symptoms into three syndromes has been confirmed in several independent studies (Arndt et al., 1991; Pantelis et al., 1991; Sauer et al., 1991). Two of these syndromes appear to reflect volitional disorders: psychomotor poverty reflects a difficulty initiating activity and disorganisation reflects a difficulty in the selection of appropriate activity.

In accordance with this view, both psychomotor poverty and disorganisation are associated with impairment in neuropsychological tests of frontal lobe function (Liddle & Morris, 1991). Furthermore, each syndrome is associated with different aspects of impairment. Psychomotor poverty is correlated with impairment of word generation in a manner suggesting a reduced speed of mental processing. Disorganisation is associated with impairment in the Stroop task, Trails B, and word generation, in a manner that suggests an underlying difficulty in suppressing inappropriate responses. Both psychomotor poverty and disorganisation are correlated with poor occupational and social function, whereas severity of reality distortion is not significantly associated with impairment in the activities of daily living (Liddle, 1987).

In a recent study, my colleague Karl Friston and I used the oxygen steady-state inhalation PET technique to measure the pattern of rCBF associated with each of the three syndromes of persistent schizophrenic symptoms (Liddle et al., 1992a). We found that each syndrome was associated with a specific pattern of rCBF in association cortex of the frontal, parietal, and temporal lobes, and in related subcortical nuclei. Although the patients were medicated at the time, the patterns could not be accounted for by the direct effects of medication. For our present purposes, we will consider the rCBF patterns associated with the psychomotor poverty and disorganisation syndromes.

BRAIN ACTIVITY ASSOCIATED WITH PSYCHOMOTOR POVERTY

We found the psychomotor poverty syndrome to be associated with decreased perfusion of the left dorsolateral prefrontal cortex and of a region of parietal association cortex that has strong reciprocal connections with dorsolateral prefrontal cortex. There is also an association with increased perfusion of the head of the caudate nucleus bilaterally. Figure 3.1

PSYCHOMOTOR POVERTY

Decreases in rCBF ≣

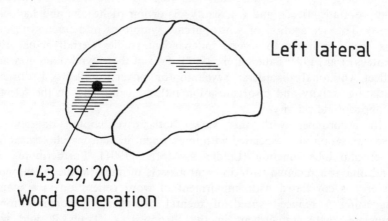

Left lateral

(-43, 29, 20)
Word generation

FIG. 3.1   Locus of maximal activation of the prefrontal cortex during the internal generation of words superimposed on the areas of decreased cortical blood flow associated with psychomotor poverty. Co-ordinates refer to the reference frame defined in the atlas of Talairach and Tournoux (1988) and specify distance in millimeters from the origin at the midpoint of the anterior commissure (after Liddle et al., 1992b, and reproduced by permission of the Royal Society of Medicine).

demonstrates that the left dorsolateral prefrontal region, in which there is a negative correlation between psychomotor syndrome and rCBF, coincides with the site of maximal activation during word generation in normal individuals.

Thus the features of schizophrenia that appear to reflect a difficulty in the initiation of spontaneous activity are associated with cerebral underactivity at the prefrontal site that is active in normal individuals during the performance of self-directed activity.

BRAIN ACTIVITY ASSOCIATED WITH DISORGANISATION

We found the disorganisation syndrome to be associated with decreased perfusion in the right vental prefrontal cortex and contiguous insular cortex, and with increased perfusion in the right anterior cingulate cortex. Figure 3.2 demonstrates that the site of increased perfusion in the right anterior cingulate cortex associated with the disorganisation syndrome coincides

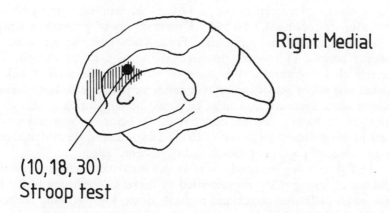

DISORGANIZATION

Increases in rCBF ||||

Right Medial

(10,18, 30)
Stroop test

FIG. 3.2   Locus of maximal activation of the anterior cingulate cortex during the Stroop task superimposed on the areas of increased cortical blood flow associated with disorganisation (after Liddle et al., 1992b, and reproduced by permission of the Royal Society of Medicine).

with the site of maximal activation associated with performance of the Stroop task in normal individuals.

These findings suggest the hypothesis that patients with the disorganisation syndrome have an abnormality of orbital prefrontal cortex, which generates a tendency to engage in inappropriate activity, leading to overactivity of the right anterior cingulate cortex at a location that is implicated in the suppression of inappropriate responses.

CATATONIA

In the classic account of schizophrenia, disturbance of volition was perhaps most clearly illustrated by catatonia. Catatonia embraces a variety of abnormalities of voluntary motor activity. Some of these abnormalities, such as catatonic stupor, entail a deficit of normal motor activity, and hence might be described as negative catatonic phenomena. Others, such as catatonic excitement, entail an excess of apparently purposeless activity and might be described as positive catatonic phenomena.

Cases exhibiting marked catatonia are seen rarely in contemporary practice. Although there is no clear evidence linking the change in prevalence of catatonia with the introduction of neuroleptic medication, it is possible that neuroleptic medication has attenuated the expression of catatonia, so that it now appears in the guise of the psychomotor poverty syndrome. This proposal is supported by a study of the pattern of rCBF in a patient who exhibited classical catatonia.

Case report. Our patient was a 44-year-old man, satisfying DSMIIIr criteria for schizophrenia, who had a 17-year history of schizophrenia prior to his third admission to hospital. Three years later, he remained an inpatient because of severely impaired ability to care for himself. The principle clinical feature at this stage of his illness was marked lack of spontaneous motor activity and classic catatonic phenomena. For example, at times when approaching a door he would become frozen in the act of putting out his hand to turn the door handle. On occasions he would remain frozen in this posture for a period of 10 minutes or longer. He exhibited only a mild degree of poverty of speech and of flattened affect.

A PET study using the steady-state oxygen inhalation technique revealed a pattern of resting rCBF characterised by decreased perfusion in the left dorsolateral prefrontal cortex and parietal cortex, together with increased perfusion in the head of the caudate nucleus on both right and left. Figure 3.3 illustrates the rCBF at these sites in this catatonic patient, in a group of ten patients with no overt evidence of psychomotor poverty, and also in a group of eight patients with substantial psychomotor poverty but without classic catatonia. The group of patients with psychomotor poverty had syndrome scores, assigned by summing scores for flat affect, poverty of speech, and decreased spontaneous movement in the manner described by Liddle and Morris (1991) in the range 5 to 11, with a mean of 8. At all sites, the rCBF in the catatonic patient is near to the mean value observed in the patients with psychomotor poverty, but lies more than a standard deviation from the mean value for patients without psychomotor poverty. Thus, this patient with atypical psychomotor poverty (insofar as lack of spontaneous movement was more pronounced than either poverty of speech or flattened affect), and suffering from classic catatonia, exhibited the pattern of rCBF characteristic of psychomotor poverty.

THE MODULATORY ROLE OF DOPAMINE

There is substantial evidence that dopamine plays a role in the modulation of voluntary activity, in animals and in man. In rats, the level of locomotor activity produced by administration of dopaminergic agonists follows a U-shaped curve. As dose increases there is initially an increase in amount of activity but, at higher doses, total activity decreases as the animals become engaged in repetitive, stereotypic activity. Lyon and Robbins (1975) have suggested that this pattern of response implies that the effect of increasing

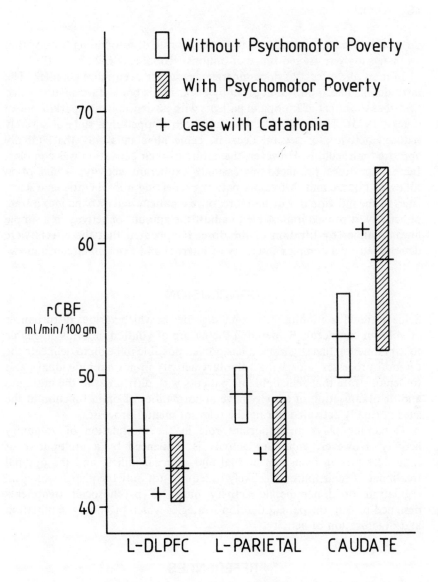

FIG. 3.3 Normalized RCBF in the left dorsolateral prefrontal cortex (L-DLPFC), left parietal lobe (L-PARIETAL) and in the caudate nucleus (mean of left and right) in a schizophrenic patient with catatonia, compared with the mean rCBF at these sites in a group of ten schizophrenic patients without significant evidence of psychomotor poverty and a group of eight schizophrenic patients with psychomotor poverty. The bars indicate a spread of one standard deviation about the mean.

dose of dopaminergic agents is an increased rate of responding from within an increasingly restricted range of options (Robbins & Sahakian, 1983).

In man, the effects of dopaminergic agents are even more complex. The most detailed account is that given by Sacks in his book *Awakenings*, which describes the effect of L-dopa in patients with postencephalitic parkinsonism (Sacks, 1973). These patients, who had been trapped in a state of severely reduced activity for several decades, came alive in a way that initially appeared miraculous. However, the nature of their activation was complex. Increasing doses produced increasingly exuberant activity, which often followed bizarre and distressing patterns reflecting idiosyncratic characteristics of the individual. Furthermore, once a patient had awoken into a state of activity, it proved impossible to adjust the amount of activity in a simple linear manner by titration of the dose. It appeared that the effects were determined by a complex interplay of internal and external circumstances.

CONCLUSION

Schizophrenia is a multidimensional disorder in which various disturbances of volition can occur. By defining the nature of volition in terms amenable to experimental investigation, it has proven possible to begin to delineate the cerebral processes underlying voluntary activity in normal individuals, and to demonstrate that schizophrenic patients with difficulties in the initiation and/or organisation of activity have abnormalities of brain function at the sites normally activated during the relevant mental processes.

Dopamine plays an important role in the modulation of voluntary activity. However, voluntary activity is influenced by a multiplicity of influences arising from the internal and external milieu, and the optimal treatment of schizophrenia is likely to require not only the pharmacological regulation of dopaminergic activity but also psychosocial treatments designed to help the patient develop strategies which promote the initiation and organisation of activity.

REFERENCES

American Psychiatric Association. (1980). *Diagnostic and statistical manual of mental disorders* (3rd ed.). Washington DC: American Psychiatric Association.
Andreasen, N.C. (1982). Negative symptoms in schizophrenia: Definition and reliability. *Archives of General Psychiatry, 39*, 784–788.
Arndt, S., Alliger, R.J., & Andreasen, N.C. (1991). The distinction of positive and negative symptoms. The failure of a two-dimensional model. *British Journal of Psychiatry, 158*, 317–322.
Blumer, D., & Benson, D.F. (1975). Personality changes with frontal lobe lesions. In D.F. Benson and D. Blumer (Eds.), *Psychiatric aspects of neurological disease* (pp. 151–170). New York: Grune & Stratton.

Crow, T.J. (1980). Molecular pathology of schizophrenia: more than one disease process? *British Medical Journal, 280*, 1–9.

Frith, C.D., Friston, K.J., Liddle, P.J., & Frackowiak, R.S.J. (1991). Willed action and prefrontal cortex in man: A study with PET. *Proceedings of the Royal Society B, 244*, 241–246.

Fuster, J.M. (1989). *The prefrontal cortex* (2nd ed.). New York: Raven Press.

Kraepelin, E. (1919). *Dementia praecox and paraphrenia* (R.M. Barclay, Trans.). New York: Kreiger. (Facsimile edition published 1971).

Kraepelin, E. (1974). Die Erscheinungsformen des Irresciens. (H. Marshall, Trans.). In S.R. Hirsch and M. Shepherd (Eds.), *Themes and Variations in European Psychiatry*. Bristol: John Wright. (Original work published 1920).

Liddle, P.F. (1984). *Schizophrenic symptoms, cognitive performance and neurological dysfunction.* Presented at Second Bienniel Winter Workshop at Schizophrenia, Davos, Austria.

Liddle, P.F. (1987). The symptoms of chronic schizophrenia: A re-examination of the positive–negative dichotomy. *British Journal of Psychiatry, 151*, 145–151.

Liddle, P.F., & Barnes, T.R.E. (1990). Syndromes of chronic schizophrenia. *British Journal of Psychiatry, 157*, 558–561.

Liddle, P.F., & Morris, D.L. (1991). Schizophrenic syndromes and frontal lobe performance. *British Journal of Psychiatry, 158*, 340–345.

Liddle, P.F., Friston, K.J., Frith, C.D., Jones, T., Hirsch, S.R., & Frackowiak, R.S.J. (1992a). Patterns of cerebral blood flow in schizophrenia. *British Journal of Psychiatry, 160*, 179–189.

Liddle, P.F., Friston, K.J., Frith, C.D., Hirsch, S.R., & Frackowiak, R.S.J. (1992b). Cerebral blood flow and mental processes in schizophrenia. *Journal of the Royal Society of Medicine, 85*, 224–227.

Lyon, M., & Robbins, T.W. (1975). The action of central nervous system stimulant drugs: A general theory concerning amphetamine effects. In W. Essman & L. Valzelli (Eds.), *Current Developments in Psychopharmacology, Vol. 2* (pp. 79–163). New York: Spectrum.

Pantelis, C., Harvey, C., Taylor, J., & Campbell, P.G. (1991). The Camden schizophrenia surveys; symptoms and syndromes in schizophrenia. *Biological Psychiatry, 29* (Suppl.), 656A.

Pardo, J.V., Pardo, P.J., Janer, K.W., & Raichle, M.E. (1990). The anterior cingulate mediates processing selection in the Stroop attentional conflict paradigm. *Proceedings of the National Academy of Sciences, 87*, 256–259.

Robbins, T.W., & Sahakian, B.J. (1983). Behavioural effects of psychomotor stimulant drugs: clinical and neuropsychological implications. In I. Creese (Ed.), *Stimulants: neurochemical, behavioural and clinical perspectives*. New York: Raven Press.

Sacks, O. (1973). *Awakenings*. London: Duckworth.

Sauer, H. Geider, F.J., Binkert, M., Reitz, C., & Schroder, J. (1991). Is chronic schizophrenia heterogeneous? *Biological Psychiatry, 29* (Suppl.), 661S.

Strauss, J., Carpenter, W.T., & Bartko, J.J. (1974). The diagnosis and understanding of schizophrenia. Part 3: speculations on the processes that underlie schizophrenic symptoms and signs. *Schizophrenia Bulletin, 11*, 61–75.

Talairach, J., & Tournoux, P. (1988). *Co-planar stereotactic atlas of the human brain*. Stuttgart: Thieme.

II INFORMATION PROCESSING

4 Neuropsychological Vulnerability to Schizophrenia

Keith H. Nuechterlein
University of California, Los Angeles, U.S.A.

Monte S. Buchsbaum
University of California, Irvine, U.S.A.

Michael E. Dawson
University of Southern California, U.S.A.

Increasing evidence indicates that certain of the abnormalities of processing information that occur in schizophrenia are not limited to the periods of active positive symptoms, but rather may be enduring indicators of vulnerability to schizophrenic episodes. This chapter will focus on deficits on tachistoscopic measures of vigilance or sustained, focused attention, one of the most prominent impairments found across offspring of schizophrenic patients, actively psychotic schizophrenic patients, and clinically remitted schizophrenic patients. The evidence for similar signal detection impairment during demanding vigilance conditions before, during, and after schizophrenic psychotic episodes will be examined. We will also review recent data on the stability of these impairments within schizophrenic patients across psychotic and remitted periods. The potential neuropsychological significance of these tachistoscopic signal detection deficits during vigilance will be discussed in the light of recent research using positron emission tomography (PET) and EEG coherence procedures. A PET study suggests that a vigilance task involving identification of blurred stimuli, the degraded-stimulus Continuous Performance Test, activates prefrontal cortex and produces differential right hemisphere activation in normal subjects. Schizophrenic patients performing this vigilance task show less prefrontal activation and less differential activation of right compared to left temporoparietal areas than normal subjects. An analysis of EEG coherence completed with R. Hoffman during the same task activation condition extends these results. EEG coherence examines similarity of EEG waveforms between spatially distributed brain modules and may thereby clarify functional interrelationships. During activation by the degraded-stimulus Continuous Performance Test, schizophrenic patients were found to have reduced EEG coherence from right prefrontal to right occipital regions and from right prefrontal to posterior temporal regions. The possible implications of these findings for neuropsychological vulnerability to schizophrenia are examined. The possibility that a specific right hemisphere impairment is implicated in vulnerability to schizophrenia is considered. The hypothesis of specific right-hemisphere impairment is contrasted with an alternative interpretation that emphasizes the role of a prefrontal supervisory attentional system interacting with task-specific demands.

INTRODUCTION

The investigator seeking to identify the key disturbances in processing information in schizophrenia and to elucidate their neuropsychological significance is faced with a fundamental dilemma. Clinical and experimental approaches to this problem have converged to provide evidence of a myriad of deficits in attention, perception, memory, thinking, language, and movement during the active psychotic period (Chapman & Chapman, 1973; Cutting, 1985; Neale & Oltmanns, 1980). The investigator suffers not from a lack of evidence of psychological and neuropsychological deficits in schizophrenia, but rather from evidence of such a wide range of deficits that it is difficult to determine which are of greatest significance. Indeed, it is not only the schizophrenic patient but also the investigator of schizophrenia who could easily suffer from a state of information overload (Buchsbaum & Silverman, 1968; Hemsley, 1977; Venables, 1964).

Although several approaches to this problem are possible, one prominent strategy has been to distinguish psychological deficits in schizophrenia that occur during active psychotic periods and then return to normal levels from deficits that extend beyond the psychotic period and are characteristic of the individual before, during, and after psychotic periods (Cromwell & Spaulding, 1978; Zubin & Spring, 1977). We have extended this dichotomy, as shown in Fig. 4.1, to a tripartite distinction among episode indicators, mediating vulnerability factors, and stable vulnerability indicators (Nuechterlein & Dawson, 1984a; Nuechterlein et al., 1991). Episode indicators are defined as measures that reveal abnormalities only during acute psychotic periods, returning to normal levels between psychotic episodes. These measures may reveal much about the psychological and neuropsychological structure of schizophrenic psychotic episodes, and will include measures that tap disturbances in elementary cognitive processes that are closely connected to the positive symptoms of schizophrenia. Abnormalities in some episode indicators might even immediately precede specific positive symptoms and contribute to the development of these symptoms. However, episode indicators are not likely to provide evidence of factors in the initial vulnerability to schizophrenia or of factors contributing to ongoing vulnerability to psychotic relapses.

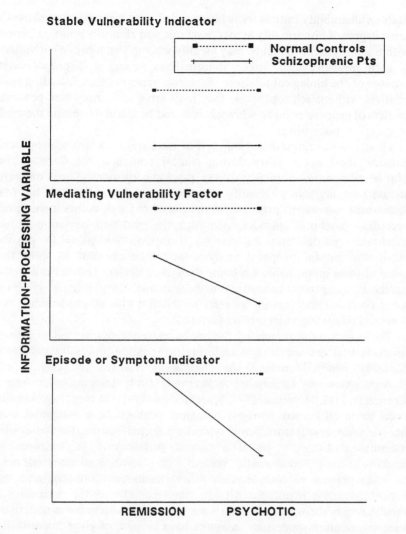

FIG. 4.1 Characteristic patterns of information-processing performance across clinical states for stable vulnerability indicators, mediating vulnerability factors, and episode or symptom indicators. Reprinted with permission from Nuechterlein et al. (1991).

A continuing level of abnormality would be expected for measures that index vulnerability factors for schizophrenia. For variables related to vulnerability to relapse, this continuing abnormality should be present in periods of clinical remission in schizophrenic patients. In the case of vulnerability factors relevant to aetiology as well as to relapse, evidence of abnormality before the initial psychotic episode would also be expected.

Stable vulnerability indicators, which we define as measures that show the same degree of abnormality across psychotic and clinically remitted periods within schizophrenic patients, may identify schizophrenia-prone individuals. If such measures also detect abnormalities among a disproportionate number of the biological relatives of schizophrenic patients, including some relatives without schizophrenia, they may serve to identify non-penitrant carriers of genes relevant to schizophrenia and be useful for testing the mode of genetic transmission.

Finally, we distinguish a third class of measures on which schizophrenic patients show abnormality during clinical remission but deviate from normal even more extremely during psychotic episodes. These measures should not only help to identify schizophrenia-prone individuals but may also reveal component processes in the causal chain of events immediately preceding psychotic episodes. Although the increased deviation during psychotic episodes may be due to disruption secondary to positive symptoms, careful temporal analyses would be expected to show that some of these abnormalities become even more deviant before the onset of psychotic symptoms, consistent with a contributory role in symptom formation. For this reason, we refer to this last type of abnormality as a potential mediating vulnerability factor.

The search for vulnerability factors in schizophrenia has led to a focus on tasks that are sensitive to enduring information-processing deficits in clinically remitted patients and biological relatives of schizophrenic patients (Asarnow, Granholm, & Sherman, 1991; Erlenmeyer-Kimling & Cornblatt, 1987; Holzman, 1987; Nuechterlein, 1991). Rather than choosing tasks based on known neuropsychological localization, investigators seeking vulnerability factors have typically selected information-processing measures that clearly detect abnormal performance in schizophrenic patients during symptomatic periods, that have particular relevance to schizophrenia as compared to other psychiatric disorders, and that concern domains hypothesised to be fundamental ones for psychological functioning in schizophrenia. The brain regions and mechanisms underlying such information-processing measures have become of great interest after initial studies indicate that a measure is sensitive to an ongoing vulnerability factor for schizophrenia. This chapter will focus on studies of signal detection during rapidly-paced vigilance tasks that followed this research sequence.

The clinical observations that led to an interest in vigilance within schizophrenia were captured by Emil Kraepelin (1913/1919, pp. 5–6), who noted a possible connection in schizophrenic patients between perseveration and increased randomness during verbal reports of perceptions and problems in maintaining attention:

This behaviour is without doubt nearly related to the disorder of attention which we very frequently find conspicuously developed in our patients. It is quite common for them to lose both inclination and ability on their own initiative to keep their attention fixed for any length of time.

It is noteworthy that this early observation linked the disordered maintenance of attention to disturbed continuity of speech and thought rather than to the delusions and hallucinations, which are the most prominent episodic aspects of schizophrenia. Another key aspect of Kraepelin's early clinical observations was that he viewed disordered attention as an aspect of a disturbance of volition or will. Avolition is now often included among the negative symptoms of schizophrenia, which are generally considered to be more persistent than the episodes of delusions and hallucinations. Eugen Bleuler (1991/1950), in a somewhat related vein, argued that disordered attention within schizophrenia was secondary to a disturbance of affect, particularly a lack of normal emotional investment in the attended stimuli. Thus, even these early observations suggested possible ties of attentional disturbance to clinical features of schizophrenia that are often more enduring than delusions and hallucinations.

VIGILANCE AND CONTINUOUS PERFORMANCE TESTS

Attempts to elucidate the nature of attentional deficit in schizophrenia have been clouded by difficulties in delineating the form of attention that is under study, as this term has been applied to diverse phenomena (Mirsky, 1989; Posner & Boies, 1971; Zubin, 1975). This chapter emphasises vigilance, which was defined by Norman Mackworth (1957, pp. 389–390) as "a state of readiness to detect and respond to certain small changes occurring at random time intervals in the environment...". Sustained attention, a closely related concept, refers to maintaining focus on a stimulus or a certain dimension of a stimulus over a period of time. The typical measure of a deficit is sustained attention in experimental psychology is the decrement in signal/noise discrimination within the vigilance period (Parasuraman, 1986). However, the vigilance level, or level of signal/noise discrimination across the entire vigilance period, appears thus far to be the more sensitive measure of a disturbance related to schizophrenia (Nuechterlein, 1991). Thus, although readiness to detect and respond to unpredictable occurrences of target stimuli in a series of incoming stimuli is an important element in schizophrenic performance on these tasks, an abnormally large progressive decrement in sustained attention over time is probably not the underlying process to which these impairments in schizophrenia should be attributed.

Rather, as we discuss elsewhere (Nuechterlein, 1991; Nuechterlein & Dawson, 1984b), difficulties in the rapid processing of the very brief stimulus presentations under time pressure may be the source.

In research on psychopathology, the primary measures of vigilance have been versions of the Continuous Performance Test (CPT), the original version of which was developed by Rosvold et al. (1956). The various versions of the CPT typically involve tachistoscopic presentations (40–200 ms) of a quasirandom series of letter or numeral stimuli at a rapid, fixed rate (e.g. 1/s) over 5–15 min with instructions to respond to a predesignated letter or number or sequence of letters or numerals each time that it appears. Beyond these basic features, some variants of the conventional CPT have been developed to increase processing load and to place particular burden on certain aspects of information processing. Two notable features of more recently developed CPT tasks have been the use of visually degraded stimuli to burden initial stimulus encoding and analysis processes (Nuechterlein, 1983; Nuechterlein, Parasuraman, & Jiang, 1983) and the use of successive identical stimuli as the target to burden active, short-term memory processes (Erlenmeyer-Kimling & Cornblatt, 1978; Cornblatt et al., 1988).

CPT ANOMALIES IN ACTIVELY SYMPTOMATIC AND REMITTED SCHIZOPHRENIC PATIENTS

An initial study of schizophrenic patients showed that chronic, drug-free schizophrenic patients obtain a lower target detection rate than normal or alcohol subjects (Orzack & Kornetsky, 1966). Although schizophrenic patients are not the only psychopathological group to show abnormal performance on CPT tasks, signal detection theory analyses have provided support for the view that schizophrenic CPT performance is more distinctive than would be apparent from examination of the target detections (hits) or incorrect responses (false alarms) alone. Signal detection theory analyses separate a signal/noise discrimination, or sensitivity, dimension from a response criterion dimension. Schizophrenic patients typically show impaired signal/noise discrimination but not altered response criterion levels (Cornblatt, Lenzenweger, & Erlenmeyer-Kimling, 1989; Nuechterlein et al., 1991). Although children with attention deficit disorder also sometimes show impaired signal/noise discrimination levels, they usually have response criterion levels that are abnormally low, consistent with an impulsive style of CPT responding (Nuechterlein, 1983; O'Dougherty, Nuechterlein, & Drew, 1984). An initial study of affective disorder patients indicated that inpatients with affective disorder or schizoaffective disorder had significantly less impairment in CPT hit rates than schizophrenic inpatients (Walker, 1981). A more recent signal detection analysis of CPT versions using numeral or nonsense-shape stimuli and successive identical stimuli as the target (Cornblatt et al., 1989) demonstrated that schizophrenic patients had poorer signal/noise discrimination levels under both stimulus conditions than either normal or depressed subjects. Depressed patients showed significant impairment during the nonsense-shape condition but not the numeral condition. Thus, although additional evaluation of diagnostic specificity relative to other psychopathological groups is clearly needed, signal detection theory analyses thus far suggest that actively symptomatic schizophrenic patients show an impairment in signal/noise discrimination or sensitivity on CPT tasks that is distinguished by its severity, pervasiveness across types of stimulus input, and lack of accompanying lowering of response criterion.

As indicated earlier, impairment during clinically remitted periods is an essential feature of potential vulnerability indicators for schizophrenia. Three cross-sectional studies have now demonstrated such impairment on CPT tasks, particularly for those CPT versions that make relatively high demands on either initial stimulus analysis processes by degrading stimuli or on active, short-term memory by using targets that involve successive stimuli (Asarnow & MacCrimmon, 1978; Steinhauer et al., 1991; Wohlberg & Kornetsky, 1973). The Wohlberg and Kornetsky (1973) result is particularly striking because the schizophrenic subjects were selected for a return to a premorbid level of functioning, were tested at least a year after their only psychiatric hospitalisation, and were in all but one case off medication without indication of deterioration.

We recently presented preliminary analyses from the first longitudinal study of schizophrenic CPT performance across clinically remitted and psychotic states (Nuechterlein et al., 1991). The longitudinal design allows direct examination of the distinction between stable vulnerability indicators and mediating vulnerability factors discussed earlier. This longitudinal, collaborative study, entitled Developmental Processes in Schizophrenic Disorders, involves patients who have recently had a first episode of schizophrenia and demographically matched normal comparison subjects (Nuechterlein et al., 1992). For this analysis we selected 17 patients who were tested during both clearly remitted and psychotic states while on the same dosage of the standard antipsychotic medication, fluphenazine decanoate, as part of this project (Nuechterlein et al., 1991). Our symptomatic criteria for clinical remission involved the absence of any rating in the pathological range (4 to 7 on 7-point scales) on any item of the Expanded Brief Psychiatric Rating Scale (Expanded BPRS; Lukoff, Nuechterlein, & Ventura, 1986) for at least 1 month, while psychotic states were defined as periods in which delusions, hallucinations, or conceptual disorganisation were present based on the Expanded BPRS ratings (4 or greater) on the day of testing. Normal comparison subjects were examined at comparable time intervals. As shown in the left panel of Fig. 4.2, these schizophrenic patients moved from a clearly non-psychotic clinical state like that of the comparison subjects to a psychotic state characterised by increased scores on the Thought Disturbance factor of the BPRS. Most psychotic periods involved return of delusions (see right panel, Fig. 4.2) or hallucinations rather than conceptual disorganisation.

One version of the CPT required that the subject detect presentations of a highly blurred 0 numeral (see Fig. 4.3) within an 8-min series of other highly blurred single digits, such as the 6 shown in Fig. 4.4. Stimuli were presented 1/s with a 0.25 target rate and a 40 ms exposure duration. The signal/noise discrimination (d') levels of the 17 schizophrenic patients on this degraded-stimulus CPT were very clearly impaired relative to the 17 normal subjects at both the clinically remitted and the psychotic points (see Fig. 4.5). The small clinical state component of performance was not significant in this analysis and reasonably high test-retest stability within schizophrenic patients was also evident ($r = 0.57$). Thus, this analysis suggests that rapid discrimination of these blurred characters within a vigilance paradigm may index a deficit that is a relatively stable vulnerability factor in schizophrenia.

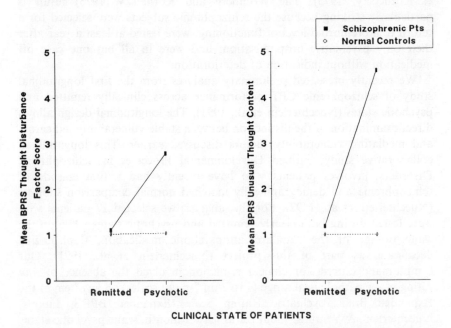

FIG. 4.2   Mean symptom ratings of 17 schizophrenic subjects and 17 normal subjects on two test occasions for the Brief Psychiatric Rating Scale (BPRS) Thought Disturbance factor and the Unusual Thought Content item. Reprinted with permission from Nuechterlein et al. (1991).

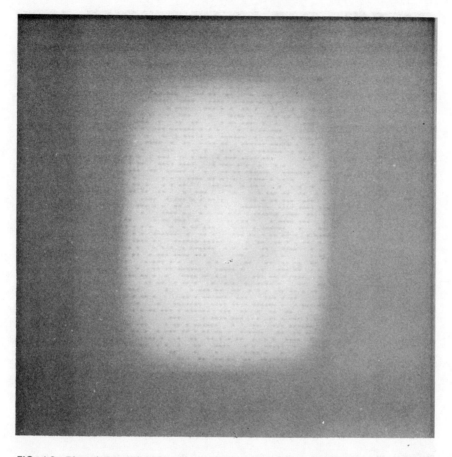

FIG. 4.3 Blurred numeral 0 that serves as the target (signal) stimulus for the degraded-stimulus Continuous Performance Test.

For comparison purposes, we also examined performance on a CPT version that demands active, short-term memory but not discrimination of degraded visual images. In this condition, the target within a quasirandom series of clearly focused single digits was the 7 only if immediately preceded by the digit 3. As shown in Fig. 4.6, signal/noise discrimination was also impaired among the schizophrenic patients on this memory-load version of the CPT during clinically remitted and psychotic states, but the state component of performance was also strong, yielding a highly significant interaction between diagnostic group and test occasion. In terms of the tripartite distinction discussed earlier, this memory-load CPT appears to tap a potential mediating vulnerability factor for schizophrenia. This finding is also consistent with Hemsley's (1987) hypothesis that positive symptoms of

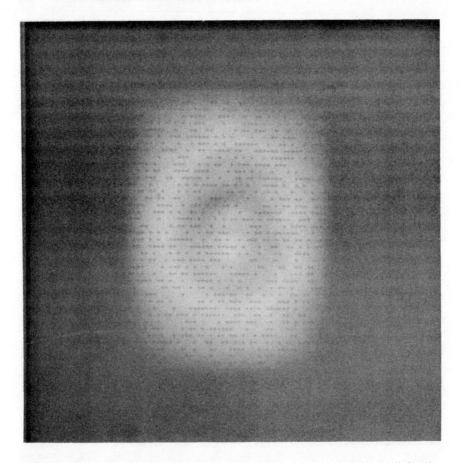

FIG. 4.4   Blurred numeral 6 that serves as one of the nontarget (noise) stimuli for the degraded-stimulus Continuous Performance Test. This nontarget stimulus is one of the numerals that is most similar perceptually to the target numeral 0.

schizophrenic patients are characterised by decreased influence of memory as a guide to interpretation of sensory input, because this memory-load CPT uses the remembered context in which the present stimulus occurs as a cue to significance (the 7 is the target only in the context of a preceding 3). Considered together with the degraded-stimulus CPT results, these memory-load CPT analyses suggest an interesting possibility: disturbances in use of active memory may be more closely linked to active psychotic periods in schizophrenia, while initial stimulus analysis aspects of perceptual discrimination may be more stably impaired across clinical state. Beyond this specific possibility, these longitudinal analyses provide additional support for the hypothesis that CPT signal/noise discrimination deficits

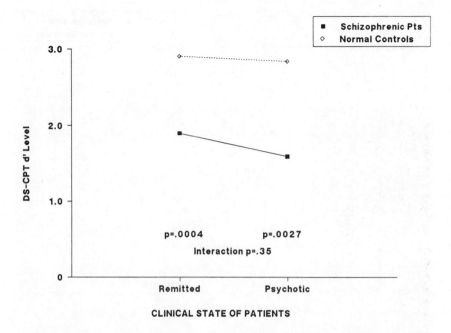

FIG. 4.5   Mean signal/noise discrimination level (d') in the degraded-stimulus Continuous Performance Test for 17 schizophrenic patients and 17 normal subjects on occasions selected for remitted and psychotic states within the same patients. Reprinted with permission from Nuechterlein et al. (1991).

endure beyond symptomatic periods in schizophrenia and are indices of ongoing vulnerability factors.

CPT DEFICITS AMONG CHILDREN AT RISK FOR SCHIZOPHRENIA

If CPT signal/noise discrimination deficits index vulnerability factors relevant to schizophrenia, these abnormalities should also be present before schizophrenia develops. Although systematic selection of individuals who will shortly have an initial schizophrenic episode is not possible, a related hypothesis is that this CPT deficit should be evident at abnormally high rates or to a greater degree in populations with increased risk for schizophrenia. To test this hypothesis, the offspring of schizophrenic patients, who have a 5 to 15% risk of developing schizophrenia as compared to a general population risk of 0.5 to 1% (Gottesman & Shields, 1982), have been compared to children who do not have this genetic relationship to a schizophrenic patient.

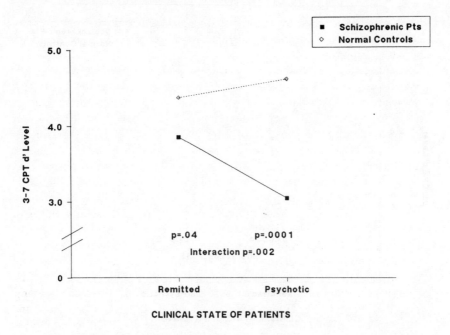

FIG. 4.6 Mean signal/noise discrimination level (d') in a memory-load Continuous Performance Test for 17 schizophrenic patients and 17 normal subjects on occasions selected for remitted and psychotic states within the same patients. Reprinted with permission from Nuechterlein et al. (1991).

Data from several samples now indicate that a signal/noise discrimination deficit is present among a disproportionate number of children born to schizophrenic patients before they enter the typical period of risk for onset of schizophrenia. In particular, Rutschmann, Cornblatt, and Erlenmeyer-Kimling (1977) of the New York High-Risk Project found decreased signal/noise discrimination levels among 7- to 12-year-old children of schizophrenic patients in a CPT that used successive identical stimuli as the target. We extended this initial result in the Minnesota High-Risk Study by demonstrating that scores on a signal/noise discrimination factor drawn from five CPT conditions were impaired among 9- to 16-year-old children born to schizophrenic patients, including three conditions with degraded numeral stimuli, but not among children born to mothers with nonpsychotic disorders outside the schizophrenia spectrum (Nuechterlein, 1983). The signal detection deficit during the CPT was found to be present across conditions differing in informational and motivational feedback (Nuechterlein, 1983). In a second New York sample, Rutschmann, Cornblatt, and Erlenmeyer-Kimling (1986) again found impaired CPT signal/noise discrimination among offspring of schizophrenic patients and demonstrated that offspring of patients with major affective disorder do not show this impairment.

Results from the New York High-Risk Project have also indicated the predictive value of CPT signal/noise discrimination deficits in childhood for later psychiatric disturbance among children born to a schizophrenic parent. In their first sample, Erlenmeyer-Kimling and Cornblatt (1987) found lower signal/noise discrimination on a memory-load CPT at age 7–12 years among offspring of schizophrenic patients who were hospitalised or in psychiatric treatment in late adolescence (not all with diagnoses of schizophrenia), as compared to the rest of the children with schizophrenic parents. The early CPT signal/noise discrimination levels of these remaining children of schizophrenic patients did not differ significantly from those of children of normal parents or children of affectively disordered parents. In other words, the subgroup of children of schizophrenic parents who show psychopathology in late adolescence are the source of CPT differences at 7–12 years of age between the entire sample of children of schizophrenic patients and children of normal or affectively disordered parents. In the second sample from the New York High-Risk Project, Rutschmann, Cornblatt, and Erlenmeyer-Kimling (1986) found that late childhood CPT discriminability factor scores were low for 41% of 17 offspring of schizophrenic parents who developed psychopathology by mid-adolescence, compared to only 6% of 18 offspring of schizophrenic parents without later psychopathology. This predictive relationship between early CPT deviance and midadolescent psychopathology was not present for the children of normal parents or of affectively disordered parents, so it appears to be tied to familial presence of genetic vulnerability to schizophrenia.

These results within children of schizophrenic patients solidify further the view that CPT signal/noise discrimination deficits may serve as an index of vulnerability factors for schizophrenia. The overall picture that emerges is that a very similar CPT deficit can be detected among symptomatic schizophrenic patients, clinically remitted schizophrenic patients, and children at genetic risk for schizophrenia.

POSITRON EMISSION TOMOGRAPHY STUDIES OF CPT PERFORMANCE

The possibility that impaired signal/noise discrimination in high-processing-load versions of the CPT indexes a vulnerability factor for schizophrenia has recently led to attempts to determine which brain regions are implicated. The possible role of arousal and the ascending reticular pathways had been suggested in early views of CPT deficits in schizophrenia (Mirsky, 1969), but interest has more recently centered on cortical involvement in information processing during the CPT. In particular, positron emission tomography (PET) research has recently allowed preliminary identification of cortical regions that are activated during CPT performance and that may be involved in schizophrenic CPT deficits. Given the greater stability of performance on the degraded-stimulus CPT as compared to a conventional CPT with clearly focused single-letter targets and the related potential for this CPT to tap trait-like vulnerability factors (Nuechterlein, 1985; Nuechterlein et al., 1991), the degraded-stimulus version of the CPT has been used as an activation task in PET research involving a collaboration among University of California, Irvine; UCLA; and University of California, San Diego, investigators. In an initial study conducted in the UC Irvine PET center directed by Monte Buchsbaum, we contrasted cortical activation of normal subjects during performance of the degraded-stimulus CPT with that of normal subjects focusing on the same blurred stimuli without instructions to process the images or to respond selectively to target stimuli (Buchsbaum et al., 1990). In addition, we have contrasted cortical activation of schizophrenic patients and normal subjects during performance of this task. We focused on three cortical slices, as shown in Fig. 4.7, and on a 2-cm-thick ring of cortex for these initial analyses.

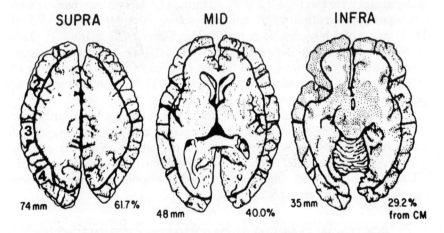

FIG. 4.7   Three slice levels used in the analysis of the cortical surface. PET images were selected to match these levels and then a computer algorithm was applied to delineate the four cortical sectors on each hemisphere that are designated R1 to R4 for the right and L1 to L4 for the left in anteroposterior sequence. The supraventricular slice comprises (1) superior and middle frontal gyrus, (2) inferior frontal, pre-central, and post-central gyrus, (3) parietal lobe, supramarginal and angular gyrus, and (4) occipital lobe. The midventricular slice comprises (1) middle frontal and some superior frontal gyrus, (2) pre-central gyrus, insula, and some superior temporal gyrus, (3) middle and inferior temporal gyrus, and (4) occipital pole. The infraventricular slice comprises (1) inferior frontal gyrus and some middle frontal gyrus, (2) tip of temporal lobe and some superior and middle temporal gyrus, (3) middle temporal gyrus, and (4) inferior occipital pole. Reprinted with permission from Buchsbaum et al. (1990).

Comparison of 18 normal subjects performing the degraded-stimulus CPT with 19 normal subjects passively focusing on the same highly blurred stimuli revealed significant differential activation of the right hemisphere during task performance, including frontal, temporal, and parietal regions (Buchsbaum et al., 1990). An example of PET images from the task and no-task conditions for normal subjects is shown in Fig. 4.8. Occipital activation did not differ for the active task and passive focal point conditions, as might be expected for matched visual stimulation situations.

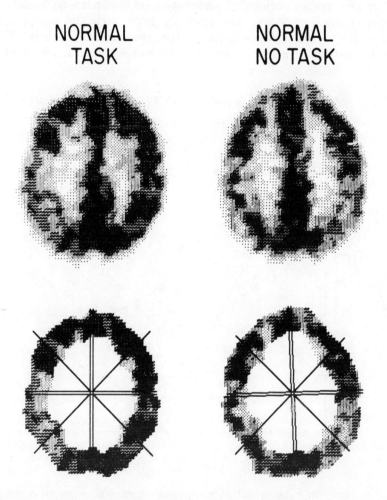

NORMAL TASK   NORMAL NO TASK

FIG. 4.8 Examples of PET scans from two normal subjects, showing supraventricular level. Metabolic rate is represented as slice maximum (darkest) to slice minimum (lightest) in nine steps of grey. Top left shows a normal subject during degraded-stimulus CPT performance and top right shows a normal subject during passive viewing of same blurred stimuli. Bottom illustrates the cortical sectors used in the analyses.

Next, the initial 13 schizophrenic patients were contrasted with the normal subjects under CPT task conditions (Buchsbaum et al., 1990). The schizophrenic patients had relatively less metabolic activity than normal subjects in prefrontal cortex (bilaterally) but normal or greater than normal activity in the occipital cortex, leading to a significant hypofrontal pattern for schizophrenic patients, as shown in Fig. 4.9. Furthermore, a significant diagnostic group by hemisphere by anteroposterior sector interaction was present. As seen in Fig. 4.9 for anteroposterior sector 3, part of this differing pattern of activation during CPT performance involves relatively higher left temporoparietal activation and relatively lower right temporoparietal activation for schizophrenic patients than for normal subjects. This differing pattern of activation can also be seen in the example of PET

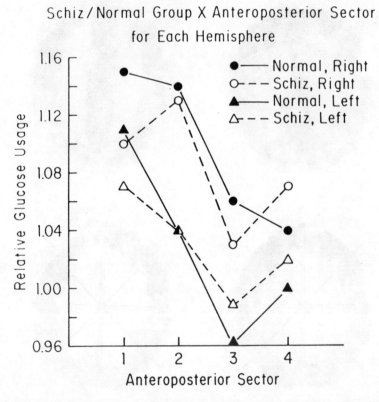

FIG. 4.9   Mean relative glucose metabolic rate for each hemisphere from front (1) to back (4) across scan levels during degraded-stimulus CPT performance. For schizophrenic patients compared to normal subjects note the hypofrontal pattern and also the smaller metabolic rate difference between right and left hemisphere in sector 3. Reprinted with permission from Buchsbaum et al. (1990).

scans from a schizophrenic and a normal subject during degraded-stimulus CPT performance in Fig. 4.10.

Thus, the primary visual sensory cortex was at least normally activated in schizophrenic patients during CPT performance. However, schizophrenic

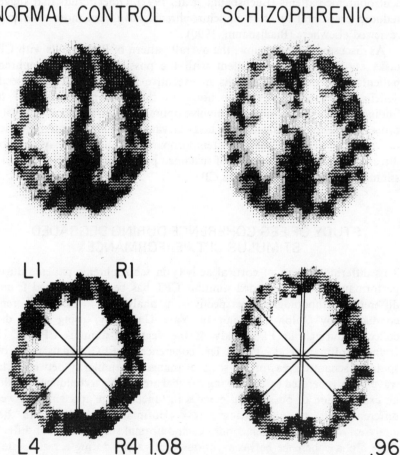

FIG. 4.10 Examples of PET scan of a normal subject and a schizophrenic patient showing metabolic rate at supraventricular level during degraded-stimulus CPT. Metabolic rate is represented as slice maximum (darkest) to slice minimum (lightest) in nine steps of grey. Top left shows a normal subject and top right shows a schizophrenic subject. Bottom illustrates the cortical sectors used in the analyses and the frontal-to-occipital ratio for the two subjects.

patients showed deficient activation of regions of the prefrontal and right temporoparietal cortex that appear to subserve sustained attention (Mesulam, 1985; Mirsky & Duncan, 1989; Pardo, Fox, & Raichle, 1991; Posner & Petersen, 1990). Correlations between signal/noise discrimination levels (d') and relative metabolic rate within groups indicated that normal subjects with the best CPT performance had high right temporoparietal activation, while for schizophrenic patients this relationship was reversed (Buchsbaum et al., 1990). Recently, the prefrontal findings during the degraded-stimulus CPT have been extended to a sample of never-medicated schizophrenic patients (Buchsbaum et al., 1992). Other results that suggest reduced prefrontal function in schizophrenia have been more extensively reviewed elsewhere (Buchsbaum, 1990).

As discussed further below, the overall pattern of PET results with CPT tasks at this point is consistent with the possibility that schizophrenic patients have prefrontal deficits in executive functions and task-specific deficits in temporoparietal functions. In this conceptualization of the findings, the executive functions involve optimal organisation and control of processing resource allocation to task-relevant brain areas across a variety of voluntary tasks, while right temporoparietal functions may be more directly tied to the effectiveness of sustained processing of the blurred visual stimuli of the degraded-stimulus CPT.

STUDY OF EEG COHERENCE DURING DEGRADED-STIMULUS CPT PERFORMANCE

This differing pattern of cortical activity in schizophrenic patients during performance of the degraded-stimulus CPT has been approached from a different methodological perspective in analyses of EEG coherence conducted by Ralph Hoffman of Yale University, using EEG data collected during our PET study of the degraded-stimulus CPT at UC Irvine (Hoffman et al., 1991). The coherence of EEG signals from two spatially separate areas of the scalp examines the similarity between EEG waveforms generated by underlying cortical areas. This technique may allow an examination of possible differences in functional relationships between different brain modules during a task (Hoffman et al., 1991). In these analyses, we found that schizophrenic and normal subjects did not differ in EEG alpha coherence between various brain areas during a resting state. However, during performance of the degraded-stimulus CPT, the schizophrenic patients showed weaker alpha coherence between right prefrontal region and the right occipital region and also between the right prefrontal cortex and right posterior temporal region. These areas are shown in the top panel of Fig. 4.11.

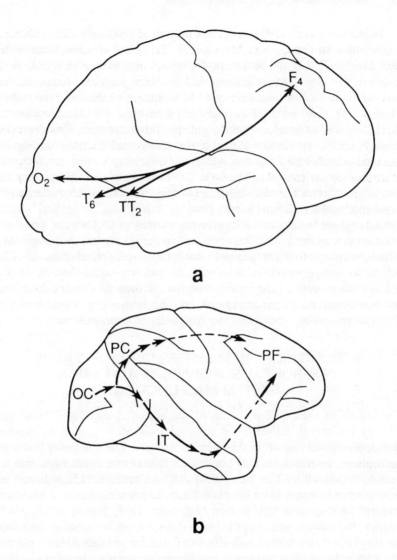

FIG. 4.11 a) Spatial distribution of alpha coherences demonstrating significant reductions in schizophrenia during degraded-stimulus CPT activation that could not be accounted for by changed alpha power. b) Visual information processing pathways identified within the monkey, as reported by Macko et al. (1982). OC = occipital cortex; PC = parietal cortex; IT = inferior temporal cortex; PF = prefrontal cortex. The parietal pathway is active during object localization, and the inferior temporal pathway is active during object identification. Reprinted with permission from Hoffman et al. (1991).

As Hoffman et al. (1991) note, this pattern of weakened EEG coherence is consistent with research by Macko et al. (1982) and Mishkin, Ungerleider, and Macko (1983) on pathways for visual processing in monkeys. A pathway for object identification that involves occipital, temporal, and prefrontal cortex has been delineated in monkeys, as shown in the bottom panel of Fig. 4.10, which is distinct from a pathway for object localisation that involves occipital, parietal, and prefrontal cortex. The degraded-stimulus CPT demands identification of numeral stimuli that are ambiguous in shape but not location, so it would be expected to involve the occipital–temporal–frontal pathway. Thus, the combination of the PET studies and the EEG coherence study suggest that schizophrenia is characterised by lower prefrontal activation and possible disruption of cortical circuits during degraded-stimulus CPT performance that extend beyond prefrontal areas to connections with temporal and occipital cortex. Although these initial studies of brain regions involved in degraded-stimulus CPT performance have examined schizophrenic patients rather than subjects at risk for schizophrenia, the results raise the question of whether disordered neural circuits in the same regions may be relevant to vulnerability to schizophrenia or to a subset of the symptoms of schizophrenia.

SPECIFIC RIGHT HEMISPHERE DEFICITS VERSUS PREFRONTAL SUPERVISORY ATTENTION SYSTEM MALFUNCTION

The results of these recent studies of the degraded-stimulus CPT suggest lowered prefrontal activation in schizophrenia accompanied by possible disrupted cortical circuits in the right hemisphere. The possibility that right hemisphere abnormalities may play an important role in schizophrenia has been hypothesised by Venables (1984) and by Cutting (1985), although left hemisphere abnormalities have played a more prominent role in models of schizophrenic cortical dysfunction (e.g. Gur, 1978; Posner et al., 1988). Studies that have found degraded-stimulus CPT performance to be mildly but significantly correlated with affective flattening in schizophrenic patients and with anhedonia in persons at risk for schizophrenia (Grove et al., 1991; Nuechterlein, 1985) are also consistent with right hemisphere involvement, as this hemisphere probably is specialised in certain aspects of emotional processing (Hellige, 1990). Given these findings and the presence of signal discrimination deficits in the degraded-stimulus CPT in children of schizophrenic patients and during remission of psychotic symptoms, one possible hypothesis is that weak right hemisphere pathways integrating right prefrontal cortex, temporal cortex, and primary sensory cortex is a predispositional factor and contributes to enduring affective flattening in schizophrenia. Recent findings suggest that information-processing disturbances is left hemisphere functioning, on the other hand, might be present during periods of active psychosis in schizophrenia but normalise during clinically remitted periods (Posner et al., 1988; Strauss et al., 1991).

Another important possibility is that the specific nature of the stimuli of this version of the CPT is contributing to the right hemisphere focus of most of our results to date. Although the right hemisphere is differentially involved in maintenance of concentration and in attentional tone (Dimond, 1976; Mesulam, 1985; Pardo et al., 1991; Posner & Petersen, 1990; Wilkins, Shallice, & McCarthy, 1987), considerable evidence also suggests that it is specialized in processing of degraded, low-spatial-frequency images (Hellige, 1990; Sergent & Hellige, 1986). Thus, at present we cannot determine whether the right hemisphere emphasis in our results is intrinsic to the vigilance demands of the CPT or is linked to the use of degraded visual images. The recent PET findings by Pardo et al. (1991) of differential right hemisphere activation in normal subjects during two other vigilance procedures strengthens the case for intrinsic right hemisphere specialisation in vigilance (in their report, especially right prefrontal and right superior parietal cortex). Direct manipulation of stimulus degradation level of vigilance activation tasks with schizophrenic and normal subjects will be needed to clarify further the localisation role played by the low-spatial-frequency images of the degraded-stimulus CPT.

The possibility that a prefrontal dysfunction is the most generalisable locus of CPT deficit in schizophrenia and in vulnerability to schizophrenia needs further consideration, particularly in light of regional cerebral blood flow findings during activation by the Wisconsin Card Sorting Task (Weinberger et al., 1986; 1988) and PET findings during an auditory analogue of the CPT (Cohen et al., 1987). The auditory analogue of the CPT used by Cohen et al. (1987) required that the subject respond to a low intensity tone among a random series of tones of three intensities. Compared to normal subjects, schizophrenic patients showed less metabolic activity in the middle prefrontal cortex (bilaterally) and the left anterior temporal cortex. Significant correlations between relative metabolic rates in the middle prefrontal cortex areas and vigilance performance level were found among normal subjects, but not among schizophrenic patients. Thus, the results with an auditory CPT analogue converge with those from the degraded-stimulus CPT in their emphasis on deficient metabolic activity in prefrontal cortex in schizophrenia during conditions demanding vigilance to briefly presented stimuli.

In summary, these findings of abnormally low prefrontal metabolic activity among schizophrenic patients during vigilance conditions (Buchsbaum et al., 1990, 1992; Cohen et al., 1987) are consistent with earlier literature regarding cerebral blood flow (Ingvar & Franzen, 1974) and metabolism (Buchsbaum et al., 1982) in schizophrenia. Brain metabolic activity and electrical activity of schizophrenic and normal subjects during a visual degraded-stimulus CPT suggest that another cortical region of particular interest is the right temporal cortex. This right temporal area might be related to the specific processing demands of the visual vigilance task used, because a PET study with auditory stimuli (Cohen et al., 1987) found that schizophrenic patients differed in metabolic rate in left temporal cortex but not in right hemisphere areas. However, other research with normal subjects does support the differential specialization of right hemisphere areas for vigilance.

Prefrontal dysfunction is the common denominator in these PET studies of vigilance in schizophrenia, which emphasises the role of the prefrontal cortex in executive functions and in what Shallice (1988) has termed a supervisory attentional system. This alternative to a specific role for right hemisphere abnormalities in schizophrenia would view the prefrontal cortex dysfunction as leading to failure to organise optimal strategies for task completion and, therefore, failure to activate the brain regions that are most specialised for processing the specific types of stimuli that a given task involves.

Studies of clinically remitted schizophrenic patients and biological relatives of schizophrenic patients will be critical to determining whether these same patterns of anomalous regional brain activation during vigilance are part of the neuropsychological vulnerability to schizophrenia.

REFERENCES

Asarnow, R.F., & MacCrimmon, D.J. (1978). Residual performance deficit in clinically remitted schizophrenics: A marker of schizophrenia? Journal of Abnormal Psychology, 87, 597–608.
Asarnow, R.F., Granholm, E., & Sherman, T. (1991). Span of apprehension in schizophrenia. In S.R. Steinhauer, J.H. Gruzelier, & J. Zubin (Eds.), Handbook of schizophrenia, Vol. 5: Neuropsychology, psychophysiology, and information processing (pp. 335–370). Amsterdam: Elsevier.
Bleuler, E. (1950). Dementia praecox or the group of schizophrenias (J. Zinkin, Trans.). New York: International Universities Press. (Original work published 1911).
Buchsbaum, M.S. (1990). The frontal lobes, basal ganglia, and temporal lobes as sites for schizophrenia. Schizophrenia Bulletin, 16, 377–387.
Buchsbaum, M.S., Haier, R.J., Potkin, S.G., Nuechterlein, K., Bracha, S., Katz, M. Lohr, J., Wu, J., Lottenberg, S., Jerabek, P.A., Trenary, M., Tafalla, R., Reynolds, C., & Bunney, W.E., Jr. (1992). Frontostriatal disorder of cerebral metabolism in never-medicated schizophrenics. Archives of General Psychiatry, 49, 935–942.
Buchsbaum, M.S., Ingvar, D.H., Kessler, R., Waters, R.N., Cappelletti, J., van Kammen, D.P., King, A.C., Johnson, J.J., Manning, R.G., Flynn, R.M., Mann, L.S., Bunney, W.E., Jr., & Sokoloff, L. (1982). Cerebral glucography with positron tomography in normals and in patients with schizophrenia. Archives of General Psychiatry, 39, 251–259.
Buchsbaum, M.S., Nuechterlein, K.H., Haier, R.J., Wu, J., Sicotte, N., Hazlett, E., Asarnow, R., Potkin, S., & Guich, S. (1990). Glucose metabolic rate in normals and schizophrenics

during the continuous performance test assessed by position emission tomography. *British Journal of Psychiatry, 156*, 216–227.

Buchsbaum, M.S., & Silverman, J. (1968). Stimulus intensity control and the cortical evoked response. *Psychosomatic Medicine, 30*, 12–22.

Chapman, L.J., & Chapman, J.P. (1973). *Disordered thought in schizophrenia.* New York: Appleton–Century–Crofts.

Cohen, R.M., Semple, W.E., Gross, M., Nordahl, T.E., DeLisi, L.E., Holcomb, H.H., King, A.C., Morihisa, J.M., & Pickar, D. (1987). Dysfunction in a prefrontal substrate of sustained attention in schizophrenia. *Life Sciences, 40*, 2031–2039.

Cornblatt, B.A., Risch, N.J., Faris, G., Friedman, D., & Erlenmeyer-Kimling, L. (1988). The Continuous Performance Test, Identical Pairs Version (CPT-IP): I. New findings about sustained attention in normal families. *Psychiatry Research, 26*, 223–238.

Cornblatt, B.A., Lenzenweger, M.F., & Erlenmeyer-Kimling, L. (1989). The Continuous Performance Test, Identical Pairs Version: II. Contrasting attentional profiles in schizophrenic and depressed patients. *Psychiatry Research, 29*, 65–85.

Cromwell, R.L., & Spaulding, W. (1978). How schizophrenics handle information. In W.E. Fann, I. Karacan, A.D. Pokorny, & R.L. Williams (Eds.), *Phenomenology and treatment of schizophrenia* (pp. 127–162). New York: Spectrum Press.

Cutting, J. (1985). *The psychology of schizophrenia.* Edinburgh: Churchill Livingstone.

Dimond, S.J. (1976). Depletion of attentional capacity after total commissurotomy in man. *Brain, 99*, 347–356.

Erlenmeyer-Kimling, L., & Cornblatt, B. (1978). Attentional measures in a study of children at high risk for schizophrenia. In L.C. Wynne, R.L. Cromwell, & S. Matthysse (Eds.), *The nature of schizophrenia: New approaches to research and treatment.* New York: Wiley.

Erlenmeyer-Kimling, L., & Cornblatt, B. (1987). The New York High-Risk Project: A follow up report. *Schizophrenia Bulletin, 13*, 451–461.

Gottesman, I.I., & Shields, J. (1982). *Schizophrenia: The epigenetic puzzle.* New York: Cambridge University Press.

Grove, W.M., Lebow, B.S., Clementz, B.A., Certi, A., Medus, C., & Iacono, W.G. (1991). Familial prevalence and coaggregation of schizotypy indicators: A multitrait family study. *Journal of Abnormal Psychology, 100*, 115–121.

Gur, R.E. (1978). Left hemisphere dysfunction and left hemisphere overactivation in schizophrenia. *Journal of Abnormal Psychology, 87*, 226–238.

Hellige, J.B. (1990). Hemispheric asymmetry. *Annual Review of Psychology, 41*, 55–80.

Hemsley, D.R. (1977). What have cognitive deficits to do with schizophrenic symptoms? *British Journal of Psychiatry, 130*, 167–173.

Hemsley, D.R. (1987). An experimental psychological model for schizophrenia. In Häfner, W.F. Gattaz, & W. Janzarik (Eds.), *Search for the causes of schizophrenia.* Heidelberg: Springer-Verlag.

Hoffman, R.E., Buchsbaum, M.S., Escobar, M.D., Makuch, R.W., Nuechterlein, K.H., & Guich, S.M. (1991). EEG coherence of prefrontal areas in normal and schizophrenic males during perceptual activation. *Journal of Neuropsychiatry and Clinical Neurosciences, 3*, 169–175.

Holzman, P.S. (1987). Recent studies of psychophysiology in schizophrenia. *Schizophrenia Bulletin, 13*, 49–75.

Ingvar, D.H., & Franzen, G. (1974). Abnormalities of cerebral blood flow distribution in patients with chronic schizophrenia. *Acta Psychiatrica Scandinavica, 50*, 425–462.

Kraepelin, E. (1919). *Dementia praecox and paraphrenia* (R.M. Barclay, Trans.). Edinburgh: E. & S. Livingston. (Original work published 1913).

Lukoff, D., Nuechterlein, K.H., & Ventura, J. (1986). Appendix A: Manual for the Expanded Brief Psychiatric Rating Scale (BPRS). *Schizophrenia Bulletin, 12*, 594–602.

Mackworth, N.H. (1957). Some factors affecting vigilance. *Advancement of Science*, *53*, 389–393.

Macko, K.A., Jarvis, C.D., Kennedy, C., Miyaoka, M., Shinohara, M., Sokoloff, L. & Mishkin, M. (1982). Mapping the primate visual system with [2-^{14}C]Deoxyglucose. *Science*, *218*, 394–397.

Mesulam, M-M. (1985). Attention, confusional states, and neglect. In M-M. Mesulam (Ed.), *Principles of behavioural neurology* (pp. 125–168). Philadelphia: F.A. Davis.

Mirsky, A.F. (1969). Neuropsychological bases of schizophrenia. *Annual Review of Psychology*, *20*, 321–348.

Mirsky, A.F. (1989). The neuropsychology of attention: Elements of a complex behavior. In E. Perecmen (Ed.), *Integrating theory and practice in clinical neuropsychology* (pp. 75–91). Hillsdale, N.J.: Lawrence Erlbaum, Associates Inc.

Mirsky, A.F., & Duncan, C.C. (1989). Attention impairment in human clinical disorders: Schizophrenia and petit mal epilepsy. In D.E. Sheer & K.H. Pribram (Eds.), *Attention: Theory, brain functions and clinical applications*. Hillsdale, N.J.: Lawrence Erlbaum Associates Inc.

Mishkin, M. Ungerleider, L.G., & Macko, K.A. (1983). Object vision and spatial vision: Two cortical pathways. *Trends in Neurosciences*, *6*, 414–417.

Neale, J.M., & Oltmanns, T.F. (1980). *Schizophrenia*. New York: Wiley.

Nuechterlein, K.H. (1983). Signal detection in vigilance tasks and behavioral attributes among offspring of schizophrenic mothers and among hyperactive children. *Journal of Abnormal Psychology*, *92*, 4–28.

Nuechterlein, K.H. (1985). Converging evidence for vigilance deficit as a vulnerability indicator for schizophrenic disorders. In M. Alpert (Ed.), *Controversies in schizophrenia: Changes and constancies* (pp. 175–198). New York: Guildford Press.

Nuechterlein, K.H. (1991). Vigilance in schizophrenia and related disorders. In S.R. Steinhauer, J.H. Gruzelier, & J. Zubin (Eds.), *Handbook of schizophrenia, Vol. 5: Neuropsychology, psychophysiology, and information processing* (pp. 397–433). Amsterdam: Elsevier.

Nuechterlein, K.H., & Dawson, M.E. (1984a). A heuristic vulnerability/stress model of schizophrenic episodes. *Schizophrenia Bulletin*, *10*, 300–312.

Nuechterlein, K.H., & Dawson, M.E. (1984b). Information processing and attentional functioning in the developmental course of schizophrenic disorders. *Schizophrenia Bulletin*, *10*, 160–203.

Nuechterlein, K.H., Dawson, M.E., Gitlin, M., Ventura, J., Goldstein, M.J., Snyder, K.S., Yee, C.M., & Mintz, J. (1992). Developmental Processes in Schizophrenic Disorders: Longitudinal studies of vulnerability and stress. *Schizophrenia Bulletin*, *18*, 387–425.

Nuechterlein, K.H., Dawson, M.E., Ventura, J., Fogelson, D., Gitlin, M., & Mintz, J. (1991). Testing vulnerability models: Stability of potential vulnerability indicators across clinical state. In H. Häfner & W.F. Gattaz (Eds.), *Search for the causes of schizophrenia* (Vol. II, pp. 177–191). Heidelberg: Springer-Verlag.

Nuechterlein, K.H., Parasuraman, R., & Jiang, Q. (1983). Visual sustained attention: Image degradation produces rapid sensitivity decrement over time. *Science*, *220*, 327–329.

O'Dougherty, M., Nuechterlein, K.H., & Drew, B. (1984). Hyperactive and hypoxic children: Signal detection, sustained attention, and behavior. *Journal of Abnormal Psychology*, *93*, 178–191.

Orzack, M.H., & Kornetsky, C. (1966). Attention dysfunction in chronic schizophrenia. *Archives of General Psychiatry*, *14*, 323–326.

Parasuraman, R. (1986). Vigilance, monitoring, and search. In K.R. Boff, L. Kaufman, & J.R. Thomas (Eds.), *Handbook of perception and human performance. Vol. II: Cognitive processes and performance* (pp. 43-1–43-39). New York: Wiley.

Pardo, J.V., Fox, P.T., & Raichle, M.E. (1991). Localization of a human system for sustained attention by positron emission tomography. *Nature, 349,* 61–64.

Posner, M.I., & Boiès, S.J. (1971). Components of attention. *Psychological Review, 78,* 391–408.

Posner, M.I., Early, T.S., Reiman, E., Pardo, P.J., & Dhawan, M. (1988). Asymmetries in hemispheric control of attention in schizophrenia. *Archives of General Psychiatry, 45,* 814–821.

Posner, M.I., & Petersen, S.E. (1990). The attention system of the human brain. *Annual Review of Neuroscience, 13,* 25–42.

Rosvold, H.E., Mirsky, A., Sarason, I., Bransome, E.D., Jr., & Beck, L.H. (1956). A continuous performance test of brain damage. *Journal of Consulting Psychology, 20,* 343–350.

Rutschmann, J., Cornblatt, B., & Erlenmeyer-Kimling, L. (1977). Sustained attention in children at risk for schizophrenia: Report on a continuous performance test. *Archives of General Psychiatry, 34,* 571–575.

Rutschmann, J., Cornblatt, B., & Erlenmeyer-Kimling, L. (1986). Sustained attention in children at risk for schizophrenia: Findings with two visual continuous performance tests in a new sample. *Journal of Abnormal Child Psychology, 14,* 365–385.

Sergent, J., & Hellige, J.B. (1986). Role of input factors in visual-field asymmetries. *Brain and Cognition, 5,* 174–199.

Shallice, T. (1988). *From neuropsychology to mental structure.* New York: Cambridge University Press.

Steinhauer, S.R., Zubin, J., Condray, R., Shaw, D.B., Peters, J.L., & van Kammen, D.P. (1991). Electrophysiological and behavioral signs of attentional disturbance in schizophrenics and their siblings. In C.A. Tamminga & S.C. Schulz (Eds.), *Schizophrenia research: Advances in neuropsychiatry and psychopharmacology* (Vol. 1). New York: Raven.

Strauss, M.E., Novakovic, T., Tien, A.Y., Bylsma, F., & Pearlson, G.D. (1991). Disengagement of attention in schizophrenia. *Psychiatry Research, 37,* 139–146.

Venables, P.H. (1964). Input dysfunction in schizophrenia. In B.A. Maher (Ed.), *Progress in experimental personality research* (Vol. 1). New York: Academic Press.

Venables, P.H. (1984). Cerebral mechanisms, autonomic responsiveness, and attention in schizophrenia. In W.D. Spaulding & J.K. Cole (Eds.), *Nebraska Symposium on Motivation, 1983: Theories of schizophrenia and psychosis.* Lincoln, NB: University of Nebraska Press.

Walker, E. (1981). Attentional and neuromotor functions of schizophrenics, schizoaffectives, and patients with other affective disorders. *Archives of General Psychiatry, 38,* 1355–1358.

Weinberger, D.R., Berman, K.F., & Zec, R.F. (1986). Physiologic dysfunction of dorsolateral prefrontal cortex in schizophrenia. I. Regional cerebral blood flow evidence. *Archives of General Psychiatry, 43,* 114–124.

Weinberger, D.R., Berman, K.F., & Illowsky, B.P. (1988). Physiological dysfunction of dorsolateral prefrontal cortex in schizophrenia. III. A new cohort and evidence for a monoaminergic mechanism. *Archives of General Psychiatry, 45,* 609–615.

Wilkins, A.J., Shallice, T., & McCarthy, R. (1987). Frontal lesions and sustained attention. *Neuropsychologia, 25,* 359–365.

Wohlberg, G.W., & Kornetsky, C. (1973). Sustained attention in remitted schizophrenics. *Archives of General Psychiatry, 28,* 533–537.

Zubin, J. (1975). Problem of attention in schizophrenia. In M.L. Kietzman, S. Sutton, & J. Zubin (Eds.), *Experimental approaches to psychopathology* (pp. 139–166). Orlando, Fl: Academic Press.

Zubin, J., & Spring, B. (1977). Vulnerability – a new view of schizophrenia. *Journal of Abnormal Psychology, 86,* 103–126.

5 Mechanisms of Backward Masking in Schizophrenia

Michael Foster Green
West Los Angeles Veterans Affairs Medical Center and Department of Psychiatry and Biobehavioral Sciences, Universtiy of California, Los Angeles, U.S.A.

Keith H. Nuechterlein
Department of Psychiatry and Biobehavioral Sciences, University of California, Los Angeles, U.S.A.

Backward masking is a technique that assesses early visual information processing. Schizophrenic patients consistently require longer interstimulus intervals to identify target stimuli than normal controls. However, the interpretation of this masking deficit has been difficult, mainly because the masking methods used with schizophrenic patients typically combined two masking mechanisms (integration and interruption) and two types of visual channels (transient and sustained). The present project altered the masking procedures to allow better specification of the nature of the deficit. First, we increased the target:mask energy ratio to obtain a non-monotonic masking function. Such a function would indicate that masking occurred primarily through interruption. Second, we lowered the spatial frequency of the target to reduce reliance on sustained visual channels during target identification. Manic patients were included to examine the specificity of the masking deficit to schizophrenia. Schizophrenic patients differed significantly from normal controls on the non-monotonic function, with targets of both high and low spatial frequency. Manic patients performed comparably to the schizophrenic patients. The results suggest that the masking deficits in schizophrenia are: (1) not entirely due to increased susceptibility to masking by integration; (2) not explained solely by deficits in sustained visual channels; and (3) present in manic patients to a comparable extent.

INTRODUCTION

Since the writings of Kraepelin (1913/1919) and Bleuler (1911/1950), information processing deficits have been considered to be integral to schizophrenia. The assessment of information processing in experimental psychopathology has usually depended on developments in experimental psychology. For example, the attentional filtering model of Broadbent (1958) inspired a series of studies looking at distractibility in schizophrenic patients (e.g. McGhie & Chapman, 1961). More recent experimental developments that have been incorporated into experimental psychopathology include the distinction between selective and sustained attention, models of sequential stages of processing, and processing resource considerations (Nuechterlein & Dawson, 1984).

In another example, developments from normal human information processing have been used by schizophrenia researchers to focus on the initial stages of visual processing. In a seminal paper, Sperling (1960) reported that the initial representation or "sensory register" is a stage of unlimited capacity and very brief duration. Neisser (1967) later coined the term "icon" to describe this stage. Although the actual role of the icon in normal visual processing is not well understood (Haber, 1983), this literature has yielded several excellent procedures for testing early visual processing. One of these procedures is backward masking.

Backward Masking

Backward masking is a special condition of the general technique of visual masking. Visual masking "refers to the reduction of visibility of one stimulus, called the target, by a spatiotemporally overlapping or contiguous second stimulus, called the mask" (Breitmeyer, 1984, p. 2). Historically, masking has been used to identify the temporal stages and parameters of visual perception. Following in the tradition of physical scientists, the psychologists of the late nineteenth century were interested in parsing sensation and perception into its elemental components.

The backward masking procedure involves tachistoscopic presentation of an initial stimulus (the target) that is followed, after a certain interstimulus interval (ISI), by a second stimulus (the mask). The target is usually a simple stimulus such as a single letter. The mask is often a pattern such as overlapping letters, but it could also be a meaningful form, or even a flash of light without form. The target is always presented at a duration that is sufficient for accurate detection in the absence of the mask. In most paradigms, the luminances of the target and mask are held constant, and the duration of the mask is greater than the duration of the target.

If the ISI is sufficiently brief, subjects are unable to identify the target. In fact, at very brief ISIs, subjects might be sceptical that a target was even presented. Because the masking occurred after the presentation of the target, it is referred to as *backward* masking. In the case of forward masking, the mask temporarily precedes the target.

Some theorists have argued that higher level cognitive processes can influence the information selected for processing at an early stage

(McClelland & Rummelhart, 1981). In other words, the generation of expectancies or strategies by higher-level processes impact the selection of certain sensory features for more extensive processing (i.e. top-down processing). Such top-down processing influences are likely to be strongest in letter perception, when letters are examined in the context of other letters that together form a word. The backward masking procedures involve a basic perceptual discrimination of single letters for which few higher-level cognitive strategies come into play. Hence, researchers have commonly referred to these as tests of early visual information processing (Saccuzzo & Braff, 1981). Knight (1984) also considers deficits on the backward masking procedure to reflect difficulties in early processing, which he attributes to deficits in perceptual organization (e.g. the ability to schematise the target stimuli).

Backward Masking in Schizophrenia

Backward masking research in schizophrenia (Braff, 1981; Saccuzzo & Braff, 1981, 1986) has found consistently that schizophrenic patients require a longer ISI between target and mask to identify a target. This finding has been interpreted to indicate that these patients suffer from a slowing of information processing (Braff, 1981).

The masking deficit in schizophrenia is not due to antipsychotic medication that seems to reduce, not exacerbate, the deficit (Braff & Saccuzzo, 1982). The masking deficit in schizophrenia also appears unlikely to be simply due to a generalised information processing deficit. First, normal elderly subjects demonstrate deficits on backward masking, but these deficits are qualitatively different from those shown by schizophrenic patients (Brody, Saccuzzo, & Braff, 1980). Second, backward masking deficits have been found in individuals with no psychiatric history but who are at hypothesised risk for schizophrenia (Balogh & Merritt 1985, 1987; Merritt & Balogh, 1984; Saccuzzo & Shubert, 1981; Steronko & Woods, 1978), so generalised deficits associated with chronicity do not account for the masking anomaly.

Although the masking deficit does not seem to be associated with severity of symptoms in general, it seems to be related to the presence of negative symptoms. Our finding of a relationship between masking deficits and negative symptoms (Green & Walker, 1984, 1986) has been supported in two subsequent studies (Braff, 1989; Weiner et al., 1990).

The question of specificity of backward masking deficits to schizophrenia remains unresolved. Saccuzzo and Braff (1981) found that patients with affective disorders did not show deficits in backward masking. However, Saccuzzo and Braff (1986) found backward masking deficits in schizoaffective and bipolar patients who showed active psychotic symptoms. In our previous work (Green & Walker, 1986), we found a non-significant trend for bipolar patients to perform worse than normal controls.

The typical masking paradigm used in schizophrenia research yields a monotonic or Type A masking function (Saccuzzo & Braff, 1981; Braff, 1981; Braff & Saccuzzo, 1981, 1982). In this paradigm, the mask (usually a pattern mask such as overlapping Xs) has greater "energy" than the target, and it occupies the same area on the screen. Energy is defined as intensity × duration (within a certain range of durations) and is usually manipulated on a tachistoscope by changing the duration of the stimuli. The monotonic function yields a plot in which the masking effect is maximal when the interstimulus interval (ISI) is 0, and drops off with increasing ISI. Under certain conditions, masking yields a non-monotonic, U-shaped function (also referred to as Type B masking) in which the masking effect is maximal at some ISI longer than 0. As we will see, the results from monotonic (Type A) masking are difficult to interpret as being related to a specific process. Type B masking is easier to interpret, but has not been used previously in research with schizophrenic patients. Figure 5.1 shows stylised Type A and Type B masking functions.

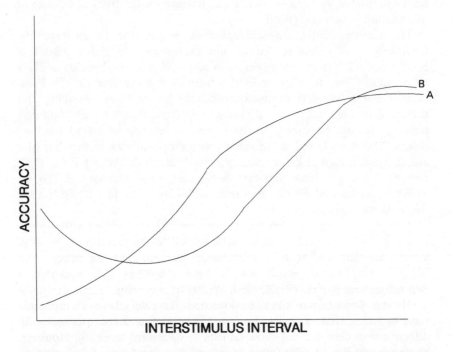

FIG. 5.1   Stylised graphs of monotonic (Type A) and a non-monotonic (Type B) masking functions.

Mechanisms of the Mask

Although several researchers have reported that schizophrenic patients show poorer performance relative to controls on backward masking (Braff & Saccuzzo, 1981; Green & Walker, 1986; Saccuzzo & Miller, 1977; Schwartz, Winstead, & Adinoff, 1983) there has been little agreement on the interpretation of this finding. Braff and Saccuzzo have suggested that this reflects "slower processing". However, this term may be more descriptive than explanatory. To understand the nature of the deficit, we first need to understand the mechanism of the mask.

Two general models have been proposed to explain masking: integration and interruption. *Integration* refers to a process in which the icons from the target and mask become fused, much like photographic film that has been double exposed; the result is an unintelligible icon. Masking by *interruption* has typically assumed that the icon is clear and intact, but that the processing is halted by the mask before the information from the icon can be transferred to a more permanent store (Turvey, 1973). It has been argued that Type A backward pattern masking occurs both by integration and interruption (Turvey, 1973). This situation makes it difficult to determine from Type A masking whether a particular mechanism is dysfunctional. If schizophrenic patients do poorly on this test, it could be either because they are slow at moving the information to a durable store or because they are poor at interpreting fused images (Nuechterlein & Dawson, 1984).

The non-monotonic masking function eliminates some of this confusion because interruption is the predominant mechanism. In the case of masking by integration, the masking effect should be greatest when the temporal overlap of the stimuli is largest (ISI = 0). However, masking by interruption can result in a maximal masking effect at an ISI greater than 0. The information necessary to identify a target might be contained in visual channels of relatively high spatial frequency. As we will see below (see Fig. 5.2), visual channels of higher spatial frequency have longer onset latencies, and these channels could be more disrupted by a mask that occurs later in time. Despite the increase in interpretive power, no study has used a masking procedure designed to yield a U-shaped function with schizophrenic patients.

Spatial Frequency

Breitmeyer and Ganz (1976; Breitmeyer, 1984) have proposed an intriguing theory for Type B backward masking that involves the interactions of sustained and transient visual channels. The sustained channels originate in the retinal X-cells, are sensitive to high spatial frequency, and show a sustained response to a stationary stimulus. The transient channels originate from the retinal Y-cells, are sensitive to low spatial frequency, and respond to the onset or offset of a stimulus. Breitmeyer and Ganz (1976) proposed that with masking by interruption, the target first initiates transient channel activity followed by sustained channel activity. Next, the mask stimulates transient activity, which interferes with the ongoing sustained channel activity initiated by the target. Hence, we have transient channels of the mask interfering with (interrupting) sustained channel activity of the target. Masking deficits in schizophrenia could be due to problems with transient channels and/or sustained channels (Schuck & Lee, 1989; Schwartz & Winstead 1982). For example, one study (Schwartz & Winstead, 1988) implicated sustained visual channels in an abnormality of early visual processing in schizophrenia.

The visual channels respond differentially to stimuli according to the spatial frequency involved. A high spatial frequency target relies heavily on the sustained channels. In contrast, a low spatial frequency (e.g. blurry) target relies on transient channels and only those sustained channels that have relatively short latency. Diagrams from Breitmeyer and Ganz in Fig. 5.2 help illustrate this concept.

This chapter summarises a portion of the data from a study of backward masking in psychotic disorders. The methods and data are reported in more detail elsewhere (Green, Nuechterlein, & Mintz, submitted a, b). By manipulating the target : mask ratio, we intended to obtain a non-monotonic masking function that would help in interpreting the nature of the masking deficit (i.e. interruption versus integration). By manipulating the spatial frequency of the target, we intended to remove a subset of the sustained channels from the task. If the masking deficit is due to sustained channels, this manipulation might alter the type or degree of the masking deficit.

METHOD

Subjects

Schizophrenic ($n = 64$) and manic ($n = 32$) subjects were drawn from the inpatient units of Camarillo State Hospital. All patients were diagnosed according to DSM-III-R criteria based on an expanded version of the Present State Exam (PSE; Wing, Cooper, & Sartorius, 1974) that was supplemented with items from the Schedule for Affective Disorders and Schizophrenia (Endicott & Spitzer, 1978). Interviewers were trained to a sensitivity of at least 0.85 and a specificity of at least 0.90 for key psychotic and affective symptoms by the Diagnosis and Psychopathology Unit of the UCLA Clinical Research Center for the Study of Schizophrenia (R.P. Liberman, Principal Investigator). Potential subjects were excluded if they had a history of drug or alcohol dependence, an identifiable neurological disorder, any signs of mental retardation, or were over 55 years of age. The

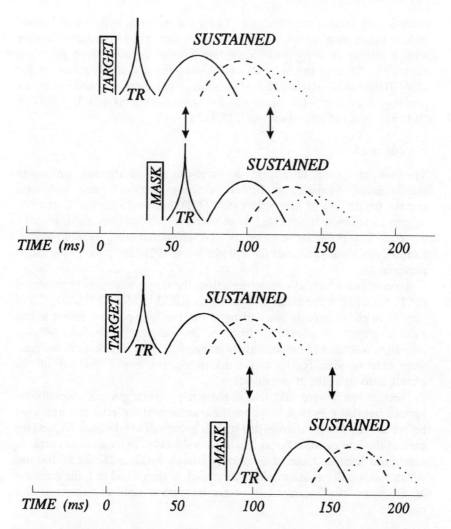

FIG. 5.2 Hypothetical time course of transient and sustained channels activated by target and mask. The transient channels (TR) are represented by a spike and the sustained channels are represented by curves which increase in spatial frequency from left to right (from Breitmeyer & Ganz, 1976).

mean years of age were 33.2 (SD = 6.2) and 37.7 (9.2); mean years of education were 11.7 (2.0) and 13.3 (2.3); and the number of years since first hospitalisation were 14.0 (6.3) and 14.5 (7.5) for the schizophrenic and manic patients, respectively.

The normal controls (n = 48) were drawn from the Psychiatric Technician training programme at Camarillo State Hospital. The exclusionary criteria were the same as for the patients, with the additional criteria that normal controls were excluded if they had a first-degree relative with a history of a psychotic disorder. Normal controls were given the expanded PSE and the sections of the Structured Clinical Interview for DSM-III-R (SCID-II) that probed for schizotypal, paranoid, and borderline personality disorder. The mean age for normal controls was 33.5 (SD = 10.1) and years of education was 13.8 (1.8).

Procedures

The subjects were tested on a three-channel Gerbrands projection tachistoscope. Subjects sat behind a rear-projection screen and were presented with one of four letters (S,C,O,Q) that could appear at any one of four locations that were slightly eccentric to fixation (top, right, bottom, or left). The presentations (letters and locations) were randomised. A fixation point was presented for 400 ms; it ended 200 ms prior to the target presentation.

To establish a subject's target duration, the target was initially presented for 10 ms without the mask. Subjects were asked to identify the target and they were encouraged to guess if not sure (the four possible target letters were displayed on a card in front of the subjects). This forced-choice paradigm was used to reduce any differences in response criterion. Subjects were able to identify the target accurately (at least eight out of ten identifications) at the 10 ms duration.

Next, subjects were told that a pattern of overlapping Xs would also appear, but that they were to ignore these and report the letter that appeared before the Xs. The mask consisted of four groups of overlapping Xs, one for each of the four possible target locations. Subjects were required to correctly identify at least four out of five target stimuli with the ISI set at 100 ms, which was usually above masking threshold. If they could not, the duration of the target was increased by 4 ms increments until subjects met this criterion.

Conditions

This chapter reports data from three masking conditions: (1) a high-energy mask; (2) a low-energy mask; and (3) a blurred target. The conditions were administered in a counterbalanced order across subjects. The ISIs were fixed at 5, 10, 20, 40, 70, and 100 ms, with 12 presentations at each ISI. Both targets and the ISIs were presented in a block-randomized fashion.

1. High-energy mask. This procedure is commonly used in schizophrenia research and it typically generates a monotonic masking function (Braff & Saccuzzo, 1981, 1982). The energy of the mask was set at twice the energy of

the target (e.g. if the duration of the target was 10 ms, the duration of the mask was 20 ms).

2. Low-energy mask. This condition was designed to generate a non-monotonic, U-shaped masking function. To obtain a U-shaped function, the energy of the mask should be equal to, or less than, the energy of the target (Breitmeyer, 1984). For this condition, the duration of the mask was one half the duration of the target (e.g. 5 ms duration for a 10 ms target).

3. Blurred target. This condition was designed to reduce the reliance on sustained visual channels. By reducing the high spatial frequency component of the target, a subset of the sustained visual channels (those with longer latency) were no longer required for identification of the target. The target was blurred to a standardised degree by moving the rear projection screen a set distance (which defocuses the stimuli) and then refocusing the mask, but not the target. The intention of blurring the stimulus was to eliminate high spatial frequency information. As a byproduct of blurring, the visual discrimination became more difficult. To obtain a test of comparable difficulty to the low-energy condition, the target duration was doubled (e.g. set at 20 ms) and the mask duration was set at one-quarter the duration of the target (e.g. 5 ms for a 20 ms target).

RESULTS AND DISCUSSION

For each of the three masking conditions, an analysis of variance was initially conducted for three groups (normal controls, schizophrenic patients, and manic patients) and the six ISIs. A Greenhouse–Geisser correction was used for the main effect of ISI, and for group by ISI interactions.

High-energy Mask

The results for this condition are shown in Fig. 5.3. The effect of group ($F = 25.37$; df $= 2, 139$; $P < 0.0001$), ISI ($F = 429.58$; df $= 5, 695$; $P < 0.0001$), and the group by ISI interaction ($F = 6.29$; df $= 10, 695$; $P < 0.0001$) were all significant.

The significant interaction was due to the fact that all groups performed close to chance for the shortest ISIs, but the normal controls performed better than patients in the last four ISIs. This finding replicates the traditional masking deficit of schizophrenic patients. In a series of contrasts, the schizophrenic patients performed significantly worse than the normal controls in every ISI except the first. The manic patients performed significantly worse than normal controls at every ISI except the first two. The two patient groups did not differ significantly from each other at any ISI.

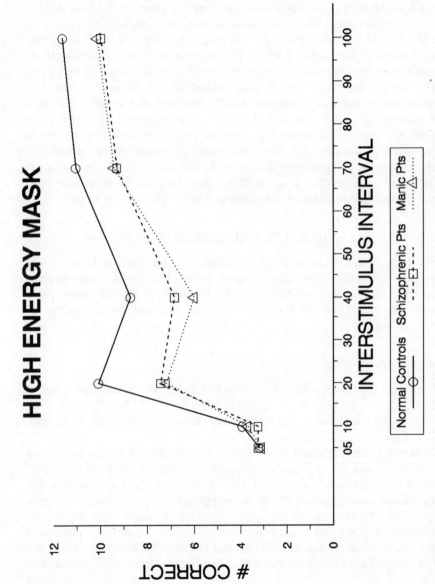

HIGH ENERGY MASK

 # CORRECT

INTERSTIMULUS INTERVAL

Normal Controls   Schizophrenic Pts   Manic Pts

FIG. 5.3 Masking functions for schizophrenic patients, manic patients, and normal controls for a high-energy mask.

Low-energy Mask

The results from the low-energy mask are shown in Fig. 5.4. The effect of group ($F = 21.21$; def $= 2$, 139; $P < 0.0001$) and ISI ($F = 142.31$; df $= 5$, 695; $P < 0.0001$) were significant. The group by ISI interaction showed a trend toward significance ($F = 1.58$; df $= 10$, 695; $P < 0.12$). For the contrasts, normal controls differed significantly from both the schizophrenic and the manic patients for every ISI. The manic patients did not differ significantly from the schizophrenic patients at any ISI.

Blurred Target

The results from the blurred target are shown in Fig. 5.5. The effects of group ($F = 10.00$; df $= 2$, 138; $P < 0.0001$) and ISI ($F = 122.12$; df $= 5$, 690; $P < 0.0001$) were significant. The group by ISI interaction was marginally significant ($F = 1.94$; df $= 10$, 690; $P = 0.06$). For the contrasts, normal controls differed significantly from the schizophrenic patients at all ISIs except the second (10 ms) and fourth (40 ms) ISIs. The normal controls differed from the manic patients on all except the second ISI. The manic patients did not differ significantly from the schizophrenic patients at any ISI.

Comparison of Normal Controls and Schizophrenic Patients

As expected, the normal controls differed from the schizophrenic patients in the high-energy mask condition, which is consistent with several previous reports that have used a high-energy mask to yield a monotonic function (Braff & Saccuzzo, 1981, 1982).

In the low-energy condition we also found a significant difference between normal controls and schizophrenic patients. We were somewhat surprised to find that the function had two dips (at 10 and 40 ms) for all groups. The function was much closer to a N-shaped function, instead of the more common U-shaped function (Michaels & Turvey, 1979). This pattern remained after we rotated the target stimuli, and did not seem to be the result of the particular target slides presented at those ISIs. The N-shaped function is believed to represent a strong interruption process with a weaker integrative component at the very early ISIs (Michaels & Turvey, 1979). If so, we would expect to obtain a smoother function (i.e. more U- shaped) by either changing the characteristics of the mask, or by decreasing the target : mask ratio (e.g. from 1 : 2 to 1 : 4). The reason for the expectation is because these manipulations would reduce luminance summation (the integrative component), but would maintain the transient on sustained interruption. We retested two samples of schizophrenic patients ($n = 10$

90

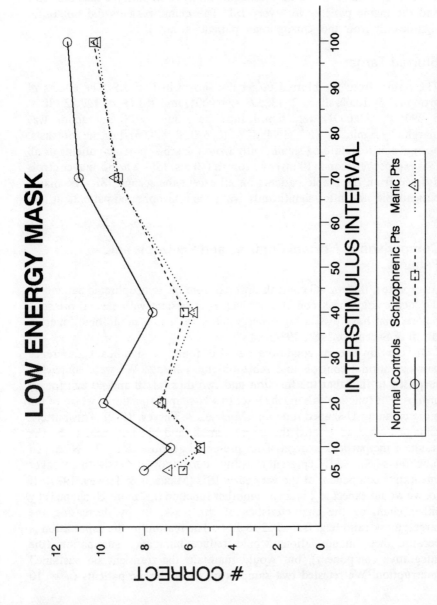

FIG. 5.4 Masking functons for schizophrenic patients, manic patients, and normal controls for a low-energy mask.

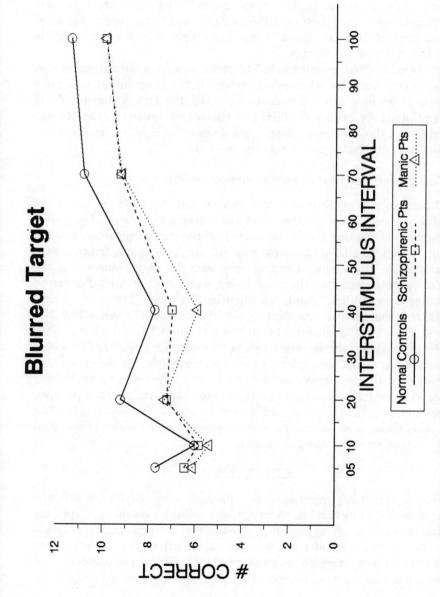

Blurred Target

FIG. 5.5   Masking functions for schizophrenic patients, manic patients, and normal controls for a blurred target.

each). One group had the target: mask ratio changed to 1 : 4, and the other group received a mask of overlapping circles instead of overlapping Xs. In both of the retested samples, the dip at 10 ms was sharply reduced, but the dip at 40 ms remained. As the dip at 40 ms remained when these manipulations reduced the integrative effects (but not the effects of interruption), we interpret these manipulations to indicate that the second dip (at 40 ms) involved masking by interruption. The schizophrenic patients differed from normal controls at ISIs of 20, 40, and 70 ms. Hence, it appears that schizophrenic patients show masking deficits when the mechanism is largely restricted to interruption.

The schizophrenic patients showed differences from normal controls in the blurred condition. Although the group effect was significant, it was not as large as in the previous conditions; and the groups did not differ significantly for two of the ISIs. The reliance on sustained channels was reduced in this condition, which might account for a smaller group effect. However, the results are equivocal at this time.

Comparison of Manic and Schizophrenic Patients

The manic patients showed a performance that was close to that of the schizophrenic patients across all of the masking conditions. The results suggest that masking deficits are found in chronic manic inpatients and are not entirely specific to schizophrenia. Although the manic patients were hospitalised at the time of testing, they were not as symptomatic as the schizophrenic patients. They had lower scores on the Brief Psychiatric Rating Scale (BPRS; Lukoff, Nuechterlein, & Ventura, 1986). The groups differed significantly on the thinking disturbance index (7.6 versus 10.9; $t = 3.94$; $P < 0.0002$), withdrawal/retardation factor (4.2 versus 7.6, $t = 5.99$; $P < 0.0001$), and the depressive index (3.9 versus 5.3; $t = 3.15$; $P < 0.005$) for the manic and schizophrenia patients respectively. To the extent that masking deficits are associated with psychiatric symptoms, we might have expected the manic patients to perform better than schizophrenic patients, but they clearly did not. It should be emphasised that the manic patients had a fairly chronic and severe illness, so the generalisability of these findings to a healthier sample is an open question.

CONCLUSIONS

The current study represents an approach for studying information processing deficits in schizophrenia, which follows a tradition of applying developments from experimental psychology to experimental psychopathology. The current effort was directed at refining our understanding of the commonly-reported backward masking deficit in schizophrenia. Two manipulations were attempted. The first was designed to restrict the masking mechanism largely to interruption. We believe this was accomplished for the latter part (ISIs of 40–100 ms) of the masking function. Schizophrenic patients showed deficits on this part of the masking function in which the mechanism was largely restricted to interruption. The second manipulation was designed to reduce the role of sustained visual channels in target discrimination. The deficit remained in this condition. Lastly, the masking deficits appeared in a group of chronic manic patients, even though the manic patients were less symptomatic than the schizophrenic patients.

ACKNOWLEDGEMENTS

The authors thank Maryam Aslani, David Chavez, Cynthia Christenson, Donna Gaier, Daniel Gutkind, Robert Kern, Ph.D., David King, Ph.D., Susan Hellman, Sharon Mitchell, M.S., Chad Nelson, Julie Van Sickle, M.A. and Jennifer Smith for their help in subject recruitment and data collection. Bruno Breitmeyer, Ph.D. consulted on the design of this project and the interpretation of the results. The statistical analyses were conducted by Sun Hwang, M.S., M.P.H. of the Methodology and Statistical Support Unit of the UCLA Clinical Research Center for the Study of Schizophrenia. Funding for this project came from NIMH grant MH-43292 to Dr. Green. The sample was obtained through the excellent co-operation of the staff and administration of Camarillo State Hospital.

REFERENCES

Balogh, D.W., & Merritt, R.D. (1985). Susceptibility to Type A backward pattern masking among hypothetically psychosis-prone college students. *Journal of Abnormal Psychology, 94*, 377–383.

Balogh, D.W., & Merritt, R.D. (1987). Visual masking and the schizophrenia spectrum. *Schizophrenia Bulletin, 13*, 679–698.

Bleuler, E. (1911/1950). *Dementia praecox or the group of schizophrenias*. (J. Zinken, Trans.). New York: International Universities Press, Inc.

Braff, D.L. (1981). Impaired speed of information processing in non-medicated schizotypal patients. *Schizophrenia Bulletin, 7*, 499–508.

Braff, D.L. (1989). Sensory input deficits and negative symptoms in schizophrenic patients. *American Journal of Psychiatry, 146*, 1006–1011.

Braff, D.L., & Saccuzzo, D.P. (1981). Information processing dysfunction in schizophrenia: A two factor deficit theory. *American Journal of Psychiatry, 138*, 1051–1056.

Braff, D.L., & Saccuzzo, D.P. (1982). Effect of antipsychotic medication on speed of information processing in schizophrenic patients. *American Journal of Psychiatry, 139*, 1117–1130.

Breitmeyer, B.G. (1984). *Visual masking: An integrative approach*. New York: Oxford University Press.

Breitmeyer, B.G., & Ganz, L. (1976). Implications of sustained and transient channels for theories of visual pattern masking, saccadic suppression, and information processing. *Psychological Review, 83*, 1–36.

Broadbent, D.E. (1958). *Perception and Communication*. London: Pergamon Press, Ltd.

Brody, D., Saccuzzo, D.P., & Braff, D.L. (1980). Information processing for masked and unmasked stimuli in schizophrenia and old age. *Journal of Abnormal Psychology, 89,* 617–622.

Endicott, J., & Spitzer, R.L. (1978). A diagnostic interview: The Schedule for affective disorders and schizophrenia. *Archives of General Psychiatry, 35,* 837–844.

Green, M.F., Nuechterlein, K.H., and Mintz, J. (submitted a). Backward masking in schizophrenia and mania: I Specifying a mechanism. *Archives of General Psychiatry.*

Green, M.F., Nuechterlein, K.H., and Mintz, J. (submitted b). Backward masking in schizophrenia and mania: II. Specifying the visual channels. *Archives of General Psychiatry.*

Green, M., & Walker, E. (1984). Susceptibility to backward masking in schizophrenic patients with positive and negative symptoms. *American Journal of Psychiatry, 141,* 1273–1275.

Green, M., & Walker, E. (1986). Symptom correlates of vulnerability to backward masking in schizophrenia. *American Journal of Psychiatry, 143,* 181–186.

Haber, R.N. (1983). The impending demise of the icon: A critique of the concept of iconic storage in visual information processing. *The Behavioural and Brain Sciences, 6,* 1–54.

Knight, R. (1984). Converging models of cognitive deficit in schizophrenia. In W.D. Spaulding, J.K. Cole (Eds.), *Theories of schizophrenia and psychosis* (pp. 93–156). Lincoln, NB: University of Nebraska Press.

Kraepelin, E. (1919). *Dementia praecox and paraphrenia* (R.M. Barclay, Trans.). Edinburgh: E & S Livingston.

Lukoff, D., Nuechterlein, K.H., & Ventura, J. (1986). Appendix A: Manual for the Expanded Brief Psychiatric Rating Scale (BPRS). *Schizophrenia Bulletin, 12,* 594–602.

McClelland, J.L., & Rummelhart, D.E. (1981). An interactive model of context effects in letter perception. I. An account of basic findings. *Psychological Review, 88,* 375–407.

McGhie, A., & Chapman, J. (1961). Disorders of attention and perception in early schizophrenia. *British Journal of Medical Psychology, 34,* 103–116.

Merritt, R.D., & Balogh, D.W. (1984). The use of a backward masking paradigm to assess information-processing deficits among schizotypics: A re-evaluation of Steronko and Woods. *Journal of Nervous and Mental Diseases, 172,* 216–224.

Michaels, C.F., & Turvey, M.T. (1979). Central sources of visual masking: Indexing structures supporting seeing at a single, brief glance. *Psychological Research, 41,* 1–61.

Neisser, U. (1967). *Cognitive psychology.* New York: Appleton–Century–Crofts.

Nuechterlein, K.H., & Dawson, M.E. (1984). Information processing and attentional functioning in the developmental course of schizophrenic disorders. *Schizophrenia Bulletin, 10,* 160–203.

Saccuzzo, D.P., & Braff, D.L. (1981). Early information processing deficit in schizophrenia. *Archives of General Psychiatry, 38,* 175–179.

Saccuzzo, D.P., & Braff, D.L. (1986). Information-processing abnormalities. *Schizophrenia Bulletin, 12,* 447–459.

Saccuzzo, D.P., & Miller, S. (1977). Critical interstimulus interval in delusional schizophrenics and normals. *Journal of Abnormal Psychology, 86,* 261–266.

Saccuzzo, D.P., & Schubert, D.L. (1981). Backward masking as a measure of slow processing in schizophrenia spectrum disorders. *Journal of Abnormal Psychology, 90,* 305–312.

Schuck, J.R., & Lee, R.G. (1989). Backward masking, information processing, and schizophrenia. *Schizophrenia Bulletin, 15,* 491–500.

Schwartz, B.D., & Winstead, D.K. (1982). Visual processing deficits in acute and chronic schizophrenics. *Biological Psychiatry, 17,* 1377–1387.

Schwartz, B.D., & Winstead, D.K. (1988). Visible persistence in paranoid schizophrenics. *Biological Psychiatry, 23,* 3–12.

Schwartz, B.D., Winstead, D.K., & Adinoff, B. (1983). Temporal integration deficit in visual information processing by chronic schizophrenics. *Biological Psychiatry, 18,* 1311–1320.

Sperling, G. (1960). The information available in brief visual presentations. *Psychological Monographs, 74*, Whole No. 498.

Steronko, R.J., & Woods, D.J. (1978). Impairment in early stages of visual information processing in nonpsychotic schizotypic individuals. *Journal of Abnormal Psychology, 87*, 481–490.

Turvey, M.T. (1973). On peripheral and central processes in vision: Inferences from an information-processing analysis of masking with patterned stimuli. *Psychological Review, 80*, 1–52.

Weiner, R.U., Opler, L.A., Kay, S.R., Merriam, A.E., & Papouchis, N. (1990). Visual information processing in positive, mixed, and negative schizophrenic syndromes. *Journal of Nervous and Mental Disease, 178*, 616–626.

Wing, J.K., Cooper, J.E., & Sartorius, N. (1974). *The measurement and classification of psychiatric symptoms.* London: Cambridge University Press.

Assessment of significance is dependent
upon whether S input are~~not~~ predictable (to the O) or novel.
Predictability (regularity) is assessed by Ⓞ
comparing the ~~current~~ S input with stored schematic
representation of past events. When S's fit the
schema, O responds accordingly, with little perceptual
effort, ~~quite~~ Only when S's are novel is attention
aroused & the S judged as significant. This leads
to a more active problem solving. Arousal is maximised

It is argued that in slide, there is a
failure to identify predictability, & every ~~sru~~
S is regarded as novel. The root cause is
suggested to be neurological.

6 Perceptual and Cognitive Abnormalities as the Bases for Schizophrenic Symptoms

David R. Hemsley
Professor of Abnormal Psychology, Institute of Psychiatry, London University.

An approach which views schizophrenia as a disturbance of information processing appears promising as a way of linking biological and social aspects of the disorder. There are, however, a number of difficulties associated with research into schizophrenics' abnormalities of perception and cognition. First, a variety of models of normal cognitive functioning have been employed. Second, schizophrenics perform poorly on most cognitive tasks. Third, the studies are difficult to relate to biological abnormalities, and to possible animal models of the disorder. A review of research in this area led to the suggestion (Hemsley, 1987) that the basic disturbance in schizophrenia is "a weakening of the influences of stored memories of regularities of previous input on current perception". This formulation leads to the prediction that in certain circumstances, schizophrenics may perform better than normal subjects. In addition it may be related to recent studies of selective attention in animals, and abnormalities resulting either from the administration of amphetamine or hippocampal lesions. Thus, a link between information processing disturbances and biological abnormalities may be possible. Three experimental studies which provide evidence in favour of the basic formulation are presented. Of the paradigms employed, two are derived from animal learning theory (latent inhibition and Kamin's blocking effect) and the third from human experimental psychology. In all three, the pattern of performance of acute schizophrenics was consistent with the model. The ways in which such an information processing disturbance may lead to schizophrenic symptomatology are outlined, with particular reference to the formation and maintenance of delusional beliefs. Recent studies suggest an abnormal reasoning style in some deluded subjects, in addition to well established perceptual disturbances.

INTRODUCTION

In 1914 Berze wrote that in schizophrenia "perception and memory have become so hopelessly intermingled". This observation still appears relevant to a number of phenomena that are prominent in the disorder. One would therefore expect models of normal information processing to assist us in specifying the psychological dysfunction which is "still the elusive core of the schizophrenia syndrome" (Shepherd, 1987, p. 37). An approach that views schizophrenia as a disturbance of information processing appears promising as a means of linking biological and social factors relevant to the disorder.

The aim has therefore been to relate "the concepts and objects of clinical observation to the concepts and experimental data from general psychology" (Cohen & Borst, 1987, p. 189) and thence to specify a single cognitive dysfunction, or pattern of dysfunction, from which the various abnormalities resulting in a diagnosis of schizophrenia might be derived.

This endeavour has proved far from straightforward. In part this is due to methodological problems associated with schizophrenia research generally (Hemsley, 1988, pp. 104–105). However, it is also apparent that there is no agreed large-scale model of normal cognitive functioning. Models are frequently designed to explain performance on a small range of tasks, and each uses a somewhat different conceptual framework. Their more general applicability (or ecological validity?) has yet to be demonstrated. As Shallice (1988, p. 32) notes, 'large scale information processing theories are very loosely characterised; adding a connection, a constraint or another subsystem to a model is unfortunately only too easy". There is the further problem that many of the key symptoms of schizophrenia represent alterations in conscious experience, and there are obvious difficulties in mapping constructs that have been generated to explain task performance onto experiential phenomena. As Anscombe (1987, p. 291) has noted, "there remains a gap between the computer terminology in which attentional theories are quoted and the patient's experience of schizophrenia". This issue is made more complex by Shallice's (1988, p. 321) argument that, "in most operations that have a conscious correspondence, many systems are involved".

The issue of selectivity of information processing has always been central to psychology, and reports by schizophrenics about their functioning during the early stage of the condition led McGhie and Chapman (1961) to suggest that the primary dysfunction is a decrease in the selective and inhibitory functions of attention. The difficulties associated with this formulation are well known; in particular the concept of "selective attention" is often ill defined. More recently there has been a renewed interest in even earlier descriptions of the ways in which schizophrenics' perceptions and/or

THIS BE LINKED TO HURLBURT'S PT'S ACCOUNTS?

thinking are disturbed. As Cutting (1989) points out, Matussek (1952) and Conrad (1958) were among the first to argue that the early stage of schizophrenia could be explained in terms of a breakdown of Gestalt perception, and that such a disturbance could form the basis of delusional perception. Matussek (1952, p. 92) describes a patient who was aware of "a lack of continuity of his perceptions both in space and over time. He saw the environment only in fragments. There was no appreciation of the whole. He saw only details against a meaningless background". Arieti (1966) later used the term "perceptual and apperceptual fragmentation" for such phenomena. Matussek (1952, p. 92) also noted another patient's report that, "I may look at a garden, but I don't see it as I normally do. I can only concentrate on details. For instance I can lose myself in looking at a bud on a branch, but then I don't see anything else". In similar vein, Shakow's experimental work had led him to the conclusion that a schizophrenic "... can't see the wood for the trees ... and examines each tree with meticulous care" (Shakow, 1950).

My own early research was influenced considerably by Broadbent (1971). It eventually led to the suggestion that schizophrenics fail to establish appropriate response biases and hence do not make use of temporal and spatial redundancy to reduce information processing demands (Hemsley, 1985). Collicutt and Hemsley (1985) suggested that such redundancy is involved in giving consciousness the distinctive "stream like" attributes emphasised by James (1890). Matussek's (1952) observation of a patient's "lack of continuity of his perceptions...", is therefore intriguing.

In a general sense, models of normal cognition accept that perception is dependent on an interaction between the presented stimuli and stored memories of regularities in previous input. The latter, in conjunction with the current context, result in "expectancies" or "response biases". Norman and Bobrow (1976) therefore make a distinction between "conceptually driven" and "data driven" processing. If schizophrenics are indeed less able to make use of the redundancy and patterning of sensory input, it should be possible to construct tasks at which schizophrenics perform better than normals; this would be due to the latter forming expectancies that were inappropriate to the stimulus presented. It is this approach that characterises some of the experiments to be described below. The aim is to overcome one of the methodological problems in this area, the existence of a generalised deficit, i.e. the poorer performance of schizophrenics on almost any task. This can make the interpretation of group differences in performance very problematic due to the confounding effects of such factors as poor motivation.

Clearly in considering schizophrenics disturbances of perception and cognition, a number of theoretical models have been drawn upon. In addition to that of Broadbent (1971) the models of Schneider and Shiffrin

Schiz's performance better than controls when perceptual set. Schiz pts don't have a perceptual set .˙. have the occasional advantage. task demands involves disengaging from

in normal processing

(1977) and Posner (e.g. Posner, 1982) have been influential. Both suggest that awareness of redundant information is inhibited to reduce processing demands on a limited capacity system. Thus the change from controlled to automatic processing on a task as a result of prolonged practice may be seen as involving a gradual inhibition of awareness of redundant information. A related position (Posner, 1982) distinguishes automatic processes and conscious attention, the former not giving rise to awareness, the latter involving awareness and closely associated with "a general inhibitory process" (Posner, 1982, p. 173). It is therefore tempting to link certain of the perceptual abnormalities prominent in schizophrenia to a weakening of the inhibitory processes crucial to conscious attention.

It is obviously hazardous to attempt to interpret studies in a different framework from that in which each was designed. Nevertheless in 1987 a review of influential views as to the nature of schizophrenics' cognitive impairment was suggestive of important common features (Table 6.1). There is an emphasis on a weakening of the influence of spatial and temporal regularities on perception, together with the suggestion of a disruption of performance by the intrusion of material normally below awareness. It was argued that although these views were based on a range of cognitive models, all acknowledged the importance of the role of spatial and temporal regularities of past experience on the processing, and more speculatively awareness, of current sensory input. The 1987 model therefore suggested that, "it is a weakening of the influence of stored memories of

TABLE 6.1
Current views on the nature of schizophrenics' cognitive impairment (from Hemsley, 1987)

"The basic cognitive defect ... it is an awareness of automatic processes which are normally carried out below the level of consciousness" (Frith, 1979, p. 233)

"There is some suggestion that there is a failure of automatic processing in schizophrenia so that activity must proceed at the level of consciously controlling sequential processing" (Venables 1984, p. 75)

Schizophrenics "concentrate on detail, at the expense of theme" (Cutting, 1985, p. 300)

Schizophrenics show "some deficiency in perceptual schema formation, in automaticity, or in the holistic stage of processing" (Knight, 1984, p. 120)

Schizophrenics show a "failure of attentional focusing to respond to stimulus redundancy" (Maher, 1983, p. 19)

"Schizophrenics are less able to make use of the redundancy and patterning of sensory input to reduce information processing demands" (Hemsley, 1985)

Schizophrenics do not maintain a strong conceptual organisation or a serial processing strategy ... nor do they organise stimuli extensively relative to others" (Magaro, 1984, p. 202)

regularities of previous input on current perception which is basic to the schizophrenic condition (Hemsley, 1987a, p. 182). The model is illustrated in Fig. 6.1. The dotted line represents the proposed "weakening". A closely related position was put forward independently by Patterson (1987), who suggested that there is "a failure in the automaticity with which prior experience may be recreated in parallel with current stimulus input in schizophrenia (with concomitant failures in future orientation or contextually generated expectancy)." It is important to note that it is not claimed that the "memories of past regularities" are not stored, nor that they are inaccessible. They may indeed be accessed by consciously controlled processing. Rather, the suggestion is that it is the rapid and automatic assessment of the significance or lack of significance of aspects of sensory input (and their implications for action) is impaired as a result of a weakening of the influence of stored past regularities. Minkowski's (1927) report of a schizophrenic patient's experience of the disorder is relevant, "Things present themselves in isolation, on their own, without evoking any response in me. Some things which ought to bring back a memory, or conjure up a thought, or give rise to a picture, remain isolated".

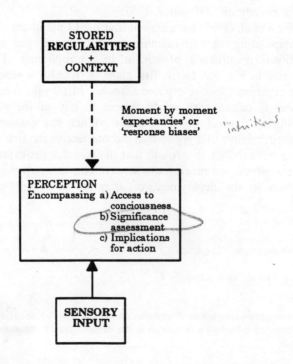

FIG. 6.1 The proposed disruption in the influence of past regularities on perception.

The proposed disorder would also influence the awareness of redundant information, and result in the intrusion into sensory experience of aspects of the environment not normally perceived, as noted by Matussek (1952).

Recent evidence relevant to this proposal will now be presented, and be followed by a more detailed exposition of the way in which it might result in the emergence of psychotic symptoms.

RECENT EXPERIMENTAL STUDIES

Our current research programme continues to draw upon the literature on normal cognition, but has increasingly looked to animal learning theory in devising the experimental paradigms. The latter has become increasingly "cognitive", and the setting up of a viable animal model for schizophrenia no longer seems an impossibility. Clearly this would facilitate research into the biological bases of schizophrenic cognitive dysfunction, as Weiner (1990, p. 442) has noted, "there is a growing interest in the study of the neural mechanisms of learned behaviours". We have focused on two behavioural phenomena, latent inhibition (LI) (Lubow, Weiner, & Feldon, 1982) and Kamin's (1969) blocking effect, both of which can be regarded as instances of the "influence of stored memories of regularities of previous input on current perception" (Hemsley, 1987a).

Lubow et al. (1982) have argued that the LI paradigm is an effective way of manipulating attention in animals and that it may provide a link with the attentional disturbance prominent in schizophrenia. The paradigm is illustrated in Fig. 6.2. In the first stage, a stimulus is repeatedly presented to the organism (the pre-exposed stimulus; PE). In the second stage, the PE stimulus is paired with reinforcement in any of the standard learning procedures, classical or instrumental. When the amount of learning is measured, relative to a group that did not receive the first stage of stimulus pre-exposure (NPE), it is found that the stimulus-pre-exposed group learns the new association much more slowly. This is interpreted as indicating a reduction in the deployment of attention to a predictable redundant

		Test
Pre-exposure (PE) group	A – A – – – – A – A	A – X
No pre-exposure group (NPE)	– – – – – – – – – – –	A – X

In normals, pre-exposure to 'A' reduces rate of learning A-X association. This is usually interpreted as reflecting a reduction in the deployment of attention to a redundant stimulus.

FIG. 6.2   Latent inhibition paradigm. From Hemsley (1990). Reproduced with permission.

stimulus. The "regularity" operating is that the stimulus has no consequence.

Lubow (1989) has argued that, "given the broad range of species and conditions (in which it has been demonstrated), one would expect that LI would be a biologically significant phenomenon, i.e. that it would serve an important adaptive function". It has been shown in animals that LI is disrupted if amphetamine is administered in both the pre-exposure and test phase (Solomon et al., 1981), and this effect can be reversed with neuroleptics. Interestingly, it is also disrupted by damage to the hippocampal formation (Kaye & Pearce, 1987), a point that will be returned to in the final section of this chapter. Lubow et al. (1982, p. 103) write, "output is controlled, not like in the intact animal, by the integration of previous stored inputs and the prevailing situational conditions, but only by the latter". The distinction between "data-driven" and "conceptually-driven" processing was discussed above, optimal performance being dependent on an interaction between the stimulus presented and stored memories of regularities in previous inputs which result in expectancies or response biases. Lubow et al. (1982) suggest that animals under the influence of amphetamine may be viewed as unable to utilise acquired knowledge in a newly encountered situation. They write, "Not having the capacity to 'use' old stimuli, all stimuli are novel. Therefore such an organism will find itself endlessly bombarded with novel stimulation, resulting perhaps in the perceptual inundation phenomena described in schizophrenia" (Lubow et al., 1982, p. 104).

Clearly this is similar to the suggestion that schizophrenics fail to make use of the redundancy and patterning of sensory input to reduce information processing demands, and the prediction is therefore of disrupted LI in acute schizophrenia. This we have recently demonstrated (Baruch, Hemsley, & Gray, 1988) and the results are presented in Fig. 6.3, where higher scores represent more rapid learning.

The acute schizophrenics tend to perform better in the pre-exposure condition, and it was argued that these results are consistent with their being in a hyperdopaminergic state. Chronic medicated patients performed more normally. In addition, LI for the acute group normalised after 6–7 weeks of antipsychotic medication, as can be seen from Fig. 6.4. All expect the acute pre-exposure group showed a simple practice effect.

The performance of the acute group on the first occasion of testing was particularly interesting because in the pre-exposure condition they performed better than normal subjects, due to their continuing to attend to the redundant stimulus. It cannot, therefore, be attributed to a non-specific loss of efficient cognitive functioning.

It is important to note that LI does not simply represent a form of habituation. There is a major difference between the two: LI is disrupted by

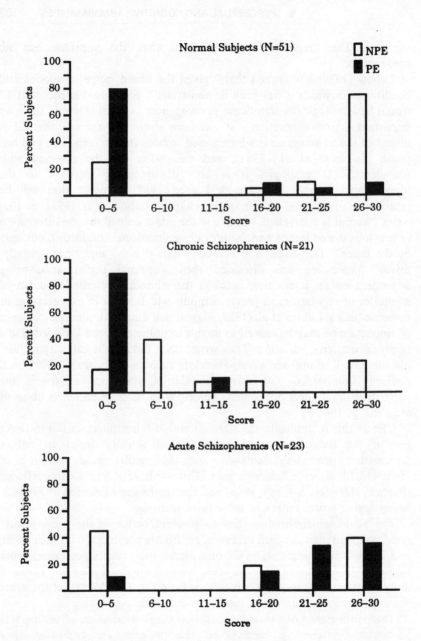

FIG. 6.3 Comparison of three groups on LI task. From Baruch et al., 1988. Reproduced with permission. © by Williams & Wilkins.

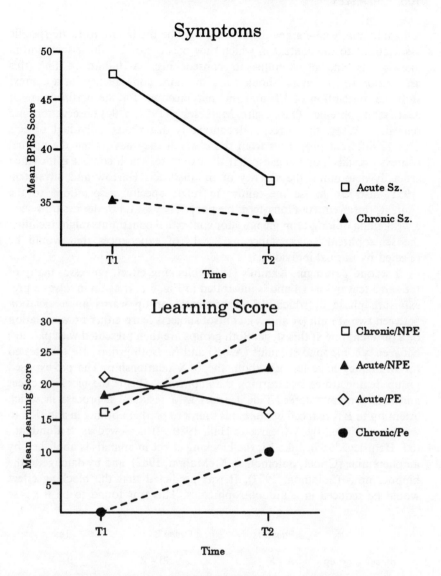

FIG. 6.4   Changes on LI over time for schizophrenic groups. From Baruch et al., 1988. Reproduced with permission. © by Williams & Wilkins.

a change in context, whereas habituation is not. Mayes (1991, p. 293) suggests that, "context may be defined as that which typically lies at the periphery of attention during learning and which either affects the meaningful interpretation of the target (interactive context) or does not (independent context)". This may prove important for our understanding of schizophrenia, where a key disturbance may be the failure to relate specific associations to the context in which they occur. For LI, the association in question is one of stimulus–no consequence. A failure to link this association to its context should have the same consequences as a context shift, i.e. disruption of LI, and this may account for the performance of acute schizophrenics. Once again, Matussek's (1952, p. 94) observations are relevant: "When the perceptual context is disturbed, individual objects acquire different properties from those which they have when the normal context prevails", and suggest that the extent to which context is loosened crucially determines the severity of the disorder. Harrow and Silverstein (1991) also emphasise the failure to relate specific associations to the context, retrieved from long-term memory. They go on to discuss how such a weakening of long-term memory for contextual constraints might facilitate the schizophrenic's acceptance as "real" of experiences that would be rejected by normal individuals.

A second paradigm, Kamin's (1969) blocking effect, possesses many of the same features as LI and is illustrated in Fig. 6.5. It again involves a pre-exposure phase in which the experimental group learns an association between two stimuli (A and X); control subjects learn either no association or a different one at this stage. Both groups are then presented with pairings between a compound stimulus (A + B) and X. Both groups are then tested for what they have learned about the B–X relationship. The pre-exposed group demonstrates less learning than controls. This is the blocking effect and it is generally agreed that it arises as a result of a process in which attention to B is reduced because it is found to predict nothing in addition to what is predicted by A (Pearce & Hall, 1980). It is viewed as "redundant" (c.f. Hemsley, 1985). Like LI, the blocking effect in animals is abolished by amphetamine (Crider, Solomon, & McMahon, 1982), and by damage to the hippocampus (Solomon, 1977). It was predicted that the blocking effect would be reduced in acute schizophrenics. This was found to be the case

	Phase 1	Phase 2	Test
Blocking group	A – X	(A + B) – X	B – X
Control group	– – – – – – –	(A + B) – X	B – X

In normals, the control group learns B–X faster than the blocked group. This finding is usually interpreted as reflecting reduction in attention to B in phase 2 for the blocked group, because it is found to predict nothing additional to that predicted by A, i.e. it is "redundant".

FIG. 6.5   "Blocking" paradigm. From Hemsley (1990). Reproduced with permission.

(Jones, Gray, & Hemsley, 1992), and the results are summarised in Fig. 6.6, which presents rank means on trials to criterion; here higher scores represent slower learning.

Acute schizophrenics actually performed worse in the control condition, whereas normals showed the usual blocking effect. The scores of the chronic patients were somewhat difficult to interpret as they performed very poorly in both conditions. A second experiment therefore employed a simpler blocking task. On this, both normals and chronic schizophrenics exhibited a blocking effect; there was no effect, however, of pre-exposure in the acute schizophrenic group.

One further study relevant to these issues has recently been conducted (Jones, Hemsley, & Gray, 1991b). It is relevant both to the role of context in determining schizophrenic performance and to the question of whether it is correct to describe the cognitive abnormalities of acute schizophrenia as a disturbance of "selective attention". Hemsley's 1987 model deliberately avoided this terminology and instead emphasised the "weakening of the influence of past regularities", as there are tasks in which different predictions are generated by the two formulations. The experiment used a choice reaction time paradigm developed by Miller (1987) from one devised by Eriksen and Eriksen (1979). Subjects were required to make one of two responses to two visually presented letters (A or B). These targets were regularly accompanied by two flanking letters (X and Y, making displays of the form XAX or YBY). Occasionally the flanking letters were interchanged

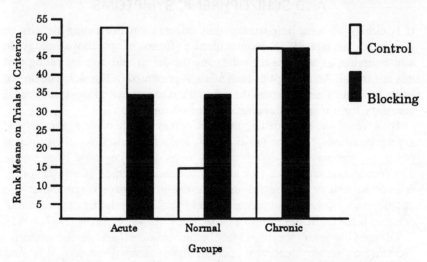

FIG. 6.6 Old blocking performance of schizophrenics and normals. Reprinted by permission of Elsevier Science Publishing Company, Inc. from *Loss of Kamin Blocking effect in acute but not chronic schizophrenics*, by Jones et al., BIOLOGICAL PSYCHIATRY, vol. 32, pp. 739–755. © 1992 by the Society of Biological Psychiatry.

(making YAY or XBX) but the correct response was still cued by the target (A or B). Normal subjects show a reliable slowing of reaction time on such context shift trials; clearly their performance is being influenced by the "past regularities" within the task. If acute schizophrenics were simply to demonstrate a broader span of attention they should be more aware of the flankers, and hence show a greater than normal slowing of reaction time on context shift trials. However, if they are less influenced by past associations between focal stimuli and context, they should be less affected than normal subjects by context shift. The latter is the result found by Jones et al. (1991b) for acute but not chronic schizophrenics. Subsequent analyses by hand of response have unfortunately somewhat complicated the picture. Only with right-hand responses did we observe the effect described above, which was interpreted as indicating that acute schizophrenics fail to integrate context with target stimulus–response association. The result is, however, consistent with research indicating primarily left hemisphere dysfunction in schizophrenia. It is of interest that Kinsbourne (1988, p. 248) suggests that "it takes left hemisphere damage to impair the depth of conscious analysis... By depth I mean relation of present to previous (and prospective) relevant experiences". We are currently exploring laterality effects within the latent inhibition paradigm.

INFORMATION PROCESSING DISTURBANCES AND SCHIZOPHRENIC SYMPTOMS

It is clearly of some importance that information processing deficits be shown to be related to more complex forms of psychopathology in schizophrenia, as a means for validating the deficit and demonstrating that it is not trivial. An attempt at such a link is presented in Fig. 6.7. The dotted line represents a modification that our recent experimental work suggests is necessary for our understanding of delusion formation.

It is convenient to distinguish two areas of theorising and related experimentation. The first (Frith, 1979) seeks to account for the principal positive symptoms of schizophrenia in terms of the cognitive impairment. The second argues that certain aspects of schizophrenics' functioning may reflect the action of control mechanisms that "involve conscious and unconscious psychological processes that focus on regulating the amount of demand faced to fit the adaptive capacity available" (Strauss, 1987, p. 85).

Of possible relevance to schizophrenic hallucinations is the extensive literature on sensory/perceptual deprivation in normal subjects. It is clear that unstructured input may result in abnormal perceptual experiences, which Leff (1968, p. 1507) suggested "overlap considerably with those of mentally ill patients". It has also been possible to demonstrate the short term manipulation of auditory hallucinations in a group of schizophrenic

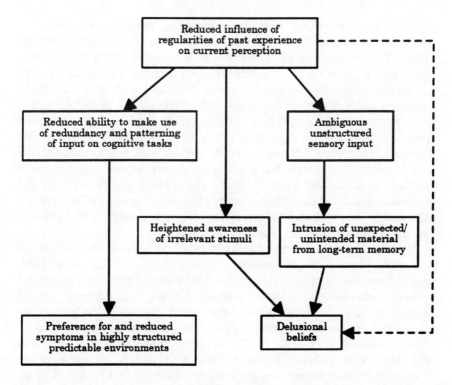

FIG. 6.7 Model of cognitive abnormalities and symptoms of schizophrenia (modified from Hemsley, 1987).

patients by means of alterations in auditory input (Margo et al., 1981). The experiences reported were inversely related to the structure and attention commanding properties of the input.

The present model proposes that the schizophrenic condition is characterised by a reduction in the influence of the regularities of past experience on current perception. This, it is suggested, results in ambiguous, unstructured sensory input. One might therefore argue that hallucinations are related to a cognitive impairment that, even under normal conditions, results in ambiguous messages reaching awareness and hence fails to inhibit the emergence of material from long-term memory (LTM) (Hemsley, 1987b). George and Neufeld (1985, p. 268) have referred to an interaction between the "spontaneous retrieval of information stored in LTM and sensory processing, the latter having an inhibitory effect on the former". A similar argument is put forward by Rund (1986, p. 532): "Schizophrenics, possibly because of a sensory overload ... are more susceptible to such a direct flow between long term storage and the sensory storage level".

Abnormal perceptual experiences, including hallucinations, have frequently been accorded a central role in the formation of delusions (Maher,
1988). This emphasis is also prominent in Matussek's (1952) observations.
Following a loosening of the perceptual context, attention may be captured
by incidental details of the environment. Normally such an aspect of the
situation would not reach awareness, but its registration prompts a search
for reasons for its occurrence. Frith's (1979) model adopts a similar
position. More recently Anscombe (1987) has extended this to suggest that
certain of the patient's thoughts may be imbued with a significance that is
out of proportion to their real importance, simply because they happen to
capture the attentional focus. He goes on to argue that both internally and
externally generated perceptions "are not placed in a context of background
knowledge" and that this "results in the coming to awareness of hasty and
alarming appraisals by pre-attentive processes".

Among the most prominent features of delusional thinking is an
abnormal view of the relationships between events. As Schneider (1930)
put it, "meaningful connections are created between temporarily coincident
external impressions, external impression with the patient's present
condition, or perceptions with thoughts which happen to be present, or
events and recollections happening to occur in consciousness about the same
time". Similarly Arieti (1974, p. 231) observed "patients see non-fortuitous
coincidences everywhere". Matussek (1952, p. 96) quotes a patient as saying
"out of these perceptions come the absolute awareness that my ability to see
connections had been multiplied many times over". For example, objects
sharing certain qualities that had become prominent were seen as being
linked in some significant way. Such feelings of relatedness, based on
temporal or spatial contiguity between experiences, may proceed to an
assumption of a causal relationship between them. Meehl (1964, cited in
Eckblad & Chapman, 1983), claims that schizophrenia-prone individuals
"entertain the possibility that events which, according to the causal concepts
of this culture cannot have a causal relation with each other, might
nevertheless do so". A patient of the present author, recalling his psychotic
experiences, noted that the co-occurrence of two events often led
immediately to an assumption of a causal relationship between them. It
was as if previous non-co-occurrences were completely ignored.

How might such clinical observations relate to the present model? In
reviewing the processes that underlie the judgement of causation, Einhorn
and Hogarth (1986, p. 5) note that normal people engage in causal reasoning
to make sense of the world, and that this is more likely to happen when
perceptions violate expectations and become prominent. Spatial and
temporal contiguity are clearly of great importance in concluding that
there exists a causal relationship. However, in assessing the strength of such
a relationship, account is also taken of instances of the occurrence of X in

the absence of Y, and Y in the absence of X (i.e. past regularities). Consider now the case of the schizophrenic patient. Not only does the "weakened influence of past regularities of current perception" result in the intrusion of redundant material into awareness, it also influences the assessment of the covariation between X and Y. Hence abnormal causal relationships may be inferred on the basis of a single co-occurrence. This is illustrated more formally in Table 6.2.

However, in emphasising failures to make use of "background knowledge" (Anscombe 1987), and alterations in the judgement of covariation (Hemsley, 1991), there has clearly been a move away from Maher's (1974, 1988) view of delusions as essentially a product of normal reasoning, serving as explanations that the deluded individual uses to account for abnormal perceptual experience. Recent research suggests an abnormal reasoning style in some deluded subjects in addition to well established perceptual disturbances.

A problem that is encountered in exploring the reasoning style of deluded subjects is in setting a standard for "correct" or "incorrect" reasoning. Fischoff and Beyth-Marom (1983) suggest that Bayesian inference provides a general framework for evaluating beliefs in the normal population, and that it may be used to describe a person's consistency with, or departure from, the model. Hemsley and Garety (1986) extended this approach to the inferences of deluded subjects. Employing a probabilistic inference task, two studies have demonstrated that deluded subjects require less information before reaching a decision (Garety, Hemsley & Wessely, 1991; Huq, Garety, & Hemsley, 1988). The first of these also indicated that, after certainty is reached, deluded subjects are more likely to make a dramatic change in probability estimate following an item of disconfirmatory information. This is consistent with those models of schizophrenia that

TABLE 6.2
A Possible Pathway to the Perception of Abnormal Causal Relationships

A search for causal explanations takes place to "make sense" of the world. This frequently occurs when events violate expectations and achieve prominence.

Temporal order and contiguity tends to indicate causal relationship (e.g. X-Y) but in addition normal subjects take into account the covariation between X and Y. Thus for a particular conjunction of X and Y, consideration is also given to the occurrence of X without Y, and Y without X on previous occasions (i.e. past regularities).

If schizophrenia is characterised by:
(a) awareness of aspects of the environment not normally attended to
(b) a reduction of the influence of past regularities on current perception, *then abnormal causal relationships may be inferred on the basis of a single co-occurrence*

From Hemsley (1990). Reproduced with permission.

emphasise the greater influence of immediate environmental stimuli compared with the effects of prior learning (Hemsley, 1987; Salziner, 1984). Hence the modification to Table 6.1.

The present discussion has been concerned primarily with models of positive symptomatology. However, it is rare for schizophrenics to show only positive or negative symptoms. It remains unclear whether the distinction represents: (1) two underlying and distinct disorders; (2) differing severity of the same disorder; (3) individual differences in reaction to the same disorder; (4) different stages of the same disorder (acute chronic); or (5) a combination of (2), (3), and (4). Thus Pogue-Geile and Harrow (1988, p. 437) conclude that, "the evidence is supportive of the view that negative symptoms may represent a severity threshold on a continuum of liability to schizophrenia". Within the present formulation, a more drastic weakening of the influence of stored regularities on current perception might result in a level of disorganisation such as to render difficult any goal-directed activities.

Relevant to (3) is Strauss' (1987) argument that certain aspects of schizophrenics' functioning may reflect the action of conscious and unconscious regulatory processes. Such control processes were seen by Hemsley (1977) as crucial to negative symptomatology. Schizophrenics were viewed as being in a state of "information overload". Symptoms such as poverty of speech, social withdrawal, and retardation, represented adaptive strategies learnt over time so as to minimise the effects of the cognitive impairment. One may also speculate that the search for meaning in the altered experiences may diminish over time, as actions based on these prove ineffective or counterproductive. As Anscombe (1987, p. 254) puts it, "less and less the subject forms his own impressions, and more and more he is impinged upon by his environment".

POTENTIAL LINKS WITH BIOLOGICAL MODELS

It has frequently been suggested (Huber, 1986; Weinberger, Wagner, & Wyatt, 1983) that pathology of the limbic system is associated with schizophrenia. In particular, the hippocampus has been discussed as a possible region of the brain that might be affected. Although neuropathological studies have provided some support for this view (Falkai & Bogerts, 1986), the findings are far from straightforward, and many other brain regions have been implicated. However, the possible functions of the hippocampus appear very relevant to the present model. Olton, Wible, & Shapiro, (1986, p. 354) have suggested that, "The hippocampus may be the brain structure that allows each of the various components of a place and an event to be linked together, and compared with other places and events". In a related formulation, Gray (1982) has argued for the role of the hippocampus in the comparison of actual and expected stimuli; if there is a mismatch, there is increasing attention to that input. A defect in this system could relate to a weakening of the effect of past regularities on current perception. Interestingly, an important further consequence of a mismatch between actual and expected stimuli is considered to be an increase in arousal. Whether this is experience as "pleasurable excitement" or "anxiety" is in part dependent on cognitive appraisal. Chapman's (1966) study of schizophrenics' reports of their experiences in the early stage of the disorder is most often referred to as evidence for early perceptual/cognitive changes. However, Chapman observed that these alterations in perceptual quality were sometimes expressed initially as pleasant, and patients were even mildly elated. However, as the disturbances of perception and cognition developed, the reaction changed to one of intense anxiety. Chapman (1966, p. 245) notes "Taking the group as a whole, every kind of neurotic symptom was encountered in the early stage of the disease—in particular intense anxiety reactions were almost invariable".

Our most recent model (Gray et al. 1991a, b) has attempted to link dopaminergic hyperactivity with temporal lobe pathology, and to relate both to the disturbances of information processing considered to underlie schizophrenic symptoms. Anatomically, the model emphasises the projections from the septohippocampal system, via the subiculum, to the nucleus accumbens, and their interaction with the ascending dopaminergic projection to the accumbens. Psychologically, the model emphasises a disturbance, in acute schizophrenia, in the normal integration of stored memories of past regularities of perceptual input with ongoing motor programmes and the control of current perception. Biological and psychological models appear to be converging in intriguing ways.

cf Beck's schemata.

REFERENCES

Anscombe, R. (1987). The disorder of consciousness in schizophrenia. *Schizophrenia Bulletin 11*, 241–260.

Arieti, S. (1966). Schizophrenic cognition. In P.H. Hoch & J. Zubin (Eds.), *Psychopathology of schizophrenia* (pp. 37–48). New York: Grave & Stratton.

Arieti, S. (1974). *Interpretation of schizophrenia* (2nd ed.). London: Crosby, Lockwood, Staples.

Baruch, J., Hemsley, D.R., & Gray, J.A. (1988). Differential performance of acute and chronic schizophrenics in a latent inhibition task. *Journal of Nervous and Mental Diseases, 176*, 598–606.

Berze, J. (1914). *Primary insufficiency of mental activity.* Leipzig: F. Deuticke.

Broadbent, D.E. (1971). *Decision and stress.* London: Academic Press.

Chapman, J. (1966). The early symptoms of schizophrenia. *British Journal of Psychiatry, 112*, 225–251.

Cohen, R., & Borst, V. (1987). Psychological models of schizophrenic impairments. In H. Hafner, W.F. Gattaz, & W. Janzarik (Eds.), *Search for the causes of schizophrenia.* Heidelberg: Springer-Verlag.

Collicutt, J.R., & Hemsley, D.R. (1985). *Schizophrenia: A disruption of the stream of thought.* Unpublished manuscript.

Conrad, K. (1958). *Die Beginnende Schizophrenie.* Stuttgart: G. Thieme.

Crider, A., Solomon, P.R., & McMahon, M.A. (1982). Attention in the rat following chronic d-amphetamine administration: relationship to schizophrenic attention disorder. *Biological Psychiatry, 17*, 351–361.

Cutting, J. (1989). Gestalt theory and psychiatry: Discussion paper. *Journal of the Royal Society of Medicine, 82*, 429–431.

Eckblad, M., & Chapman, L.J. (1983). Magical ideation as an indicator of schizotypy. *Journal of Consulting and Clinical Psychology, 51*, 215–225.

Einhorn, H.J., & Hogarth, R.M. (1986). Judging probably cause. *Psychiatry Bulletin, 99*, 3–19.

Eriksen, B.A., & Erikson, C.W. (1974). Effects of noise letters upon the identification of a target letter in a nonsearch task. *Perception and Psychophysics, 16*, 143–149.

Falkai, P., & Bogerts, B. (1986). Cell loss in the hippocampus of schizophrenics. *European Archives of Psychiatry and Neurological Science, 236*, 154–161,

Fischoff, B., & Beyth-Marom, R. (1983). Hypothesis evaluation from a Bayesian perspective. *Psychological Review, 90*, 239–260.

Frith, C.D. (1979). Consciousness, information processing and schizophrenia. *British Journal of Psychiatry, 134*, 225–235.

Garety, P.A., Hemsley, D.R., & Wessely, S. (1991). Reasoning in deluded schizophrenic and paranoid patients. *Journal of Nervous and Mental Disease, 179*, 194–201.

George, L., & Neufeld, R.W.J. (1985). Cognition and symptomatology in schizophrenia. *Schizophrenia Bulletin, 11*, 264–285.

Gray, J.A. (1982). *The neuropsychology of anxiety.* Oxford: University Press.

Gray, J.A., Feldon, J., Rawlins, J.N.P., Hemsley, D.R., & Smith, A.D. (1991a). The neuropsychology of schizophrenia. *Behavioural and Brain Sciences, 14*, 1–20.

Gray, J.A., Hemsley, D.R., Gray, N., Feldon, J., & Rawlins, J.N.P. (1991b). Schiz. Bits: Misses, mysteries and hits. *Behavioural and Brain Sciences, 14*, 56–84.

Harrow, M., & Silverstein, M. (1991) The role of long term memory and monitoring in schizophrenia: Multiple functions (Commentary to Gray et al. 1991a). *Behavioural and Brain Sciences, 14*, 30–31.

Hemsley, D.R. (1977). What have cognitive deficits to do with schizophrenic symptoms? *British Journal of Psychiatry, 130*, 167–173.

Hemsley, D.R. (1985). Information processing and schizophrenia. Paper presented at EABT Conference, Munich. In E. Straube, & K. Hahlireg (Eds.), *Schizophrenia, concepts, vulnerability and intervention.* Heidelberg: Springer.

Hemsley, D.R. (1987a). An experimental psychological model for schizophrenia. In H. Hafner, W.F. Gattaz, & W. Janzarik (Eds.), *Search for the causes of schizophrenia.* Heidelberg: Springer.

Hemsley, D.R. (1987b). Hallucinations: Unintended or unexpected? *Behavioural and Brain Sciences, 10*, 532–533.

Hemsley, D.R. (1988). Psychological models of schizophrenia. In E. Miller, & P. Cooper (Eds.), *Adult Abnormal Psychology*, p. 101–127. London: Churchill Livingstone.

Hemsley, D.R. (1990). What have cognitive deficits to do with schizophrenia? In G. Huber (Ed.), *Idiopathische Psychosen*, p. 111–125. Stuttgart: Schattauer.

Hemsley, D.R., & Garety, P.A. (1986). The formation and maintenance of delusions: A Bayesian analysis. *British Journal of Psychiatry, 149*, 51–56.

Huber, G. (1986). Negative or basic symptoms in schizophrenia and affective illness. In Shagass, C. et al. (Eds.), *Biological psychiatry.* New York: Elsevier.

Huq, S.F., Garety, P.A., & Hemsley, D.R. (1988). Probabilistic judgements in deluded and non-deluded subjects. *Journal of Experimental Psychology, 40A* (4), 801–812.

James, W. (1890). *The principles of psychology.* London: MacMillan.

Jones, S.H., Hemsley, D.R., & Gray, J.A. (1991. Contextual effects on reaction time and accuracy in acute and chronic schizophrenia: Impairment in selective attention or in the influence of prior learning. *British Journal of Psychiatry, 159,* 415–421.

Jones, S., Gray, J.A., & Hemsley, D.R. (1992). Loss of the Kamin Blocking effect in acute but not chronic schizophrenics. *Biological Psychiatry, 32,* 739–755.

Kamin, L.J. (1969). Predictability, surprise, attention and conditioning. In B.A. Campbell & R.M. Church (Eds.), *Punishment and aversive behaviour.* New York: Appleton–Century–Crofts.

Kaye, H., & Pearce, J.M. (1987). Hippocampal lesions alternate latent inhibition and the decline of the orienting response in rats. *Quarterly Journal of Experimental Psychology, 39B,* 107–125.

Kinsbourne, M. (1988). Integrated field theory of consciousness. In A.J. Marcel, & E. Bisiach (Eds.), *Consciousness in contemporary science,* pp. 239–256. Oxford: Clarendon Press.

Leff, J.P. (1968). Perceptual phenomena and personality in sensory deprivation. *British Journal of Psychiatry, 114,* 1499–1508.

Lubow, R.E. (1989). *Latent inhibition and conditioned attention theory.* New York: Cambridge University Press.

Lubow, R.E., Weiner, I., & Feldon, J. (1982). An animal model of attention. In M.Y. Spiegelstein & A. Levy (Eds.), *Behavioural models and the analysis of drug action,* pp. 89–107. Amsterdam: Elsevier.

Maher, B.A. (1974). Delusional thinking and perceptual disorder. *Journal of Individual Psychology, 30,* 98–113.

Maher, B.A. (1988). Anomalous experience and delusional thinking: The logic of explanations. In T.F. Oltmann, & B.A. Maher (Eds.). *Delusional beliefs.* New York: Wiley.

Margo, A., Hemsley, D.R., & Slade, P.D. (1981). The effects of varying auditory input on schizophrenic hallucinations. *British Journal of Psychiatry, 139,* 122–127.

Matussek, P. (1952). Studies in delusional perception. *Psychiatrie und Zeitschrift, Neurologie, 189,* 279–318.

Mayes, A. (1991). Amnesia: lesion location and functional deficit—what is the link? *Psychological Medicine, 21,* 293–297.

McGhie, A., & Chapman, J. (1961). Disorders of attention and perception in early schizophrenia. *British Journal of Medicine and Psychology, 34,* 103–115.

Miller, J. (1987). Priming is not necessary for selective attention failures: Semantic effects of unattended, unprimed letters. *Percept Psychology, 41*(5), 419–434.

Minkowski, E. (1927). *The essential disorder underlying schizophrenia and schizophrenic thought.* Paris: Payot.

Norman, D.A., & Bobrow, D.G. (1976). On the role of active memory processes in perception and cognition. In C.N. Cofer (Ed.). *The structure of human memory.* San Francisco: Freeman.

Olton, D.S., Wible, C.G., & Shapiro, M.L. (1986). Mnemonic theories of hippocampal function. *Behavioural Neuroscience, 100,* 852–855.

Patterson, T. (1987). Studies towards the subcortical pathogenesis of schizophrenia. *Schizophrenia Bulletin, 13,* 555–576.

Pearce, J.M., & Hall, G. (1980). A model for Pavlovian learning: Variations in the affectiveness of conditioned but not of unconditional stimuli. *Psychiatry Revue, 87,* 532–552.

Pogue-Geile, M.F., & Harrow, M. (1988). Negative symptoms in schizophrenia: Their longitudinal course and prognostic importance. *Schizophrenia Bulletin, 11,* 427–439.

Model of normal attention — an inf processing model in normal O's.

116 HEMSLEY

Posner, M. (1982). Cumulative development of attentional theory. *American Psychologist, 37,* 168–179.

Rund, B.R. (1986). Verbal hallucinations and information processing. *Behavioural and Brain Sciences, 9* (3), 530–531.

Schneider, C. (1930). *Die Psycholgie der Schizophrenen.* Leipzig: G. Thieme.

Schneider, W., & Shiffrin, R.M. (1977). Controlled and automatic human information processing. Detection, search and attention. *Psychiatry Revue, 84,* 1–66.

Shakow, D. (1950). Some psychological features of schizophrenia. In M.L. Reyment (Ed.). *Feelings and emotions,* 383–390. New York: McGraw Hill.

Shallice, T. (1988). Information processing models of consciousness: Possibilities and problems. In A.J. Marcel and E. Bisiach (Eds.), *Consciousness in contemporary science.* Oxford: Clarendon Press.

Shepherd, M. (1987). Formulation of new research strategies on schizophrenia. In A. Hafner, W.F. Gattaz, & W. Janzavik (Eds.), *Search for the Causes of Schizophrenia.* Heidelberg: Springer.

Solomon, P.R. (1977). Role of the hippocampus in blocking and conditioned inhibition of rabbits nictating membrance response. *Journal of Physiological Psychology, 91,* 407–417.

Solomon, P.R., Crider, A., Winkelman, J.W., Tuvi, A., Kamer, R.M., & Kaplan, L.T. (1981). Disrupted latent inhibition in the rat with chronic amphetamine or halopendol induced supersensitivity: Relationship to schizophrenic attention disorder. *Biological Psychology, 16,* 519–537.

Strauss, J. (1987). Processes of healing and chronicity in schizophrenia. In H. Hafner, W.F. Gattaz, & W. Janzavik (Eds.), *Search for the causes of schizophrenia,* (Vol. 11, pp. 75–87). Heidelberg: Springer.

Weinberger, D.R., Wagner, R.L., & Wyatt, R.J. (1983). Neuropathological studies of schizophrenia—a selective review. *Schizophrenia Bulletin, 9,* 193–212.

Weiner, I. (1990). Neural substrates of latent inhibition: the switching model. *Psychiatry Bulletin, 108,* 442–461.

III
NEUROPSYCHOLOGY AND NEURODEVELOPMENT

7

Neurodevelopmental Precursors of Schizophrenia

Elaine F. Walker
Emory University, Atlanta, U.S.A.

In our archival-observational study of the precursors of schizophrenia, we are using childhood home-movies, as well as other sources of data, to identify the very earliest signs of vulnerability. This research takes a developmental approach in that it assumes that the neuropathological process subserving schizophrenia is a gradually unfolding one whose manifestations vary as the individual matures. The ultimate goal is to document the developmental course as a foundation for generating neurodevelopmental models of etiology. In this presentation, we will report on the results of our preliminary analyses of neuromotor functions from the first to the 15th year of life. *Neuromotor functions* are considered important because their development is reflective of the integrity of the central nervous system. Moreover, findings from high-risk research suggest that abnormalities in early motor development may characterise children at risk for schizophrenia.

INTRODUCTION

Developmental changes in behavioural manifestations may hold important clues to the aetiological processes underlying various forms of psychopathology (Walker, 1991). Unfortunately, data on the childhood development of schizophrenic patients have been so scarce that few writers have accepted the challenge of proposing a developmental model of the aetiology of the disorder. The models that have been proposed attempt to integrate what little is currently known about the developmental course of schizophrenia with evidence from research on normal neurodevelopment (Benes, 1989; Feinberg, 1983; Saugstad, 1989; Taylor, 1991; Weinberger,

1987). Although the models differ in the nature of the neuropathological process they describe, all but one (Taylor, 1991) of those cited above share the assumption that the organic dysfunction subserving schizophrenia has its onset in adolescence (i.e. the onset of the prodromal phase). In other words, the somatophene (biological phenotype) or somatophenocopy (an acquired biological abnormality) does not manifest itself prior to that point.

If it is the case that schizophrenia is due to a disruption in CNS functioning that is triggered by the biological changes accompanying adolescence, then we would expect to see a relatively unremarkable course of development up to that point. This does not, of course, preclude the existence of CNS abnormality prior to adolescence, but it does imply that any such abnormality is silent because it lay in a structure or system that is essentially non-functional prior to the onset of puberty.

However, findings from high-risk and follow-back research suggest that abnormalities predate the onset of the clinical symptoms of schizophrenia by many years (Walker, 1991). In fact, there is suggestive evidence that neuromotor abnormalities may be observable as early as infancy (Walker & Emory, 1983). Infant offspring of schizophrenic parents show greater abnormalities in fine and gross motor development as measured by standardised instruments (see Watt et al., 1984, for a review). However, the fact that most of these children are being reared by a schizophrenic parent raises the possibility that their motor impairments are environmentally induced, rather than reflecting organic vulnerability to schizophrenia. Unfortunately, only one of the high-risk studies that directly assessed infant functioning has followed subjects through the early adult risk period for schizophrenia to determine psychiatric outcome. In this study of 12 high-risk subjects, Fish (1977, 1984) diagnosed one as schizophrenic and six as schizotypal or paranoid personality. These seven ill subjects all showed developmental abnormalities in infancy (Fish, 1984, 1992). Consistent with the findings from high-risk research, follow-back studies that have examined the childhood records of adult psychiatric patients find evidence of delays in early motor development (Offord & Cross, 1969; Watt, 1972). In sum, although data on the relation between childhood characteristics and adult psychiatric outcome are limited, the findings are consistent in showing early abnormalities.

It is reasonable to speculate that four of the five neurodevelopmental theorists cited above posit a functional onset of neuropathology in adolescence because the clinical and empirical evidence for behavioural dysfunction at this point in the life course of schizophrenia is so well established. In contrast, as Pogue-Geile (1991) notes, although high-risk and follow-back research suggests the existence of dysfunction long before adolescence, the evidence is non-specific. The limitations of past research methods may, therefore, be influencing the nature of our aetiological models. If, however, further research verifies the existence of neuromotor and behavioural abnormalities in preschizophrenic infants and children, it will be necessary to incorporate these findings into future neurodevelopmental models. In other words, we will be compelled to develop models that account for the varying manifestations of dysfunction across the life-span.

In the preliminary study reported here, we further examine the relation between early neuromotor development and adult-onset schizophrenia. This study is part of a larger project, described below, that uses a novel methodology to explore the childhood precursors of schizophrenia (Walker & Lewine, 1990).

We believe that neuromotor factors are an important area for investigation because motor development is highly sensitive to CNS abnormalities (Kreusser & Volpe, 1984), and because the emergence of various motor milestones is assumed to be at least partially determined by developmental changes in CNS structures (Saint-Anne Dargassies, 1986; Sarnat, 1984). Further, as Meehl (1989, 1990) has noted, soft neurological signs are presumably closer, in the causal chain, to the biological substrate of schizophrenic pathology than are psychometrics, symptoms and social behaviour. In this sense, neuromotor indicators are less subject to the cumulative effects of social learning, which would be expected to contribute significantly to individual differences in cognitive functions and social behaviour.

AN ARCHIVAL–OBSERVATIONAL APPROACH TO RESEARCH ON THE DEVELOPMENT OF SCHIZOPHRENIA

By better documenting the ontogenesis of behaviour in individuals who succumb to adult-onset psychopathology, we may be able to identify modal developmental trajectories. Moreover, by relating these trajectories to potential sources of constitutional vulnerability and moderating factors, it may be possible to identify subtypes that will inform the generation of more precise developmental models of aetiology (Walker, Cudeck, Mednick, & Schulsinger, 1981; Walker, Downey, & Bergman, 1989). Obtaining data on the life-span development of schizophrenic patients will be particularly important if our assumption of a final common pathway with multiple aetiological origins is correct. After the clinical onset of the disorder, we are presumably seeing the pervasive consequences and sequelae of impairment in this common pathway. The period prior to the clinical onset, however, may be the optimal one for the manifestation of signs that correspond to specific aetiological origins.

To obtain such data, we must have a research method that will yield reliable information on premorbid characteristics, preferably beginning in infancy, as well as adult psychiatric outcome. We have recently initiated a research programme that uses such a method. It is best described as an "archival observational" study because the primary source of information is childhood home movies of subjects who were first diagnosed as having schizophrenia in late adolescence or early adulthood. The technology for making home movies became widely available in the 1950s, so individuals born during this decade have now passed through the major risk period for schizophrenia.

The archival–observational method has several advantages over previous approaches to the study of childhood antecedents of schizophrenia. First, as indicated, it allows for direct observation of behaviour. Researchers have demonstrated that observational procedures can be used to study a broad range of characteristics, and that they can yield reliable data on microlevel behaviours (Sackett, 1978). We will, therefore, be able to study the behaviour of preschizophrenic children without reliance on secondary sources (academic records or informants) that may serve to introduce biases, filter information, or provide only gross impressions (Yarrow, Campbell, & Burton, 1970). Second, the adult psychiatric outcome of the subjects is known, so we can readily ascertain the relation between antecedents and outcome. Related to this, the data were collected independent of knowledge of developmental outcome, which eliminates the problem of examiner or informant bias. Third, unlike follow-up studies, the patient sample in the present study is not restricted to those with clinical conditions in childhood (Offord & Cross, 1969) and, in contrast to high-risk studies, the sample is not restricted to those with schizophrenia in a first-degree relative (Watt et al., 1984). Given that the overwhelming majority of schizophrenic patients (about 90%) do not have first-degree relatives with the disorder, this is a clear advantage (Gottesman & Shields, 1982). Not only is sample representativeness enhanced, but genotype–environment confounds are reduced (Walker, Downey, & Nightingale, 1988; Walker, Downey, & Caspi, 1990). In sum, the sample is potentially more representative of the general population of schizophrenic patients.

Through the use of three comparison groups—healthy siblings of patients, patients with affective disorders, and subjects from families with no mental illness—we will ultimately be able to address a variety of important questions. Healthy siblings of patients are particularly informative as comparison subjects because they appear in the same films and, consequently, the same behavioural contexts as the patients. And, of course, they are reared by the same parents. This imposes some control for environmental factors when patients are compared with siblings.

Prior to applying microlevel, observational coding schemes to the childhood films, we felt it was important to address the question of whether observers (psychologists and psychiatrists) would be capable of identifying the preschizophrenic children without the benefit of specific criteria. We conducted a preliminary study, using a subset of the films, to answer this question (Walker & Lewine, 1990). The films featured five patients with diagnoses (DSM III-R) of schizophrenia (four males and one female) and their healthy siblings from infancy to 8 years of age. The siblings are all now past the age of 25 years and have no history of psychiatric disorder. In every case, the patient was the only one in his/her nuclear family who succumbed to a psychiatric disorder. None of the patients was referred for or received treatment for psychiatric problems prior to 17 years, nor were any characterised by physical illnesses or handicaps that would set them apart from their siblings.

Viewers were 12 clinicians who were informed that they would be viewing videotape segments of sibships in which only one child developed schizophrenia, and their task was to identify that child. They were able to do so at above-chance levels. These findings lend support to the notion that vulnerability to schizophrenia is manifested early in life.

In this paper, we present the preliminary results from our microlevel analyses of the neuromotor development of preschizophrenic children and their healthy siblings. The goals are to test the hypothesis that preschizophrenic children evidence more signs of neuromotor dysfunction than their healthy siblings, and, if the hypothesis is supported, to specify the precise nature of this dysfunction.

METHOD

Subjects

The subjects of this report are four male and three female schizophrenic patients and seven healthy siblings of the patients.

Structured diagnostic interviews (Schedule for Affective Disorders and Schizophrenia) were conducted and diagnoses are based on DSM III-R criteria. This sample is a subset of a larger group of schizophrenic patients ($n = 30$) participating in the research programme. The subset includes all subjects on whom neuromotor data are currently available. The nearest-in-age, same-sex healthy sibling of each patient was chosen as the comparison subject. In cases where there was no same-sex sibling, the nearest-in-age, opposite-sex sibling served as the comparison. None of the healthy siblings had received psychiatric treatment and none met lifetime criteria for any psychiatric disorder. Demographic characteristics of the subjects are listed in Table 7.1.

None of the subjects manifested any neurological or psychiatric disorder in childhood. All have now experienced at least one hospitalisation and are currently on antipsychotic medication. With one exception (number 6), all of the patients have been chronically unemployed and dependent on others

TABLE 7.1
Demographic Characteristics of the Subjects

Sibship pair number	Year of birth	Sex	Diagnosis	Age at onset of illness
1	1961	F	Schizophrenic	22 years
	1963	F	Healthy	
2	1940	M	Schizophrenic	18 years
	1946	M	Healthy	
3	1957	F	Healthy	24 years
	1962	M	Schizophrenic	
4	1954	F	Schizophrenic	17 years
	1955	M	Healthy	
5	1966	M	Schizophrenic	19 years
	1968	M	Healthy	
6	1966	M	Healthy	21 years
	1967	M	Schizophrenic	
7	1953	F	Schizophrenic	17 years
	1955	F	Healthy	

for care since the onset of their illness. For all of the families in this sample, the patient is the only psychiatrically ill family member.

Procedures

All available home movies of the subjects were submitted for study; the films span from infancy to 15 years of age. The films were transferred to videotape and the age of subjects in each segment was documented.

Measure

The neuromotor rating scale used in the present study was designed to assess the presence of neurological soft signs and to document the presence of delays and abnormalities in motor development. It contains two subscales: (1) neurological soft signs; and (2) quality of movement.

All 34 items contained in the neurological signs subscale are rated as present or absent, and the 24 items in the Qualities of Movement subscale are rated below average, average, or above average. The neurological soft signs subscale contains items such as hypotonicity, associated movements, morphological asymmetries, hand posturing, and akinesia. The qualities of movement subscale rates functions such as head control, transitional movements, crawling, bimanual skill, and gait. The ages of occurrence of all signs and abnormalities are also recorded. The neuromotor ratings were made by a specialist in neurodevelopmental assessment. The ratings were made in the absence of knowledge about the diagnostic outcome of the subjects.

RESULTS

The aggregated data from the neuromotor ratings are presented in Table 7.2. Mean comparisons revealed that for the preschizophrenic subjects significantly more neurological abnormalities were present ($t = 2.89$; $P < 0.01$) and their motor abilities were more often rated in the below average range ($t = 2.36$; $P < 0.025$). In contrast, the healthy siblings were more likely to receive ratings of "above average" for motor abilities ($t = 2.05$; $P < 0.05$).

Patient 1 showed musculoskeletal anomalies (genu valgus), postural abnormalities in sitting (predominant W-sitting), associated reactions in the left arm, and apparent weakness of the left side of the body, all during the first two years of life. She was rated below average on motor alignment, weightshift, smoothness of transitional movements, posture and crawling.

Patient 2, a male, showed involuntary movements, posturing, associated reactions, and rigidity in the left hand during the first four years. He was rated below average on equilibrium reactions, activity level, gait, grasp, manipulation, sitting without support, and walking.

Patient 3, a male, showed involuntary movements, posturing, and associated reactions in the left hand through the first three years. He was generally hypotonic. He was rated below average on shoulder stability, alignment, weight shift, motor planning, strength, age at acquisition of milestones, i.e. crawling and walking.

Patient 4, a female, manifested mild athetosis beginning at 8 months, musculoskeletal abnormality (genu valgus), primitive reflexes (asymmetric tonic neck reflex at 8 months), bilateral associated reactions, left hand posturing, and hypotonicity, especially in the oral region; hand flapping was repeatedly noted. Rated below average were righting reactions, shoulder

TABLE 7.2
Neuromotor Scale Ratings for Preschizophrenics and Sibling Controls

	Mean number of neurological signs present	Mean number of motor abilities above average	Mean number of motor abilities below average
Preschizophrenics	5.00 (1.00)*	1.00 (1.78)	9.90 (3.8)
Sibling controls	0.71 (1.31)	5.57 (5.5)	2.29 (3.64)

* Standard deviations in parentheses.

stability, antigravity movements, equilibrium reactions, activity level, weight shift, smoothness, dissociation, posture, head control, sitting, and age at acquisition of motor milestones.

Patient 5, a male, showed associated reactions and posturing in both hands, but predominantly in the left. There was also evidence of neglect of the left hand. Abnormal oral movements and sitting posture were also noted. Activity level, shoulder and girdle stability, and crawling were below average.

Patient 6, a male, showed musculoskeletal abnormality (genu vagus), hypotonicity, postural asymmetry (right side preference), and abnormal oral movements. He was below average in righting reactions, equilibrium reactions, activity level, alignment, weight shift, posture, gait, smoothness, dissociation of movement, crawling, and walking.

Patient 7, a female, showed extreme hypotonicity in the first two years, retained primitive reflexes (ATNR at 6 months), left-side musculoskeletal abnormality during infancy (left leg bowed), and postural abnormalities (sitting and left-hand position). She was rated as below average on almost all motor abilities and milestones.

DISCUSSION

Consistent with previous findings, the present results indicate that preschizophrenic children, beginning in infancy, manifest significant neuromotor abnormalities. Thus, the notion that schizophrenia is associated with a central nervous system defect that is present at birth receives strong support (Meehl, 1989, 1990; Mirsky & Duncan, 1986).

The abnormalities observed in the preschizophrenic children show striking consistency across subjects. Six of the seven patients showed abnormalities in the left hand/arm during the first two years of life. Although previous high-risk and follow-back studies have not examined lateral asymmetries in neuromotor functions, a recent report on adult schizophrenic patients indicated that deficient left-hand precision grip was associated with poor clinical course in the two years subsequent to hospitalisation (Johnstone et al., 1990).

The finding of greater left-side abnormalities would not be predicted by theories that posit left-hemisphere defects in schizophrenia (Walker, Lewine, & Lucas, 1991). Instead, damage to the right hemisphere is typically suspected when there is evidence of left-upper-limb weakness or dyscontrol. If the assessments of remaining schizophrenic subjects continue to reveal left-sided abnormalities, we will be compelled to explore the potential aetiological implications of these signs. To shed light on this issue, the morphological symmetry of brain structures will be examined via magnetic resonance imaging (MRI) scans recently conducted on the patients in this study.

Most of the other specific signs yielded by the present study have been noted by previous investigators in studies of children at risk for schizophrenia. For example, delays in musculoskeletal development and in the age at acquisition of motor milestones have been noted by previous investigators (Fish, 1977, 1991); hypotonicity has also been observed (Walker & Emory, 1983).

It is important to note that the abnormalities observed in the preschizophrenic subjects can be interpreted in at least two ways. First, they might be reflective of the same neuropathological process that will ultimately lead to the expression of the schizophrenic syndrome. Alternatively, they may be indicative of a generalised CNS vulnerability that enhances the likelihood that the individual will succumb to the neuropathology of schizophrenia. For example, the neuromotor abnormalities may be a manifestation of hypersensitivity to CNS insults of many varieties, such as prenatal and postnatal infections (Mednick, 1988) or obstetrical injury.

Related to this, we plan to explore the relation between early neuromotor factors and potential etiologic agents, such as obstetrical complications and genetic vulnerability (family history of schizophrenia). Because obstetrical complications are known to be linked with childhood motor abilities (Abel, 1989; Kreusser & Volpe, 1984) and schizophrenia (Walker & Emory, 1983), it will be of particular interest to explore these relations in the present study.

When neuromotor data are available on the entire sample of subjects, it will be possible to examine variability in the neurodevelopmental characteristics among schizophrenic patients. Of particular interest is the identification of subtypes based on neuromotor variables. As mentioned above, the relation between early neuromotor characteristics and adult brain morphology will also be examined. Finally, the specificity of the motor signs to schizophrenia will be explored by comparing the development of schizophrenic and affective patients.

Clearly, our ability to generate plausible developmental models of schizophrenia hinges on knowledge of the entire premorbid life course of the disorder. Rapidly accumulating data in the fields of developmental neurobiology, psychobiology, and neuroendocrinology are illuminating the changing nature of CNS structure and function across the life-span, particularly in early and middle childhood (Goldman-Rakic, 1987). However, despite rapid advances in the neurosciences, it is important to note that we still know very little about the development of the CNS in humans. Most research on neurodevelopment involves animal subjects (Goldman-Rakic, 1987; Nowokowski, 1987), so current speculations about human neurodevelopment are based on just a few post-mortem investigations (e.g. Benes, 1989). There is reason, however, to expect that the revolution in technology for visualising structural and physiological brain characteristics *in vivo* (e.g. computerised tomography, magnetic resonance imaging) will contribute to a dramatic increase in our knowledge of developmental changes in the human CNS.

ACKNOWLEDGEMENTS

Supported by grant numbers K02MH00876 and R01MH46496 from the National Institute of Mental Health.

REFERENCES

Abel, E.L. (1989). *Behavioral teratogenesis, behavioral mutagenesis: A primer of abnormal development.* New York: Plenum.

Benes, F.M. (1989). Myelination of cortical–hippocampal relays during late adolescence. *Schizophrenia Bulletin, 15*, 585–594.

Feinberg, I. (1983). Schizophrenia: Caused by a fault in programmed synaptic elimination during adolescence. *Journal of Psychiatric Research, 17* 319–334.

Fish, B. (1977). Neurologic antecedents of schizophrenia in children: Evidence for an inherited, congenital neurointegrative deficit. *Archives of General Psychiatry, 34*, 1297–1313.

Fish, B. (1984). Characteristics and sequelae of the neurointegrative disorder in infants at risk for schizophrenia. In N.F. Watt, E.J. Anthony, L.C. Wynne, & J.E. Rolf (Eds.), *Children at risk for schizophrenia* (pp. 423–439). New York: Cambridge University Press.

Fish, B. (1992). Infants at risk for schizophrenia: Sequelae of a genetic neurointegrative defect. *Archives of General Psychiatry, 49*, 221–235.

Goldman-Rakic, P.S. (1987). Development of cortical circuitry and cognitive function. *Child Development, 58*, 601–622.

Gottesman, I., & Shields, P. (1982). *Schizophrenia: The epigenetic puzzle.* New York: Cambridge University Press.

Johnstone, E.C., MacMillan, J.F., Frith, C.D., Benn, D.K., & Crow, T.J. (1990). Further investigation of the predictors of outcome following first schizophrenic episodes. *British Journal of Psychiatry, 157*, 182–189.

Kreusser, K.L., & Volpe, J.J. (1984). The neurological outcome of perinatal asphyxia. In C.R. Almli & S. Finger (Eds.), *Early brain damage.* New York: Academic Press.

Mednick, S. (1988). Adult schizophrenia following prenatal exposure to an influenza epidemic. *Archives of General Psychiatry, 45*, 189–192.

Meehl, P. (1989). Schizotaxia revisited. *Archives of General Psychiatry, 46*, 935–944.

Meehl, P. (1990). Toward an integrated theory of schizotaxia, schizotypy and schizophrenia. *Journal of Personality Disorders, 4*, 1–99.

Mirsky, A., & Duncan, C. (1986). Etiology and expression of schizophrenia: Neurobiological and psychosocial factors. *Annual Review of Psychology, 37*, 291–319.

Nowakowski, R.S. (1987). Basic concepts of CNS development. *Child Development, 58*, 568–595.

Offord, D., & Cross, L. (1969). Behavioral antecedents of adult schizophrenia. *Archives of General Psychiatry, 21*, 267–283.

Pogue-Geile, M. (1991). The development of liability to schizophrenia: Early and late developmental models. In E. Walker (Ed.), *Schizophrenia: A life-course developmental perspective* (pp. 277–299). New York: Academic Press.

Sackett, E. (1978). *Observing behavior: Volume I: Data collection and analysis of methods.* Baltimore: University Park Press.

Saint-Anne Dargassies, S. (1986). *The neuro-motor and psycho-affective development of the infant.* New York: Elsevier.

Sarnat, H.B. (1984). Anatomic and physiologic correlates of neurologic development in prematurity. In H.B. Sarnat (Ed.), *Topics in neonatal neurology.* New York: Grune and Stratton.

Saugstad, L. (1989). Social class, marriage and fertility in schizophrenia. *Schizophrenia Bulletin, 15*, 9–44.

Taylor, M.A. (1991). The role of the cerebellum in the pathogenesis of schizophrenia. *Neuropsychiatry, Neuropsychology, and Behavioral Neurology, 4*, 251–280.

Walker, E. (1991). *Schizophrenia; A life- course developmental perspective.* New York: Academic Press.

Walker, E., Cudeck, R., Mednick, S.A., & Schulsinger, F. (1981). The effects of parental absence and institutionalization on the development of clinical symptoms in high-risk children. *Acta Psychiatrica Scandinavica, 63*, 95–109.

Walker, E., Downey, G., & Bergman, A. (1989). The effects of parental psychopathology and maltreatment on child behavior: A test of the diathesis-stress model. *Child Development, 60*, 313–321.

Walker, E., Downey, G., & Caspi, A. (1990). Twin studies of psychopathology: Why do the concordance rates vary? *Schizophrenia Research, 44*, 1–12.

Walker, E., Downey, G., & Nightingale, N. (1988). The nonorthogonal nature of risk factors: Implications for research on the causes of maladjustment. *Journal of Primary Prevention, 9*, 143–163.

Walker, E., & Emory, E. (1983). Infants at risk for schizophrenia: Offspring of schizophrenic parents. *Child Development, 54*, 1269–1285.

Walker, E., & Lewine, R.J. (1990). Prediction of adult-onset schizophrenia from childhood home-movies of the patients. *American Journal of Psychiatry, 147*, 1052–1056.

Walker, E., Lewine, R.J., & Lucas, M. (1991). Neuropsychological aspects of schizophrenia. In T. Puente & B. McCaffrey (Eds.), *Psychobiological factors in clinical neuropsychological assessment.* New York: Plenum.

Watt, N. (1972). Longitudinal changes in the social behavior of children hospitalized for schizophrenia as adults. *Journal of Nervous and Mental Disease, 155*, 42–54.

Watt, N., Anthony, E.J., Wynne, L., & Rolf, R. (Eds.) (1984). *Children at risk for schizophrenia.* New York: Cambridge.

Weinberger, D.R. (1987). Implications of normal brain development for the pathogenesis of schizophrenia. *Archives of General Psychiatry, 44*, 660–670.

Yarrow, M.R., Campbell, J.D., & Burton, R.V. (1970). Recollections of childhood: A study of the retrospective method. *Monographs of the Society for Research in Child Development, 35*, no. 5.

8 Low Intelligence and Poor Educational Achievement Precede Early Onset Schizophrenic Psychosis

Peter Jones, Christian Guth, Shôn Lewis, and Robin Murray
Institute of Psychiatry and King's College Hospital, London.

Our recent clinical and epidemiological studies show that the more strictly schizophrenia is defined, the fewer females qualify for the diagnosis. In particular, there is a huge excess of DSM-3 schizophrenia in young men while later onset schizophreniform disorders are much commoner in woman. The later onset female cases show normal premorbid functioning, more affective and fewer negative symptoms, a better outcome, and less structural brain abnormalities. The evidence that their relatives have an increased risk of affective disorder, and that they show the same summer peak of admissions as manic patients, suggests that they have much in common with affective disorder. On the other hand, evidence will be presented that early onset, predominantly male schizophrenia is associated with premorbid personality, social under achievement and structural brain abnormalities. Adult schizophrenics seen previously at the Maudsley Children's Department had low IQ as children. In addition, mentally handicapped individuals who develop schizophrenia have an earlier onset of psychosis than schizophrenics without mental handicap; they also show an excess of males. It is suggested that neurodevelopmental schizophrenia has its origins in abnormal brain development during foetal or neonatal life. Aberrant genetic control of brain development and early environmental hazards are both implicated.

INTRODUCTION

Much evidence suggests that there is heterogeneity in the antecedents, form, and outcome of schizophrenic psychosis (reviewed by Lyons et al., 1989). Indeed, it has been proposed that the term "schizophrenia" may subsume several conditions—different pathological processes may produce distinct illnesses, which share similar psychotic and manifestations at some time in their course (Murray et al., 1992). We have argued elsewhere (Jones & Murray, 1991) that the vagaries of psychotic phenomena are unlikely to yield a sufficiently valid phenotype for genetic research, and that researchers should take into account demonstrated abnormalities in brain structure when defining the phenotype for genetic analyses. Similarly, we believe that attempts to model a unitary psychological disturbance underlying schizophrenia are unlikely to succeed unless the particular form of schizophrenia is defined; the different conditions sheltering under the umbrella of the schizophrenia syndrome may have distinct neuropsychological characteristics.

Early psychological theorists (Bleuler, 1950/1911; Jaspers, 1936/1913; Stransky, 1987/1904) took an opposing view, concentrating on analyses of the phenomenological characteristics of schizophrenic psychosis in an attempt to distil a basic psychological understanding of the whole clinical syndrome. Most recent attempts have concentrated on the explanation of particular phenomena (see Gray et al., 1991, for discussion) but continue to assume that their findings will be generalisable. Some workers, however, have incorporated concepts of heterogeneity into their research. For instance, Liddle and colleagues have used latent variable analysis to divide the phenomena of chronic schizophrenia into three syndromes (Liddle 1987, a,b; Liddle & Barnes, 1990). They have demonstrated associations between the severity of individual syndromes and both neuropsychological test performance (Liddle & Morris, 1991) and functional neuroimaging (Frith & Liddle, 1991; see Chapter 3). These results suggest that particular types of schizophrenic impairment can be localised in terms of neuropsychological dysfunction and brain activity *in vivo*.

Evidence from diverse areas suggests that schizophrenia can usefully be divided in terms of the presence or absence of abnormalities presumed to arise *in utero* or during early childhood. Abnormal development of brain structure (Jakob & Beckman, 1986; Falkai & Bogerts, 1986; Bruton, Crow, & Frith, 1990; Roberts, 1991), obstetric difficulties (Lewis & Murray, 1987; Eagles et al., 1990), minor physical developmental defects (Gualtieri, Adams, & Chen, 1982; Guy, Majorski, & Wallace, 1983; see Chapter 7), abnormal childhood personality traits (Foerster, Lewis, Owen, & Murray, 1991, a,b; Watt, 1978), poor scholastic achievement (Watt, 1978), and lower childhood IQ than controls (Offord & Cross, 1971) all appear to exist in a proportion of schizophrenics prior to the onset of frank psychosis. The occurrence of these development abnormalities has given rise to the concept of neurodevelopmental schizophrenia (Murray & Lewis, 1987; Weinberger, 1987) in which a lesion occurring during early brain development is postulated to manifest itself in different ways with increasing maturity, and most dramatically as psychosis during adolescence or adult life.

No characteristic pattern of association has yet been demonstrated between these features when they occur in preschizophrenic individuals. However, they have all been found most frequently in early onset, severe psychosis, particularly among males, in whom this form of schizophrenia predominates (Castle, Wessely, Der, & Murray, 1991). Thus, a syndrome of neurodevelopmental schizophrenia has been differentiated from the more benign, later onset disorder commoner in females, in which markers of abnormal development are rare (see Castle & Murray, 1991, for discussion). It is of considerable interest that other neurodevelopmental disorders also predominate in males.

It seems likely that the neuropsychology of this early onset, developmental schizophrenia will be distinct from that of later onset forms. Thus, conflation of the different forms of schizophrenia may be one cause of contradictory results in the neuropsychological literature.

Some evidence to support this view comes from studies that have demonstrated that premorbid IQ levels of schizophrenic subjects, obtained in childhood and adolescence, are lower than those of either their peers or siblings (Lane & Albee, 1968; Offord & Cross, 1971; Watt & Lubensky, 1976). Of particular interest is the finding that these premorbid IQ deficits are more marked in males. Aylward, Walker, and Bettes (1984) performed a meta-analysis of retrospective (Offord, 1974; Watt & Lubensky, 1976) and prospective, high-risk studies (Rieder, Broman, & Rosenthal, 1977; Lane, Albee, & Doll, 1970), and demonstrated that the proportion of males in each sample predicted the size of the reduction in IQ of the preschizophrenics. Aylward et al. considered that this may indicate the possibility of differential occurrence of subtypes of schizophrenia between the sexes. Unfortunately, they were unable to account for the possibly confounding effect of the earlier age at onset of males. Our view is that the more schizophrenic subjects with late onset psychosis included in a sample, the more females with the non-developmental form of the disorder will be analysed; this in turn will lead to apparent sex differences.

We hypothesise that premorbid deficits in intelligence are most marked in early onset, neurodevelopmental schizophrenia where they are secondary to the structural brain abnormalities (Falkai, Bogerts, & Rozumek, 1988; Murray, Lewis, Owen, & Foerster) that underlie the disorder. We present results from two studies of early onset schizophrenia. The first estimates premorbid IQ, social functioning, and scholastic achievement in a cross-sectional survey of adults with psychosis. The second is a follow-back study of adult schizophrenic and affective disorder patients who had psychological tests performed when they attended a child psychiatry department.

CROSS-SECTIONAL SURVEY OF ADMISSIONS FOR PSYCHOSIS

Evidence in favour of the existence of prepsychotic cognitive abnormalities comes from analysis of the scholastic achievement and premorbid social functioning of subjects in the Camberwell Collaborative Psychosis Study. This sample is described in detail by Jones et al. (1992). Briefly, admissions to three psychiatric hospitals were screened over 2 years to identify all those with delusions, hallucinations, or formal thought disorder not due to an obvious organic precipitant. All such first admissions were included ($n = 68$) but readmissions were only included if they had a living mother, as the study was directed at assessing premorbid functioning from maternal interviews. A total of 195 subjects (125 males) were included. According to DSM-III criteria, there were 100 subjects with schizophrenia, 15 with schizophreniform disorder, 18 with depressive psychosis, 49 with bipolar disorder, and 13 with other psychotic conditions. Here, we confine ourselves to a comparison of schizophrenia and schizophreniform disorder combined ($n = 115$; 86 males) versus affective psychosis ($n = 67$; 30 males).

Data on educational achievement were available on all but three subjects and are shown in Table 8.1, broken down by sex for the two diagnostic groups. Certificate of Secondary Education (CSE), Ordinary level (O level), Advanced level (A level), and university degree, represent progressively higher levels of attainment in the educational examinations in use at the time of the study.

TABLE 8.1
Breakdown of Educational Achievement by Sex for Schizophrenic and Affective Disorder Subjects

Gender	Educational achievement				
	Total	No. qualifications	CSE	O level	A level/degree
Schizophrenic subjects					
Males (% in category)	86 (76.1)	36 (87.8)	16 (76.2)	20 (71)	14 (60.9)
Females	27 (23.9)	5 (12.2)	5 (23.8)	8 (29)	9 (39.1)
Male : female ratio	3.2:1	7.2:1	3.2:1	2.5:1	1.5:1
Affective disorder subjects					
Males (% in category)	30 (45)	8 (50)	2 (50)	10 (40)	10 (47.6)
Females	36 (55)	8 (50)	2 (50)	15 (60)	11 (52.4)
Male : female ratio	0.8:1	1:1	1:1	0.67:1	0.9:1

For both sexes combined, those with affective disorder achieved higher qualifications than the schizophrenic subjects (χ^2 = 11.2; P = 0.01). In the affective disorder group, there was little difference between males and females, with no evidence of any trend (χ^2 = 0.5; P = 0.9; χ^2 for trend = 0.06). This was not the case for those with schizophrenia, where there was a marked difference between the sexes in the level of educational achievement. There was a strong trend for the M:F ratio to increase as educational achievement declined (χ^2 for trend = 6.2; P = 0.01). Almost 90% of schizophrenic subjects leaving school with no formal qualifications were male, compared to 61% of the few subjects qualifying for university. Poor educational outcome was not a consequence of low age at onset of psychosis (mean 22.6 years, 95% confidence interval 21.6–23.6) as there was no difference in age at onset between the educational outcome groups (F = 1.04; P = 0.37). The gender effect, too, was unlikely to be due to age at onset or socio-economic class differences because these variables do not show sex differences in this series (Jones et al., 1993). Thus, in terms of educational outcome, males appeared to be disadvantaged some years before the onset of their psychosis.

Were the males less intelligent than the females? If so, this would provide a simple answer to the question as to why the males fared worse in formal examinations. We used the National Adult Reading Test (NART; Nelson & O'Connell, 1978) to estimate premorbid intelligence. Data were available on 100 schizophrenic and 57 affective subjects.

Subjects with affective diagnoses had significantly higher mean NART scores than the schizophrenics (111.9 versus 103.3; F = 28.0; P = 0.0001) but the scores for males and females within each category were virtually identical. As expected, there was a strong positive relationship between educational achievement and NART score, as this is what the test is based upon (Nelson & O'Connell, 1978). However, within the qualification strata, there were no significant or consistent sex differences in NART score for either diagnostic category.

It is possible that our measure of intelligence, the mean NART score, is too crude and too dependent upon education to differentiate between males and females. A more subtle way of investigating psychological functioning antedating both secondary school failure and psychosis is to assess the abnormal premorbid social and personality traits found in developmental schizophrenia (Foerster et al., 1991a,b). We hypothesised that these traits would be found particularly in those schizophrenics who failed at school because some, at least, of the failure is allied to their schizophrenic diathesis, betrayed in childhood and adolescence by these personality traits.

Two measures of premorbid social functioning were completed during interviews with the mothers of our subjects, and are described in detail by Foerster et al. (1991a). The PSA1 and PSA2 rating scales measure

Premorbid Social Adjustment between the ages of 8 and 11 years and 12 and 16 years, respectively, higher scores representing greater abnormality. Premorbid Schizoid and Schizotypal Traits are measured by the PSST rating scale (Foerster et al., 1991b). Previous analyses on a subgroup of the present sample demonstrated that male, early onset schizophrenics in particular had high (i.e. abnormal) scores on the PSA1 (Foerster et al., 1991a), and that schizoid and schizotypal traits were more common when there was a family history of schizophrenia, or low birth weight (Foerster et al., 1991b). Both the PSA1 and PSA2 scales include a question on scholastic performance. Analyses were performed both including and excluding the scholastic performance item with no substantial effect on the results obtained. Data are presented here including this item, allowing comparison with previous studies.

Scores for PSA1, PSA2, and PSST in the different educational outcomes in the schizophrenic group are shown in Table 8.2. Distributions were approximately normal, and similar results were obtained with log-transformed data. As we predicted, PSA1 and PSA2 scores were both progressively more abnormal in those with fewer qualifications (ANOVA by school qualifications: PSA1, $F = 9.2$; $P = 0.0001$; PSA2, $F = 6.7$; $P = 0.0005$). However, there was no such effect for PSST scores. The strongest association was for the PSA1 scale, which measures abnormal social functioning many years before the examinations by which educational performance was assessed. It is therefore unlikely that the poor examination performance was due merely to an insidious onset of psychosis.

Once again, we could not differentiate between males and females. Neither did the diagnostic category have an effect on the strong relationship between abnormal premorbid social functioning and educational achievement. An analysis of PSA1, PSA2, and PSST by educational achievement,

TABLE 8.2
PSA1, PSA2, and PSST Scores for Schizophrenic Subjects Broken Down by Educational Achievement (For Each Scale, a Higher Score Represents More Abnormality)

Educational category	PSA1 score	PSA2	PSST score
No qualifications (n = 23)	14.0 (0.9)	18.6 (1.0)	8.7 (0.6)
CSE (n = 16)	14.6 (1.2)	18.4 (1.6)	9.3 (0.6)
O level (n = 21)	11.2 (0.8)	13.8 (0.9)	8.0 (0.5)
A level or degree (n = 19)	8.7 (0.6)	12.5 (1.2)	8.9 (0.5)
Total schizophrenia group (n = 79)	12.1 95% c.i. 11.1–13.0 range 5–26	15.9 95% c.i. 14.6–17.2 range 11–31	8.7 95% c.i. 8.1–9.2 range 0–15

Figures in brackets are the standard deviations; c.i., confidence interval.

sex, and diagnosis, with age at onset of psychosis as a covariate, indicated that high (more abnormal) scores on the PSA1 (main effect $F = 9.9$; $P = 0.0001$) and PSA2 (main effect $F = 5.4$; $P = 0.004$) were both associated with poor educational achievement but that deviant PSST scores were not ($F = 1.79$; $P = 0.12$). In none of these analyses was either sex or diagnosis significant, nor was age at onset a significant covariate. There were no interactions.

Thus, both schizophrenic and affective disorder patients who perform poorly in their late teenage years at school are characterised by abnormal social functioning. This is already apparent before 11 years of age and it not an early manifestation of the psychosis *per se*. We have demonstrated that such a scenario is more common before schizophrenic than affective psychosis.

To pursue this link between psychological abnormality in childhood, IQ, and adult psychiatric disorder, we then studied a group of adult psychotic subjects who were sufficiently abnormal in childhood to have been referred to a child psychiatry department. Here, we present data concerning IQ measurements performed in childhood, data unbiased by knowledge of the adult diagnosis.

A FOLLOW-BACK STUDY OF CHILDHOOD INTELLIGENCE IN ADULT SCHIZOPHRENIA AND MAJOR AFFECTIVE DISORDERS

The case summaries of all adults discharged between 1965 and 1987 from the Bethlem Royal and Maudsley Hospitals, some 49,000 were reviewed. Subjects who, up to the age of 16 years, had been seen (for any reason) in the children's department of the same hospitals were identified. This was done using information contained in the hospital code number and the past psychiatric history; 156 subjects had adult discharge diagnoses of schizophrenia, depression, manic depressive psychosis, or unspecified psychosis. The Research Diagnostic Criteria (RDC; Spitzer, Endicott, & Robbins, 1978) were applied to clinical information in the adult case notes and case summaries; 52 subjects fulfilled the RDC for schizophrenia, 24 for bipolar-1 disorder, and 23 for major depressive disorder. Two subjects (females) fulfilled the criteria for bipolar-1 disorder and for schizophrenia at different stages of their adult illnesses; they were excluded. The childhood records of the remaining 95 subjects were then assessed blind to adult diagnosis. Age at childhood presentation ranged from 3 to 16.9 years (mean 13.5). Subjects with adult schizophrenia were compared to those with either bipolar disorder or depression.

Presenting illness in childhood was rated according to criteria developed by Rutter, Schaffer, & Sturge (1983): (1) psychotic symptoms; (2) emotional disorder with or without disturbance of conduct; or (3) conduct disorder alone. Results according to adult diagnosis are displayed in Table 8.3. Psychosis was the most common childhood presentation in those who developed either schizophrenia or bipolar-1 disorder. Presentation with emotional problems was most often associated with subsequent adult major depression, whereas conduct disorder was much more common in those who went on to develop schizophrenia than adult affective disorders. These differences were statistically significant ($\chi^2 = 17.5$; $P = 0.002$). There were too few subjects to further breakdown childhood presentation by sex but, in general, males were more likely to have presented with psychosis, and females with affective symptoms.

Intelligence test results (WISC or WISC-R) from the time of childhood presentation were obtained wherever possible. Data on full-scale IQ were available for 64 subjects, and performance and verbal IQ data were available for 63. Their distributions appeared approximately normal.

Childhood IQ and Adult Diagnosis

Table 8.4 shows the breakdown of full scale, performance, and verbal IQ by adult outcome and by childhood presentation. While all three IQ measures were similar for those with the two adult affective diagnoses, those for

TABLE 8.3
Adult Diagnosis Broken Down by Sex and Childhood Presentation

Adult diagnosis		Childhood presentation		
	No. males	Psychosis	Emotional	Conduct
Schizophrenia ($n = 50$)	36 (72%)	24 (48%)	14 (28%)	12 (24%)
Bipolar 1 ($n = 22$)	13 (59%)	10 (45.5%)	10 (45.5%)	2 (9%)
Major depression ($n = 23$)	7 (30%)	3 (13%)	18 (78%)	2 (9%)

Figures in brackets are standard deviations; BP-1, bipolar 1.

TABLE 8.4
Childhood IQ Broken Down by Adult Outcome and by Childhood Presentation

IQ	Adult outcome			Childhood Presentation		
	Schizophrenia	BP-1	Depression	Psychosis	Emotional	Conduct
Full-scale	85.4 (2.5)	93.8 (4.9)	96.9 (3.5)	87.0 (3.5)	96.4 (3.4)	83.6 (3.5)
Performance	85.7 (2.7)	94.2 (4.2)	97.9 (3.0)	86.0 (3.2)	98.3 (2.8)	87.9 (4.2)
Verbal	90.1 (3.4)	101.4 (4.6)	100.0 (2.7)	86.3 (3.9)	97.4 (2.9)	76.9 (4.2)

Figures in brackets are standard deviations; BP-1, bipolar 1.

subjects with schizophrenia were consistently lower. Analyses of variance indicated that these differences were likely to be statistically significant (F = 2.7–3.8; P = 0.07–0.03). However, IQ level also varied significantly with presentation, those presenting with emotional symptoms having higher scores than those presenting with psychosis or conduct disorder. As presenting complaint was related to both adult outcome and IQ, it was necessary to include it as a possible confounder in an analysis of these two variables. This proved not to be the case for sex; girls and boys had similar results, although this result could have been due to small sample size (95% confidence intervals for difference between means: full-scale –6 to 12.4; performance –2.5 to 13.9; verbal –4.9 to 13.7).

Analysis of variance was performed, including adult diagnosis, recorded as schizophrenia or affective disorder to increase the cell sizes, *and* presenting complaint in childhood. The main effect of adult outcome decreased below conventional significance but an effect of presentation persisted for full scale (F = 2.7; P = 0.08) and verbal IQ (F = 3.3; P = 0.05) but not for the performance subscale (F = 1.6; P = 0.3). There was no evidence of a significant interaction.

These results indicate that presentation with either psychotic symptoms or conduct disorder in childhood was associated with low performance IQ score when there was an adult outcome of schizophrenia or severe affective disorder. This effect was reflected in lower full scale scores. Those destined to become schizophrenic did have lower IQ, but this was partly explained by their more common presentation in childhood with psychotic symptoms or conduct disorder. This is unlikely to be a complete explanation; when presentation was controlled for in an analysis of variance, a consistent effect of adult diagnosis remained, albeit below conventional statistical significance. The study is small and larger numbers of subjects might have increased the size of the effect and its associated statistical significance.

To some extent, the problem of childhood presentation as a confounder is spurious. It assumes that childhood presentation in these subjects was quite separate from their adult diagnosis. On the contrary, in terms of a developmental model, these preschizophrenic children had a common cause for both their childhood and adult disorders, and their IQ deficits. Presumably this cause was a brain lesion, or lesions, occurring during early development, and it was merely its manifestation that changed as the individuals' compromised nervous systems matured. In other words, all the clinical phenomena in developmental schizophrenia are on the same causal pathway. Regarding the affective disorder controls, the link between childhood affective symptoms and adult affective disorder is well recognised (Zeitlin, 1986) although its mechanism is little understood in terms of development (see Rodgers, 1990). we argue that the normal IQ levels in our affective sample are evidence against an underlying disorder of gross brain structure.

Socio-economic class was a possible confounder but we did not have sufficient data to control for this. Observer bias was minimised by the follow-back design. Some examinations used the WAIS, others the WAIS-R, and in others it was not clear which was used. However, we have no reason to believe that either version was used more extensively in any one group, so our comparisons of group differences should be unbiased. None of the children had a diagnosis of schizophrenia when first examined despite the presence of psychotic symptoms in some.

The sample is, of course, highly selected. All subjects had to have been referred to a child psychiatrist, so the sample is biased towards preschizophrenics so deviant that they had traversed the complex filter system that such referral entails (Zeitlin, 1986). Although this means that the results cannot be generalised as an estimate of the childhood IQ of all those who will later be diagnosed as schizophrenic, this was never our intention. On the contrary, we believe that this mainly male group, which manifests abnormality at an early age, represents a relatively homogeneous category, distinct from later onset schizophrenic subjects in whom females predominate.

Once at the child psychiatry clinic, we assume that IQ testing was most likely to have been carried out on those in whom some abnormality was suspected. A higher proportion of preschizophrenics was tested (70%) than affectives (64%) and so our results may underestimate the true IQ deficit in early onset schizophrenia. We are presently undertaking a follow-up study of these subjects which should shed light on this point.

Regarding the IQ subscales, each childhood presentation showed similar results for full-scale, performance, and verbal subscales. The exception was conduct disorder where, regardless of adult outcome, verbal IQ was particularly low. This may be a chance finding but it is also compatible with the idea that there is a link between verbal cognitive problems and conduct disorder (Rutter & Hersov, 1985). There was no differential association between any adult outcome and score on either verbal or performance scales. This is in accord with findings reviewed by Aylward et al. (1984), who concluded that schizophrenia and other psychiatric disorders are associated with variable, but not specific, patterns in terms of verbal and non-verbal subtests.

CONCLUSIONS

What do the results of these two studies tell us about the neuropsychology of schizophrenia? Both studies concentrated on early onset psychosis and found evidence of prepsychotic cognitive abnormalities and deviant behaviour. We have to turn to the literature for data regarding late onset subjects in order to assess the specificity of our findings to early onset disease. The majority of relevant studies are retrospective, often giving anecdotal reports of premorbid functioning, but it appears that there is no evidence of a prepsychotic IQ decline in late onset schizophrenia. Kay and Roth (1947) commented that many subjects with late-onset schizophrenia functioned well at work, and no study has found poor educational achievement in these individuals (Castle & Murray, 1992; Kay, 1963; Post, 1982).

Both studies reported here demonstrated intellectual deficits predating schizophrenia rather than affective disorder. The Camberwell Collaborative data is predominantly centred around verbal skills; the NART and most school examinations we considered predominantly test such skills. Neither study found major sex differences in IQ despite good exam performance being more common in females. This is likely to have been the result of the sampling procedure, which resulted in schizophrenics of both sexes being early onset and so constrained to be similar in other ways.

Most interestingly, both studies indicated that it was prepsychotic phenomena that best predicted IQ or scholastic achievement. The follow-back study demonstrated that childhood presentation accounted for most of the variance in contemporary IQ. In the Collaborative Study, abnormal premorbid social adjustment in early childhood was associated with educational attainment more strongly than it was with diagnosis. In both studies, therefore, the finding of low IQ in schizophrenia was largely due to the fact that particular childhood presentations, or personality attributes, were more common in schizophrenia than affective psychosis.

At first glance such conclusions appear facile; performance in tests depends on level of psychological functioning at the time, not on level of functioning in the future. However, on reflection, the implications for psychological researchers are clear. Investigators need to ensure that their schizophrenic subjects are homogeneous with respect to prepsychotic, developmental characteristics, otherwise difficulty may arise in interpreting their data. It is evident from the above that some of the conflicting findings, as well as the marked sex differences reported in the IQ literature (Aylward et al., 1984) may have been due to such heterogeneity in the condition under study. Studies sampling subjects with developmental abnormalities and early onset psychosis (i.e. the neurodevelopmental syndrome) are likely to yield very different results from those studies examining samples that include substantial numbers of late onset patients. This has been shown to be the case in other areas of schizophrenia research including epidemiology (Castle et al., 1991; Loranger, 1984), clinical research (Lewine, 1981) and neuropathology (Bogerts, 1991); neuropsychology is unlikely to provide an exception to this trend.

REFERENCES

Aylward, E., Walker, E., & Bettes, B. (1984). Intelligence in schizophrenia: Meta-analysis of the research. *Schizophrenia Bulletin*, 10, 430–459.

Bleuler, E. (1950). *Dementia praecox or the group of schizophrenias*, (J. Zinkin, Trans.). New York: International University Press. (Original work published 1911).

Bogerts, B. (1991). The neuropathology of schizophrenia: Pathophysiological and neurodevelopmental implications. In *Fetal Neural Development and Adult Schizophrenia*. S.A. Mednick, T.D. Cannon, C.E. Barr, & M. Lyon (Eds.), Cambridge: Cambridge University Press.

Bruton, C.J., Crow, T.J., Frith, C.G., Johnstone, E.C., Owens, D.G.C., & Roberts, G.W. (1990). Schizophrenia and the brain. *Psychological Medicine*, 20, 285–304.

Castle, D.J., & Murray, R.M. (1991). The neurodevelopmental basis of sex differences in schizophrenia. *Psychological Medicine*, 21, 565–575.

Castle, D.J., & Murray, R.M. (1992). Schizophrenia: Etiology and genetics. In J.R.M. Copeland, M.T. Abou-Saley, & D.G. Blazer (Eds.), *The psychiatry of old age: An international text book*. Chichester: John Wiley & Sons.

Castle, D.J., Wessely, S., Der, G., & Murray, R.M. (1991). The incidence of operationally defined schizophrenia in Camberwell, 1965–1984. *British Journal of Psychiatry* 159, 790–794.

Eagles, J.M., Gibson, I., Bremner, M.H., Clunie, F., Ebmeier, K.P., & Smith, N.C. (1990). Obstetric complications in DSMIII schizophrenics and their siblings. *Lancet*, 335, 1139–1141.

Falkai, P., & Bogerts, B. (1986). Cell loss in the hippocampus of schizophrenics. *European Archives of Psychiatry and Neurological Science*, 236, 154–161.

Falkai, P., Bogerts, B., & Rozumek, M. (1988). Limbic pathology in schizophrenia. The entorhinal region—a morphometric study. *Biological Psychiatry*, 24, 515–521.

Forster, A., Lewis, S.W., Owen, M.J., & Murray, R.M. (1991a). Premorbid adjustment and personality in psychosis. Effects of sex and diagnosis. *British Journal of Psychiatry*, 158, 171–176.

Foerster, A., Lewis, S.W., Owen, M.J., & Murray, R.M. (1991b). Low birth weight and a family history of schizophrenia predict a low premorbid functioning in psychosis. *Schizophrenia Research*, 5, 13–20.

Frith, C., & Liddle, P.F. (1991, July). *Conference on PET scanning in neurology and psychiatry*. Guy's Hospital and St. Thomas's Medical School.

Gray, J.A., Feldon, J., Rawlins, J.N.P., Hemsley, D.R., & Smith, a.D. (1991) The neuropsychology of schizophrenia. *Behavioral and Brain Sciences*, 14:1, 34–41.

Gualtieri, C.T., Adams, A., & Chen, C.D. (1982). Minor physical abnormalities in alcoholic and schizophrenic adults and hyperactive and autistic children. *American Journal of Psychiatry*, 139, 640–643.

Guy, J.D., Majorski, L.V., Wallace, C.J., & Guy, M.P. (1983). The incidence of minor physical anomalies in adult male schizophrenics. *Schizophrenia Bulletin*, 9, 571–582.

Jakob, H., & Beckman, H. (1986). Prenatal developmental disturbances in the limbic allocortex in schizophrenics. *Journal of Neural Transmission*, 65, 303–326.

Jaspers, K. (1963). *General psychopathology*. (J. Hoenig & M.W. Hamilton, Trans.) (Original work published 1913.) Manchester: Manchester University Press.

Jones, P.B., Bebbington, P., Foerster, A., Lewis, S.W., Murray, R.M., Russell, A., Sham, P.C., Toone, B.K., & Wilkins, S. (1993) Premorbid social underachievement in schizophrenia: Results from the Camberwell Collaborative Psychosis Study. *British Journal of Psychiatry*, 162, 65–71.

Jones, P.B., & Murray, R.M. (1991). The genetics of schizophrenia is the genetics of neurodevelopment. *British Journal of Psychiatry*, 158, 615–623.

Kay, D.W. (1963). Late paraphrenia and its bearing on the etiology of schizophrenia. *Acta Psychiatrica Scandinavica, 39,* 159–169.

Kay, D.W., & Roth, M. (1961). Environmental and hereditary factors in the schizophrenias of old age ("late paraphrenia") and their bearing on the general problem of causation in schizophrenia. *Journal of Mental Science, 107,* 649–686.

Lane, E., & Albee, G. (1968). Childhood intellectual decline of adult schizophrenics: A reassessment of an earlier study. *Journal of Abnormal and Social Psychology, 73,* 174–177.

Lang, E., Albee, G., & Doll, L. (1970). The intelligence of children of schizophrenics. *Developmental Psychology, 2,* 315–317.

Lewine, R.R.J. (1981). Sex differences in schizophrenia: Timing or subtypes? *Psychological Bulletin, 90* (3), 433–444.

Lewis, S.W., & Murray, R.M. (1987). Obstetric complications, neurodevelopmental deviance, and risk of schizophrenia. *Journal of Psychiatric Research, 21,* 413–421.

Liddle, P.F. (1987a). The symptoms of chronic schizophrenia: A re-examination of the positive–negative dichotomy. *British Journal of Psychiatry, 151,* 145–151.

Liddle, P.F. (1987b). Schizophrenic syndromes, cognitive performance and neurological dysfunction. *Psychological Medicine, 16,* 49–57.

Liddle, P.F., & Barnes, T.R.E. (1990). Syndromes of chronic schizophrenia. *British Journal of Psychiatry, 157,* 558–561.

Liddle, P.F., & Morris, D. (1991). Schizophrenic syndromes and frontal lobe performance. *British Journal of Psychiatry, 158,* 340–345.

Loranger, A.W. (1984). Sex difference at age at onset of schizophrenia. *Archives of General Psychiatry, 41,* 157–161.

Lyons, M.J., Kremen, W.S., Tsuang, M.T., & Faraone, S.V. (1989). Investigating putative genetic and environmental forms of schizophrenia: Methods and findings. *International Review of Psychiatry, 1,* 259–275.

Murray, R.M., & Lewis, S.W. (1987). Is schizophrenia a neurodevelopmental disorder? *British Medical Journal, 295,* 681–682.

Murray, R.M., Lewis, S.W., Owen, M.J., & Foerster, A. (1988). The neurodevelopmental origins of dementia praecox. In P. Bebbington & P. McGuffin (Eds.), *Schizophrenia: The major issues* (pp. 90–107). London: Heinemann.

Murray, R.M., O'Callaghan, E., Castle, D.J., & Lewis, S.W. (1992). A neurodevelopmental approach to the classification of schizophrenia. *Schizophrenia Bulletin, 18,* 319–332.

Nelson, H.E., & O'Connell, A. (1978). Dementia: The estimation of premorbid intelligence levels using the new adult reading test. *Cortex, 14,* 234–244.

Offord, D. (1974). School performance of adult schizophrenics, their siblings and age mates. *British Journal of Psychiatry, 125,* 12–19.

Offord, D., & Cross, L. (1971). Adult schizophrenia with scholastic failure or low IQ in childhood. *Archives of General Psychiatry, 24,* 431–435.

Post, F. (1982). Functional disorders. In R. Levy & F. Post (Eds.) *The psychiatry of late life.* Oxford: Blackwell.

Rieder, R., Broman, S., & Rosenthal, D. (1977). The offspring of schizophrenics. *Archives of General Psychiatry, 34,* 789–799.

Roberts, G.W. (1991). Schizophrenia: A neuropathological perspective. *British Journal of Psychiatry, 158,* 8–17.

Rodgers, B. (1990). Behavioural and personality in childhood as predictors of adult psychiatric disorder. *Journal of Child Psychology and Psychiatry, 31,* (3), 393–414.

Rutter, M.L., & Hersov, L. (1985). *Child and adolescent psychiatry: Modern approaches* (2nd ed.). London: Blackwell.

Rutter, M.L.,Schaffer, D., & Sturge, C. (1983). *A guide to a multi-axial classification scheme for psychiatric disorders in childhood and adolescence.* London: Institute of Psychiatry.

Spitzer, R.L., Endicott, J., & Robbins, E. (1978). *Research diagnostic criteria for a selected group of functional disorders* (3rd ed.). New York: New York State Psychiatric Institute.

Stransky, E. (1987). Towards an understanding of certain symptoms of dementia praecox. In J.C. Cutting & M. Shepherd (Eds.), *The clinical roots of the schizophrenia concept.* Cambridge: Cambridge University Press. (Original work published 1904. Zur Auffassung Gewisser Symptome der Dementia Praecox. *Neurologisches Centralblatt, 23,* 1137–43.)

Watt, N.F. (1978). Patterns of childhood social development in adult schizophrenics. *Archives & General Psychiatry, 35,* 160–165.

Watt, N., & Lubensky, A. (1976). Childhood roots of schizophrenia. *Journal of Consulting and Clinical Psychology, 44,* 363–375.

Weinberger, D.R. (1987). Implications of normal brain development for the pathogenesis of schizophrenia. *Archives of General Psychiatry, 44,* 660–669.

Zeitlin, H. (1986). *The natural history of psychiatric disorder in children.* Maudsley Monograph No. 29. Oxford: Oxford University Press.

IV COGNITION AND METACOGNITION

9 Theory of Mind in Schizophrenia

Chris Frith
CRC Psychiatry, Harrow & MRC Cyclotron Unit, London and University College, London.

[handwritten: Theory of mind - being able to introspect and .: say "I think x..." Therefore, also being able to understand = that "She thinks y..." , also understand]

We do not interpret each other's speech and actions in terms of surface meaning and behaviour, but in terms of intentions, knowledge and beliefs. This is called "having a theory of mind" and is essential for successful social interactions. Theory of mind has been studied intensively and experimentally in the developing child and has been shown to be grossly impaired in autism. Many of the signs and symptoms of schizophrenia can be understood as arising from impairments in processes underlying "theory of mind" such as the ability to represent beliefs and intentions. Patients with delusions of reference and persecution can represent that other people have different beliefs and intentions from themselves, but have difficulty inferring the content of these beliefs and intentions. This difficulty is the basis of their erroneous beliefs about the intentions of others. Patients with auditory hallucinations and delusions of control cannot distinguish between representations of beliefs and intentions (their own and others) and representations of directly perceived events. As a consequence representations of their own intentions are experienced as alien forces controlling their actions. Representations of the beliefs of others are experienced as auditory hallucinations. Patients with lack of volition and social withdrawal can no longer represent their own wishes and beliefs, or those of others. Being unable to represent their own goals, they have difficulty with spontaneous willed acts and instead show perseverative and stimulus driven behaviour. Lesion studies suggest that successful social interactions require intact frontal and temporal lobes. I propose that representation of a belief requires an interaction between posterior structures and frontal cortex. Posterior structures hold representations of perceptions (such as "it is raining"). Interactions between frontal cortex and appropriate posterior structures permit (a) awareness of perceptions (I know, "it is raining") and (b) marking of representations as beliefs (John believes, "it is raining"). Schizophrenic symptoms are a consequence of abnormalities in these interactions.

[handwritten margin notes: alternative views, (not in Asperger's, not suggested by Frith in schiz]

147

"THEORY OF MIND" IN ANIMALS, CHILDREN, AND AUTISTIC INDIVIDUALS

Happy the hare at morning, for she cannot read the Hunter's waking thoughts
(Auden, 1935)

The term "theory of mind" was first used by Premack and Woodruff (1978) in relation to the understanding of deception in chimpanzees. The theory in question is not one held by psychologists, but one held by us all. When we communicate with others we assume that they have minds just like ours. It is necessary to have a "theory of mind" if we are to base our behaviour on what we know about the beliefs and intentions of others. Without a "theory of mind" we would not even begin to try and alter the beliefs and intentions of others. In particular, the ability to deceive critically depends on having a "theory of mind", because deception depends upon inducing a false belief in someone. There are some reports of deception in higher primates (Byrne & Whiten, 1988), but in every case other explanations of the behaviour in question cannot be ruled out. Having a "theory of mind" is a uniquely human ability except, possibly, in a very primitive form.

A large number of experimental techniques have been devised for studying theory of mind in children (Astington & Gopnik, 1991). A particularly elegant example involves contrasting *deception* and *sabotage*. In this experiment the aim of the child is to prevent someone from getting a sweet (Sodian & Frith, 1992). This can be achieved by sabotage (putting the sweet in a box and locking it) or by deception (putting the sweet in a box and then saying "the box is empty"). Deception requires the child to have a "theory of mind" while sabotage does not. Experiments like this have demonstrated that the ability to handle false beliefs in others develops at around 4 years of age. Research in this area has received special impetus from the discovery that children with early childhood autism are grossly impaired on a wide range of "theory of mind" tasks (U. Frith, 1989), but can perform other tasks of similar complexity (Baron-Cohen, Leslie, & Frith, 1985; Leslie & Thaiss, 1992; Leekham & Perner, 1991). These studies have led to the hypothesis that a cognitive "module" evolved to enable the development of a 'theory of mind". Underlying this cognitive module there is likely to be a brain system concerned specifically with "theory of mind" problems (U. Frith, Morton, & Leslie, 1991).

THE CARDINAL FEATURES OF AUTISM FOLLOW FROM THE LACK OF A THEORY OF MIND

According to Wing and Gould (1979), the three cardinal features of early childhood autism are (1) autistic aloneness; (2) poor communication; and (3) lack of pretend play. It has been proposed that all of these features are a consequence of a faulty "theory of mind" module.

Leslie (1987) has argued convincingly that understanding pretence depends on the ability to represent the mental state of the other player, for example, *Mum is pretending the banana is a telephone.* Without such an ability, the behaviour of the player will be incomprehensible.

It is generally agreed that the problems that autistic children have with language are in the realm of pragmatics rather than syntax or semantics (U. Frith, 1989). Several writes (e.g. Sperber & Wilson, 1986) have pointed out that successful communication (the pragmatic aspect of language) depends on inferring the beliefs and intentions of our partner in the conversation. This applies especially in situations where the literal meanings of the words do not directly correspond to the meaning of the speaker. The classic example of such a discrepancy between literal and intended meaning is the question 'Can you pass the salt?' In this case, responding only to the literal meaning by saying "Yes" is, in most circumstances, inadequate. Figures of speech, such as metaphor and irony, are other examples in which meaning cannot be derived simply from the words uttered (decoding), but has to be inferred on the basis of the speaker's intentions. Happé (1991) has shown that the ability to understand metaphor and irony is closely linked with the ability to solve "theory of mind" tasks. Autistic children have great difficulty in understanding these figures of speech.

The child who is unable to conceive that other people have minds is necessarily alone in a world in which there is no essential difference between people and things.

Lack of a "theory of mind" module can explain all the cardinal features of autism. There is, however, disagreement about what underlies this deficit. Some (e.g. Hobson, 1990) propose that it is secondary to a fundamental defect of emotional contact; there is as yet little evidence for this proposal. According to Leslie and Frith (1990) the "theory of mind" module involves several fundamental cognitive mechanisms, any of which may be faulty in autism. All these mechanisms crucially involve metarepresentation. I shall consider the nature of this mechanism briefly at the end of this chapter.

AUTISM AND SCHIZOPHRENIA

Traditionally, autism and schizophrenia have been rigidly segregated for diagnostic purposes. In DSM-III-R (American Psychiatric Association, 1987) the presence of positive symptoms rules out a diagnosis of autism. However, the term "autism" was originally coined by Bleuler (1987/1913) to describe a feature of schizophrenia and the cardinal features of autism are strikingly similar to some of the negative features of schizophrenia. Paralleling autistic aloneness, communication difficulties and lack of pretend play, patients with chronic schizophrenia show social withdrawal, poverty of speech, and stereotyped rather than spontaneous behaviour. Language difficulties in schizophrenia, as in autism, involve pragmatics rather than syntax or semantics (Andreasen, Hoffman, & Grove, 1985; Frith & Allen, 1988). In terms of test performance also, there are similarities in that both groups perform badly on "frontal" tests rather than those localising to other parts of the brain (Rumsey & Hamburger, 1988; Shallice, Burgess, & Frith, 1991). I have argued elsewhere that the differences between autism and schizophrenia might be analogous to the differences between early and late acquired disorders (Frith & Frith, 1991). This could account for the same underlying cognitive disorder being manifested in different ways and would be consistent with different aetiologies in the two groups. However, it may be that there are even closer similarities between autism and schizophrenia. Murray and Lewis (1987) have presented evidence suggesting that there is a "neurodevelopmental" subgroup of schizophrenia. This subgroup has an early onset, a high proportion of males, and defects in premorbid IQ, behaviour, and sociability that can be identified even in early childhood. These observations lead me to wonder how many of the patients in this group would have met criteria for autism or Asperger's syndrome before their psychotic breakdown (Watkins, Asarnow, & Tanguay, 1988). Conversely, one can ask how many children diagnosed with autism or Asperger's syndrome develop positive symptoms in later life (Petty, Ornitz, Michelman, & Zimmerman, 1984).

NEGATIVE SIGNS AND THEORY OF MIND

As yet there are no published studies designed explicitly to examine theory of mind in schizophrenia. However, some studies have used tasks dependent on this ability. Pilowsky and Bassett (1980) asked patients to describe photographs of people. They found that, in contrast to controls, schizophrenic patients described the physical appearance of the people rather than their mental states. In a similar study based on personal construct theory, Bodlakova, Hemsley, & Mumford (1974) found that failure to use psychological constructs related to flattening of affect, social withdrawal, and duration of illness. Allen (1984) also asked patients to describe pictures and found that patients with poverty of speech failed to make inferences about these pictures, especially in relation to the mental states of the people shown. These results suggest that schizophrenic patients, especially those with negative features, fail to attend to the mental states of other people. The relationship with flattening affect suggests that they may also have an associated lack of awareness of their own mental states. If these patients cannot or do not know about the mental states of others, then, as in autism, this would explain the extreme impoverishment of all their social interactions. This account does not explain the other major feature of negative schizophrenia: their impoverishment of will.

I have suggested that schizophrenic patients lack awareness of their own mental states, as well as the mental states of other people. Of course, mental states include not only affects and emotions, but also goals and intentions. A person who was unaware of their goals could, on the one hand be a slave to every environmental influence or, on the other hand, be prone to perseverative or stereotyped behaviour, because they would not have the insight to recognise that certain goals were unobtainable or inappropriate.

INCOHERENCE AND THEORY OF MIND

From the many studies of language disorder in schizophrenia, perhaps the major finding is that this is a disorder of expression rather than comprehension. This is shown most elegantly in the studies of Cohen (1978). In these studies, patients and controls were asked to describe coloured discs in such a way that a listener could pick out the disc described. It was found that normals (and schizophrenics) could not understand schizophrenic descriptions, while schizophrenics could understand normal descriptions. What is it that makes schizophrenic speech so hard to understand? Detailed linguistic studies suggest that one cause of the difficulty is a lack of referents (Rochester & Martin, 1979). In normal speech markers are used to indicate: (1) that a protagonist is being introduced for the first time; and (2) to refer back to that protagonist. For example, "There was *a stranger* in my garden this morning. *He* was stealing the goldfish from the pond". In this example the indefinite article *a* indicates that the stranger is being introduced for the first time and the pronoun *he* refers back to the stranger. One feature of incoherent speech is that referents appear without anything to refer back to. For example, "Ever studied this sort of formation, block of ice in the ground? Well, it fights the permafrost, it pushes it away and lets things go up around it. You can see they're like, they're almost like a pattern with a flower. They start from the middle" (from Rochester & Martin, 1979). In this example there is no antecedent for the pronoun they. In their description of the purpose of referents, Rochester and Martin say, "speakers tell listeners new things on the basis of what they assume are old things for the listener". The lack of referents in the speech of some schizophrenic patients suggests that these patients are assuming that certain things are old for the listener when they are in fact new. In other words the patient assumes that their knowledge is shared by the listener when this is not, in fact, the case. This is precisely the error that autistic children make when they fail false belief tasks. They assume that if they know something everyone else must know it too. Other aspects of incoherence can also be explained in these terms. This applies in particular to the lack of cohesive ties and to failures of discourse planning. In these cases, because patients know how the different topics in their discourse are linked together, they assume that the listener also knows, and do not provide explicit links. This failure to take account of the listener's knowledge has been commented on previously. For example, Rutter (1985) concluded, "the central problem lies ... in the social process of taking the role of the other". Harrow and Miller (1985) concluded that schizophrenics do not use "conventional social norms" to guide their speech, implying a lack of shared knowledge.

I conclude that one reason for schizophrenic speech being incoherent is that the patient fails to take account of his listeners lack of knowledge. In other words the incoherent speaker has an inadequate theory of mind. (Of course there are additional reasons for incoherence. These are discussed fully in Frith (1992).

POSITIVE SYMPTOMS

The obvious difference between autism and schizophrenia, is that the cognitive defect associated with autism is present from birth. In most cases of schizophrenia, on the other hand, the onset of symptoms has been preceded by a period in which social interactions have been relatively normal. Thus, unlike the autistic person the schizophrenic has had experience in using theory of mind abilities, knows that other people have different knowledge and beliefs, and knows that it is important to find out what these are. Thus the schizophrenic will continue trying to infer something about the mental states of others, but will find that these inferences are difficult to make. Furthermore, the inferences are likely to be wrong.

FALSE INFERENCES

By definition, certain delusions concern false inferences about the intentions of other people. Patients with delusions of persecution infer that others have evil intentions towards them; patients with delusions of reference falsely infer that others are communicating with them. However there are more subtle consequences of having an unexpected difficulty in inferring the mental states of others. Normally we have an immediate feeling of contact with others. In most cases we do not have to work hard to find out what is in the minds of others; we *know* it almost in the manner of a direct perception. Indeed the lack of theory of mind in autism has sometimes been referred to as 'mind blindness" (Frith & Frith, 1991). If we found ourselves unable to "read" people in this way, how would we react? People would seem wooden, actors without real emotions (derealisation). In extreme cases, we might even think that our loved one had been replaced by a robot, as the creature did not have real mental states (Capgras syndrome). Likewise, if we could no longer "read" our own mental states then we would feel ourselves to be unreal (depersonalisation). If we found it so difficult to read other people's intentions we might conclude that this was a deliberate ploy; that people were deliberately disguising their intentions in order to gain some secret end. This could be the basis of a paranoid belief in a general conspiracy. This would apply particularly to people we knew well, as in these cases we would have gained some facility in reading their intentions. We would not expect to read the intentions of strangers. However, as we got to know people, they too would become part of the conspiracy of deliberately disguising their intentions. I propose, then, that certain delusions can be explained as the consequence of losing the ability to "read" the intentions and beliefs of others. This can be seen as the most minor of a sequence of failures in "theory of mind" mechanisms. I shall now show how a more severe failure can explain certain first rank symptoms.

FAILURE OF "DECOUPLING"

To have a "theory of mind", we must be able to represent propositions like "Chris believes that 'It is raining'". Leslie (1987) has proposed that a major requirement for such representations is a mechanism that decouples the content of the proposition (It is raining) from reality. This decoupling is necessary because a critical feature of such propositions is that their content is neither true nor false, and thus critically different from representations of reality. Decoupling of this type is represented conventionally by quotation marks, a technique much used by newspapers to avoid the libel laws. I propose that, in certain cases of schizophrenia, something goes wrong with this decoupling process. As a consequence, first the content (It is raining) becomes detached from the rest of the proposition (Chris believes that...) and, second, the content is perceived as a representation of the real world, rather than someone's belief about it. As beliefs and reality frequently do not coincide, this would be very confusing. However, more pertinently, much of the content of propositions is not simply concerned with the current state of the real world. For example, I am very much concerned to know what my friends and colleagues think about me. This concern will give rise to propositions like, "Eve thinks that 'Chris drinks too much.'" If the content of this proposition becomes detached, then I would have floating in my mind the unattached statement "Chris drinks too much" apparently emanating from outside my mind, although not necessarily outside my head. I suggest that it is these "free-floating" representations that are the origin of experiences such as third-person hallucinations. The precise nature of the experience depends on the proposition from which the content has become detached. For example, the patient's immediate intentions (I want to "make a cup of tea") might be perceived as voices commenting on the patient's actions. Table 9.1 lists a series of propositions and the abnormal experiences that might arise if the decoupling mechanism failed.

TABLE 9.1
The Abnormal Experiences that Occur When the Content of a Proposition Becomes
"Detached"

Normal proposition	Detached content	Abnormal experience
I know that "my car is faulty"	My car is faulty	Thought insertion
I intend to "make a cup of tea"	Make a cup of tea	Delusion of control
Eve thinks "Chris drinks too much"	Chris drinks too much	Third-person hallucination

Failure of the decoupling mechanism would give rise not only to free-floating representations of mental states, an equally serious consequence would be that the patient would no longer be able to represent mental states, either their own or those of others. I have suggested previously (Frith, 1987) that patients have passivity experiences (such as delusions of control and thought insertion) because of a defect in central monitoring. Central monitoring depends on our being aware of our intention to make a particular response before the response is made. In the absence of central monitoring, responses and intentions can only be assessed by peripheral feedback. For example, if we were unable to monitor our intentions with regard to speech, we would not know what we were going to say until after we had said it. I now propose that this failure of central monitoring is the consequence of an inability to represent our own mental states, including our intentions.

This loss of ability to represent mental states and the associated loss of awareness is not an all or nothing phenomenon. There is a continuum of difficulty underlying these representations. We are beginning to get an idea of the nature of this continuum from studies of the development of the ability to represent mental states in children. Perner (1991) has reviewed the development of the "representational mind". I believe that this development is intimately associated with the development of awareness of mental states. This awareness of our own mental states and those of others must depend on our ability to represent these states. I shall therefore describe these developmental trends in terms of awareness, even though Perner, and others who write on this topic, talk only in terms of representation and metarepresentation.

At around 18 months infants develop an awareness of their own goals. Prior to this stage infants have goals, but are not aware of them. As a consequence they show what Piaget (1936/1953) has called *reactions circulaires*. This is a form of perseverative behaviour in which the infant repeatedly makes responses, even though they no longer achieve the desired goal. Perner (1991) proposes that only when infants have an awareness of their own goals are they able to overcome these perseverative responses: "To engage in goal-directed action, one need not be aware of being engaged in it. But without such awareness, what happens when the action meets with success or failure? The infant will simply repeat the action or, if the internal motivation changes, go on to some other activity." Without awareness of having a goal "children do not expect completion of a planned action to produce the goal. And without this expectation they do not experience failure or success." During the second year of life there is evidence that children start to be aware of having goals. For example, there is a sharp increase in the percentage of children commenting on their success or failure in a task. At this age children also start to use words like "want".

Awareness of goals and goal-directed actions concerns what people will do in certain situations. This does not involve having a theory of mind. However, there is a closely related mental level, which concerns desires and intentions. At this level, which appears between 3 and 5 years of age, children are not only aware of having goals, they are also aware of having intentions. Without such awareness, they cannot distinguish between intentional and accidental responses. This is most strikingly illustrated in an experiment using the knee-jerk reflex. Children below the age of five could not distinguish between an intended movement of their lower leg and the reflexive movement initiated by a gentle tap on the knee (Shultz, Wells, & Sarda, 1980). Similarly children at a somewhat younger age cannot tell whether they have found a sweet in a box by accident or by design (Perner, 1991).

The final stage in this progress towards a sophisticated theory of mind requires that we have the ability to represent the mental states of other people. I have already mentioned experiments showing that children below the age of four cannot appreciate that others have false beliefs. There are more complex tasks concerning the beliefs of ours, which cannot be solved until children are between seven and nine. For example, second-order false-belief tasks require the child to represent that person A has a false belief about person B's beliefs (Perner & Wimmer, 1985).

My interpretation of these developmental trends is that three stages can be identified: (1) awareness of our goals; (2) awareness of our own intentions and other mental states; and (3) awareness of other peoples mental states. These stages can be identified with different classes of schizophrenic signs and symptoms. Table 9.2 shows such a scheme.

A DISORDER OF CONSCIOUSNESS

All the abnormalities listed in Table 9.2 involve lack of awareness. It follows that we would expect schizophrenic patients to have a general abnormality of conscious experience quite apart from their symptoms. Hurlburt (1990)

TABLE 9.2
Abnormalities of Awareness at Various Levels and Some Associated Signs and
Symptoms

Loss of awareness of ...	Positive features	Negative features
Own goals	Grandiose ability	Depersonalisation lack of will
Own intentions	Delusions of control thought insertion	Poverty of thought loss of affect
Others' intentions	Delusions of persecution third person hallucinations	Derealisation social withdrawal

has developed a technique for studying the contents of consciousness and
has applied this to the study of a small number of patients with
schizophrenia. Even in remission these patients experienced some difficulty
switching to the introspective mode required to describe the contents of their
consciousness. In addition, this content was somewhat abnormal. In
particular, the patients (they were American) described some of their
images as "goofed up". For example, one patient described looking at a
man holding a yellow glass while at the same time having the mental image
of the man holding a blue glass. Two patients who were examined during
acute episodes seemed to be unable to describe the contents of their
consciousness at all. These preliminary results are consistent with the notion
that schizophrenic patients do have a fundamental problem of self-
awareness. It would be of considerable interest to apply Hurlburt's
technique to larger numbers of patients selected to have particular signs
and symptoms.

THEORY OF MIND AND THE BRAIN

U. Frith et al. (1991) argue that the case of autism strongly suggests that
there is a specific brain module that instantiates the mechanisms that make
it possible to have a theory of mind. As yet, no studies relate specifically to
"theory of mind" and brain function. However, certain types of social
interaction have been studied in animals and humans which probably do
involve "theory of mind".

SOCIAL COGNITION AND THE BRAIN

Brothers (1990) has reviewed in detail studies of "social cognition" in man
and animals. "Social cognition" is precisely the sort of ability that is likely
to depend on "theory of mind" mechanisms. Brothers considers three
aspects: (1) perceiving faces; (2) perceiving emotions; and (3) engaging in

social interactions. (1) She concludes that an area of the superior temporal sulcus is specialised for the recognition of faces. This evidence has recently been reinterpreted by Campbell et al. (1990), who concluded that cells in this region are specialised in detecting direction of eye-gaze. This ability is especially important in social interactions. For example, eye-gaze is used to control turn-taking in dialogues (Hedge, Everitt, & Frith, 1978). (2) Brothers suggests that the amygdala is concerned with processing emotions. This is consistent with work in animals showing that the amygdala is involved in attaching *value* to objects (i.e. this object is nice, that object is nasty). In humans the amygdala handles much more subtle emotional distinctions (Gloor, 1986). (3) There is evidence, in both man and monkeys, that lesions of frontal cortex, especially the orbital cortex, produce impairments of social interaction. Brothers concludes that a distributed brain system including frontal cortex, amygdala, and superior temporal sulcus underlies social cognition.

Social cognition concerns our ability to infer and represent the mental states of others and is almost certainly impaired in some schizophrenic patients. The other major problem associated with schizophrenia, especially the negative features, involves the ability to represent our own mental states. Willed action, in which our acts are determined by our own conscious intentions, rather than external stimuli, depends upon such representations. Goldberg (1985), Passingham (1987), and others have proposed that there is a specific brain system underlying willed actions. This system includes prefrontal cortex, supplementary motor area, and caudate. Here again we find a distributed brain system including frontal cortex.

PREFRONTAL CORTEX AS PART OF A DISTRIBUTED BRAIN SYSTEM

Goldman-Rakic (1987) has studied the connections between one area of dorsolateral prefrontal cortex (Brodmann's area 46) and other parts of the brain. She has revealed a wealth of reciprocal interconnections between this area and many other areas such as superior temporal sulcus and parahippocampal gyrus. Goldman-Rakic points out that "frontal" tasks, such as spatial delayed responding, depend not just on intact prefrontal cortex, but also on the more posterior area relevant to the particular task. She proposes that visuospatial problems involve parietal-prefrontal connections, while problems that involve the use of memory involve limbic–prefrontal connections. At the MRC Cyclotron Unit we have proposed a similar account of willed action on the basis of positron emission tomography (PET) in humans (C.D. Frith, Friston, Liddle, & Frackowiak, 1991). In one task, subjects had to choose deliberately which finger to move, and this was contrasted with the same finger movements elicited by an external stimulus. The wild finger movements revealed an interaction of area 46 (dorsolateral prefrontal cortex) with motor cortex (finger area) and area 39 (an area associated with finger identification). In the second task subjects had to choose which word to say, this was contrasted with shadowing a word that was given by the experimenter. The willed speaking task revealed an interaction of area 46 with Wernicke's area, which is concerned with auditory word forms. Thus, in both studies, the prefrontal area (which is presumably concerned with non-specific willed actions) interacted with different posterior areas which related to the specific modality of the response.

DISTRIBUTED BRAIN SYSTEMS AND METAREPRESENTATION

There are obvious parallels between these physiological systems and the mechanisms of metarepresentation that I discussed earlier. The tasks used in the PET scanner could be formulated as propositions thus: (1) I intend to "say the word wolf"; (2) I intend to "move my first finger". In these examples the functional relationship of the proposition to the content (intending) maps onto area 46, while the content maps onto posterior regions specific to the particular response. I propose that there is general mapping of this sort between frontal cortex and metarepresentation. The different functions (intending, knowing, feeling, and so on) may relate to different parts of frontal cortex. The content of the propositions (knowledge about objects, people, movement, and so on) is instantiated in the same cortical areas as the primary representation of this knowledge. Thus, hearing a word and intending to say a word both involve Wernicke's area, but the intending task requires interaction with frontal cortex as well. I propose that it is these reciprocal interactions that underlie the cognitive mechanism of metarepresentation.

BRAIN ABNORMALITIES IN SCHIZOPHRENIA

On the basis of these speculations about the brain systems underlying theory of mind, I would propose that the signs and symptoms of schizophrenia occur because of disconnections between frontal cortex and posterior regions. In the case of negative features the connections are almost entirely lost and the patient behaves in many ways like a patient with a frontal lesion. In the case of positive experiential features the disconnection is only partial. For example, "I intend to 'move my finger'", the appropriate modulation of the finger-moving areas is achieved and the finger movement takes place. However, the feedback to area 46 does not occur, or is abnormal, and the movement is perceived as alien. In this context it is interesting to note that the areas of abnormal brain structure observed in post-mortem studies are not in dorsolateral prefrontal cortex but connected areas such as parahippocampal gyrus (Brown et al., 1986), anterior cingulate cortex (Benes & Bird, 1987), and superior temporal sulcus.

REFERENCES

Allen, H.A. (1984). Positive and negative symptoms and the thematic organisation of schizophrenic speech. *British Journal of Psychiatry, 144*, 611–617.

American Psychiatric Association (1987). *Diagnostic and statistical manual of mental disorders (3rd revised edition) DSM-III-R.* Washington D.C.: American Psychiatric Association.

Andreasen, N.C., Hoffman, R., & Grove, W. (1985). Mapping abnormalities in language and cognition. In A. Alpert (Ed.), *Controversies in Schizophrenia: Changes and constancies.* New York: Guildford Press. (pp. 199–226).

Astington, J.W., & Gopnik, M. (1991). Theoretical explanations of children's understanding of mind. *British Journal of Developmental Psychology, 9*, 7–31.

Baron-Cohen, S., Leslie, A.M., & Frith, U. (1985). Does the autistic child have a "theory of mind"? *Cognition, 21*, 37–46.

Benes, F.M., & Bird, E.D. (1987). An analysis of the arrangement of neurones in the cingulate cortex of schizophrenic patients. *Archives of General Psychiatry, 44*, 608–616.

Bleuler, E. (1986). Dementia praecox or the group of schizophrenias (J. Zinkin, Trans., New York, 1950). In J. Cutting & M. Shepherd (Eds.), *The clinical routes of the schizophrenia concept.* Cambridge: Cambridge University Press. (Original work published 1911.)

Bodlakova, V., Hemsley, D.R., & Mumford, S.J. (1974). Psychological variables and flattening of affect. *British Journal of Medical Psychology, 47*, 227–234.

Brothers, L. (1990). The social brain: A project for integrating primate behaviour and neurophysiology in a new domain. *Concepts in Neuroscience, 1*, 27–51.

Brown, R., Colter, N., Corsellis, J.A.N., Crow, T.J., Frith, C.D., Jagoe, R., Johnstone, E.C., & Marsh, L. (1986). Post-mortem evidence of structural brain changes in schizophrenia. *Archives of General Psychiatry, 43*, 36–42.

Byrne, R., & Whiten, A. (1988). *Machiavellian intelligence: Social expertise and the evolution of intellect in monkeys, apes and humans.* Oxford: Oxford University Press.

Campbell, R., Heywood, C.A., Cowey, A., Regard, M., & Landis, T. (1990). Sensitivity to eye gaze in prosopagnosic patients and monkeys with superior temporal sulcus ablation. *Neuropsychologia, 28*, 1123–1142.

Cohen, B.D. (1978). Referent communication disturbances in schizophrenia. In S. Schwartz (Ed.), *Language and cognition in schizophrenia.* Hillsdale, New Jersey: Lawrence Erlbaum Associates Inc.

Frith, C.D. (1987). The positive and negative symptoms of schizophrenia reflect impairment in the perception and initiation of action. *Psychological Medicine, 17*, 631–648.

Frith, C.D. (1992). *The cognitive neuropsychology of schizophrenia.* Hillsdale, New Jersey: Lawrence Erlbaum Associates Inc.

Frith, C.D., & Allen, H.A. (1988). Language disorders in schizophrenia and their implications for neuropsychology. In P. Bebbington and P. McGuffin (Eds.), *Schizophrenia: The major issues.* (pp. 172–186). Oxford: Heinemann.

Frith, C.D., Friston, K.J., Liddle, P.F., & Frackowiak, R.S.J. (1991). Willed action and the prefrontal cortex in man: a study with PET. *Proceedings of the Royal Society of London, Series B, 244*, 241–246.

Frith, C.D., & Frith, U. (1991). Elective affinities in schizophrenia and childhood autism. In P. Bebbington (Ed.), *Social psychiatry: Theory, methodology and practice.* New Brunswick, New Jersey: Transactions Press.

Frith, U. (1989). *Autism: Explaining the enigma.* Oxford: Blackwell.

Frith, U., Morton, J., & Leslie, A.M. (1991). The cognitive basis of a biological disorder: Autism. *Trends in Neurosciences, 14,* 433–438.

Gloor, P. (1986). Role of the human limbic system in perception, memory and affect. In B.K. Doane & K.E. Livingstone (Eds.), *The limbic system: Functional organisation and clinical disorders.* New York: Raven Press. (pp. 165–169).

Goldberg, G. (1985). Supplementary motor area structure and function: Review and hypotheses. *The Behavioral and Brain Sciences, 8,* 567–616.

Goldman-Rakic, P.S. (1987). Circuitry of primate prefrontal cortex and regulation of behavior by representational memory. In V. Mountcastle & F. Plum (Eds.), *Handbook of physiology: The nervous system* (vol. 5, pp. 373–417). Baltimore: Williams & Wilkins.

Happé, F. (1991). *Theory of mind and communication in Autism.* Unpublished PhD thesis, University College, London.

Harrow, M., & Miller, J.G. (1985). Schizophrenic thought disorders and impaired perspective. *Journal of Abnormal Psychology, 89,* 717–727.

Hedge, B.J., Everitt, B.S., & Frith, C.D. (1978). The role of gaze in dialogue. *Acta Psychologia, 42,* 453–475.

Hobson, R.P. (1990). On acquiring knowledge about people and the capacity to pretend: response to Leslie (1987). *Psychological Review, 97,* 114–121.

Hurlburt, R.T. (1990). *Sampling normal and schizophrenic inner experience.* New York: Plenum Press.

Leekam, S., & Perner, J. (1991). Does the autistic child have a metarepresentational deficit? *Cognition,* 40, 203–218.

Leslie, A.M. (1987). Pretence and representation: The origins of "Theory of Mind". *Psychological Review, 94,* 412–426.

Leslie, A.M., & Frith, U. (1990). Prospects for a cognitive neuropsychology of autism: Hobson's choice. *Psychological Review, 97,* 122–131.

Leslie, A.M., & Thaiss, L. (1992). Domain specificity in cognitive development: Evidence from Autism. *Cognition, 43,* 225–251.

Murray, R.M., & Lewis, S.W. (1987). Is schizophrenia a developmental disorder? *British Medical Journal, 295,* 681–682.

Passingham, R.E. (1987). Two cortical systems for directing movement. In *Motor areas of the cerebral cortex* (pp. 151–161). Chichester: Wiley.

Perner, J. (1991). *Understanding the representational mind.* Cambridge, MA: MIT Press.

Perner, J., & Wimmer, H. (1985). "John thinks that Mary thinks that...": attribution of second-order false beliefs by 5- to 10-year-old children. *Journal of Experimental Child Psychology, 39,* 437–471.

Petty, L.K., Ornitz, E.M., Michelman, J.D., Zimmerman, E.G. (1984) Autistic children who become schizophrenic. Archives of General Psychiatry, 41, 129.

Piaget, J. (1953). The origin of intelligence in the child. London: Routledge & Kegan Paul. (Original work published 1936.)

Pilowsky, I., & Bassett, D. (1980). Schizophrenia and the response to facial emotions. *Comprehensive Psychiatry, 21,* 236–244.

Premack, D., & Woodruff, G. (1978). Does the chimpanzee have a theory of mind? *Behavioural and Brain Sciences, 4,* 515–526.

Rochester, S., & Martin, J.R. (1979). *Crazy talk: A study of the discourse of schizophrenic speakers.* New York: Plenum Press.

Rumsey, J.M., & Hamburger, S.D. (1988). Neuropsychological findings in high-functioning men with infantile autism, residual state. *Journal of Clinical and Experimental Neuropsychology, 10,* 201–221.

Rutter, D.R. (1985). Language in schizophrenia: The structure of monologues and conversations. *British Journal of Psychiatry, 146,* 399–404.

Shallice, T., Burgess, P., & Frith, C.D. (1991). Can the neuropsychological case-study approach be applied to schizophrenia? *Psychological Medicine, 21*, 661–673.

Shultz, T.R., Wells, D., & Sarda, M. (1980). The development of the ability to distinguish intended actions from mistakes, reflexes and passive movements. *The British Journal of Social and Clinical Psychology, 19*, 301–310.

Sodian, B., & Frith, U. (1992). Deception and sabotage in autistic, retarded and normal children. *Journal of Child Psychology and Psychiatry, 33*, 591–605.

Sperber, D., & Wilson, D. (1986). *Relevance: Communication and Cognition.* Oxford: Blackwell.

Watkins, J.M., Asarnow, R.F., & Tanguay, P.E. (1988). Symptom development in childhood onset schizophrenia. *Journal of Child Psychology & Psychiatry, 29*, 865–878.

Wing, L., & Gould, J. (1979). Severe impairments of social interaction and associated abnormalities in children: Epidemiology and classification. *Journal of Autism and Developmental Disorders, 9*, 11–30.

10 Semantic Memory and Schizophrenia

Peter J McKenna
Fulbourn Hospital, Cambridge, CB1 5EF.

Ann M. Mortimer
Charing Cross Hospital Medical School and St Bernard's Hospital, Ealing, Middlesex, UB1 3EU.

John R Hodges
Addenbrooke's Hospital, Cambridge, CB2 2QQ.

Semantic memory, the long term storage of knowledge without personal time and place connotations, may be relevant to schizophrenia for a number of reasons. First, there is a growing feeling that a dysfunction of "real world knowledge" (Cutting & Murphy, 1988), "stored regularities" (Gray et al., 1991; Hemsley, 1987) or "second order representations" (Frith & Frith, 1992) is central to the phenomenology of schizophrenia. Secondly, the neuropsychology of semantic memory, with its emphasis on executive/frontal and mnestic/temporal mechanisms, shows obvious overlap with putative areas of disorder in schizophrenia. Finally, the existence of episodic memory impairment in schizophrenia is well established and this has been argued to be selective and disproportionate to the overall level of intellectual impairment. The theoretical construct of semantic memory lacks a coherent conceptual framework, hampering developing of experimental tests. In the present studies, the commonly used existing tests of semantic memory were administered to groups of schizophrenic patients with and without memory impairment. In addition, a detailed, wide ranging, and theoretically sophisticated semantic memory battery, recently developed by Hodges, was applied to 46 schizophrenic patients classified into three groups: acutely ill, non-elderly chronic/severe, and elderly chronically hospitalised. The performance of the schizophrenic patients on the standard tests pointed to a marked semantic memory impairment. On the Hodges battery, all three groups showed evidence of substantial impairment in many of the aspects of semantic memory probed. There was evidence that the impairment was present in patients without evidence of overall intellectual impairment. Preliminary analysis suggested a pattern of impairment more consistent with "impaired access" rather than "degraded store".

INTRODUCTION

In 1972, in a chapter he appended to the proceedings of a conference he was editing, Tulving (see Tulving, 1983) drew attention to a conceptual distinction that seemed to exist between two types of long-term or secondary memory. On the one hand there was memory for personally experienced events, the recollection of individual happenings and doings that were accompanied by a "when and where" specification. Tulving termed this episodic memory; examples would include remembering what one had for breakfast, or who one met on holiday last year. On the other hand, there was memory for information which was held without any personal "it happened to me" connotations and which was devoid of any reference to the time and place at which it was acquired. Examples here would include knowing the chemical formula for salt or the capital of France. Tulving referred to this as semantic memory, because it seemed primarily to be memory for the use of language, a sort of mental thesaurus of organised knowledge about words and other verbal symbols, their meanings and referents, and the relations among them.

Following Tulving's distinction and other influential work, semantic memory became an area of considerable psychological interest. At a theoretical level, the focus of the concept gradually broadened to include not just memory for the meaning of words, but also memory for facts, concepts, and abstract categorisations—until it became, in fact, synonymous with the concept of knowledge itself. The experimental investigation of semantic memory has also developed. This has proceeded along two largely independent lines, which can be referred to as the psychology of semantic memory—what can be learnt about it from the study of normal individuals—and the neuropsychology of semantic memory—what can be deduced from its abnormal function in patients with neurological disorders.

THE PSYCHOLOGY OF SEMANTIC MEMORY

It is clear from recent reviews (Baddeley, 1990; Kintsch, 1980; Tulving, 1983) that semantic memory is a somewhat fragmentary psychological construct whose limits remain poorly defined. The current state of knowledge can be organised under three rough headings: that which is assumed, that which is based on experimental findings, and that which is accepted chiefly by force of argument.

It is assumed (e.g. see Baddeley, 1990; Kintsch, 1980) that semantic memory, like episodic memory, consists of a vast store of information, which is operated upon by processes of registration and retrieval so that its contents are updated continually. It is also assumed that the representation of knowledge in semantic memory spans a continuum from the simple meaning of words; through the more complex concepts that can be described in words but need several to do so; to the most abstract conceptualisations or categories, which define the logical relations between concepts. Semantic memory is also considered to contain so-called frames, scripts, and schemas, organised structural frameworks necessary to comprehend stories and deal with situations like going out to a restaurant, etc. It is possible, even likely, that there are subdivisions of semantic memory, but so far there has been little speculation about where the lines of demarcation should be drawn.

The experimental investigation of semantic memory has been almost exclusively devoted to study of simple concepts like dog, animal, fruit and vegetable and the relationships between them (see reviews by Baddeley, 1990; Kintsch, 1980). The experimental design invariably employed has been the sentence verification task, in which a statement (e.g. "A robin is a bird"; "a canary has gills") is shown to be a subject, who then has to respond true or false as quickly as possible; the time taken to respond is the variable of interest. This has yielded a robust and powerful finding—the so-called semantic relatedness effect: the more closely related the items in a proposition are, the faster subjects are able to verify it. This organisational principle within semantic memory seems to embody what might be termed both horizontal and vertical elements. Thus it takes less time to verify "a robin is a bird" than "an ostrich is a bird", indicating that the interlinking of concepts within a particular category is a function of how prototypical they are or how many features they have in common. It has also been found that "a canary is a canary" is verified faster than "a canary is a bird", which is in turn verified faster than "a canary is an animal"; this suggests that there is some sort of hierarchical structure to semantic memory.

Simple views of the organisation of semantic memory have, however, been undermined by further investigation of the semantic relatedness effect. Any model of horizontal organisation faces difficulties with the verification of negative statements. For instance, "a rifle is a bird" is verified faster than "a potato is a bird", despite the fact that it is undoubtedly more semantically distant. Similarly, if there is a vertical structure to semantic memory, it does not follow a very logical pattern. Thus the statement "a dog is a mammal" takes longer to verify than "a dog is an animal", even though mammals, as a subset of the larger category animals, is presumably lower in the hierarchy.

It has been argued, chiefly by Tulving (1983), that episodic and semantic memory should be regarded as functionally distinct cognitive systems. This argument rests on the large number of apparent differences between them both in the nature of the information held and in the mode of operation of each of them. As summarised in Table 10.1, which is taken from Tulving's (1983) book, information held in episodic memory is based directly on perceptual experiences. These are organised as events or episodes with a beginning and an end, and their correctness is judged almost exclusively by

TABLE 10.1
Differences Between Episodic and Semantic Memory (Modified from Tulving, 1983)

	Episodic	Semantic
Information		
Source	Sensation	Comprehension
Units	Events, episodes	Facts, ideas, concepts
Organisation	Temporal	Conceptual
Reference	Personal	Universe
Veridicality	Personal belief	Social agreement
Operations		
Retrieval query	Time? place?	What?
Retrieval report	Remember	Know
Recollective experience	Remembered past	Actualised knowledge
Registration	Experiental	Symbolic
Inferential capacity	Limited	Rich
Context dependency	More pronounced	Less pronounced
Affect	More important	Less important

the strong feeling of intrinsic veridicality that they evoke. In contrast, the information that makes up semantic memories has to be comprehended, i.e. related to existing knowledge, before it can be stored. The unit of information is the fact or idea; the organisation of the store is conceptual rather than being ordered in time; and finally, when retrieved, the knowledge evokes no automatic feeling that it must be true—rather, an intellectual judgment about its validity has to be made.

Some of the differences in the operation of episodic and semantic memory shown in Table 10.1 are self-evident. Others, however, are not so obvious.While it is not possible to do justice to these latter here, it is worth pointing out that several of the input and output differences relate to the fact that episodic memory is experiential, in the sense that it takes information immediately from experience, whereas to be taken into semantic memory, information has to be recoded into language or some other symbolic representation and is thus second-hand. This is intriguingly reminiscent of the theory of first- and second-order representations of knowledge developed by Frith in Chapter 9.

Tulving (1983) also argued that although they were functionally distinguishable, episodic and semantic memory were also highly inter-dependent and interacted with one another virtually all the time. Episodic memories almost always contain a core of semantic information, and a reasonable case can be made that the store of semantic knowledge is built up from memories that are first acquired by the episodic system and then transferred to the semantic system. Conversely, episodic memory also depends to some extent on semantic memory: episodes are perceived and interpreted in the context of existing semantic memory, and it seems highly probable that the recall of episodic memories is routinely enhanced by bringing relevant semantic information to bear on them.

THE NEUROPSYCHOLOGY OF SEMANTIC MEMORY

Along with many other domains of neuropsychological function, semantic memory has been found to be impaired in Alzheimer's disease. As the disease progresses, patients show mild to moderate breakdown in the performance of many tasks dependent on semantic memory, including object naming, generation of definitions for words, word–picture matching, and category fluency—the generation of words in categories like animals or household items (Hodges, Salmon, & Butters, 1992; Huff, Corkin, & Growden, 1986; Martin & Fedio, 1983). This impairment, of course, is accompanied by and usually overshadowed by deficits in episodic memory, and the study of Alzheimer's disease has not in itself shed much light on the episodic:semantic distinction.

A selective impairment in semantic memory was first described by Warrington (1975) in three patients who developed progressive dysphasia in association with a cerebral atrophic process. Detailed neuropsychological examination of these patients revealed that the language difficulty affected mainly vocabulary, both receptive and expressive, and that phonology, syntax, and speech output were relatively intact; there was also impoverishment of conceptual knowledge about a wide range of animate and inanimate objects. Subsequently a similar syndrome has been documented following herpes simplex encephalitis or in patients with progressive dementing illnesses, which are probably subsumable under the aetiological heading of Pick's disease (Hodges, Patterson, Oxbury, & Funnell, 1992; Shallice, 1988). The pattern of neuropsychological performance of these patients is best understood as a relatively pure and progressive breakdown in semantic memory, which disrupts language, object recognition, and factual knowledge. Episodic memory can be surprisingly well preserved (De Renzi, Liotti, & Nichelli, 1987; Hodges et al., 1992). Some of these patients (as well as others with less pure syndromes) also show the highly counterintuitive phenomenon of category specific deficits—disastrous performance on knowledge in one category, e.g. animals, being coupled with near-normal performance in another, e.g. inanimate objects (Damasio, 1990; Shallice, 1988).

Whether semantic memory is affected in the classical (Korsakoff's) amnesic syndrome has been a matter of some debate. The observation that it was apparently spared was first made by Kinsbourne and Wood (1975) who noted, among other things, that while amnesic patients might not recall events that had happened the same day, they remained obviously able to use language and still had access to considerable general knowledge. It was soon pointed out, however, that this pathological dissociation might be more apparent than real, as it is confounded by the making of comparisons from two different time periods. The semantic memories that appear to remain intact in the amnesic syndrome are largely acquired in the remote past, a time period for which episodic memories are also substantially preserved, even when the retrograde deficit is extensive. As far as the acquisition and retention of new semantic memories is concerned, the impression is that amnesic patients fail conspicuously to update their general knowledge, not knowing their whereabouts, the name of the Prime Minister, and so on (Baddeley, 1984). This impression has, with minor reservations, been supported by a number of studies (reviewed by Ellis & Young, 1988; Squire, 1987), which have demonstrated deficits in the acquisition of new semantic memories prior to and following the onset of amnesia.

SEMANTIC MEMORY IN SCHIZOPHRENIA

It might at first sight seem somewhat arbitrary to single out semantic memory for investigation in schizophrenia when there is no shortage of other candidates for psychological abnormality. There are, however, both theoretical and practical reasons for considering this particular domain of neuropsychological function to be peculiarly relevant to the disorder.

Theoretically, three of the most recent attempts to account for the symptomatology of schizophrenia have invoked dysfunction in a psychological construct very similar to semantic memory. Hemsley (1987) and Gray, Rawlins, Hemsley, and Smith (1991) have argued that schizophrenic symptoms result from a weakening of the influence of what they term "stored regularities" about the world on moment-to-moment mental functioning. Cutting and Murphy (1988) have suggested that at the heart of various forms of thinking disturbance in schizophrenia, including delusions and formal thought disorder, is a disorder they term "deficient real world knowledge". Most recently, Frith and Frith (1992, see also Frith, Chapter 9) have proposed that virtually the entire range of positive and negative schizophrenic symptoms can be understood as different types of failure in a cognitive system that represents knowledge. All these general theories home in on an abnormality of knowledge in schizophrenia, but the concept of knowledge, as described above, is essentially synonymous with that of semantic memory. Semantic memory abnormality has also been implicated directly in a recent approach to delusions (McKenna, 1991), and is also discernible in a theory of auditory hallucinations (Hoffman, 1987, see also Chapter 16).

A practical reason for studying semantic memory in schizophrenia is provided by the finding that its counterpart, episodic memory, is not only impaired but seems to be emerging as the leading neuropsychological deficit associated with the disorder. Several studies over the last 30 years have found that memory impairment is present in schizophrenia, and can become quite marked in chronic patients (see Cutting, 1985). More recently it has been documented that memory deficits are by no means restricted to chronic, institutionalised, or generally intellectually impaired schizophrenic patients (McKenna et al., 1990; Chapter 12). Very recent evidence suggests that memory impairment is disproportionately pronounced in comparison to other neuropsychological deficits in schizophrenia, including executive or frontal lobe dysfunction (Braff et al., 1991; Saykin et al., 1991). As well as being prevalent and substantial, schizophrenic memory impairment also conforms to the classic amnesic syndrome pattern: recall, recognition, and other aspects of secondary/long-term memory are affected, whereas primary/short-term memory is spared (Tamlyn et al., 1992), as are procedural and implicit memory (Clare, McKenna, & Baddeley, in press).

Before proceeding to review the investigation of semantic memory in schizophrenia, a potential pitfall needs to be pointed out and dealt with. It is widely accepted that, as a group, schizophrenic patients can be relied on to perform more poorly than normal individuals on virtually any task that is set them. In addition, or perhaps merely looked at another way, there is good evidence that schizophrenia is associated with intellectual deterioration: this commonly manifests itself as a decline in IQ (Nelson et al., 1990; Payne, 1973), and in some cases it attains the levels of severity seen in organic dementia (Owens & Johnstone, 1980)—25% of chronically hospitalised patients show age-disorientation (Stevens, Crow, Bowman, & Coles, 1978). It follows that precautions need to be taken to ensure that when a specific neuropsychological impairment is found in schizophrenia it is not merely a function of the overall tendency to poor performance, and it is present over and above any wider pattern of impairment. Influenced by the techniques and disciplines of cognitive neuropsychology, the following series of steps is tentatively suggested as a way of establishing that a particular neuropsychological dysfunction, in this case involving semantic memory, is central to the disease process of schizophrenia:

1. *Demonstration of impairment.* The first and minimal requirement that has to be met is that the neuropsychological abnormality in question is in fact present in schizophrenic patients. The most straightforward way of achieving this is by showing impaired performance on standard tests of the neuropsychological function. The degree of impairment should preferably be more than minor, at least in some patients.

2. *Demonstration that the impairment is disproportionate to the overall level of intellectual impairment.* Having established that a deficit is present, it

is next necessary to document that this is not merely part of a pattern of general intellectual deterioration. Ideally, poor performance on tests of the neuropsychological function under investigation should be demonstrable against a background of wholly intact performance on a wider battery of tests. However, as schizophrenia is associated with a variety of deficits, and in some patients the process of impairment seems to become quite generalised, in practice it is likely that no more than a relative isolation can ever be realised.

3. *Demonstration that the impairment follows a recognised neuropsychological pattern.* The overall credibility of the deficit, as well as the argument that it is fundamental to schizophrenia, is strengthened considerably if it can be shown that the pattern of test performance mirrors that observed in an established neuropsychological syndrome. This boils down to demonstrating the kinds of associations, dissociations, and, if possible, double dissociations that have become the standard means of delineating specific impairments in neurological patients.

4. *Demonstration of anomalous rather than just impaired function.* At a clinical level schizophrenia is characterised not just by deficits, in the shape of negative symptoms, but also by productive or positive symptoms like delusions, hallucinations, and formal thought disorder. While it is plausible to assume that negative symptoms will turn out to bear some direct relationship to neuropsychological (and perhaps neurological) deficits, it is much less clear that it will ever be possible to understand positive symptoms in such a way. To account for these, it may be necessary to take the unprecedented step of beginning to think in terms of a neuropsychological function that is heightened, biased, distorted, or otherwise deranged rather than merely being compromised.

In the remainder of this chapter the available studies on semantic memory functioning in schizophrenia are reviewed within the above framework.

IS SEMANTIC MEMORY IMPAIRED IN SCHIZOPHRENIA?

The first study to explicitly examine semantic memory in schizophrenia was carried out by Koh and co-workers (see Koh, 1978). They used a sorting task in which words were required to be categorised according to common features; some of the words were related to each other (e.g. lake, hill, valley, canyon) and some were unrelated to any of the others. When young, acute schizophrenic patients who were in remission were compared to non-schizophrenic psychiatric patients and normal controls, no major differences were found. However, the schizophrenics showed a tendency to utilise fewer categories and to put more words in each category. Koh concluded that any impairment in semantic memory was minor and a reflection of the organising processes acting upon it rather than of the store *per se*. Broga and Neufeld (1981) reviewed a number of studies in a similar vein and came to the same conclusion.

Later studies have painted a rather different picture. Tamlyn et al. (1992) applied the most widely known semantic memory task—the "Silly Sentences" Test of Collins and Quillian (1969)—to a sample of schizophrenic patients of all grades of severity and chronicity. In this test the subject has to state whether each of 50 spoken sentences (e.g. "Rats have teeth", "Desks wear clothes") are true or false as quickly as they can; the verifications are all extremely easy and normals generally make no more than two errors. As a group, the schizophrenics were slower than a control group of normal individuals (schizophrenic mean 5.72 s/sentence; control mean 3.5 s/sentence; $P < 0.001$). Even the fastest patients were slower than the average normal individual, and two- thirds fell outside the normal range altogether. A further surprising finding was the tendency of the schizophrenic patients to make errors in their verifications, usually but not always misclassifying false statements as true. Nearly one-quarter of the sample made three or more semantic errors, and five patients made more than ten.

Hodges, Salmon, and Butters (1992) have recently devised a comprehensive battery of tests dependent on semantic memory. This is constructed around 48 carefully matched living items (animals, birds, sea or water creatures) and man-made items (household items, musical instruments, and vehicles). Knowledge of these is probed in the following ways: (1) *category fluency*, subjects are asked to generate items in the above categories for one minute; (2) *naming*, they then have to name pictures of each of the 48 items presented in turn; (3) *sorting*, they are then asked to sort cards showing the 48 pictures different categories at the three putative levels in the semantic hierarchy—living versus man-made, superordinate/category (e.g. animals versus birds versus sea/water creatures), and subordinate/attributional (e.g. fierce versus non-fierce animals or electrical versus non-electrical household items); (4) *word-to-picture matching*, next, the subjects are given the names of each of the 48 items and asked to point the named item out from an array containing distractor items in the same category; (5) *definition*, finally the subjects are required to generate defining features of a subset of 12 of the 48 items over 1 minute. The present authors (McKenna, McKay, Mortimer, & Hodges, unpublished data) applied this battery to a group of 20 non-elderly schizophrenic patients with chronic, severe illnesses. These formed part of a larger sample of 46 patients of all grades of severity and chronicity. The performance of these patients was compared to 26 normal individuals and 22 patients with Alzheimer's disease originally studied by Hodges et al. (1992). The chronic, severe schizophrenic patients performed significantly worse than the normals on almost all the subtests; in some subtests the level of impairment approached that seen in the Alzheimer's patients. However, in word-to-picture matching, the differences were slight. The findings are shown in Table 10.2. A group of 12 elderly, largely chronically hospitalised patients performed even more poorly, whereas a group of 12 younger patients with more acute and episodic illnesses showed a pattern of impairment that was less severe but still significantly worse than that of the normals.

IS THE SEMANTIC MEMORY IMPAIRMENT DISPROPORTIONATE TO OVERALL INTELLECTUAL IMPAIRMENT?

A simple and quick test of overall intellectual function is the Mini-Mental State Examination (MMSE), on which a score of 23–24 out of the maximum of 30 provides a sensitive and specific cut-off for dementia or delirium (Anthony et al., 1982). Clare et al., (unpublished data) examined 12 patients meeting RDC (Research Diagnostic Criteria) for schizophrenia who showed some degree of memory impairment but who scored 24 or more on the

TABLE 10.2

Scores on the Hodges Semantic Memory Battery for Normals, Patients with Alzheimer's Disease and Schizophrenics

	Mean score		
Subtest	Normals ($n = 26$)	Alzheimer pts ($n = 22$)	Chronic, severe schizophrenic patients ($n = 20$)
Category fluency (words/min)			
Animals	19.7	9.9***	11.9***
Birds	14.1	5.4***	9.0***
Sea/water creatures	13.0	4.4***	8.0***
Naming (maximum 48)			
Total	46.4	35.3***	42.5***
Sorting (% correct)			
Living versus man-made	100.0	99.9	97.5*
Superordinate	95.6	88.3*	91.7*
Subordinate	96.4	86.8***	87.6***
Word-to-picture matching (maximum 48)			
Total	47.9	43.1***	47.5
Definitions (facts/item)			
Total	7.2	4.9***	5.7***
Correct	6.8	3.8***	4.3***

* $P < 0.05$; *** $P < 0.001$, normal versus patient group.

MMSE. These patients were individually matched with 12 normal controls for age, sex, and estimated premorbid IQ, and both groups were administered three standard tests of semantic memory: (1) the "Silly Sentences" test of Collins and Quillian (1969); (2) the Categories test (Baddeley, et al., 1987) in which subjects are required to say whether pairs of words (e.g. house–mansion, apple–night) belong to the same or different conceptual group; and (3) the Mill Hill Vocabulary test (Raven, 1960), which, as well as giving an estimate of IQ, is sensitive to semantic memory impairment. In addition to having memory impairment, the schizophrenic patients were found to perform significantly worse than controls on all the three measures of semantic memory. On the "Silly Sentences", processing time was slower to the extent that there was no overlap between the groups, and the error rate was significantly higher (means and significance levels were similar to those found in Tamlyn et al., 1992). The schizophrenics' errors were also significantly higher in the Categories test (mean error scores 8.42 and 1.67 out of 60; $P < 0.01$). Performance on the Mill Hill Vocabulary test was also significantly impaired in the schizophrenic patients (at $P < 0.05$), a particularly striking finding since the patients were matched for estimated premorbid IQ.

A more sensitive way of gauging overall intellectual decline is by utilising measures of premorbid and current IQ. In the study by McKenna et al. (unpublished data) described above, the WAIS was administered to a substantial majority of the whole sample of 46 schizophrenic patients. Twenty patients with a score on the MMSE of 24 or greater and who also had a current IQ of 85 or greater (i.e. within one standard deviation of the normal mean) were compared to the control group. Their performance remained significantly poorer on almost all of the subtests of the Hodges battery. The only exceptions were on word-to-picture matching, as also found in the original schizophrenic group, and on the first two levels of the sorting subtest, which are very easy. These findings are shown in Table 10.3. The same pattern of significantly impaired performance was found in the subset of these patients who, in addition to having a current IQ in the average range, showed no great IQ decline, i.e. a fall from estimated premorbid levels of 15 points or less.

DOES SEMANTIC MEMORY IMPAIRMENT IN SCHIZOPHRENIA CONFORM TO A RECOGNISED NEUROPSYCHOLOGICAL PATTERN?

According to Shallice (1988), patients with semantic memory impairment caused by neurological disease tend to show one of two alternative patterns of impairment, as judged by their performance on tests of knowledge about words.

TABLE 10.3
Performance of 20 Schizophrenic Patients with Preserved IQ on the
Hodges Semantic Memory Battery

	Mean score	
Subtest	Normals (n = 26)	Schizophrenic patients with preserved IQ (n = 20)
Category fluency (words/min)		
Animals	19.7	13.3**
Birds	14.1	10.6**
Sea/water creatures	13.0	9.2**
Naming (maximum 48)		
Total	46.4	42.6***
Sorting (% correct)		
Living versus man-made	100.0	99.5
Superordinate	95.6	93.5
Subordinate	96.4	89.1***
Word-to-picture matching (maximum 48)		
Total	47.9	47.8
Definitions (facts/item)		
Total	7.2	5.3**
Correct	6.8	4.6***

** $P < 0.01$; *** $P < 0.001$, normal versus patient group.

In the degraded store type of disorder, it is argued that when information cannot be retrieved from semantic memory this is because it is lost altogether. These patients show deficits that are consistent over test sessions (i.e. the same items are affected). Techniques like priming and cueing of the item are ineffective and, for reasons to do with redundancy and size of representations, less frequent words, and words in subordinate rather than superordinate categories, tend to be particularly affected.

In the impaired access type of disorder, it is postulated that the information still exists in semantic memory but the retrieval process is compromised and can only operate inefficiently. Such patients show an inconsistent pattern of performance from session to session; priming and cueing tend to be helpful; and word frequency and superordinate/subordinate category effects, though still present, are considerably less marked.

The unusually poor performance of some of the patients in the study by McKenna et al. (unpublished data) on the Hodges battery provided an opportunity to examine the pattern of semantic memory impairment in schizophrenia, albeit rather crudely. For this purpose, four patients with chronic, severe illnesses but who were not elderly (and hence unlikely to also be suffering from a coincidental dementia) and who were among the worst performers on the naming subtest of the Hodges battery, were selected. Three of these showed no overall cognitive impairment as defined by a score on the MMSE above the cutoff of 23–24; however, one was just in the impaired range. All showed some decline in IQ. The findings on the naming subtest are shown in Table 10.4. It can be seen that the test–retest consistency was not high: all four patients were able to name words on the second testing occasion that they were unable to name or had misnamed on the first occasion, and inconsistent errors were more frequent than consistent ones. Frequency effects were present but the differences were, on the whole, not marked. When given a semantic cue for words they were unable to name or misname (e.g. "It crawls in the sea" for lobster), all patients showed some improvement, and this was substantial in two cases. These findings can only be regarded as preliminary and comparison with the neurological cases reviewed by Shallice (1988) is not possible for methodological and other reasons. Nevertheless, the interpretation of schizophrenic semantic memory impairment seems consistent with impaired access and so falls into line with one of the two types of neurological semantic memory syndrome.

TABLE 10.4
Performance of Four Schizophrenic Patients with Marked Semantic Memory Deficits

	DH (age 52)	SR (age 48)	TC (age 34)	MT (age 53)
General				
Estimated premorbid IQ (NART)	96	105	113	102
Current IQ (WAIS)	74	93	66	82
MMSE score	29	25	25	23
Naming of 48 items				
Errors session 1	6	14	12	10
Errors session 2	6	15	5	8
Inconsistent errors	4	9	7	5
High versus low frequency words	3 versus 3	5 versus 9	5 versus 7	2 versus 8
Improvement with cueing	28%	40%	20%	62%

IS THERE ANOMALOUS SEMANTIC MEMORY
FUNCTION IN SCHIZOPHRENIA?

Very little work has addressed this issue directly. Just about the only relevant example is the study of Manschreck et al. (1988), in which a "semantic priming" task was employed. Normal, depressed, and schizophrenic subjects were required to respond by pressing keys after deciding whether a word displayed on a screen was a real word or a non-word. In these conditions, speed of responding is known to be increased when the target word is preceded ("primed") by a semantically related word. The schizophrenic patients seemed to show an exaggeration of this priming effect compared to the control groups, the effect being most pronounced in those showing formal thought disorder. However, although in this particular case the task involved semantic memory, priming in general is not usually considered to be a semantic memory phenomenon (see Baddeley, 1984). The results of this study were also unusual in that the schizophrenic patients tended to respond more quickly than the controls across all the conditions.

It is possible to speculate, however, that something understandable as a semantic memory anomaly was unwittingly documented in schizophrenia some years ago. The concept of overinclusive thinking was proposed as a unifying explanation of the various aspects of schizophrenic formal thought disorder by Cameron (1947). It refers to a tendency for concepts to become pathologically large, their boundaries loose and blurred, and their content accordingly broad, vague, and overlapping. As a disorder of concept formation, overinclusiveness thus involves knowledge about the world and its representation in semantic memory. The occurrence of overinclusive thinking was exhaustively investigated by Payne and co-workers (Payne, 1973). Payne concluded that, whilst somewhat elusive, the phenomenon could be demonstrated in schizophrenia using several different test procedures. Of particular note were the findings that it was more characteristic of acute than chronic patients—the only psychological abnormality for which this has ever been shown—and that it was associated with presence of formal thought disorder. It may not be stretching a point too far to claim that overinclusiveness fulfils the requirements for an anomaly of semantic memory functioning, an anomaly that may underlie at least one class of productive or positive symptom.

CONCLUSION

Not all patients with schizophrenia show evidence of neuropsychological impairment. When they do, however, there is good evidence that semantic memory is affected along with other domains of function. A case can also be made that the semantic memory impairment seen in schizophrenia—like that in episodic memory and perhaps also in that executive/frontal function—stands out from the general background of poor cognitive performance that characterises the disorder. The application of cognitive neuropsychological methods suggests that the impairment is one of access to the semantic store. This makes it plausible to speculate on the possibility of a wider disturbance, which might go beyond semantic memory hypofunction to, in some circumstances, disorganised function and even, perhaps, hypofunction.

It would be premature to claim that the positive and negative symptoms of schizophrenia might be explicable in terms of abnormal semantic memory. Nevertheless, the idea of a fundamental disorder of knowledge has considerable theoretical precedent and, from the findings cited in this chapter, arguably not a little experimental support.

REFERENCES

Anthony, J.C., LeReche, L., Niaz, U., Von Korff, M.R., & Folstein, M.F. (1982). Limits of the "Mini- Mental State" as a screening test for dementia and delirium among hospital patients. *Psychological Medicine, 12*, 397–408.

Baddeley, A.D. (1984) Neuropsychological evidence and the semantic/episodic distinction. *Behavioral and Brain Sciences, 7*, 238–239.

Baddeley, A.D. (1990). *Human memory: Theory and practice*. Hove: Lawrence Erlbaum Associates Ltd.

Baddeley, A.D., Harris, J., Sutherland, A., Watts, K.P., & Wilson, B.A. (1987). Closed head injury and memory. In H.S. Levin, J. Grafman & H.M. Eisenberg (Eds.), New York: Oxford University Press.

Braff, D.L., Heaton, R., Kuck, J., Cullum, M., Moranville, J., Grant, I., & Zisook, S. (1991). The generalized pattern of neuropsychological deficits in outpatients with chronic schizophrenia with heterogeneous Wisconsin Card Sorting Test results. *Archives of General Psychiatry, 48*, 891–898.

Broga, M.I., & Neufeld, R.W.J. (1981). Evaluation of information sequential aspects of schizophrenic performance I: Framework and current findings. *Journal of Nervous and Mental Disease, 169*, 558–568.

Cameron, N. (1947). *The psychology of behavior disorders*. Boston: Houghton Mifflin.

Clare, L., McKenna, P.J., Mortimer, A.H., & Baddeley, A.D. (in press). Memory in schizophrenia: What is impaired and what is preserved? *Neuropsychologia*.

Collins, A.M., & Quillian, M.R. (1969). Retrieval time from semantic memory. *Journal of Verbal Learning and Verbal Behaviour, 8*, 240–247.

Cutting, J. (1985). *The psychology of schizophrenia*. Edinburgh: Churchill Livingstone.

Cutting, J., & Murphy, D. (1988). Schizophrenic thought disorder: A psychological and organic interpretation. *British Journal of Psychiatry, 152*, 310–319.

Damasio, A.R. (1990). Category-related recognition deficits as a clue to the neural substrates of knowledge. *Trends in Neuroscience, 13*, 95–98.

De Renzi, E., Liotti, M., & Nichelli, N. (1987). Semantic amnesia with preservation of autobiographical memory: A case report. *Cortex, 23*, 575–597.

Ellis, A.W., & Young, A.W. (1988). *Human cognitive neuropsychology*. Hove: Lawrence Erlbaum Associates Ltd.

Frith, C.D., & Frith, U. (1992). Elective affinities in schizophrenia and childhood autism. In P. Bebbington (Ed.), *Social psychiatry: Theory, methodology and practice*. New Brunswick, New Jersey: Transactions.

Gray, J.A., Rawlins, J.N.P., Hemsley, D.R., & Smith, A.D. (1991). The neuropsychology of schizophrenia. *Behavioral and Brain Sciences, 14*, 1–84.

Hemsley, D.R. (1987). An experimental psychological model for schizophrenia. In H. Hafner, W.F. Gattaz & W. Janzarik (Eds.), *Search for the causes of schizophrenia.* Heidelberg: Springer Verlag.

Hodges, J.R., Salmon, D.P., & Butters, N. (1992). Semantic memory impairment in Alzheimer's disease: Failure of access or degraded knowledge? *Neuropsychologia, 30*, 301–314.

Hodges, J., Patterson, K., Oxbury, S., & Funnell, E. (1992). Semantic dementia: progressive fluent aphasia with temporal lobe atrophy. *Brain, 115*, 1783–1806.

Hoffman, R.E. (1987). Computer simulations of neural information processing and the schizophrenia-mania dichotomy. *Archives of General Psychiatry, 44*, 178–188.

Huff, F.J., Corkin, S., & Growden, J.H. (1986). Semantic impairment and anomia in Alzheimer's disease. *Brain and Language, 28*, 235–249.

Kinsbourne, M., & Wood, F. (1985). Short-term memory processes and the amnesic syndrome. In D. Deutsch & J.A. Deutsch (Eds.), *Short-term memory.* New York: Academic Press.

Kintsch, W. (1980). Semantic memory: A tutorial. In R.S. Nickerson (Ed.). *Attention and performance, VIII.* Hillsdale, New Jersey: Lawrence Erlbaum Associates Inc.

Koh, S.D. (1978). Remembering of verbal materials by schizophrenic young adults. In S. Schwartz (Ed.), *Language and cognition in schizophrenia.* New York: Wiley.

Manschreck, T.C., Maher, B.A., Milavetz, J.J., Ames, D., Weisstein, C.C., & Schneyer, M.L. (1988). Semantic priming in thought disordered schizophrenic patients. *Schizophrenia Research, 1*, 61–66.

Martin, A., & Fedio, P. (1983). Word production and comprehension in Alzheimer's disease: The breakdown of semantic knowledge. *Brain and Language, 19*, 124–141.

McKenna, P.J. (1991). Memory, knowledge and delusions. *British Journal of Psychiatry, 159* (suppl. 14), 36–41.

McKenna, P.J., Tamlyn, D., Lund, C.E., Mortimer, A.M., Hammond, S., & Baddeley, A.D. (1990). Amnesic syndrome in schizophrenia. *Psychological Medicine, 20*, 967–972.

Nelson, H.E., Pantelis, C., Carruthers, K., Speller, J., Baxendale, S., & Barnes, T.R.E. (1990). Cognitive functioning and symptomatology in chronic schizophrenia. *Psychological Medicine, 20*, 357–365.

Owens, D.G.C., & Johnstone, E.C. (1980). The disabilities of chronic schizophrenia: Their nature and the factors contributing to their development. *British Journal of Psychiatry, 136*, 384–93.

Payne, R.W. (1973). Cognitive abnormalities. In H.J. Eysenck (Ed.), *Handbook of abnormal psychology.* London: Pitman.

Raven, J.C. (1960). *Extended guide to using the Mill Hill vocabulary scale with the progressive matrices scales.* London: H.K. Lewis.

Saykin, A.J., Gur, R.C., Gur, R.E., Mozley, P.D., Mozley, L.H., Resnick, S.M., Kester, D.B., & Stafiniak, P. (1991). Neuropsychological function in schizophrenia: Selective impairment in memory and learning. *Archives of General Psychiatry, 48*, 618–624.

Shallice, T. (1988). *From neuropsychology to mental structure.* Cambridge: Cambridge University Press.

Squire, L.R. (1987). *Memory and brain.* New York: Oxford University Press.

Stevens, M., Crow, T.J., Bowman, M.J., & Coles, F.C. (1978). Age disorientation in schizophrenia: A constant prevalence of 25% in a chronic mental hospital population. *British Journal of Psychiatry, 133*, 130–136.

Tamlyn, D., McKenna, P.J., Mortimer, A.M., Lund, C.E., Hammond, S., & Baddeley, A.D. (1992). Memory impairment in schizophrenia: Its extent, affiliations and neuropsychological character. *Psychological Medicine, 22*, 101–115.

Tulving, E. (1983). *Elements of episodic memory.* Oxford: Clarendon/Oxford University Press.

Warrington, E.K. (1975). The selective impairment of semantic memory. *Quarterly Journal of Experimental Psychology, 27*, 635–657.

V CLINICAL NEUROPSYCHOLOGY

11 The Cognitive Impairment of Severe Psychiatric Illness: A Clinical Study

Gillian Dunkley and Daniel Rogers
*West Dorset Psychology Services, Dorchester and Burden
Neurological Hospital, Bristol, U.K.*

The results of a neuropsychological study of 102 patients with severe psychiatric illness, 96 of whom had a diagnosis of schizophrenia, are described. A third of the patients were aged 20 to 40, a third 40 to 60 and a third 60 to 80, but all were comparable in terms of severity of illness. The study confirmed that severe psychiatric illness, manifested by prolonged hospitalisation, is associated with severe cognitive impairment comparable to that found in known neurological disorders. This cannot be attributed to the effects of hospitalisation or previous physical treatment. It is associated with indices of neurological disorder. It is most likely an integral part of the psychiatric disorder. It appears soon after the onset of the psychiatric disorder. It is not necessarily progressive, but is apparently progressive in a substantial subgroup of such patients possibly due to an interaction with the ageing process.

INTRODUCTION

Nearly every study of cognitive functioning in patients with severe psychiatric illness since the introduction of standardised cognitive testing a century ago has found significant cognitive impairment in a considerable proportion of patients. However, because this implied cerebral disorder in these patients, at a time when psychological interpretations of psychiatric disorder were favoured, the findings were largely ignored (Rogers, 1991).

These studies suggested that cognitive impairment associated with psychiatric disorder had certain characteristics. It was:

1. Related to the severity of the psychiatric illness—the more severe the psychiatric disorder, the more severe the cognitive impairment— with

severe psychiatric illness it approached the severity found in known neurological disorders.

2. Not necessarily progressive.
3. Reversible with improvement in the psychiatric illness.
4. Characterised more by slowness of, and difficulty with access to, cognitive functions rather than loss of such functions.

This chapter describes a neuropsychological study of patients selected for severity of psychiatric illness by the criterion of length of current admission to a psychiatric hospital. The aim was to confirm the presence of significant cognitive impairment in such patients and to examine in detail its nature and severity at different stages.

Patients in three age groups—young (20–39 years), middle-aged (40–59 years), and elderly (60–79 years), with comparable severity of illness—were examined. A neuropsychological battery commonly used with neurological disorders was employed to allow comparison with the cognitive impairment found in known neurological disorders. A wide range of tests was used to allow the maximum number of patients to achieve a score on at least some tests rather than being eliminated as "untestable".

The patients' case notes were reviewed independently for evidence of previous cognitive impairment, as well as any association with features of possible neurological disorder and history of previous and current physical treatments. The pattern of impairment found with the different tests used was also assessed.

METHOD

Patient Population

102 inpatients of a large multidistrict psychiatric hospital were selected for study. There were 34 patients in each of the three age groups, with, on a given day, the earliest dates of current admission to the hospital. These three groups are referred to as 1, 2, and 3, respectively.

Neuropsychological Assessment

Each patient was asked to come, or was brought by nursing staff, to the psychologist's office. Any patient who refused or failed to come was approached again. In the event of two failures, an attempt was made to locate the patient and administer the tests wherever they were found. A refusal was only recorded if the patient failed to remain with the psychologist on three different occasions.

The following assessments were attempted with each patient, in the order given:

1. *CAPE tests.* Two subtests of the CAPE (Clifton Assessment Procedures for the Elderly; Pattie & Gilleard, 1979), a simple assessment of general cognitive ability, were used—the Information/Orientation (I/O) and Mental Ability (MAb) subtests. Although the patients' ages ranged from 21 to 80, and these tests were designed for use with elderly subjects, the authors of the CAPE tests had reported their usefulness with younger patients. One of the questions asked is the subject's age, so that in addition "age disorientation" (difference between reported age and true age) could be assessed.

2. *Premorbid IQ.* Two reading tests, levels on which reliably indicate premorbid IQ (Nelson & McKenna, 1975; Nelson & O'Connell, 1978), were used—the NART (National Adult Reading Test; Nelson, 1982) and Schonell graded word reading test (Schonell, 1942). To obviate difficulty with visual acuity, the reading tests were presented one word at a time in letters 1.5 cm high on individual white cards. An estimate of premorbid IQ was also derived from the occupational history obtained independently in the case note review, by taking the lower end of the IQ range equivalent for that occupation, i.e. manual, 80; semiskilled, 90; skilled, 100; supervisory, 110; and managerial, 120.

3. *Current IQ.* To obtain a full-scale IQ (FSIQ), seven subtests of the Wechsler Adult Intelligence Scale (WAIS; Wechsler 1955) were used: vocabulary, similarities, digit span, arithmetic, picture completion, block design, and digit symbol. With one exception, these were the subtests used by Nelson (1982) to develop and standardise the reading test used to assess premorbid IQ. Any patient, who was unable to score on the WAIS, was offered the first three subtests (bead threading, memory for colour, and picture identification) of the Hiskey–Nebraska Test (Hiskey, 1966). This was developed for assessing deaf children and has norms for hearing children; little verbal comprehension is required. A mental age from 3 years is produced. Where these Hiskey–Nebraska subtests could not be performed, mental age was assessed on ability to copy simple shapes or scribble from the Terman–Merrill scale (1973) and Griffiths scale for babies (Griffiths, 1954).

4. *Memory.* Four tests were used. The logical memory subtest of the Wechsler Memory Scale (WMS; Wechsler, 1945) was presented for immediate recall before the "current IQ" test. Delayed recall (Russell, 1975) was attempted at the end of the interview. Both parts (verbal and visual) of the Recognition Memory Test (RMT; Warrington, 1984) were also administered.

5. *Perceptual categorisation, object naming and praxis.* The 20 unusual view (UV) photographs of Warrington (1982) were presented for identification, with no time limit imposed. These are misperceived by patients with non-dominant hemisphere involvement. The 15 objects, such

as a key, a ring, and a candle, used by Coughlan and Warrington (1978) as a simple test of language, were presented for naming (NOb) and responses produced within 15 seconds were accepted. A screening battery for praxis modified from the Boston Diagnostic Aphasia Examination (Goodglass & Kaplan, 1983) by Maria Wyke (personal communication) was used. The patient was required to copy a series of hand positions and carry out a number of simple requests, such as "Show me how to salute, wave goodbye, light a cigarette...". Each of the 27 required responses performed correctly scored 1 point.

To obtain a global index of cognitive impairment, scores on different tests were rated on a 5-point cognitive impairment scale (CIS). Scores for individual tests were corrected for age where possible (WAIS IQ, RMT, UV); where age norms were not available, group norms were used (NOb, WMS delayed recall, praxis, CAPE I/O, and MAb). Compared to the performance of a normal population, a CIS score of 0 represents a score at or above the 10th percentile (equivalent to IQ 80 or above); a CIS score of 1 scores between the 9th and 5th percentiles (IQ equivalent 70–79); a CIS score of 2 scores between the 4th and 2nd percentiles (IQ equivalent 60–69); a CIS score of 3 scores at the first percentile (IQ equivalent 50–59); and a CIS score of 4 scores below the 1st percentile (IQ equivalent under 50).

Case Records

Examination of the patients' case notes was carried out independently by the medical co-author and was not available to the psychologist carrying out current evaluations. Educational and occupational history, and evidence of cognitive impairment in the history or on previous examination, was recorded. The psychiatric diagnoses made, physical treatments administered and current medication were noted. Any of the following eight features of possible neurological disorder were also noted:

1. History of possible cerebral insult preceding first admission.
2. Abnormality on routine neurological examination.
3. Abnormality on neurological investigation with electroencephalography (EEG), air encephalography (AEG), computerised brain tomography (CT), or examination of cerebro- spinal fluid (CSF).
4. Spontaneous epileptic fits, i.e. not related to physical treatment.
5. Disorientation noted within 5 years of first admission.
6. Incontinence noted within 5 years of first admission.
7. Case note secondary diagnosis of mental subnormality.
8. Case note secondary diagnosis of dementia.

RESULTS

Patient Characteristics and Case Note Findings

Age and Length of Admission (Table 11.1). Because of the selection criteria, the mean current age and lengths of current admission for patients in groups 1, 2, and 3 differed significantly. The mean ages on first psychiatric and current admission for the three groups, however, were comparable.

School and work record (Table 11.2). Seventy-one of the 102 patients had histories of having completed a normal secondary school education. Only two patients had ever started higher education. Twenty-one patients had histories of having required special schooling or having failed to complete their secondary education. The scholastic history was unavailable in ten. Eighty-two patients had histories of being in paid employment at some time. Only three had ever been employed in a supervisory or managerial capacity. Sixteen patients had a history of never having worked. The occupational history was unavailable in four.

Diagnosis (Table 11.3). Although diagnosis was not a selection criterion, 96 of the 102 patients had a current primary diagnosis of schizophrenia. The remaining six patients had diagnoses of manic-depressive psychosis (two), delusional psychosis, hysterical personality, post-traumatic dementia and postencephalitic defect state.

In addition to their primary diagnosis, 40 patients had had a diagnosis of mental handicap or equivalent made. This secondary diagnosis was made on

TABLE 11.1
Means and Ranges for Current Age, Length of Current Admission, Age on First Psychiatric Admission and Age on Current Admission

	Group 1	Group 2	Group 3
Number of patients	34	34	34
Current age	33.6	52.9	74.6
(range)	(21–39)	(40–59)	(60–79)
Length of current admission (years)	7.0	27.3	53.4
(range)	(2–22)	(19–44)	(49–61)
Age on first psychiatric admission	19.2	22.7	19.7
(range)	(11–36)	(14–34)	(3–29)
Age on current admission	26.6	25.6	21.1
(range)	(17–36)	(15–38)	(15–29)

TABLE 11.2
Patient Characteristics—Number with Different School and Work Record

	Group 1	Group 2	Group 3
Special schooling or failure to complete secondary education	6	9	6
Normal secondary education	24	19	26
Higher education	2	0	0
Scholastic record unavailable	2	6	2
Never employed	8	5	3
Unskilled, semiskilled or skilled employment	24	26	29
Supervisory or managerial employment	2	0	1
Occupational record unavailable	0	3	1

TABLE 11.3
Patient Characteristics—Number with Diagnosis of Schizophrenia, Number with Secondary Diagnosis of Mental Handicap and Estimation of Premorbid IQ

	Group 1		Group 2		Group 3	
Diagnosis of schizophrenia	32		32		32	
Secondary diagnosis of mental handicap	8		15		17	
Estimated premorbid IQ	No.	IQ	No.	IQ	No.	IQ
Reading	23	97.8	21	93.8	11	93.2
Occupation	8	92.2	10	89.4	20	95.0

or up to 24 years (median 1 year) after first admission. Nineteen patients had had a secondary diagnosis of dementia (one in group 1, four in group 2 and 14 in group 3). This was distinct from a diagnosis of primary dementia or dementia praecox, which were historical precursors of schizophrenia. This secondary diagnosis of dementia was made 1–57 years (median 13 years) after first admission. Nine patients had had diagnoses of both mental handicap and dementia made at different stages of their admissions.

Only 46 of the 102 patients (29 in group 1, 13 in group 2, and four in group 3) had had a previous cognitive assessment by a psychologist.

TABLE 11.4
Patient Characteristics—Number Who Received Different Physical Treatments

	Group 1	Group 2	Group 3
Cardiazol or electroconvulsive therapy	16	27	14
Insulin coma therapy	0	19	1
Leucotomy	0	3	1
Current neuroleptic medication			
none	1	3	20
1 drug	6	20	12
2 drugs	12	8	2
3 or more drugs	15	3	0

Physical Treatments (Table 11.4). Fifty-seven patients had had cardiazol induced fits or electro-convulsive therapy (ECT), but in none within 3 years of current testing. Twenty patients had had insulin coma therapy (ICT); four patients had had a leucotomy; and 78 were currently taking neuroleptic medication, the distribution being uneven between the three groups.

Features of Possible Neurological Disorder (Table 11.5). Ninety-one of the 102 patients had at least one of the eight features of possible neurological disorder (Table 11.5).

TABLE 11.5
Patient Characteristics—Number With the Following Features of Possible Neurological Disorder

History of possible cerebral insult before first admission
Abnormality on neurological examination within 5 years of first admission
Abnormality on neurological investigation
History of spontaneous fits
Disorientation within 5 years of first admission
Incontinence within 5 years of first admission
Secondary diagnosis of mental handicap
Secondary diagnosis of dementia

	Group 1	Group 2	Group 3
0 features	9	2	0
1–2 features	18	16	14
3–4 features	6	13	13
5–6 features	1	3	7

TABLE 11.6
Neuropsychological Testing—Number with Previous and Current WAIS Estimations of Full Scale IQ, Verbal IQ, and Performance IQ, with Estimated Premobid IQ and Mean Intervals in Years Between First Psychiatric Admission and IQ Assessments

	Group 2			Group 2			Group 3		
	No.	Mean	SD	No.	Mean	SD	No.	Mean	SD
Premobid IQ	31	96.4	–	31	92.4	–	31	94.4	–
Years from first admission to first test		2.1			10.0			31.7	
First test									
WAIS FSIQ	26	86.5 ± 18.0		6	78.0 ± 21.6		2	74.5 ± 26.2	
VIQ	22	89.7 ± 16.6		4	83.5 ± 13.1		2	102.5 ± 0.7	
PIQ	20	81.5 ± 21.6		2	73.5 ± 2.1		1	82.0	
Years from first admission to second test		5.4			27.7				
Second test									
WAIS FSIQ	16	79.5 ± 16.1		3	72.0 ± 12.1				
VIQ	12	88.7 ± 17.5		3	81.3 ± 6.8				
PIQ	12	78.3 ± 15.1		3	65.0 ± 18.1				
Years from first admission to third test		6.6							
Third test									
WAIS FSIQ	7	65.4 ± 10.8							
VIQ	8	77.5 ± 12.4							
PIQ	6	63.8 ± 13.5							
Years from first admission to fourth test		9.5							
Fourth test									
WAIS FSIQ	5	70.2 ± 8.5							
VIQ	4	84.0 ± 10.6							
PIQ	3	67.7 ± 6.1							
Years from first admission to current test		15.8			35.1	56.0			
Current test									
WAIS FSIQ	19	82.8 ± 14.4		18	76.2 ± 13.7		7	79.6 ± 8.9	
VIQ	19	88.3 ± 15.2		19	78.3 ± 14.8		7	81.7 ± 10.3	
PIQ	19	76.5 ± 13.9		20	71.4 ± 22.5		7	67.9 ± 31.4	

WAIS, Wechsler Adult Intelligence Scale; FSIQ, full-scale IQ; VIQ, verbal IQ; PIQ, performance IQ.

Cognitive Impairment Noted in History. Within 5 years of first psychiatric admission, 53 patients (nine in group 1, 22 in group 2, and 22 in group 3) were described as confused, disorientated, or showing clouding of consciousness. 32 (six in group 1, seven in group 2, and 19 in group 3) were described as having an impairment of memory or giving a wrong estimate of age.

Forty-six had had a previous assessment with the WAIS, which had been performed on up to four occasions in individual patients. The results of these assessments, together with current WAIS results and the mean interval in years between first psychiatric admission and the different assessments are given in Table 11.6.

Neuropsychological Assessment

Completeness of testing.   Four patients died (one in group 1 and three in group 3) and three patients (group 1) were discharged before they could be tested. Eight patients (five in group 1 and three in group 2) refused to be

TABLE 11.7
Neuropsychological testing—Number Obtaining Scores on Different Tests: Mean and Standard Deviation of These Scores

	Group 1			Group 2			Group 3		
	No.	Mean	SD	No.	Mean	SD	No.	Mean	SD
CAPE									
I/O	23	9.1 ±	2.9	30	6.5 ±	3.8	26	3.1 ±	3.6
MAb	24	9.3 ±	2.3	29	6.2 ±	3.5	25	4.0 ±	3.8
RIQ	23	97.8 ±	10.2	21	93.8 ±	9.2	11	93.2 ±	7.1
WAIS FSIQ	19	82.8 ±	14.4	18	76.2 ±	13.7	7	79.6 ±	8.9
or									
MA	–			6	42mo ±	12.6	16	37mo ±	15.9
WMS									
Immediate	13	23.4 ±	17.4	15	18.1 ±	17.7	4	11.0 ±	11.6
Delayed	12	55.9 ±	32.7	13	40.5 ±	33.6	4	5.8 ±	11.5
FCW	15	7.9 ±	6.3	8	9.3 ±	5.5	0		
FCF	15	5.9 ±	5.0	10	5.8 ±	4.1	0		
UV	15	17.7 ±	2.9	20	9.3 ±	5.3	12	4.2 ±	2.3
ObN	15	13.9 ±	1.4	20	11.8 ±	4.0	11	10.5 ±	3.5
Praxis	17	25.8 ±	3.6	22	24.2 ±	5.6	18	18.7 ±	8.6

CAPE, Clifton Assessment Procedures for the Elderly; I/O, information/orientation; MAb, mental ability; RIQ, Reading IQ (National Adult Reading Test and Schonell); WAIS, Wechsler Adult Intelligence Scale; FSIQ, full-scale IQ; MA, mental age (in months) from Hiskey–Nebraska, Terman-Merrill or Griffith scales; WMS, Wechsler memory scale—immediate and delayed; FCW, forced choice words; FCF, forced choice faces; UV; unusual views; ObN, object naming.

tested on three occasions. Of the remaining 87 patients, considering the 11 possible individual test results shown in Table 11.7, scores were obtained for 56% of all possible data points (69% for group 1, 62% for group 2, 39% for group 3).

Test Results (Tables 11.7 and 11.8).   Eighty-five patients obtained a score on at least one test (Table 11.7). Test results were converted into cognitive impairment scores (CIS) as described previously (Table 11.8).

Cognitive Deterioration.   A premorbid IQ based on reading level was obtained from 55 patients and one based on premorbid occupational level was estimated on a further 38 (Table 11.3). Forty-four patients were able to achieve a current WAIS IQ and a further 22 an estimate of current mental age (Table 11.7).

A total of 42 patients obtained both a current and reading IQ, allowing an estimate of deterioration from premorbid IQ (Nelson, 1982). Current IQ was lower than reading IQ in all but one patient. Using Nelson's cut-off of 12 or more IQ points (found in only 4% of normal subjects), 67% of these 42 patients (11 of 19 in group 1, 14 of 16 in group 2, and three of seven in group 3) showed a significant deterioration from estimated premorbid IQ.

Estimates of premorbid IQ from either reading ability or occupational history, and current IQ from either WAIS FSIQ or mental age, allowed an estimate of cognitive deterioration in 65 patients. This was rated as a cognitive impairment score (Table 11.8).

Age disorientation.   Sixty-three patients gave an estimate of their age (22 patients in group 1, 27 patients in group 2, 14 patients in group 3). Only 34 gave an estimate within 5 years of their true age (19 patients in group 1, 11 patients in group 2, four patients in group 3). The mean and standard deviation of the difference in years by which true age exceeded estimated age was 1.9 ± 5.7 for group 1, 15.0 ± 14.9 for group 2, and 31.5 ± 26.7 for group 3.

Correlations.   Eighty-five patients could be given a mean cognitive impairment score (CIS), for the tests on which they obtained a score, of between 0.0 and 4.0. In these patients there was a positive correlation between this mean CIS and both age ($r = 0.44$; $P = 0.0001$) and length of current admission ($r = 0.5$; $P < 0.0001$). There was also a significant positive association ($P < 0.01$) between mean CIS and the number of features of possible neurological disorder, and a significant negative association ($P < 0.01$) between mean CIS and the number of neuroleptic drugs the patient was currently receiving, i.e. the greater the amount of medication the less the cognitive impairment. There was no association of mean CIS with previous treatment with ECT $P > 0.8$) or insulin coma therapy ($P > 0.9$).

TABLE 11.8
Neuropsychological Testing—Number Obtaining Scores on Different
Tests and Mean CIS Scores for These Tests

	Group 1		Group 2		Group 3	
	No.	CIS	No.	CIS	No.	CIS
CAPE						
IO	23	1.1	30	2.1	26	3.2
MAb	24	0.8	29	2.1	25	2.8
DIQ	19	1.7	23	2.6	23	3.3
WMS						
Immediate	13	1.5	15	2.4	4	2.8
Delayed	12	1.5	13	2.3	4	3.8
FCW	15	1.4	10	1.4	0	
FCF	18	2.0	17	2.4	6	4.0
UV	15	0.5	20	1.9	12	3.2
ObN	15	0.3	20	0.8	11	1.5
Praxis	17	0.1	26	0.9	27	2.0
All above tests	171	1.1	203	1.9	138	2.8

CAPE, Clifton Assessment Procedures for the Elderly; I/O, information/ orientation; MAb, mental ability; DIQ, difference between estimated premorbid IQ (from reading IQ or occupational history) and current IQ (WAIS FSIQ or mental age); WMS, Wechsler memory scale—immediate and delayed; FCW, forced choice words; FCF, forced choice faces; UV, unusual view; ObN, object naming.

CIS score represents score on a 5-five point scale (0, 1, 2, 3, 4) to allow comparison of performance on different tests to performance of normal population. The IQ equivalent of these CIS scores is:

CIS		IQ
0	:	> 80
1	:	70–79
2	:	60–69
3	:	50–59
4	:	< 50

DISCUSSION

This study set out to perform a neuropsychological assessment of patients with severe psychiatric disorder. Length of continuous admission to a psychiatric hospital was used as the criterion of severity of psychiatric illness. This was almost equivalent to a clinical diagnosis of chronic schizophrenia, the diagnosis in 94% of the 102 patients. There had been a similar finding in a previous study with a similar patient selection criterion (Rogers, 1985). In the present study, patients were selected so that patients differing in age between 20 and 80, but similar in severity of illness could be compared.

An attempt was made to test every patient, by repeated attempts if necessary and including tests for all levels of cognitive ability. The ability to scribble on a piece of paper was the simplest test used. Seven patients were discharged or died before they could be tested and eight patients refused to be tested at all on three occasions. Eighty-five of the remaining 87 patients were able to obtain a score on at least one test. This suggests that fewer severely ill psychiatric patients are "untestable" than might be expected on the basis of previous reports.

The means for estimated premorbid IQ from current reading ability or previous occupation were within the range expected in a normal population, although below rather than above average (Table 11.3). Where current IQ could be assessed there was a significant deterioration compared to the estimated premorbid IQ (Table 11.7). Where serial IQ had been assessed, this cognitive impairment was present soon after psychiatric admission was first required (Table 11.6). There was little evidence of further progression in cognitive impairment after the first 5 years.

This last statement, however, can only be made about those patients able to achieve an IQ score on the WAIS. When other tests are included in the assessment (Table 11.8), a more serious deterioration in current cognitive ability compared to estimated premorbid ability in a substantial subgroup of the patients is suggested. This becomes more common with increasing age and greater lengths of illness and hospitalisation. It could well represent a definite progressive deterioration in a subgroup of patients with schizophrenia.

The effect of the ageing process on cognitive function is well recognised, but the deterioration found in the older patients in this study seems too pronounced to be simply an effect of ageing. An interaction of disease process and ageing changes is certainly a possibility.

The contribution of prolonged admission, or institutionalisation, to cognitive impairment was seriously considered at one time when psychological theories of psychiatric disorder were favoured, but is now felt to be relatively small compared to the effects of the disease process (Goldberg et al., 1990; Goldstein, Zubin, & Pogue-Geile, 1991; Johnstone et al., 1981; Mathai & Gopinath, 1986). Long-term inpatient care is more likely to be the result than the cause of cognitive impairment in such patients.

Another possible explanation, therefore, for the greater cognitive impairment in older patients would be a selection bias, in that patients with more profound cognitive impairment from the onset of their illness would be more likely to require prolonged hospitalisation and would be over-represented in the older patients in any population with prolonged admission.

The cognitive impairment found was not related to treatment with neuroleptic medication or previous treatment with ECT or insulin coma therapy. There is general agreement that physical treatment makes only a minor, if any, contribution to the cognitive impairment of patients with severe psychiatric illness, and can in fact improve cognitive performance if there is improvement in the psychiatric illness (Cassens, Inglis, Appelbaum, & Guthell, 1990; Devanand, Verma, Tirumalasetti, & Sackeim, 1991; Rogers, 1991).

The findings of this study support the findings of Hazel Nelson and her colleagues (1990) in their study of cognitive function in a group of similar patients hospitalised with chronic schizophrenic illness. They found that these patients were functioning intellectually at a level substantially below the average for the normal population and significantly below their premorbid level estimated from current reading ability. The mean current WAIS-R full scale IQ of their 63 patients was 80.2 ± 10.6, with an estimated premorbid IQ from the NART and Schonell test of 93.1 ± 11.6. However, there was no association between age and intellectual decline, suggesting that there was no, or only slight, progressive deterioration in cognitive functioning.

Nelson and colleagues examined speed of cognitive processing and motor function, and found that their chronic schizophrenic patients scored relatively more poorly on both motor and cognitive speed tests than on the intelligence test, and relatively more poorly on the cognitive than on the motor speed test. This pattern of cognitive deficit would fit the concept of subcortical dementia. The relevance of this concept to the cognitive impairment of schizophrenia has been considered by the same authors in an extensive review (Pantelis, Barnes, & Nelson, 1992).

In the present study, a pattern of impairment emerged which would support this thesis. The object naming test, unusual views test, and praxis test assess the "posterior cortical" dysfunction of aphasia, agnosia, and apraxia. These three tests showed the least impairment of any of the tests used for patients in group 1, and naming objects and praxis the least impairment of any of the tests for patients in groups 2 and 3 (Table 11.8). "Cortical sparing" therefore seemed to be a feature of the cognitive impairment found in these patients, and a feature that held up with the increasing general impairment in cognitive function, associated with increasing age and length of admission.

A substantial impairment of memory was found in these patients, supporting the findings of recent studies (McKenna et al., 1990; Saykin et al., 1991). McKenna and colleagues examined 60 schizophrenic patients, aged 18 to 68, with differing severity of illness, and found that poor memory performance was common, sometimes substantial, and disproportionately pronounced compared to the degree of general intellectual impairment. They felt that, if anything, their study tended to underestimate the extent of the memory disorder because many patients who would in all probability be severely affected were not testable. They felt that age disorientation, shown by 10% of their patients, was a marker of severe memory impairment. In the present study, 46% of 63 patients who gave their age, gave an estimate of at least 5 years below their true age.

Interestingly from a practical point of view, the CAPE assessments, which are very easy and quick to perform, seemed as efficient in assessing overall cognitive impairment as a whole battery of more sophisticated neuropsychological tests (Table 11.8).

The presence of cognitive impairment was recognised clinically from the start of their illness in a significant proportion of these patients. After the change in name for the illness in the early part of this century, from Primary Dementia to Dementia Praecox and then Schizophrenia (Rogers, 1985), and the philosophical change in approach that went with this, cognitive impairment was no longer officially accepted as part of the illness. Thus, when cognitive impairment was obviously present, secondary diagnoses had to be provided. Forty of these 102 patients had received a diagnosis of mental handicap or equivalent in addition to their primary diagnosis, typically at the time of their first psychiatric admission. Of these 40, premorbid IQ was estimated in 33. In 32, this estimate of premorbid IQ was in the normal range; in only one patient was a subnormal premorbid IQ confirmed. Later in their admission, a secondary diagnosis of dementia could be made even when a previous one of mental handicap had been made, and with no clinical evidence of further decline in cognitive performance.

In summary, this study has confirmed that severe psychiatric illness, manifested by prolonged hospitalisation, is associated with severe cognitive impairment comparable to that found in known neurological disorders. This cannot be attributed to the effects of hospitalisation or previous physical treatment. It is associated with indices of neurological disorder, probably an integral part of the psychiatric disorder, appears soon after the onset of the psychiatric disorder, and is not necessarily progressive, but is apparently progressive in a substantial subgroup of such cases, possibly due to an interaction with the ageing process.

ACKNOWLEDGEMENTS

To all the patients who took part in the study, the consultant staff of Friern hospital who all gave permission for their patients to take part, and nursing staff for helping with patient attendance.

REFERENCES

Cassens, G., Inglis, A.K., Appelbaum, P.S. & Guthell, T.G. (1990). Neuroleptics: Effects on neuropsychological function in chronic schizophrenic patients. *Schizophrenia Bulletin, 16*, 477–99.

Coughlan, A.K., & Warrington, E.K. (1978). Word comprehension and word-retrieval in patients with localised cerebral lesions. *Brain, 101*, 163–185.

Devanand, D.P., Verma, A.K., Tirumalasetti, F., & Sackeim, H.A. (1991). Absence of cognitive impairment after more than 100 lifetime ECT treatments. *American Journal of Psychiatry, 148*, 929–932.

Goldberg, T.E., Ragland, J.D., Torrey, E.F., Gold, J.M., Bigelow, L.B., & Weinberger, D.R. (1990). Neuropsychological assessment of monozygotic twins discordant for schizophrenia. *Archives of General Psychiatry, 47*, 1066–1072.

Goldstein, G., Zubin, J., & Pogue-Geile, M.F. (1991). Hospitalisation and the cognitive deficits of schizophrenia. The influences of age and education. *Journal of Nervous and Mental Diseases, 179*, 202–206.

Goodglass, H., & Kaplan, E. (1983). *The assessment of apraxia and related disorders.* Philadelphia: Lea & Febiger.

Griffiths, R. (1954). *The abilities of babies.* London: University of London Press.

Hiskey, M.S. (1966). *Hiskey–Nebraska test of learning aptitude.* Lincoln, NB: Union College Press.

Johnstone, E.C., Owens, D.G.C., Gold, A., Crow, T.J., & Macmillan, J.F. (1981). Institutionalisation and the defects of schizophrenia. *British Journal of Psychiatry, 139*, 195–203.

Mathai, J.P., & Gopinath, P.S. (1986). Deficits of chronic schizophrenia in relation to long-term hospitalisation. *British Journal of Psychiatry, 148*, 509–516.

McKenna, P.J., Tamlyn, D., Lund, C.E. Mortimer, A.M., Hammond, S., & Baddeley, A.D. (1990). Amnesic syndrome in schizophrenia. *Psychological Medicine, 20*, 967–972.

Nelson, H.E. (1982). *The National Adult Reading Test.* Windsor: NFER-Nelson.

Nelson, H.E., & McKenna, P. (1975). The use of current reading ability in the assessment of dementia. *British Journal of Social and Clinical Psychiatry, 14*, 259–267.

Nelson, H.E., & O'Connell, A.D. (1978). Dementia: The estimation of premorbid intelligence levels using the New Reading Test. *Cortex, 14*, 234–244.

Nelson, H.E., Pantelis, C., Carruthers, K., Speller, J., Baxendale, S., & Barnes, T.R.E. (1990). Cognitive functioning and symptomatology in chronic schizophrenia. *Psychological Medicine, 20*, 357–365.

Pantelis, C., Barnes, T.R.E., & Nelson, H.E. (1991). Is the concept of frontal-subcortical dementia relevant to schizophrenia? *British Journal of Psychiatry, 160*, 442–460.

Pattie, A.H., & Gilleard, C.J. (1979). *Clifton Assessment Procedures for the Elderly (CAPE).* Buckhurst Hill, Essex: Hodder & Stoughton Educational/Chigwell Press.

Rogers, D. (1985). The motor disorders of severe psychiatric illness: A conflict of paradigms. *British Journal of Psychiatry, 147*, 221–232.

Rogers, D. (1992). The cognitive disorder of Psychiatric illness. A historical perspective. In C. Pantelis, H.E. Helson, & T.R.E. Barnes (Eds.), *The neuropsychology of schizophrenia.* Chichester: John Wiley.

Russell, E.W. (1975). A multiple scoring method for the assessment of complex memory functions. *Journal of Consulting and Clinical Psychology, 43*, 800–809.

Saykin, A.J., Gur, R.C., Gur, R.E., Mozley, P.D., Mozley, L.H., Resnick, S.M., Kester, D.B., & Stafiniak, P. (1991). Neuropsychological function in schizophrenia. Selective impairment in memory and learning. *Archives of General Psychiatry, 48*, 618–624.

Schonell, F. (1942). *Backwardness in the basic subjects.* Oxford: Oliver and Boyd.

Terman, L.M., & Merrill, M.A. (1973). *Stanford–Binet Intelligence Scale.* Boston: Houghton-Mifflin.

Warrington, E.K. (1982). Neuropsychological studies of object recognition. In D. Broadbent & L. Weiskrantz (Eds.), *The neuropsychology of cognitive function*. London: The Royal Society.

Warrington, E.K. (1984). *Recognition memory test: Manual*. Windsor, NFER-Nelson.

Wechsler, D. (1945). A standardised memory scale for clinical use. *Journal of Psychology, 19*, 87–95.

Wechsler, D. (1955). *Wechsler Adult Intelligence Scale*. New York: The Psychological Corporation.

12

Applying Working Memory Constructs to Schizophrenic Cognitive Impairment

Kirsten Fleming, Terry E. Goldberg, and James M. Gold
*Intramural Research Program, Clinical Brain Disorders Branch,
National Institute of Mental Health Neuroscience Center,
Washington D.C. U.S.A.*

In this chapter we review models of working memory and assess the utility of the construct to account for some of the core cognitive deficits in schizophrenia. Working memory appears to be a viable construct which may account for some of the disparate, and often conflicting findings in the literature entailing attentional, executive and behavioural defects that epitomise patients with schizophrenia. Based upon data from primate studies and *in vivo* neuroimaging investigations it is reasoned that the neuroanatomical region required for this function may be the prefrontal cortex in particular as it recruits activity related to medical temporal and diencephalic centres, and further, that the mesocortical dopamine system may be especially related to its workings.

INTRODUCTION

Kraepelin's original behavioural description of schizophrenia emphasised lack of attentional control, motivation defects, and disorganisation of behaviour (Kraepelin, 1913/1919). Similar defects have been documented in numerous laboratory paradigms. As related deficits have been observed in patients with frontal lobe abnormalities, many investigators have argued that these aspects of schizophrenic phenomena can be attributed to frontal dysfunction. Limiting the value of this analogy is the fact that there is little consensus on the specific cognitive functions subserved by the frontal lobe.

Recently, a number of investigators of both normal experimental psychology and of non-human primate cognition have expressed an interest in the general construct of "working memory", and the possibility

197

that the frontal cortex plays a critical role in mediating this function. Working memory may be thought of as a function of capacity involved in many different cognitive tasks that require the short-term retention and internal manipulation of information that is only relevant for specific, changing contexts. Thus, the construct appears to involve attentional, memory, and response preparation dimensions. Theoretically, impairments in working memory might produce difficulties in those aspects of behaviour specified by Kraepelin to be essential to schizophrenia.

In light of this possibility we thought it might be useful to discuss the various models of working memory that have been proposed in the experimental and animal literatures. The details of these models may be critical in evaluating more precisely the relevance of working memory to the study of prefrontal dysfunction and characterising the nature of impairment in schizophrenia. It is this chapter's goal to summarise various models of working memory and attempt to ascertain the ability of the construct to account for some of the ostensibly disparate cognitive abnormalities in schizophrenia.

The chapter is organised into several sections. First, a review of the original cognitive model of working memory is presented (Baddeley, 1986). The implications for understanding schizophrenia drawn from this model are explored, as are the limitations of such a cognitive framework. Next, working memory as conceptualised by contemporary researchers investigating the functions of prefrontal cortex from primate and cognitive neuroscience studies will be examined. Taken together, we believe that these studies appear to specify a cognitive construct from which various core cognitive abnormalities of schizophrenia might be understood. Furthermore, we attempt to provide evidence that the functions of working memory rely on the integrity of catecholamine systems, all of which may be impaired in patients with schizophrenia. Finally, the last section summarises the utility of the working memory construct.

COGNITIVE MODEL OF WORKING MEMORY.

Baddeley (1986, 1992) proposed that working memory is a general-purpose system involved in a wide range of cognitive operations requiring the simultaneous storage and processing of information. This concept of working memory involves two modality-specific short-term stores and a "central executive", which is responsible for the overall co-ordination of information processing. The storage of transient information is conducted by two peripheral "slave" systems—the articulatory loop, and the visuospatial scratch-pad—specialised for the short term retention of phonological and visual information respectively. Each of these systems will be discussed briefly; the reader is referred to Baddeley (1986, 1990) for a more detailed review.

The articulatory loop subsystem (also commonly referred to as the phonological loop), is specialised for the processing of auditory material, is of limited capacity, and is itself composed of two subsystems, a phonological store and an articulatory rehearsal mechanism (Baddeley et al., 1984; Vallar & Baddeley, 1984). The articulatory loop subsystem may account for a realm of phenomena associated with memory span (Baddeley, 1990). The subsystem thought to be responsible for the processing and short-term storage of visuospatial material including abstract patterns and matrices is called the visual sketch/scratch-pad system (Baddeley & Lieberman, 1980). In contrast to the articulatory loop, the characteristics of the visual spatial scratch-pad have been less well defined and investigated.

The central executive is the core of Baddeley's working memory system and is responsible for the co-ordination of the processing of material in the slave systems and has access to long-term memory (Baddeley et al., 1991). Furthermore, it is proposed to be of limited capacity and can be devoted flexibly to the processing of data in the peripheral slave systems according to the demands of a particular task. Baddeley has utilised the model of attention posited by Shallice (1982) and Norman and Shallice (1980) to help explain the functioning of the central executive component of working memory. According to this model, which might best be described as a theoretical account of the attentional control of action, a supervisory process is necessary for efficient response selection when more habitual and automatic forms of response generation are ineffective. According to Norman and Shallice (1980, 1986), this supervisory system is presumed to have limited processing capacity, and is utilised only for specific circumstances, which include: (1) conscious deliberation due to the failure of automatic processing; (2) situations that necessitate planning; (3) tasks that are judged to be difficult; (4) situations involving either novel or inadequately learned chains of acts; and (5) where a potent habitual reaction is implicated and must be inhibited. This theory has the advantage of being able to explain the seemingly contradictory phenomenon of both increased perseveration and increased distraction when there is a disruption of the supervisory process (Robbins et al., 1990).

According to Baddeley, patients with dysfunctional central executive processes are rendered stimulus-bound and are unable to maintain cognitive sets. Deficits of this module would probably be revealed on a broad range of tasks, which require the monitoring of behaviour by an attentional supervisor. Perhaps most salient should be deficits on dual-task para-digms, which require the co-ordination of two simultaneous acts.

Dual-task paradigms have been widely used in Alzheimer's research (Baddeley, Della Sala, Logie, & Spinnler, 1986), and have suggested that demented individuals are specifically impaired when required to partition their attention on two tasks, the magnitude of the deficit being related to the difficulty of the task. In addition, a dysfunctional central executive would also be manifest in deficient performance on Brown–Peterson tasks (Glenberg & Adams, 1978). In this task the subjects view (or hear) stimulus material and are then immediately required to perform some distractor task until signalled to stop, whereupon they are required to recall the material. The purpose of the distractor is to prevent active rehearsal of the material in a short-term slave system and to necessitate the deployment of central executive resources. This paradigm has been utilised in the study of Alzheimer's patients by using distractors of varying difficulty. Patients are particularly impaired on conditions in which the distractor task is more demanding, thereby presumably requiring more of the available processing resources (Glenberg & Adams, 1978; Morris, 1986). Interpretations of this finding must be cautious, however, as it may be the case that other variables, such as the interference of between trial material (Craik & Levy, 1976) or hindrance of distractor task material (Shiffrin, 1975; 1976) might be responsible.

The construct of working memory also provides a useful framework for understanding performance on tasks where the subjects must monitor their own behaviour as opposed to processing externally presented stimulus information. Two paradigms that have been used to assess this process are the generation of random sequences and two-choice guessing tasks. Such paradigms require a long-term strategy and the continual monitoring of prior responses to avoid the development of simple sterotyped responses (Baddeley, 1986). One way to invoke stereotypy, which is defined behaviourally as an action that is repeated incessantly and is inappropriate to the context (Frith & Done, 1990), is by employing a two-choice guessing task in which the sequence of stimuli is random, thus providing no data upon which the subject can calculate a response. Another approach is to assess the ability of subjects to produce a random series of numbers or letters, a task that requires the subject to evaluate their own responses in relationship to an internal schema of what constitutes a properly random sequence (see also Lyon & Gerlack, 1988).

An overall evaluation of the utility of Baddeley's model of working memory as it relates to schizophrenia is tentative at this point because the slave systems have yet to be analysed systematically. What can be inferred from the existing literature suggests that the slave systems may be relatively intact as compared to the functions subserved by the central executive system. A recent study by Baddeley and colleagues (McKenna et al., 1990) suggested that the memory impairment of schizophrenic patients is similar to that of the classic amnesic syndrome, with sparing of working memory. What they defined as working memory, however, involved auditory digit span, which may be a measure of the articulatory loop, and not of the central executive. We believe that the promise of this model lies in the discussion of the dysfunction of the central executive. It is noteworthy that this is not a new idea. Robbins and Sahakian (1983) applied the Norman and Shallice model (Norman & Shallice, 1980) to elucidate the psychopathology of psychosis, and Frith (1987) proposed a cognition based theory that also emphasised the supervisory role of the frontal cortex. In addition, the data might be explained with equal precision by other theoretical frameworks (Broadbent, 1983; Monsell, 1984; Nuechterlein & Dawson, 1984). Last, the model can be attacked on the grounds that two slave systems are probably too simplistic to explain the functioning of the neural networks in humans. As others have proposed (Gevins & Cutillo, in press), working memory may be comprised of numerous slave systems which vary as a function of the nature of the task.

NEUROPSYCHOLOGICAL MODELS OF WORKING MEMORY

Recently, several investigators have used the working memory construct to describe the functions subserved by the prefrontal cortex, and have suggested that this region is involved in the memory necessary for goal-directed behaviour. The recent conceptual impetus for this notion stems from primate studies, neuropsychological reports of patients with frontal lobe injuries, and from *in vivo* neuroimaging investigations.

In the 1930s, Jacobsen (1935, 1936) demonstrated that primates with lesions of the prefrontal cortex were unable to execute simple response tasks when there was a brief delay between the stimulus and the response. This task was coined the delayed response task, and it, and subsequent variants, have become the quintessential paradigms for assessing prefrontal function in primates. Recently, investigators have attempted to localise the regions activated by the delayed response task in the monkey (Friedman & Goldman-Rakic, 1988; Goldman-Rakic, 1991). By mapping metabolic activity, it was demonstrated that there was activation of a distributed neuronal network involving the dorsal prefrontal cortex, as well as other areas of posterior parietal cortex, hippocampus and ventral anterior and medial dorsal thalamus.

Despite the apparent simplicity of the delayed response (DR) task the essential cognitive demands of the paradigm remain somewhat controversial. Diamond, in evaluating the literature on DR-type tasks in both primates and human infants, has proposed that prefrontal cortex function is required whenever data must be retained over time and a prepotent response inhibited (Diamond, 1985, 1988). She arrived at this notion by documenting developmental changes in primate and human infants on Piaget's "AB" task and on delayed response tasks. Both of these tasks entail the linking together of elements in a cue–response–reward paradigm when a delay period is imposed between the two elements (Diamond, 1990) and appear to be dependent on the same neural system (Diamond & Doar, 1989; Diamond & Goldman-Rakic, 1989). Children 5 years of age and adult monkeys can complete this task successfully on delays of up to 2 minutes. Human infants less than 6 months old and primates with lesioned prefrontal cortexes can only perform the task with no delay; with delays of 2 seconds and greater they exhibit perseverative responding (Diamond & Goldman-Rakic, 1989).

Fuster (1989) suggests that the memory subserved by the prefrontal cortex is supramodal. He argues that it is not the modality, content, or temporal gap alone that defines prefrontal memory; instead, it is a contextual basis, or the "need to bridge a temporal gap in the course of behavioral action." He believes that what distinguishes prefrontal memory, which he refers to as "active memory" from other types is that it is action based (contextual), and it is the "action that gives it its content, duration and term" (1990). Further, he emphasises that the functioning of working memory is comprised not only of a "retrospective" short-term memory but two additional cognitive operations: a "prospective function/preparatory motor set", and a control of interference (Fuster, 1990). All three of these cognitive functions are mediated by the prefrontal cortex, and there is some evidence that the working memory and preparatory motor set are embodied in the dorsolateral prefrontal cortex, and the inhibition of interference in the orbitofrontal area (Fuster, 1989).

Based on neurophysiological studies from Fuster's laboratory, working memory can also be examined at the cellular level. In these early investigations, electrophysiological studies were conducted on primates executing delayed-response tasks (Fuster & Alexander, 1971; Kubota & Niki, 1971) and it was discovered that cells in the dorsolateral prefrontal cortex increased firing following a cue and maintained the activity through the delay. In addition, a subset of these cells is direction specific, in that they fire more if the cue was on the right or left (Funahashi, Bruce, & Alexander, 1989; Fuster & Alexander, 1971).

Goldman-Rakic (1988) proposes that working memory for spatial material is a fundamental prefrontal function. Her thesis is based upon evidence that primates with lesioned dorsolateral prefrontal areas exhibit less impairment on some non-spatial tasks than on tasks with spatial memory components (Mishkin et al., 1969). Goldman and Rosvold (1970) had earlier demonstrated that primates with lesions to the principal sulcus were able to execute spatial tasks, provided memory was not required. Accordingly, the prefrontal cortex directs behaviour through the access, maintenance and updating of "representations" (memories) over time when the stimuli are no longer present. A difficulty for this theory is that prefrontally lesioned primates and infants can perform accurately at the beginning of the AB task even though spatial location is required; errors occur only after the location of the reward is shifted. While this theory describes accurately the working memory of primates, it may have limitations in humans, because most tests of prefrontal function do not contain spatial components.

Studies of Working Memory in Humans

To date, there have only been a few studies investigating the human neural systems of the cognitive components that mediate the functions required by working memory tasks. One difficulty with the application of these classic primate paradigms with human subjects has been that these tasks may not be difficult enough to tax human prefrontal function, except in severely impaired patients.

In an effort to overcome this problem, we recently developed a computerised task, which combines elements of both the delayed response and delayed alternation—the Delayed Response Alternation task (DRA) (Gold et al., 1991). The task requires the subject simultaneously to keep track of the location of a visual stimulus and of an alternating principle. In other words, the perceptual information must be held in working memory and co-ordinated with an internally generated set. We applied this paradigm to a group of normal controls to confirm that the task requires prefrontal cognitive function by examining brain metabolic activity.

The metabolic pattern observed during the DRA involving enhanced dorsolateral prefrontal cortex activity was similar to that documented by Weinberger, Berman, & Zec (1986) on the Wisconsin Card Sorting (WCS) test, another test of prefrontal cortex function. Specifically, the WCS requires the identification of concepts and the maintenance of the response set in the face of distracting compound stimuli that match on more than one dimension. Mental flexibility in the use of feedback to change from a previously rewarded set is also required. All of this information must be held on-line and used to prepare the next response. Thus, the test requires the maintenance of information, without perceptual support, in an ordered temporal sequence, that will be used to guide action. Further evidence to support the validity of the WCS as a measure of working memory comes from a study of normal controls (Berman & Weinberger, 1991) in which the task was administered twice. Dorsolateral prefrontal activation on the second trial was comparable to the first trial, intimating that prefrontal activation was not due to the novelty of the task, or even to figuring out the rules of the test, but perhaps instead to the holding on-line of the rule and maintaining readiness to respond.

In an elegant study, Gevins has attempted to elucidate the areas implicated by working memory in humans by recording neuroelectric patterns while subjects were performing a complex task (Gevins & Cutillo, in press). EEG recordings from 27 scalp electrodes were recorded from five adult males while performing a difficult short-term memory task. Gevins found that prefrontal areas were activated differentially by the working memory task, which included a prestimulus preparatory interval and a delay. He concluded that working memory should not be considered to be a "store", but rather a "function of distributed neural systems by which various types of sensory, motor and higher-order information are maintained for brief periods of time until utilized in a cognitive operation or behaviour." Further, he postulated that the prefrontal cortex may be the "active node" implicated in the functional network only while the data are being utilised and manipulated by other neural areas.

Each of these definitions of "working memory" presented refers to a process whereby cognitive representations are sustained, prolonged, or maintained in the face of varying degrees of interference, distraction, or "noise" that might otherwise disrupt the representations. The process of sustaining these cognitive representations makes them available to a range of auxiliary cognitive operations or "mental manipulations". The nature of representations that may be sustained in working memory are manifold: these may be representations of sensory stimulation of one or more modalities, motor programmes, or "response sets". For example, Baddeley has distinguished components of the working memory system that are referred to as "slave" systems—the phonological loop and the visuospatial scratch-pad. These systems are capable of storing representations of only the preceding several seconds of stimulation, and this storage is subject to rapid decay. In an intact working memory system, however, storage is prolonged within these systems and rendered less vulnerable to disruption. The components of the working memory system that appear necessary for this prolongation of storage comprise frontal lobe and related mechanisms. When frontal systems are disrupted, so too is the capacity to sustain in working memory those representations which are the substrate of mental operations.

COGNITIVE DEFECTS IN SCHIZOPHRENIA INTERPRETED AS WORKING MEMORY DEFICITS

Individuals afflicted with schizophrenia often exhibit impairment on a broad variety of neuropsychological tasks (Goldberg et al, 1987). This pattern has been labelled a generalised deficit by some, underscoring the imprecision, cognitive inefficiency, and psychomotor slowing that often characterises schizophrenic patients. There are, however, some domains of functioning that appear to be differentially impaired in schizophrenia, and that exist in patients who are not globally impaired. These deficits include frontal lobe-type deficits and memory dysfunction (Goldberg et al., 1987, 1989; Saykin et al., 1991).

Both Bleuler (1911/1950) and Kraepelin (1950) highlighted the attentional deficits in schizophrenia. Consequently, the domain of attention has been among the most frequently studied deficits in schizophrenia research (Braff, 1985; Mirsky, 1969). Some investigators have gone so far as to postulate that the underlying cause of cognitive dysfunctioning is due to attentional problems (Nuechterlein & Dawson, 1984). Experimental studies have suggested that there are several distinct types of attention, including: (1) selective attention—the ability to filter relevant information from among alternatives; (2) sustained attention—also known as vigilance, referring to the capacity to maintain alertness over time; and (3) switching attention—the ability to shift attention from one modality to another. It is possible that these different types of attention may be implicated by widely distributed brain areas, with the result that a wide range of cerebral insults may lead to such attentional defects (Mesulam, 1983; Posner & Peterson 1990).

Schizophrenic patients demonstrate impaired performance across a wide variety of attentional paradigms. Some of these attentional difficulties can be explained parsimoniously in terms of a defect in working memory, as many attentional tasks involve a short-term memory component and readiness to respond. As an illustration, we shall use the Continuous Performance Test (CPT; Rosvold et al., 1956), which has long been held as a "gold standard" for measuring sustained attention or vigilance (Nuechterlein & Dawson, 1984). Versions of the CPT differ in terms of the visual quality of the stimuli, and of the memory load involved. For example, some require a response involving a fixed target sequence (e.g. respond to X when it follows A). This version clearly calls for a retention of the previous stimulus to respond correctly, and that schizophrenics perform poorly suggests an inability to hold target information and to guide action selectively over intervals. Interestingly enough, Nuechterlein noted recently that the CPT deficits might be better conceptualised as resulting from a weak supervisory attentional mechanism, representing a "difficulty in initiating a predesignated response for each detected target" (Nuechterlein, 1991). However, primary deficits in visual neural pathways are also possible.

Another attention task requiring the manipulation of short-term material is digit span. Unlike simple digits forward, which may reflect simple auditory short-term memory, variants of this paradigm require functions of working memory. Regarding forward digit span recall, Frame and Oltmans (1982) discovered that schizophrenic patients performed significantly worse on this task during the presence of distractor items, intimating that patients experience difficulty sustaining material on line in the face of interference.

Similarly, patients have been found to exhibit severe disruptions in digit recalls tasks when memory capacity is exceeded (Weiss, Vrtunski, & Simpson, 1988). On the other hand, recalling material in backward order necessitates manipulation of the material held on line. Goldberg et al. (1993) recently assessed memory in pairs of monozygotic twins discordant for schizophrenia and found that the affected group performed significantly worse on digits backward, but not on digits forward.

In addition, schizophrenic patients do not benefit from regular preparatory or warning intervals (Shakow, 1962). One example of this is the RT (Reaction Time) cross-over effect, which alludes to a "crossing" of the functions representing reaction time for predictable versus unpredictable intervals. On this task, schizophrenic patients perform faster when the interstimulus intervals are predictable and of short duration, as do normals. As the intervals increase in length, however, the performance of schizophrenic patients deteriorates significantly. This defect may be attributable to a failure in the maintenance of a readiness to respond component of working memory.

Defects in working memory would also result in an impairment in the ability to generate a random sequence of responses. For example, as noted above, on two-choice guessing tasks, schizophrenic patients often demonstrate position biases, and respond sterotypically (Frith & Done, 1983, Lyon et al., 1986, 1988). A similar pattern also emerges on tasks that require the generation of random number or letter sequences by selecting binary patterns such as might be generated by chance. Here again, schizophrenic patients demonstrate difficulties (Horne, Evans, & Orne, 1982; Rosenberg et al., 1990). Taken together, these studies suggest that schizophrenic patients do not show the ability to produce random sequences like normal controls. This might suggest that patients are unable to hold on line the requirement of the task, while at the same time inhibiting a potent response to the immediate stimulus.

Some of the neuropsychological difficulties encountered by schizophrenic patients are highlighted by tasks involving set shifting, problem solving, and response to feedback. This category of abnormalities has been widely investigated through the use of the WCS, a useful probe of prefrontal cortex functioning. Beginning with Fey (1951) it has repeatedly been shown that schizophrenic patients typically do poorly on the WCS, in that they have trouble attaining concepts and, more significantly, appear to be impervious to feedback to alter their behaviour, which often causes perseveration to incorrect responses. Goldberg et al. (1987) found that the impairment could not be readily normalised, even after explicit instructions. Conceptually related to the WCS, several studies have concluded that patients also perform poorly on the Category Test from the Halstead–Reitan Neuropsychological Test Battery (Goldberg et al., 1988; Golden, 1977).

Common to both these tests, the subject is required to identify the rules of the task by utilising feedback, hold that rule on line, and inhibit responses to dominant stimuli, the functions of the putative prefrontal working memory system. Thus, a deficiency on these tasks often results not from a lack of knowledge, but from an inability to utilise feedback to modify behaviour.

Recently, we discovered a relationship of hippocampal pathology and of prefrontal hypofunction on the WCS (Berman et al., 1992; Suddath et al., 1990; Weinberger, Berman, Suddath, & Torrey, 1992). Nine pairs of monozygotic twins discordant for schizophrenia were examined, and the more an affected twin diverged from his/her unaffected twin in left hippocampal volume, the more they differed on WCS-related prefrontal physiological activation. This result may be consistent with the view that schizophrenia involves pathology of the dysfunction within a widely distributed neocortical–limbic neural network that has been implicated in the performance of working memory tasks.

This anatomically based framework makes the investigation of dual task paradigms of great interest, as such task situations presumably demand the activity and co-ordination of several neural systems. To our knowledge, there has only been one study that utilised a dual-task paradigm in schizophrenia (Granholm, Asarnow, & Marder, 1991). In this study, patients accuracy on a multiple-frame search task was normalised through practice, after which an auditory shadow condition was added. As a consequence of the dual task, the patients exhibited a decline in performance on the shadowing measure. This was interpreted by the authors as a reduction in the available processing capacity. We believe that the results might be reinterpreted as a failure in the co-ordination of the working memory system such that multiple sources of information cannot be handled simultaneously. While we are cognisant that there are inherent difficulties associated with dual-task experiments (Somberg & Salthouse, 1982) and results are compatible with other interpretations (Brown & Marsden, 1991; Duncan, 1979), further dual-task research in schizophrenia is warranted. Specifically, it would be useful to use tasks that are thought to be mediated by different neuronal networks, thereby controlling potential interference. For example, it would be interesting to couple a reading measure with a visual–spatial task.

PUTATIVE MECHANISMS UNDERLYING WORKING MEMORY FUNCTION

There is evidence accumulating to suggest that dopamine may play an integral role in the neuronal processing of working memory (Sawaguchi et al., 1988; Sawaguchi & Goldman-Rakic, 1990). For example, depletion of dopamine in the prefrontal cortex of primates produces deficits on delayed-alternation tasks (Brozoski, Brown, Rosvold, & Goldman-Rakic, 1979). Sawaguchi and Goldman-Rakic (1991) were further able to demonstrate that local blockade of dopamine D1 receptors in the dorsolateral prefrontal cortex produced impaired performance on an oculomotor delay–response task. In contrast, a D2 antagonist did not produce comparable abnormalities, thereby supplying additional evidence that D1 receptors are involved selectively in working memory processes. It is also possible that defects in this system may be reduced—Sawaguchi et al. (1988) administered dopamine to monkeys, which led to an increase in the delay-related regional activity in the dorsolateral prefrontal cortex and function on the task. They concluded that dopamine "promotes" processing of spatial short-term memory by increasing memory-related activity, again probably by means of D1 receptors.

In addition, it has been demonstrated that putative tests of working memory in humans can be affected by dopamine agonists. As an illustration, a single administration of dextroamphetamine, an indirect dopamine agonist, in schizophrenic patients has been shown to improve performance on a measure of concept formation on the WCS (Goldberg et al., 1991). Further, it was demonstrated that the effect of amphetamine resulted in task-dependent activation of the dorsolateral prefrontal cortex, and that there was a significant correlation between activation of this neuronal area and performance on the WCS (Daniel et al., 1991). These findings may lend support to the theory that cortical dopaminergic activity underlies working memory.

SUMMARY

Patients with schizophrenia demonstrate widespread cognitive deficits which have proven difficult to explain in terms of simple anatomic localisation or stage models of information processing. In this chapter we had adopted the outlines of Baddeley's model of working memory and examined several of the important aspects of schizophrenic cognitive dysfunction. Data from tests of abstraction (WCS), vigilance (CPT), stereotypy (two-choice), and dual-task paradigms all appear to be explainable as the result of dysfunction at the level of executive control of the working memory system, thought to be mediated by the prefrontal cortex. The operation of more basic auditory and visual-spatial peripheral systems, primarily mediated by posterior cortical areas appear to be relatively intact based on available literature. Although this conceptual framework can account for many empirical observations, the more specific details of this theoretical construct remain to be tested in patients with schizophrenia, and the extent to which "executive deficits" can account for the widespread cognitive impairments observed in patients with this disorder needs to be determined. One advantage of this framework is that it is potentially testable at the level of cognitive experiments and may be of use in further specifying the "prefrontal" hypothesis of schizophrenia.

Functional neuroimaging results in schizophrenia have demonstrated failures in prefrontal metabolism in response to particular cognitive challenge paradigms such as the WCS. Recent evidence that this metabolic failure may be linked to structural abnormalities in the medial temporal lobe, suggests that the impairment in schizophrenia is probably best described as the result of abnormalities of a distributed system rather than of a single anatomic site or specific stage of information processing. Thus impairments are likely to be observed across a variety of tasks and modalities which require the simultaneous storage and processing of information in the service of action selection.

ACKNOWLEDGEMENTS

The authors would like to thank Dr Alan Gevins for allowing us to cite his unpublished data.

REFERENCES

Baddeley, A.D. (1986). *Working memory.* Oxford: Clarendon Press.

Baddeley, A.D. (1990). *Human memory: Theory and practice.* London: Lawrence Erlbaum Associates Ltd.

Baddeley, A.D. (1992). Working memory. *Science, 255,* 556–559.

Baddeley, A.D., Bressi, S., Della Sala, S., Logie, R., & Spinnler, H. (1991). The decline of working memory in Alzheimer's disease: A longitudinal study. *Brain, 114,* 2521–2542.

Baddeley, A.D., Della Sala, S., Logie, R., & Spinnler, H. (1986). Working memory and dementia. *Quarterly Journal of Experimental Psychology, 36A,* 233–352.

Baddeley, A.D., Lewis, V., & Vallar, G. (1984). Exploring the articulatory loop. *Quarterly Journal of Experimental Psychology, 36A,* 233–252.

Baddeley, A.D., & Lieberman, K. (1980). Spatial working memory. In R. Nickerson (Ed.), *Attention and performance VIII.* Hillsdale, N.J.: Lawrence Erlbaum Associates Inc.

Berman, K.F., Torrey, E.F., Daniel, D.G., & Weinberger, D.R. (1992). Regional cerebral blood flow in monozygotic twins discordant for schizophrenia. *Archives of General Psychiatry, 49,* 927–935.

Berman, K., & Weinberger, D. (1991). Functional localization in the brain in schizophrenia. In A. Tasman & S.M. Goldfinger (Eds.), *American Psychiatric Press Review of Psychiatry.* Washington D.C.: American Psychiatric Press.

Bleuler, E. (1950). *Dementia praecox, or the group of schizophrenics.* (J. Zinken, Trans.) New York: International Universities Press. (Original work published 1911).

Braff, D.L. (1985). Attention, habituation, and information processing in psychiatric disorders. In Michael, B., Cavenar, J.O., & H.K. Brodie et al. (Eds.), *Psychiatry* (Vol. 3, pp. 1–12). Philadelphia, PA: J.B. Lippincott.

Broadbent, D.E. (1983). The functional approach to memory. *Philosophical Transactions of the Royal Society of London, B302,* 239–249.

Brown, R.G., & Marsden, C.B. (1991). Dual task performance and processing resources in normal subjects and patients with Parkinson's disease. *Brain, 114,* 215–231.

Brozoski, T.J., Brown, R., Rosvold, H.E., & Goldman-Rakic, P.S. (1979). Cognitive deficits caused by regional depletion of dopamine in prefrontal cortex of rhesus monkey. *Science, 4,* 429–432.

Craik, F.M., & Levey, B.A. (1976). The concept of primary memory. In W.K. Estes (Ed.), *Handbook of learning and cognitive processes* (Vol. 4). Hillsdale, N.J.: Lawrence Erlbaum Associates Inc.

Daniel, D.G., Weinberger, D.R., Jones, D.W., Zigun, J.R., Coppola, R., Handel, S., Bigelow, L.B., Goldberg, T.E., Berman, K.F., & Kleinman, J. (1991). The effect of amphetamine on regional cerebral blood flow during cognitive activation schizophrenia. *The Journal of Neuroscience, 11*(7), 1907–1917.

Diamond, A. (1985). Development of the ability to use recall to guide action, as indicated by infants' performance on AB. *Child Development, 56,* 868–883.

Diamond, A. (1988). The abilities and neural mechanisms underlying AB performance. *Child Development, 59,* 523–527.

Diamond, A. (1990). The development and neural bases of memory functions as indexed by the AX-TO(B) and delayed response tasks in human infants and infant monkeys. In A. Diamond (Ed.), *The development and neural bases of higher cognitive functions* (pp. 267–317). New York: New York Academy of Science Press.

Diamond, A., & Doar, B. (1989). The performance of human infants on a measure of frontal cortex function, and delayed response task. *Developmental Psychobiology, 22*(3), 271–294.

Diamond, A., & Goldman-Rakic, P.S. (1989). Comparison of human infants and rhesus monkeys on Piaget's AXTO(B) task: Evidence for dependence on dorsolateral prefrontal cortex. *Experimental Brain Research, 74,* 24–40.

Duncan, J. (1979). Divided Attention: The whole is more than the sum of its parts. *Journal of Experimental Psychology: Human Perception and Performance, 5,* 216–228.

Fey, E. (1951). The performance of young schizophrenics and young normals on the Wisconsin Card Sorting Test. *Journal of Consulting Psychology, 15,* 311–319.

Frame, C.L., & Oltmanns, T.F. (1982). Serial recall by schizophrenic and affective patients during and after psychiatric episodes. *Journal of Abnormal Psychology, 91,* 311–318.

Friedman, H.R., & Goldman-Rakic, P.S. (1988). Activation of the hippocampus by working memory: a 2-deoxyglucose study of behaving rhesus monkeys. *Journal of Neuroscience, 8,* 4693–4706.

Frith, C.D. (1987). The positive and negative symptoms of schizophrenia reflect impairments in the perception and initiation of action. *Psychological Medicine, 17,* 631–648.

Frith, C.D., and Done, D.J. (1990). Stereotyped behavior in madness and in health. In S. Cooper & C. Dourish (Eds.), *The neurobiology of stereotypy* (pp. 232–260). Oxford: Clarendon Press, 25–64.

Funahasi, S., Bruce, C., & Goldman-Rakic, P.S. (1989). Mnemonic coding of visual space in the money's dorsolateral prefrontal cortex. *Journal of Neurophysiology, 36,* 61–78.

Fuster, J.M. (1989). *The prefrontal cortex* (2nd Ed.). New York: Raven Press.

Fuster, J.M., & Alexander, G.E. (1971). Neuron activity related to short-term memory. *Science, 173,* 652–654.

Gevins, A.S., & Cutillo, B.A. (in press). *Dynamic neural networks of human working memory.*

Glenberg, A., & Adams, F. (1978). Type I rehearsal and recognition. *Journal of Verbal Learning and Verbal Behavior, 17,* 455–463.

Gold, J., Berman, K., Randolph, C., Goldberg, T., & Weinberger, D. (1991). PET validation and clinical application of a novel prefrontal task. *Journal of Clinical and Experimental Neuropsychology, 13,* 81.

Goldberg, T., Bigelow, L., Weinberger, D., Daniel, D., & Kleinman, J. (1991). Cognitive and behavioral effects of the coadministration of dextroamphetamine and haloperidol in schizophrenia. *American Journal of Psychiatry, 148*(1), 78–84.

Goldberg, T., Kelsoe, J., Weinberger, D., Pliskin, N., Kirwin, P., & Berman, K. (1988). Performance of schizophrenic patients on putative neuropsychological tests of frontal lobe function. *International Journal of Neuroscience, 42,* 51–58.

Goldberg, T.E., Kelsoe, J., Weinberger, D.R., Pilskin, N.H., & Berman, K. (1988). Performance of schizophrenic patients on putative neuropsychological tests of frontal lobe function. *International Journal of Neuroscience, 42,* 51–58.

Goldberg, T.E., Weinberger, D.R., Berman, K.F., Pliskin, N.H., & Podd, M.H. (1987). Further evidence for dementia of the prefrontal type in schizophrenia? *Archives of General Psychiatry, 44,* 1043–1051.

Goldberg, T.E., Weinberger, D.R., Pliskin, N.H., Berman, K.B. & Podd, M.H. (1989). Recall memory deficit in schizophrenia. *Schizophrenia Research, 2,* 251–257.

Golden, C.J. (1977). Validity of the Halstead-Reitan neuropsychological battery in a mixed psychiatric and brain injured population. *Journal of Consulting and Clinical Psychology, 34,* 1043–1051.

Goldman, P.S., & Rosvold, H.E. (1970). Localization of function within the dorsolateral prefrontal cortex of the rhesus monkey. *Experimental Neurology, 27,* 291–304.

Goldman-Rakic, P.S. (1988). Topography of cognition: Parallel distributed networks in primate association cortex. *Annual Review Neuroscience, 11,* 136–156.

Goldman-Rakic, P.S. (1991). Prefrontal cortical dysfunction in schizophrenia: The relevance of working memory. In B. Caroll & Barrett (Eds.), *Psychopathology and the brain.* New York: Raven Press.

Granholm, E., Asarnow, R.F., & Marder, S.R. (1991). Controlled information processing resources and the development of automatic detection responses in schizophrenia. *Journal of Abnormal Psychology, 100,* 22–30.

Horne, R.L., Evans, F.J., & Orne, M.T. (1982). Random number generation, psychopathology and therapeutic change. *Archives of General Psychiatry, 39,* 680–683.

Jacobsen, C.F. (1935). Functions of the frontal association in primates. *Arch. Neurol. Psychiatry, 33*: 558–569.

Jacobsen, C.F. (1936). Studies of cerebral function in primates. *Comp Psychol Monogr, 13*: 1–68.

Kraepelin, E. (1919). *Demential praecox and paraphrenia.* (R.M. Barclay, Trans.). Edinburgh: E & S Livingston. (Original work published 1913.)

Kraeplin, E. (1950). *Dementia praecox and paraphrenia.* (J. Zinkin (Trans.). New York: International Universities Press Inc. (Original work published 1913.)

Kubota, K., & Niki, H. (1971). Prefrontal cortical unit activity and delayed cortical unit activity and delayed alternation performance in monkeys. *Journal of Neurophysiology, 34,* 337–347.

Lyon, N., & Gerlack, J. (1988). Perseverative structuring of responses by schizophrenic and affective disorder patients. *Journal of Psychiatric Research, 22*(4), 261–277.

McKenna, P.J., Tamlyn, D., Lund, C.E., Mortimer, A.M., Hammond, S., & Baddeley, A.D. (1990). Amnesic syndrome in schizophrenia. *Psychological Medicine, 20,* 967–972.

Mesulam, M.M. (1983). The functional anatomy and hemisphere specialization for directed attention. *Trends in Neuroscience, 6,* 384–387.

Mirsky, A.F. (1969). Neuropsychological bases of schizophrenia. *Annual Review of Psychology, 20,* 321–348.

Mishkin, M., Vest, B., Waxler, M., and Rosvold, E. (1969). A re-examination of the effects of frontal lesions on object alternation. *Neuropsychologia, 7,* 357–363.

Monsell, S. (1984). Components of working memory underlying verbal skills: A "distributed capacities" view. In H. Bouma & D.G. Bouwhuis (Eds.), *Attention and performance.* Hillsdale, N.J.: Lawrence Erlbaum Associates Inc.

Morris, R.G. (1986). Short-term forgetting in senile dementia of the Alzheimer's type. *Cognitive Neuropsychology, 3,* 77–97.

Morris, R.G., & Baddeley, A.D. (1988). Primary and working memory functioning in Alzheimer-type dementia. *Journal of Clinical and Experimental Neuropsychology, 10,* 279–296.

Norman, D.A., & Shallice, T. (1980). *Attention or action: Willed and automatic control of behavior.* CHIP Report 99. San Diego: University of California.

Norman, D.A., & Shallice, T. (1986). Attention and action: Willed and automatic human control of behavior. In R.J. Davidson, G.E. Schwartz, & D. Shapiro (Eds.), *Consciousness and self-regulation* (Vol. 4, pp. 1–18). New York: Plenum Press.

Nuechterlein, K.H. (1991). Vigilance in schizophrenia and related disorders. In *Handbook of Schizophrenia, Vol. 5.* Edited by H.A. Nasrallah. Amsterdam: Elsevier Science Publishers, pp. 397–433.

Nuechterlien, K.H., & Dawson, M.E. (1984). Information processing and attentional functioning in the developmental course of schizophrenic disorders. *Schizophrenia Bulletin, 10,* 160–203.

Posner, M.I., & Petersen, S.E. (1990). The attention system of the human brain. *Annual Review of Neuroscience, 13,* 25–42.

Robbins, R.W., Mittleman, G.L., O'Brien, J., & Winn, P. (1990). The neuropsychological significance of stereotypy induced by stimulant drugs. In S. Cooper & C. Dourish (Eds.), *The neurobiology of stereotypy* (pp. 25–64). Oxford: Clarendon Press.

Robbins, T.W., & Sahakian, B.J. (1983). Behavioral effects of psychomotor stimulant drugs: Clinical and neuropsychological implications. In I. Creese (Ed.), *Stimulants: neurochemical, behavioral and clinical perspectives.* New York: Raven Press, pp. 301–338.

Rosenberg, S., Weber, N., Crocq, M., Duval, F., & Macher, J. (1990). Random number generation by normal, alcoholic and schizophrenic subjects. *Psychological Medicine, 20,* 953–960.

Rosvold, K.E., Mirsky, A.F., Sarason, I., Bransome, E.D., & Beck, L.H. (1956). A continuous performance test of brain damage. *Journal of Consulting Psychology, 20*(5), 343–350.

Sawaguchi, T., & Goldman-Rakic, P.S. (1991). D1 dopamine receptors in prefrontal cortex: Involvement in working memory. *Science, 251,* 947–951.

Sawaguchi, T., Matsumara, M., & Kubota, K. (1988). Dopamine enhances the neuronal activity of spatial short term memory task in the primate prefrontal cortex. *Neuroscience Research, 5,* 465–473.

Saykin, A.J., Gur, R.C., Gur, R.E., Mozley, P.D., Mozley, L.H., Resnick, S.M., Kester, D.B., & Stafniak, P. (1991). Neuropsychological impairment in schizophrenia: Selective impairment in memory and learning. *Archives of General Psychiatry, 48,* 618–624.

Shakow, D. (1962). Segmental set: A theory of the formal psychological deficit in schizophrenia. *Archives of General Psychiatry, 6,* 60–612.

Shallice, T. (1982). Specific impairments of planning. *Philosophical Transactions Royal Society of London, 289,* 199–209.

Shiffrin, R.M. (1975). Short-term storage: The basis for a memory search. In F. Restle, R.M. Shiffrin, N.J. Catellan, H. Lindman, & D.B. Pisoni (Eds.), *Cognitive Theory* (vol. 1). Hillsdale, N.J.: Lawrence Erlbaum Associates Inc.

Shiffrin, R.M. (1976). Capacity limitations in information processing, attention and memory. In W.K. Estes (Ed.), *Handbook of learning and cognitive processes* (vol 4). Hillsdale, N.J.: Lawrence Erlbaum Associates Inc.

Somberg, T.A., & Salthouse, T.A. (1982). Divided attention abilities in young and old adults. *Journal of Experimental Psychology: Human Perception and Performance, 8,* 651–663.

Suddath, R.L., Christison, G.W., Torrey, E.F., Casanova, M.F. & Weinberger, D.R. (1990). Anatomical abnormalities in the brain of monozygotic twins discordant for schizophrenia. *New England Journal of Medicine, 322,* 789–794.

Vallar, G., & Baddeley, A.D. (1984). Fractionation of working memory: Neuropsychological evidence for a phonological short-term store. *Journal of Verbal Learning and Verbal Behavior, 23,* 151–161.

Weinberger, D.R., Berman, K.F., & Zec, R. (1986). Physiologic dysfunction of dorsolateral prefrontal cortex in schizophrenia: I. Regional cerebral blood flow evidence. *Archives of General Psychiatry*, *43*, 114–124.

Weiss, K.M., Vrtunski, P.B. & Simpson, D.M. (1988). Information overload disrupts digit recall performance in schizophrenics. *Schizophrenia Research*, *1*, 299–303.

13 Cognitive Functioning and Symptomatology in Schizophrenia: The Role of Frontal-subcortical Systems

Christos Pantelis
The Mental Health Research Institute & Royal Park Hospital, and the University of Melbourne & Royal Melbourne Hospital, Australia.

Hazel E. Nelson
Horton Hospital, Epsom, U.K.

— my heroine.

Neuropsychological

deficit → information processing problem.

Similarities between schizophrenia and disorders with known subcortical pathologies have suggested that the fronto-subcortical areas may also be implicated in cases of schizophrenia, especially those with negative or Type 2 symptoms. Recent studies from our group showed no association between measures of episodic memory or motor skills learning and symptomatology, but using the CANTAB associations were found between slowing of thinking and the disorganisation syndrome, and between tests of frontal lobe functioning and the psychomotor poverty syndrome.

INTRODUCTION

This paper deals with the interrelationships between the symptoms of schizophrenia and the neurocognitive impairments found in this condition, and how such associations might provide clues to its neurobiology. We will argue that in at least some cases of schizophrenia there is dysfunction of the fronto-thalamo-striatal pathways connecting cortex with subcortex.

The hypothesis was suggested in the first instance by the similarities between some of the clinical features of schizophrenia, notably those manifest in the Type II syndrome characterised by negative symptoms (Crow, 1980), and descriptions of patients with subcortical lesions (Pantelis, Barnes, & Nelson, 1992), and frontal lesions (Andreasen, 1987). The evidence from neuropathology, neurochemistry and brain imaging studies supporting such a hypothesis has been detailed elsewhere (Pantelis et al., 1992). In the present chapter we shall seek to evaluate the evidence by

215

reference to neuropsychological studies in schizophrenia, including some previously unpublished results from our group.

THE NATURE OF NEUROPSYCHOLOGICAL DYSFUNCTION IN SCHIZOPHRENIA

A large number of investigations of patients with schizophrenia have demonstrated impairments in cognitive functioning (see Hemsley, 1982; Goldstein, 1986, for reviews) but there is no unanimous agreement as to the extent or neurological implications of these cognitive deficits. Those studies that have compared schizophrenic patients with normal subjects or with other groups of psychiatric patients have generally found greater impairment in the group with schizophrenia. Heaton and colleagues (Heaton & Crowley, 1981; Heaton, Beade, & Johnson, 1978) reviewed the early literature examining the use of neuropsychological tests to discriminate functional from organic disorders. The evidence from these studies suggested that neuropsychological tests were well able to discriminate such conditions except for those patients with chronic schizophrenia. This latter group tended to perform essentially like diffuse brain damaged patients (Chelune, Heaton, Lehman, & Robinson, 1979) and could not be distinguished from them on any of the standard neuropsychological assessments.

More recently, the use of increasingly refined cognitive tasks has suggested that some cognitive deficits may be relatively specific to schizophrenia, or to particular types or syndromes of schizophrenia (Crow, 1980; Liddle, 1987b). In particular, there have been consistent findings of deficits in performance on tests sensitive to frontal lobe function (Kolb & Wishaw, 1983; Liddle, 1987b; Morice, 1990; Shallice, Burgess, & Frith, 1991; Weinberger, Berman, & Zec, 1986). For example, schizophrenic subjects are impaired in their performance on the Wisconsin Card Sorting Test, which is thought to implicate particularly the dorsolateral prefrontal cortex (DLPFC) (Berman, Zec, & Weinberger, 1986; Berman, Illowsky, & Weinberger, 1988; Goldberg et al., 1987; Kolb & Wishaw, 1983; Morice, 1990; Weinberger et al., 1986; Weinberger, Berman, & Illowsky, 1988). In a recent, detailed neuropsychological evaluation of five schizophrenic patients with different symptom profiles, Shallice and his colleagues (1991) used an extensive battery of tests, including a number of different frontal lobe tests, and identified a specific deficit in performance on the frontal tests in addition to a more widespread decline in cognitive functioning. Although all five patients performed poorly on some but not all frontal tests, there was no uniformity in the pattern of results, suggesting that different frontal or prefrontal impairments might be implicated in these patients.

The mechanism mediating the observed frontal deficits is ill-understood, though one possibility is disruption of the frontal–striatal neuronal circuitry (Robbins, 1990, 1991). Pantelis and colleagues (Barnes, 1988; Pantelis et al., 1989, 1992) have argued that the observed frontal lobe impairments in schizophrenia may be consequent on disruption of subcortical systems with deafferentation of prefrontal areas with which they connect. These authors have drawn parallels between some of the symptoms of schizophrenia and the description of patients with subcortical dementia. In particular, the association reported in schizophrenia, between negative symptoms, abnormal involuntary movements and cognitive deficits are similar to the descriptions of patients with lesions of subcortical structures, such as the basal ganglia and thalamus. Others, such as Crosson (1985) and McGrath (1991), have argued that the presence of thought disorder also implicates subcortical structures and the frontal–striatal pathways.

Liddle (1987a; Liddle & Barnes, 1990; Liddle & Morris, 1991) identified three syndromes in schizophrenia and has reported associations between these and specific patterns of neuropsychological impairment. On the basis of the pattern of performance on the various tests and the associations found with each of the three syndromes, Liddle has postulated the existence of three distinguishable, but related neuropathological processes in schizophrenia. Specifically, he proposes that the "psychomotor poverty syndrome", characterised by negative symptoms such as flatness of affect and poverty of speech, results from dysfunction of the left DLPFC; that the "disorganisation syndrome", manifest by such symptoms as incoherence of speech and inappropriateness of affect, involves right ventral prefrontal cortex; and that the "reality distortion syndrome", consisting of positive symptoms of delusions and hallucinations, involves abnormality of the medial temporal lobe (Liddle, 1987b; Liddle et al., 1991). It is relevant to the present hypothesis that the prefrontal areas described by Liddle have intimate connections with basal ganglia and thalamus, thus implicating these frontal–subcortical connections in the pathogenesis of certain symptoms or syndromes of schizophrenia.

FRONTAL–STRIATAL PATHWAYS

Investigations of the structure and fibre connections of the basal ganglia indicate that the frontal–striatal pathways are highly organised with parallel, segregated circuits throughout their course (Alexander, DeLong, & Strick, 1986; DeLong, Alexander, Miller, & Crutcher, 1990; Groenewegen et al, 1991). At least five distinct basal ganglia–thalamo–cortical circuits have been identified (Alexander et al., 1986), which funnel through the basal ganglia from the neocortex and allocortex (Nauta, 1986). Thus, the basal ganglia have other functions as well as being important in the control of movement via the motor and oculomotor circuits. Their role extends to the control of cognitive function via their connections with the DLPFC and orbito-frontal (OFC) areas of the prefrontal cortex. The connections with the limbic lobe via the anterior cingulate circuit also suggests a role in emotion and behaviour. Other connections with limbic structures may be relevant in this regard (Groenewegen et al., 1991). Importantly, such cortico–striato–thalamic pathways are not directed towards cortical areas caudal to the frontal lobe (Groenewegen et al., 1991).

As pointed out in a recent review (Pantelis et al., 1992), the organisation of these pathways, with their close proximity in the basal ganglia, provides a model for understanding how a disturbance of the pathophysiology in that region might generate a range of symptoms, including disorders of movement, affect and cognition. While outside the basal ganglia these pathways are not so closely aligned and lesions would be expected to produce more limited and discrete impairments of cognitive, limbic or motor function, disruption occurring within subcortical nuclei would be more likely to produce symptoms involving all of these functions. Thus, the topographical arrangement of these pathways would seem to be consistent with evidence of cognitive, psychiatric, and motor disturbance occurring together in disorders of the basal ganglia, such as Huntington's disease and Parkinson's disease. The implication of similar disturbances co-existing in schizophrenia is that basal ganglia and/or thalamic pathology are relevant in this condition (Pantelis et al., 1992).

THE RELEVANCE OF SUBCORTICAL STRUCTURES IN SCHIZOPHRENIA

The basal ganglia and/or thalami have long been considered of importance in schizophrenia (Bowman & Lewis, 1980; Buscaino, 1920; Lidsky, Weinhold, & Levine 1979; Mettler, 1955) and there has been a resurgence of interest recently (Barnes, 1988; Crosson & Hughes, 1987; McGrath, 1991; McKenna, 1990; Nelson et al., 1990; Oke & Adams, 1987; Pantelis et al., 1989, 1992; Patterson, 1987; Robbins, 1990, 1991; Sandyk & Kay 1990a, 1991; Swerdlow & Koob, 1987). Indeed, some of these authors have drawn parallels between conditions such as Parkinson's disease and schizophrenia (Pantelis et al., 1989, 1992; Reading, 1991; Robbins, 1991; Sandyk & Kay, 1990a, 1991).

In attempting to understand how these subcortical areas may be relevant to the pathogenesis of certain attributes of the disorder, the findings, referred to above from neuroanatomy, become particularly relevant, thereby implicating the frontal–striatal system. Each of the brain regions connecting with the basal ganglia in the major cortico–thalamo–striatal circuits described have been incriminated as dysfunctional in schizophrenia. Thus, the involvement of the motor system is manifest by the presence of abnormal involuntary movements (Barnes, 1988); oculomotor dysfunction is evidenced by abnormalities of eye movements (Holzman, 1987); the two cognitive circuits involve fibre connections with the DLPFC and the OFC, both of which have been inculpated as showing functional impairment in schizophrenia (Berman et al., 1986, 1988; Goldberg et al., 1987; Liddle, 1987b; Liddle et al., 1992; Weinberger et al., 1986, 1988); and, finally, emotional and behavioural disturbance and active psychotic symptoms may implicate the connections with the limbic system, possibly involving other circuits as well as the anterior cingulate projections (Groenewegen et al., 1991).

DEFICITS ON TESTS SENSITIVE TO FRONTAL–SUBCORTICAL DYSFUNCTION

It has been argued that cognitive deficits associated with subcortical disorders can be distinguished from the cognitive deficits associated with cortical disorders (Cummings, 1986; Freedman, 1990; Huber & Shuttleworth, 1990), though such distinctions are certainly not as clear cut as has been suggested by some authors. In their extensive review, Brown and Marsden (1988) found only a few studies supporting a distinction (Freedman & Oscar-Berman, 1986; Heindel, Butters, & Salmon, 1987, 1988; Sagar, Cohen, Corkin, & Growden, 1985; Sahakian et al., 1988), though perhaps a large overlap in dysfunction is not surprising in view of the anatomical and functional interrelatedness of these areas.

In comparison with cortical dementias, subcortical dementia (Albert, Feldman, & Willis, 1974) is considered to manifest a greater impairment of certain executive functions, such as set shifting (Freedman, 1990; Pillon, Dubois, Lhermitte, & Agid, 1986), greater deficit in recall memory rather than recognition memory (Butters et al., 1987; Eslinger & Damasio, 1986; Fisher, Kennedy, Caine, & Shoulson, 1983; Tweedy, Langer, & McDowell, 1982), a greater impairment of procedural learning (Butters et al, 1987; Eslinger & Damasio, 1986; Grafman et al., 1990; Heindel et al., 1988; Martone et al., 1984) and a slower speed of information processing (bradyphrenia) (Albert et al., 1974; Cummings, 1986; Dubois et al., 1988; Morris et al., 1988; Rogers, 1986).

IMPAIRMENT OF EXECUTIVE FUNCTIONS

Although impairment in set shifting is generally considered to be a function of the frontal cortex, and in particular the dorsolateral prefrontal area, deficits in set shifting may also be observed in some cases where the primary lesion is in the subcortex (Gotham, Brown, & Marsden, 1988; Lees & Smith, 1983; Pillon et al., 1986). As discussed above, the frontal and subcortical areas are so closely linked anatomically that it is probably more appropriate to consider the system as an integrated fronto-subcortical system (Pantelis et al., 1992; Robbins, 1990, 1991) so that dysfunction in one part of the system may affect, and therefore appear as dysfunction in, another part of the system. An impairment in set shifting is commonly reported in schizophrenia, as has been earlier discussed.

RECALL/RECOGNITION MEMORY

Similar to the pattern of results found in studies of memory in subcortical disorders, it is the studies of schizophrenia that have used recall measures to assess memory that have tended to find deficits, rather than the studies using recognition measures (Bauman & Murray, 1968; Cutting, 1985; Goldberg & Weinberger, 1988; Koh, 1978; Koh & Paterson, 1978; Koh, Kayton, & Schwartz, 1974; Traupman, 1975).

As part of a study to investigate the memory and learning deficits in schizophrenia and the association of these deficits with different symptom clusters we (Nelson et al., unpublished data) assessed a group of 49 chronic schizophrenic inpatients on a test of memory for a single event, memory being assessed using immediate and delayed, recall and recognition measures. The single event was the presentation of a set of 20 line drawings of objects. Following a 1-minute interval, filled to prevent rehearsal and thereby remove any short-term memory (STM) component to the task, the subjects were asked to recall the 20 objects. Following this a 40-item yes/no recognition task was employed. These tests were repeated after 45 minutes with a different set of distractor items being used in the yes/no recognition task. For the group as a whole, the recall measures (i.e. immediate and delayed) were significantly correlated ($r = 0.45$; $P < 0.01$) as were the recognition measures ($r = 0.62$; $P < 0.01$) but there was no association between any of the recall/recognition pairs, suggesting that these two ways of measuring memory for a single event were measuring essentially different aspects of the memory process.

As expected, recognition scores were substantially higher than recall scores, but as a normal control group has not yet been run on these tests it is not possible to comment on the size of the recognition/recall discrepancy in the group of schizophrenics as a whole. However, contrary to the prediction based on our previous study (Nelson et al., 1990) the negative symptom group did not show a more "subcortical" pattern of recall/recognition results. Indeed, it was those patients with high positive symptoms who showed a trend to be relatively better at recognition than recall measures ($P < 0.06$).

PROCEDURAL LEARNING

We also looked at learning on the Pursuit Rotor in this group of 49 chronic schizophrenic subjects, in view of reports of differentially impaired procedural learning in Huntington's disease (Heindel et al., 1988; Martone et al., 1984) and progressive supranuclear palsy (Grafman et al., 1990). Following three test trials of 10 seconds each, the Rotor speed was adjusted so that all subjects were "on target" for 30–50% of the time when the learning trials commenced. The learning test comprised six trials of 80 seconds each, with each trial being broken into 10-second intervals for analysis. All six trials were completed in one session, with task-filled rests being allowed between trials. All subjects showed significant learning across trials, with maximum learning between trials 1 and 4. Normal control subjects have not yet been run on this task so it is not known how the learning pattern of the schizophrenic group as a whole compares with normal subjects, but no significant associations were found between any of the measures of learning and any of the measures of symptomatology, when this was considered in terms of the syndromes described by Liddle (1987a).

In view of previous results from our group that have suggested that there might be a particular association between negative symptoms and signs of subcortical dysfunction (Nelson et al., 1990), including movement disorders (Barnes, 1988; Pantelis et al., unpublished data), the lack of any association between Pursuit Rotor learning and negative symptomatology was disappointing.

BRADYPHRENIA

Slowing of cognitive functioning has been considered the most compelling feature of a distinction between dementia of subcortical origin and cortical dementia (Cummings, 1986). The term was introduced by Naville in 1922 to describe patients with parkinsonism secondary to encephalitis lethargica. Rogers (1986) has argued that subcortical dementia is a more recent synonym for bradyphrenia.

Impaired speed on cognitive tests is a characteristic feature of schizophrenia (Babcock, 1930, 1933, 1941; Shapiro & Nelson, 1955); this appears to be disproportionately severe compared to the impaired level of intellectual functioning (Senf, Huston, & Cohen, 1955; Eysenck, Granger, & Brengelmann, 1957). Harris and Metcalfe (1956) examined the association of flattening of affect and cognitive functioning in a group of 40 schizophrenics, including tests of speed and level of functioning, and they found that only the tests involving mental speed differentiated significantly between the groups: the more severe the flattening of affect the slower the speed of cognitive functioning.

In a study of chronic schizophrenic patients Nelson et al. (1990) confirmed that speed of functioning was relatively more impaired than level of functioning, with cognitive speed being more affected than motor speed. This study also reported an association between negative symptomatology and bradyphrenia. However, in a more recent study from our group, using a simple odd-man-out cancellation task (cancelling out the odd shape or colour from a set of three), we failed to find any specific association between speed of thinking and symptomatology (Nelson et al., unpublished data).

Recent studies have suggested that bradyphrenia consists of at least two components: (1) slowness in decision making, which may reflect dysfunction of the basal ganglia; and (2) slowness of thought processes, which may relate to dysfunction of the frontal lobe (Dubois et al., 1988). These findings have received support from the group in Cambridge, using a computerised test battery. Morris et al. (1988) used a computerised version of the Tower of London task to assess speed of cognitive functioning. In the original test, Shallice (1982) demonstrated that patients with frontal lobe damage were impaired in their performance on this task. The computerised version provided measures of "initial" movement and thinking times, these reflecting the time taken to plan before making the first response, as well as "subsequent" movement and thinking times, these reflecting the times taken to complete the task subsequent to the first move. In comparison with matched controls, patients with Parkinson's disease were found to have a specific impairment in initial thinking or planning time, which was significantly longer, whereas subsequent thinking time was not significantly impaired (Morris et al., 1988). In contrast, in the next study using this computerised task, Owen and his colleagues (1990) found that frontal lobe-lesioned patients were not impaired in their initial thinking time but, compared to matched controls, they had significantly longer "subsequent" thinking times. Thus, using this test, a different pattern of impairment emerges in Parkinson's disease, a disease of the basal ganglia, compared with frontal lobe-lesioned patients.

We have recently reported the preliminary results of our investigations using this computerised Tower of London Test, in a group of 45 patients with chronic schizophrenia (Pantelis et al., 1991, unpublished data). Those patients with symptoms of the disorganisation syndrome were significantly slower in their "initial" thinking time, rather than "subsequent" thinking time—a similar pattern to that seen in patients with Parkinson's disease. These patients were well-matched on a number of variables, including age, length of illness, antipsychotic dosage, parkinsonism scores, mini-mental state scores, and both current and premorbid IQ levels. Also, the findings could not be explained by a difference in the patients' ability to complete the task, as there was no difference between the high and low disorganisation groups in the number of problems they completed in the minimum number of moves.

It is intriguing to consider what processes are involved in producing this specific impairment in initial thinking time. Although the pattern of impairment was similar to that seen in Parkinson's disease, different underlying processes may be involved in the two conditions. Thus, the prolonged initial thinking times in these patients may have been due to impairments in working memory function. Two further computerised tests were used to exclude this possibility. There was no significant difference found between the disorganisation syndrome groups in their Visual Spatial Span, which was determined using a computerised version of the Corsi Block Tapping Test (Milner, 1971). The deficit in performance is therefore not explicable by a deficit in spatial span. Patients were also assessed on a test of spatial working memory, involving finding counters in boxes on a computer screen (Morris et al., 1988). Performance on this task has been shown to be impaired in patients with frontal lobe lesions (Owen et al., 1990) whereas patients with Parkinson's disease perform normally (Morris et al., 1988). There was no difference between the high and low disorganisation groups in performance on this task, so impairments in spatial working memory could not explain the differences found in thinking times.

In seeking to explain the specific deficit seen in these patients, it is helpful to consider the two major components of the task during initial thinking or planning time, namely the time taken to formulate a plan and the time taken to put this plan into action. In our study, the patients may have difficulty in deciding on an appropriate plan of action for this novel task, a difficulty that would implicate the frontal lobes (Shallice, 1988). Frith and Done (1988) have suggested that such a deficit is important in explaining at least part of the problem in schizophrenia. Alternatively, the longer initial thinking time may have been due to a difficulty in the execution of a plan, after it had been selected, similar to the explanations that have been offered in the deficits observed in patients with Parkinson's disease and that have been attributed to dysfunction of the basal ganglia.

The results for the spatial working memory task, which allows strategy to be evaluated, found no difference in strategy between patients in the high and low disorganisation groups. This is similar to the pattern found in Parkinson's disease. In contrast, we found a significant association between performance on the spatial working memory task and the psychomotor poverty syndrome, such that those patients with high scores for the negative symptoms of flattening of affect and poverty of speech were significantly impaired on this task (Pantelis et al., unpublished data). This pattern is similar to that found in patients with frontal lobe lesions (Owen et al., 1990).

Taken collectively, the implication of these results is that patients with schizophrenia demonstrate impairments similar to those resulting from dysfunction of frontal–subcortical circuits (Alexander et al., 1986).

SUMMARY AND CONCLUSIONS

We have examined the evidence suggesting that the frontal–subcortical neuronal pathways are important in the pathogenesis of schizophrenia. Our investigations have explored the relationship of symptoms to cognitive impairment and our approach has been to focus on neuropsychological tests shown to be sensitive in establishing differences between cortical and frontal–subcortical dementias.

The results of our initial investigations suggest that negative symptoms are associated with bradyphrenia in a paper and pencil task, while a computerised test battery found an association with a test of spatial working memory, the latter test being sensitive to frontal lobe impairment. Patients scoring high on the disorganisation syndrome were demonstrated to have a prolonged initial thinking or planning time on another computerised test, this latter pattern being similar to that found in patients with Parkinson's disease.

The implications of these findings are that the frontal–subcortical system may be dysfunctional in schizophrenia and provide some clues as to the nature of the deficits in this disorder. Further work should be directed at establishing links between the various features of schizophrenia and neuropsychological impairment, particularly functions mediated by such frontal–subcortical neuronal pathways.

ACKNOWLEDGEMENTS

We would like to thank Dr Thomas Barnes, Dr Daniel Rogers and Dr Trevor Robbins for their support and helpful discussions relating to the ideas presented. We are grateful to the librarian at Horton Hospital, Mrs Kathleen Whitehead. We thank the Horton Hospital League of Friends and Westminster Association of Friends for financial support for the work being undertaken.

REFERENCES

Albert, M.L., Feldman, R.G., & Willis, A.L. (1974). The "subcortical dementia" of progressive supranuclear palsy. *Journal of Neurology, Neurosurgery, and Psychiatry*, *37*, 121–130.

Alexander, G.E., DeLong, M., & Strick, P.E. (1986). Parallel organization of functionally segregated circuits linking basal ganglia and cortex. *Annual Review of Neuroscience*, *9*, 357–381.

Andreasen, N.C. (1987). The diagnosis of schizophrenia. *Schizophrenia Bulletin*, *13* (1), 9–21.

Babcock, H. (1930). An experiment in the measurement of mental deterioration, *Archives of Psychology*, *18* (117), p. 100.

Babcock, H. (1933). *Dementia praecox, a psychological study*. Lancaster, PA: The Science Press.

Babcock, H. (1941). The level-efficiency theory of intelligence. *Journal of Psychology, 11*, 261–270.

Barnes, T.R.E. (1988). Tardive dyskinesia: Risk factors, pathophysiology and treatment. In K. Granville-Grossman, *Recent advances in clinical psychiatry, number six* (pp. 195–205). London: Churchill Livingstone.

Bauman, E., & Murray, D.J. (1968). Recognition versus recall in schizophrenia. *Canadian Journal of Psychology, 22*, 18–25.

Berman, K.F., Illowsky, B.P., & Weinberger, D.R. (1988). Physiologic dysfunction of dorsolateral prefrontal cortex in schizophrenia. IV. Further evidence for regional and behavioural specificity. *Archives of General Psychiatry, 45*, 616–622.

Berman, K.F., Zec, R.F., & Weinberger, D.R. (1986). Physiology dysfunction of dorsolateral prefrontal cortex in schizophrenia. II. Role of neuroleptic treatment, attention, and mental effort. *Archives of General Psychiatry, 43*, 126–135.

Bowman, M., & Lewis, M.S. (1980). Sites of subcortical damage in diseases which resemble schizophrenia. *Neuropsychologia, 18*, 597–601.

Brown, R.G., & Marsden, C.D. (1988) 'Subcortical dementia': The neuropsychological evidence. *Neuroscience, 25*, 363–387.

Buscaino, V.M. (1920). Le cause anatoma-pathologiche della manifestatione schizophrenica della demenza precoce. *Ric Pathologia Nervus Mental, 25*. 193–226.

Butters, N., Salmon, D.P., Granholm, E, Heindel, W., & Lyon, L. (1987). Neuropsychological differentiation of amnesic and dementing states. In S.M. Stahl, S.D. Iversen & E.C. Goodman (Eds.), *Cognitive neurochemistry*, (pp. 3–20). Oxford: Oxford University Press.

Chelune, G.J., Heaton, R.K., Lehman, R.A., & Robinson, A. (1979). Level versus pattern of neuropsychological performance among schizophrenic and diffusely brain damaged patients. *Journal of Consulting and Clinical Psychology, 47*, 155–163.

Crosson, B. (1985). Subcortical functions in language: A working model. *Brain and Languages, 25*, 257–292.

Crosson, B., & Hughes, C.W. (1987). Role of the thalamus in language: Is it related to schizophrenic thought disorder? *Schizophrenia Bulletin, 13(4)*, 605–621.

Crow, T.J. (1980). Molecular pathology of schizophrenia: More than one disease process. *British Medical Journal, 1*, 66–68.

Cummings, J.L. (1986). Subcortical dementia: Neuropsychology, neuropsychiatry, and pathophysiology. *The British Journal of Psychiatry, 149*, 682–697.

Cutting, J. (1985). *The psychology of schizophrenia*. London: Churchill Livingstone.

DeLong, M.R., Alexander, G.E., Miller, W.C., & Crutcher, M.D. (1990). Anatomical and functional aspects of basal ganglia–thalamocortical circuits. In A.J. Franks, J.W. Ironside, H.S. Mindham, R.J. Smith, E.G.S. Spokes & W. Winlow (Eds.), *Function and dysfunction in the basal ganglia*, (pp. 3–32). Manchester: Manchester University Press.

Dubois, B., Pillon, B., Legault, F., Agid, Y., & Lhermitte, F. (1988). Slowing in cognitive processing in progressive supranuclear palsy. *Archives of Neurology, 45*, 1194–1199.

Eslinger, P.J., & Damasio, A.R. (1986). Preserved motor learning in Alzheimer's disease: Implications for anatomy and behaviour. *Journal of Neuroscience, 6*, 3006–3009.

Eysenck, H.J., Granger, G.W., & Brengelmann, J.C. (1957). *Perceptual processes and mental illness*, Maudsley Monograph No. 2. London: Institute of Psychiatry.

Fisher, J.M., Kennedy, J.L., Caine, E.D., & Shoulson, I. (1983). Dementia in Huntington's disease: a cross-sectional analysis of intellectual decline. In R. Mayeux & W.G. Rosen (Eds.), *The dementias* (pp. 229–238). New York: Raven Press.

Freedman, M. (1990). Parkinson's disease. In J.L. Cummings (Ed.), *Subcortical dementia* (pp. 108–122). Oxford: Oxford University Press.

Freedman, M., & Oscar-Berman, M. (1986a). Selective delayed response deficits in Parkinson's and Alzheimer's disease. *Archives of Neurology, 43*, 886–890.

Freedman, M., & Oscar-Berman, M. (1987). Tactile discrimination learning deficits in Parkinson's and Alzheimer's disease. *Archives of Neurology, 44*, 394–398.

Frith, C.D., & Done, D.J. (1988). Towards a neuropsychology of schizophrenia. *British Journal of Psychiatry, 153*, 437–443.

Goldberg, T.E., & Weinberger, D.R. (1988). Probing prefrontal function in schizophrenia with neuropsychological paradigms. *Schizophrenia Bulletin, 14*(2), 179–183.

Goldberg, T.E., Weinberger, D.R., Berman, K.F., Pliskin, N.H., & Podd, M.H. (1987). Further evidence for dementia of the prefrontal type in schizophrenia? A controlled study of teaching the Wisconsin Card Sorting Test. *Archives of General Psychiatry, 44*(11), 1008–10014.

Goldstein, G. (1986). The neuropsychology of schizophrenia. In I. Grant & K. Adams (Eds.), *Neuropsychological assessment of neuropsychiatric disorders*, pp. 147–171. Oxford: Oxford University Press.

Gotham, A.M., Brown, R.G., & Marsden, C.D. (1988). "Frontal" cognitive function in patients with Parkinson's disease "on" and "off" levodopa. *Brain, 111*, 299–321.

Grafman, J., Weingartner, H., Newhouse, P.A., Thompson, K., Lalonde, F., Litvan, I., Molchan, S., & Sunderland, T. (1990). Implicit learning in patients with Alzheimer's disease. *Pharmacopsychiatry, 23*(2), 94–101.

Groenewegen, H.J., Berendse, H.W., Meredith, G.E., Haber, S.N., Voorn, P., Walters, J.G., & Lohman, A.H.M. (1991). Functional anatomy of the ventral, limbic system-innervated striatum. In P. Willner & J. Scheel-Kruger (Eds.), *The mesolimbic dopamine system: From motivation to action* (pp. 19–59). Chichester: John Wiley & Sons.

Harris, A., & Metcalfe, M. (1956). Inappropriate affect. *Journal of Neurology and psychiatry, 19*, 308–313.

Heaton, R.K., Baade, L.E., & Johnson, K.L. (1978). Neuropsychological test results associated with psychiatric disorders in adults. *Psychological Bulletin, 85*, 141–162.

Heaton, R.K., & Crowley, T.J. (1981). Effects of psychiatric disorders and their somatic treatments on neuropsychological test results. In S.V. Filscow, & T.J. Boll (Eds.), *Handbook of clinical neuropsychology* (pp. 481–525). New York: John Wiley & Sons.

Heindel, W.C., Butters, N., & Salmon, D.P. (1987). Impaired motor skill learning associated with neostriatal dysfunction (Abstract). *Journal of Clinical and Experimental Neuropsychology, 9*, 18.

Heindel, W.C., Butters, N., & Salmon, D.P. (1988). Impaired learning of a motor skill in patients with Huntington's disease. *Behavioural Neuroscience, 102*(1), 141–147.

Hemsley, D.R. (1982). Cognitive impairment in schizophrenia. In A. Burton (Ed.), *The pathology and psychology of cognition* (pp. 169–203). London: Methuen.

Holzman, P.S. (1987). Recent studies of psychophysiology in schizophrenia. *Schizophrenia Bulletin, 13*(1), 49–75.

Huber, S.J., & Shuttleworth, E.C. (1990) Neuropsychological assessment of subcortical dementia. In J.L. Cummings (Ed.), *Subcortical dementia* (pp. 71–86). Oxford, Oxford University Press.

Koh, S.D. (1978). Remembering of verbal material by schizophrenic young adults. In S. Schwartz (Ed.), *Language and cognition in schizophrenia*. Hillsdale, N.J.: Laurence Erlbaum Associates Inc.

Koh, S.D., Kayton, L., & Schwartz, C. (1974). The structure of word-storage in the permanent memory of nonpsychotic schizophrenics. *Journal of Consulting and Clinical Psychology, 42*, 879–887.

Koh, S.D., & Peterson, E.A. (1978). Encoding orientation and the remembering of schizophrenic young adults. *Journal of Abnormal Psychology, 87*, 303.

Kolb, B., & Wishaw, I.Q. (1983). Performance of schizophrenic patients on tests sensitive to left or right frontal, temporal or parietal function in neurological patients. *Journal of Nervous and Mental Disease, 171*, 435–443.

Lees, J., & Smith, E. (1983). Cognitive deficits in the early stages of Parkinson's disease. *Brain*, *106*, 257–270.

Liddle, P.F. (1987a). The symptoms of chronic schizophrenia: A re-examination of the positive-negative dichotomy. *British Journal of Psychiatry*, *151*, 145–151.

Liddle, P.J. (1987b). Schizophrenic syndromes, cognitive performance and neurological dysfunction. *Psychological Medicine*, *17*, 49–57.

Liddle, P.F., & Barnes, T.R.E. (1990). The symptoms of chronic schizophrenia. *British Journal of Psychiatry*, *157*, 558–561.

Liddle, P.F., Friston, K.J., Frith, C.D., Hirsch, S.R., Jones, T., & Frackowiak, R.S.J. (1992). Patterns of cerebral blood flow in schizophrenia. *British Journal of Psychiatry*, *160*, 179–186.

Liddle, P.F., & Morris, D. (1991). Schizophrenic syndromes and frontal lobe performance. *British Journal of Psychiatry*, *158*, 340–345.

Lidsky, T.I., Weinhold, P.M., & Levine, F.M. (1979). Implications of basal ganglionic dysfunction for schizophrenia. *Biological Psychiatry*, *14*, 3–12.

Martone, M., Butters, N., Payne, M., Becker, J., & Sax, D.S. (1984). Dissociations between skill learning and verbal recognition in amnesia and dementia. *Archives of Neurology*, *41*, 965–970.

McGrath, J. (1991). Ordering thoughts on thought disorder. *British Journal of Psychiatry*, *158*, 307–316.

McKenna, P.J. (1990). Basal ganglia dysfunction in schizophrenia? In A.J. Franks, J.W. Ironside, R.H.S. Mindham, R.J. Smith, E.G.S. Spoker, & W. Winlow (Eds.), *Function and dysfunction in the basal ganglia* (pp. 247–255). Manchester: Manchester University Press.

Mettler, F.A. (1955). Perceptual capacity, functions of the striatum and schizophrenia. *Psychiatric Quarterly*, *29*, 89.

Milner, B. (1971). Interhemispheric differences in the localization of psychological processes in man. *British Medical Bulletin*, *27*, 272–277.

Morice, R. (1990). Cognitive inflexibility and pre-frontal dysfunction in schizophrenia and mania. *British Journal of Psychiatry*, *157*, 50–54.

Morris, R.G., Downes, J.J., Sahakian, B.J., Evendon, J.L., Heald, A., & Robbins, T.W. (1988). Planning and spatial working memory in Parkinson's disease. *Journal of Neurology, Neurosurgery, and Psychiatry*, *51*, 757–766.

Nauta, W.J.H. (1986). A simplified perspective on the basal ganglia and their relation to the limbic system. In B.K. Doane & K.E. Livingston (Eds.), *The limbic system: Functional organization and clinical disorders* (pp. 43–54). New York: Raven Press.

Naville, F. (1992). Les complications des sequelles mentales de l'encephalite epidemique. *L'encephale*, *17*, 369–375.

Nelson, H.E., Pantelis, C., Carruthers, K., Speller, J., Baxendale, S., & Barnes, T.R.E. (1990). Cognitive functioning and symptomatology in chronic schizophrenia. *Psychological Medicine*, *20*, 357–365.

Oke, A.F., & Adams, R.N. (1987). Elevated thalamic dopamine: Possible link to sensory dysfunctions in schizophrenia. *Schizophrenia Research*, *13*(4), 589–604.

Owen, A.M., Downes, J.J., Sahakian, B.J., Polkey, C.E., & Robbins, T.W. (1990). Planning and spatial working memory following frontal lobe lesions in man. *Neuropsychologia*, *28*, 1021–1034.

Pantelis, C., Barnes, T.R.E., & Nelson, H.E. (1989). A pilot study of subcortical dementia in schizophrenia (Abstract). *Schizophrenia Research*, *2*, 69.

Pantelis, C., Barnes, T.R.E., Nelson, H.E., & Robbins, T. (1991). The nature of dementia in schizophrenia. Abstracts of The Royal College of Psychiatrists, Annual Meeting, 2–6 July 1991, *Psychiatric Bulletin of The Royal College of Psychiatrists*, *15 (Suppl. 4)*, 63–64.

Pantelis, C., Barnes, T.R.E., & Nelson, H.E. (1992). Is the concept of frontal–subcortical dementia relevant to schizophrenia? *British Journal of Psychiatry, 160*, 442–460.
Patterson, T. (1987). Studies toward the subcortical pathogenesis of schizophrenia. *Schizophrenia Bulletin, 13 (No. 4)*, 555–576.
Pillon, B., Dubois, B., Lhermitte, F., & Agid, Y. (1986). Heterogeneity of cognitive impairment in progressive supranuclear palsy, Parkinson's disease, and Alzheimer's disease. *Neurology, 36*, 1179–1185.
Reading, P.J. (1991). Frontal lobe dysfunction in schizophrenia and Parkinson's disease—a meeting point for neurology, psychology and psychiatry: Discussion paper. *Journal of the Royal Society of Medicine, 84*, 349–353.
Robbins, T.W. (1990). The case for fronto-striatal dysfunction in schizophrenia. *Schizophrenia Bulletin, 16*(3), 391–402.
Robbins, T.W. (1991). Cognitive deficits in schizophrenia and Parkinson's disease: Neural basis and the role of dopamine. In P. Willner & J.Scheel-Kruger (Eds.), *The Mesolimbic Dopamine System: From Motivation to Action* (pp. 497–528). Chichester: John Wiley & Sons.
Rogers, D. (1986). Bradyphrenia in parkinsonism: A historical review. *Psychological Medicine, 16*, 257–265.
Sagar, H.J., Cohen, N.J., Corkin, S., & Growden, J.H. (1985). Dissociations among processes in remote memory. In D.S. Olton, E. Gamzu, & S. Corkin (Eds.), *Memory dysfunctions: An integration of animal and human research from preclinical and clinical perspectives* (pp. 533–535). New York: New York Academy of Science.
Sahakian, B.J., Morris, R.G., Evendon, J.L., Heald, A., Levy, R., Philpot, M., & Robbins, T.W. (1988). A comparative study of visuospatial memory and learning in Alzheimer-type dementia and Parkinson's disease. *Brain, 111*, 695–718.
Sandyk, R., & Kay, S.R. (1990a). Is negative schizophrenia a variant of Parkinsonism? (Letter). *International Journal of Neuroscience, 53*(2–4), 235–240.
Sandyk, R., & Kay, S.R. (1990b). The relationship of negative schizophrenia to parkinsonism. *International Journal of Neuroscience, 55*(1), 1–59.
Sandyk, R., & Kay, S.R. (1991). The significance of the basal ganglia for schizophrenia (Letter). *Behavioural and Brain Sciences, 14*, 45–46.
Senf, R., Huston, P.E., & Cohen, B.D. (1955). Thinking deficit in schizophrenia and changes with amytal. *Journal of Abnormal (Soc.) Psychology, 50*, 383–387.
Shallice, T. (1982). Specific impairments in planning. *Philosophical Transactions of the Royal Society (London), B298*, 199–209.
Shallice, T. (1988). *From neuropsychology to mental structure.* Cambridge: Cambridge University Press.
Shallice, T., Burgess, P.W., & Frith, C.D. (1991). Can the neuropsychology case-study approach be applied to schizophrenia? *Psychological Medicine, 21*, 661–673.
Shapiro, M.B., & Nelson, E.H. (1955). An investigation of the nature of cognitive impairment in co-operative psychiatric patients, *British Journal of Medical Psychology, 28*, 239–256.
Swerdlow, N.R., & Koob, G.F. (1987). Dopamine, schizophrenia, mania and depression: Towards a unified hypothesis of cortic–striato–pallido–thalamic function. *Behavioural and Brain Sciences, 10*, 197–245.
Traupman, K.L. (1975). Effects of categorization and imagery on recognition and recall by process and reaction schizophrenics. *Journal of Abnormal Psychology, 75*, 182–186.
Tweedy, J.R., Langer, K.G., & McDowell, F.H. (1982). The effect of semantic relations on the memory deficit associated with Parkinson's disease. *Journal of Clinical Neuropsychology, 4*, 235–247.
Weinberger, D.R., Berman, K.F., & Illowsky, B.P. (1988b). Physiologic dysfunction of dorsolateral prefrontal cortex in schizophrenia. III. A new cohort and evidence for a monoamingergic mechanism. *Archives of General Psychiatry, 45*, 609–615.

Weinberger, D.R., Berman, K.F., & Zec, R.F. (1986). Physiologic dysfunction of dorsolateral prefrontal cortex in schizophrenia. I. Regional cerebral blood flow evidence. *Archives of General Psychiatry*, *43*, 114–124.

14 Evidence for Right Hemisphere Dysfunction in Schizophrenia

J. Cutting
Institute of Psychiatry, London.

The role of right hemisphere dysfunction in schizophrenia is reviewed in this chapter. Four categories of evidence are examined: neuropsychological analogies, neuropsychiatric analogies, neurobiological findings and neuropsychological test data. The neuropsychological analogies comprise the development of a typical schizophrenic phenomenon under conditions of definite focal brain damage, e.g. the experience of an alien quality to one's own voice with right parietal damage. The neuropsychiatric analogies are the *clinical syndromes* which occur with focal brain damage, e.g. epileptic psychoses. The neurobiological evidence comes from electrophysiological, neuropathological and scan studies. The neuropsychological test results are those in which specific one-or-other hemisphere-sensitive tests are used, rather than test batteries. I argue that right hemisphere dysfunction in schizophrenia is amply supported by the above four categories of evidence.

INTRODUCTION

Since Flor-Henry (1969) first suggested a disturbance in the usual balance of hemispheric functions in schizophrenia, there has been a growth of publications on the issue. Like Flor-Henry, the majority of these have incriminated the left hemisphere in some way. A mere handful of us have pointed to the right hemisphere as the focus of the primary, pathogenetic disturbance. I myself, in a number of publications between 1985 and 1990 (Cutting, 1985, 1990) and Oepen (Oepen et al., 1987), have most consistently espoused this viewpoint.

What I am going to do in this chapter is to review the *categories* of evidence for my belief. I do not intend to examine the detailed methodological problems surrounding each claim and counterclaim, but I shall take a broad view.

For the sake of convenience, the evidence can be considered to fall into four main categories:

1. Neuropsychological analogies. (*Actual* focal right hemisphere lesions producing identical phenomena to those of schizophrenia).
2. Neuropsychological test results. (Valid "right hemisphere" tests being impaired in schizophrenia).
3. Neurobiological findings. (Scan, post mortem, neurophysiological abnormalities in right hemisphere of schizophrenics).
4. Neuropsychiatric analogies. (*Actual* right hemisphere disease mimicking part or all of the schizophrenic syndrome).

NEUROPSYCHOLOGICAL ANALOGIES

There are a large number of neuropsychological analogies, but I am going to restrict myself only to those where the phenomenon is virtually identical to that encountered in schizophrenia. It is not correct to draw support for the theory of left-sided dysfunction in schizophrenia by pointing out that both temporal lobe epileptics with a left-sided lesion *and* schizophrenics both experience auditory hallucinations. The fact that the same proportion of temporal lobe epileptics with right-sided lesions as those with left-sided lesions also experience auditory hallucinations (Penfield & Perot, 1963) is not the main problem with this claim. The main problem is that the description given by observers or subjects of their auras or ictal experiences is quite unlike that of schizophrenics when describing *their* voices. If one reads the accounts given by Penfield and Perot's enormous collection of subjects, there is not one reference to voices in the third person commenting, voices echoing thoughts, or voices arguing about the subject. They are mainly voices of people familiar to the subject in the past saying and doing what they actually did do in the past.

This overreadiness to equate any psychotic phenomenon that occurs in someone with definite brain damage with a similar schizophrenic phenomenon extends to most, if not all, areas of phenomenology. Because someone with frontal lobe damage appears apathetic, and because some schizophrenics are also apathetic, this is interpreted as evidence that the former deficit underlies the latter condition.

In the list that appears in Table 14.1, I have tried to match the phenomena as closely as possible, and not just use broad psychopathological categories such as hallucination, delusion, apathy, etc.

TABLE 14.1
Neuropsychological Analogies with Schizophrenia

Characteristic schizophrenic phenomenon	Neuropsychological analogy
Auditory hallucinations of specific sorts of voices	Hoff and Silbermann's (1933) experiment
Disordered self-body boundaries	Bogousslavsky and Regli's (1988) "response-to-next-patient" syndrome
Annihilation of will as in catatonia	Coslett and Heilman's (1989) localisation of will to move
Flattened affect	Aprosody
Delusional misidentification	Capgras' syndrome in right-hemisphere-damaged subjects
Formal thought disorder	Incoherent speech in right-hemisphere-damaged subjects
	Incorrect proverb interpretation
	Impaired estimation of cost of common objects

Auditory Hallucinations of Specific Sorts of Voices

Hoff and Silbermann (1933) anaesthetised the right temporoparietal lobe of one subject who was about to undergo surgery for a tumour. During this procedure, the subject:

> ... had the feeling that suddenly her speech seemed strange, as if someone was in her place, speaking what she herself was thinking.

This is without doubt exactly what a schizophrenic experiences.

Disordered Self-body Boundaries

Bogousslavsky and Regli (1988) reported 11 patients, all with an acute cerebrovascular accident involving the right hemisphere, with what they called "response-to-next-patient-stimulation". The patients would obey commands, e.g. "open your mouth", that were, in fact, addressed to patients in the bed next to them. A patient that I saw myself, with an acute right middle cerebral artery infarct, had an even more specific dissolution of self/body boundaries. When I showed her a picture, she said, "It's wrapped behind me. It's all muddled up in my pillow." Her main concern was that when other patients used the ward sink, which was beside her bed, they were actually scrubbing her back.

A breakdown in the boundary of self and body is, in fact, very common in schizophrenia. Consider the following schizophrenic woman: she experienced her own face intermingled with mine as I talked to her, she felt her body melt into doors as she passed them and her head dissipate into lamp-posts as she passed them.

Annihilation of Will

Coslett and Heilman (1989) reported the results of 18 subjects—nine with a right- and nine with a left-sided middle cerebral artery infarct (paired for size and location on CT scan)—who were asked to raise first their left and then their right shoulders. Shoulder elevation was used because the motor strip responsible for this is rarely infarcted. The elevation was measured, and it was found that patients with a right hemisphere lesion were more impaired in raising the contralateral shoulder than those with a left hemisphere lesion. The results were independent of the extent of the hemiparesis. The crucial point was that the "intention" to raise the contralateral shoulder was more affected by a lesion in the *right* than in the *left* hemisphere.

The fundamental feature of schizophrenic catatonia is loss of will—whether the precise phenomenon is negativism, stereotypy, catalepsy, or ambivalence—and it is my contention that the right hemisphere is critical in supplying this component. In this neuropsychological analogy, I have strayed a little in my aim of supplying identical phenomena in neuropsychology and schizophrenia, but there seems to me an analogy all the same.

Flattened Affect

There is a powerful analogy here between the effect on speech of a right hemisphere lesion and the sort of phenomenon one sees in schizophrenia. In fact, the only difference is in the names neurologists and psychiatrists give to it.

Ross (1981) identified an abnormality in the prosodic characteristics of speech following right hemisphere lesions. Patients would have no phonemic, syntactic, or semantic problems, but would be unable to convey (if the lesion was anterior) or comprehend (if the lesion was posterior) the emotional component of speech. This aprosody was thus the right-hemisphere-damage counterpart of left-hemisphere-damage aphasia.

But flattening of affect, a characteristic (though unreliably rated) aspect of schizophrenia, is a composite of poorly modulated speech, unchanging facial expression, and impoverished bodily emotion, and so again we have a right-hemisphere-based analogy for a central feature of schizophrenia.

Delusional Misidentification

Capgras' syndrome, the belief that a familiar person has become an imposter, was, until recently, regarded as a psychiatric curiosity. Now, it is quite clear that not only is it a relatively common consequence of definite organic brain disease, but, more specifically, of right hemisphere dysfunction. In a literature review, Feinberg and Shapiro (1989) found 26 cases with unequivocal evidence of brain damage—16 bilateral, eight right-sided and only two left- sided.

Moreover, it is now considered appropriate (Joseph, 1986) to include Capgras' syndrome in the wider category of delusional misidentification syndromes, and these are very common in schizophrenia. The most common cause of Capgras' syndrome itself is schizophrenia (Kimura, 1986) and, in a series of my own schizophrenics, no less than 40% had some form of delusional misidentification.

Formal Thought Disorder

Finally, formal thought disorder, an otherwise baffling aspect of schizophrenia, can be equated with some of the speech/language sequelae of right hemisphere damage.

For virtually a century after Broca's localisation of the speech centre within the left hemisphere, the right hemisphere's possible role in speech, language, or thought was completely ruled out. In the last three decades, this remarkable oversight has been reversed, and the right hemisphere is now credited with contributing the lion's share to metaphor (Winner & Gardner, 1977) and pragmatic conversation (Foldi, 1987).

More specifically, for the purposes of my argument, there are reports that right-hemisphere-damaged subjects exhibit phenomena or psychological deficits almost exactly like those seen in schizophrenia—"incoherent and tangential speech" (Joanette et al., 1986), incorrect proverb interpretation (Benton, 1968), and even impaired common sense, in the form of a reduced capacity to estimate the cost of common objects (Smith & Milner, 1984).

Summary of Neuropsychological Analogies

Some of those quoted are anecdotal, but most are generalisable and, without exception, the phenomena exhibited in right-hemisphere-damaged patients are much more like those seen in schizophrenics than any found in their left-hemisphere-damaged counterparts.

NEUROPSYCHOLOGICAL TEST RESULTS

Here again, it is possible to select a number of studies that have demonstrated right hemisphere dysfunction in schizophrenics, using specific tests that have a high validity for picking up right hemisphere damage in those with actual focal lesions in this hemisphere.

The problem in the past has been that vast batteries of tests, e.g. Luria–Nebraska, Halstead–Reitan, have been administered without any appreciation that these batteries were designed to identify subjects with *generalised* organic brain damage. Moreover, some of these batteries were actually standardised using *schizophrenics* as *non-brain-damaged controls*!

I should like to mention three areas of dysfunction which I have personally investigated:

1. Facial–emotion perception tests.
2. Speech–emotion perception and expression tests.
3. Linguistic tests.

Facial–emotion Perception Tests

Over 10 years ago, before formulating my views on right hemisphere involvement in schizophrenia, I carried out the following experiment. It is relevant to my theme because the perception of facial emotion in others has, in the last 15 years, been specifically linked with the right hemisphere (Ley & Bryden, 1979).

The experiment (Cutting, 1981) involved 20 schizophrenics in remission (to control for the state-trait issue), 10 psychotic depressives (to control for the issue of psychosis in general) and 20 floridly acute schizophrenics (Table 14.2). Each subject was shown three sets of 20 pairs of faces—ones that standardisers had agreed on that one was more *friendly* than the other, that one was more *mean* than the other, and that one was *older* than the other. From Table 14.2 it is clear that the acutely psychotic schizophrenics differed from the other two groups in their deviant choices—relative to normal standardisation—on friendliness and meanness but not on age; these differences were statistically significant. This is illustrated in Table 14.3.

In fact, in a subsequent study (Gessler et al., 1989) we showed that schizophrenics were also deviant, relative to normals and depressed subjects, in estimating age of a face. This does not undermine my hypothesis concerning right hemisphere dysfunction in schizophrenia, because De Renzi et al. (1989) found that this was a right hemisphere function too, and the age-perception task I had originally used was probably too easy, and could be successfully completed with the aid of one or two simple cues, e.g. baldness, glasses (a possible left-hemisphere-based facility).

TABLE 14.2
Facial–emotion Perception Experiment

	Agreement on age, friendliness and meanness		
	Remitted psychotics	Psychotic depressives	Acute schizophrenics
Number	20	10	20
Age	39.6	40.0	37.9
Sex ratio (m:f)	9:11	5:5	6:14
IQ (Nelson reading test)	101.7	105.3	101.2
Age (older/20)	16.5	15.2	15.7
Friendliness (more friendly/20)	16.9	15.4	13.2
Meanness (more mean/20)	16.5	15.7	12.9

TABLE 14.3
Facial-emotion Perception Experiment

	Age			Friendliness			Meanness		
Score	Rem. psych.	Psych. dep.	Ac. schiz.	Rem. psych.	Psych. dep.	Ac. schiz.	Rem. psych.	Psych. dep.	Ac. schiz.
20		x		xxxx	x	x	x		
19	xx		xx	x		x	x		x
18	xxxx	x	xxxx	xxx	xx	x	xxxxxx	xx	x
17	xxxx	x		xxxx	x	xxxx	xxxx	xx	
16	xxxxxx	xx	xxxxxx	x	xxx	x	xxxx	xxx	xx
15	x	x	xxxx	xx	x			xx	xxx
14	xx	xx	xx	xxxxx		x	xx		x
13		x					x		xxx
12	x					xxx			xxx
11			x			x			xx
10					x	xx	x		
9		x				xxx		x	xx
8			x		x	x			x
7						x			
6									x

Rem. psych., remitted psychotics; Psych. dep., psychotic depressives; Ac. schiz., acute schizophrenics.

Speech–emotion Perception and Expression Tasks

In the following experiment (Murphy & Cutting, 1990) I attempted to establish whether schizophrenics had the sort of emotional aprosody that Ross (1981) claimed was characteristic of patients with focal right hemisphere damage.

Fifteen acute schizophrenics, 15 manics, 15 depressives, and 15 normal controls were given four tasks: (1) stress prosody comprehension (10 sentences read out to them to select which word was stressed); (2) stress prosody expression (10 sentences that they had to read out stressing an underlined word, their performance later judged by five normal raters); (3) emotional prosody comprehension (10 sentences read out to them to select which of four emotions the speaker intended—neutral, sad, happy, angry); (4) emotional prosody expression (10 sentences that they had to read out in one of the above four designated emotions, and subsequently rated by the five judges as correctly or incorrectly corresponding to the designated emotion). The results (Table 14.4) show a significant impairment, relative to normals, in the ability of schizophrenics to both comprehend and express emotional prosody, but no difference from normals on the issue of stress prosody. Relative to the depressives and manics, the schizophrenics were only statistically significantly different in their expression of emotional prosody.

Right-hemisphere-specific Linguistic Task

The contribution of the right hemisphere to thought and language is well illustrated in a study by Brownell et al. (1984), in which subjects with either left- or right-sided brain damage were asked to choose pairs of words "which went together best" from a triad. In each triad the pairings could be on the basis of a metaphorical similarity, e.g. cold and hateful from the triad "cold, warm, hateful". Or they could be based on a simple antonymic

TABLE 14.4
Speech–emotion Perception and Expression

	Schizophrenics (n = 15)	Manics (n = 15)	Depressives (n = 15)	Normals (n = 15)
Age—mean	27.9**	37.8	41.5	38.2
Sex distribution—m:f	10:5	8:7	7:8	8:7
IQ—mean	113.5	112.6	109.4	108.5
Prosody results—mean (SD)				
Stress comprehension/10	8.5 (0.7)	8.1** (0.7)	9.2 (0.6)	9.0 (0.6)
Emotion comprehension/10	7.5** (0.8)	7.9** (0.9)	7.7* (0.8)	8.8 (0.7)
Stress expression/10	7.5 (0.7)	8.1 (0.7)	7.9 (0.6)	7.5 (0.9)
Emotion expression/10	4.3* (0.9)	5.4†† (0.8)	5.3† (0.9)	5.2 (1.1)

Significance levels of *post hoc* t-test comparisons between normals and other groups * $P < 0.05$; ** $P < 0.01$.

Significance levels of *post hoc* t-test comparisons between schizophrenics and affective groups: † $P < 0.05$; †† $P < 0.01$.

relationship, e.g. cold and warm from the same triad. In Brownell et al.'s study patients with left-sided brain damage chose the metaphorical pairings significantly more often than they did the antonymic pairings; the converse was true of right-hemisphere-damaged subjects.

If my hypothesis of right-sided dysfunction in schizophrenia is correct, then schizophrenics should eschew metaphorical pairings in favour of antonymic pairings. The results (Cutting & Murphy, 1990) (Table 14.5) are in line with this. In fact, the possible pairings are more complicated, but taking these into account, there was a statistically significant difference between the schizophrenics' tendency to choose along antonymic lines and the other groups' tendency to choose along metaphorical lines.

Summary of Neuropsychological Test Results

On the basis of the few tests reported here, there is a tendency for schizophrenics to perform more like subjects with a definitive right hemisphere lesion than those with a left hemisphere lesion. The point about this category of evidence is that the tests given are designer-specific for a right hemisphere lesion and the results can be regarded as much more significant than any weighting on some hemisphere scale of a vast battery of tests.

NEUROBIOLOGICAL FINDINGS

Here, the evidence is not entirely in favour of my thesis, to say the least. However, although vast amounts of money and time have been expended in the last decade on increasingly sophisticated scanning techniques, a kind of intellectual shutter comes down when investigators start interpreting their results. I blame Flor-Henry for this, for producing the intellectual set that left-hemisphere dysfunction is at the root of schizophrenia. Although I regard Flor-Henry as a genius for introducing the notion of hemisphere imbalance in the psychoses in the first place, in the face of apathy, cynicism, and, in some cases, accusations of charlatanism, subsequent investigators have, in many instances, simply not looked carefully at their own data.

TABLE 14.5
Metaphorical/antonymic Choices of Schizophrenics and Controls

	Schizophrenics	Manics	Depressives
Number of metaphor pairs/20	7.2	8.3	8.3
Number of antonym pairs/20	7.8	5.8	6.5

I am not going to provide an exhaustive review of all the studies on this issue, but I should like to exhort investigators to take an unbiased view of their data.

NEUROPSYCHIATRIC ANALOGIES

In Flor-Henry's original report on epileptic psychoses, there were 28 patients with a schizophrenia-like psychosis: 19 with a left-sided focus and nine with a right-sided one. Several reanalyses of his cohort have since been published. In fact the temporal lobe epileptics channelled through the Maudsley Hospital Neurosurgical Unit in the last 30 years must be the most reported on patients in the history of psychiatry. There are at least ten publications on different subsets of them, each arriving at a different proportion of left/right lesions. The latest (Roberts et al., 1990) gives figures of 15 left-sided and ten right-sided lesions among 25 instances of schizophrenia-like psychoses—a non-significant left–right difference. Of particular interest to my thesis is the fact that the left–right proportions are in different directions when one divides the cases up into those whose psychosis coincides with an *active epileptogenic focus* and those whose psychosis only occurs *after a lobectomy*. Moreover, the proportions are different again when one considers the handful of cases whose psychosis disappears when a lobectomy is performed. These issues are examined in Table 14.6. The crucial points in Roberts et al.'s study are: (1) of those epileptics who first became psychotic after their lobectomy, five had right lobectomies and four had left lobectomies; (2) of those epileptics whose psychosis resolved after a lobectomy, four had a left-sided lesion and none had a right-sided lesion; (3) this leaves figures of 11 left- and five right-sided actively discharging foci being associated with a schizophrenia-like psychosis.

Two other studies support the notion that a schizophrenia-like psychosis is linked *either* with an actively discharging left-sided focus *or* a resected right-sided temporal lobe. Perez et al. (1985) reported nine patients with an actively discharging temporal focus and a schizophrenia-like psychosis—seven left-sided and two right-sided. Mace and Trimble (1991) reported six patients whose schizophrenia-like psychosis followed a temporal lobectomy, and *all* had right lobectomies.

One final study supporting my contention can be mentioned. This was carried out by Parnas et al. (1982). Of 18 patients with active temporal lobe epilepsy and a "non-affective psychosis", 12 had a left-sided lesion and six had a right-sided lesion. But when the phenomenology of these psychoses were analysed, 11 of the 12 with a left-sided lesion were strictly classified as paranoia or a paranoid–hallucinatory state (leaving only one "Bleulerian schizophrenic"). Among the right-sided instances, three had "Bleulerian

TABLE 14.6
Re-examination of Flor-Henry's Epileptic Psychosis Model of Left-hemisphere
Dysfunction and Schizophrenia

Roberts et al. *(1990)*
25 epileptics with a schizophrenia-like psychosis; altogether 15 left-sided, 10 right-sided but:
a) those with active focus—11 left-sided, 5 right-sided
b) those with postlobectomy psychosis—4 left-sided, 5 right-sided
c) those with postlobectomy resolution of psychosis—4 left-sided, 0 right-sided

Perez et al. *(1985)*
9 epileptics with active focus and schizophrenia; altogether 7 left-sided, 2 right-sided

Mace and Trimble (1991)
6 patients with postlobectomy psychosis; all 6 right-sided

Parnas et al. *(1982)*
18 patients with active focus and non-affective psychosis; altogether 12 left-sided, 6 right-sided but:
a) left-sided cases—11 paranoia or paranoid-hallucinatory state
1 "Bleulerian schizophrenia"
b) right-sided cases—3 paranoia/paranoid–hallucinatory state
3 "Bleulerian schizophrenia"

---

schizophrenia" and three had paranoia or a paranoid–hallucinatory state.

The lesson to be learnt from such detailed analyses is two-fold: (1) an abnormal but present temporal lobe has a different pathogenetic effect from an absent lobe; and (2) phenomenological differences may occur in psychoses associated with a dysfunctional/absent temporal lobe between each hemisphere.

CONCLUSION

To my mind, the evidence linking schizophrenia with right hemisphere dysfunction is overwhelming. In this paper I have tried to point out some of the positive pieces of evidence and show some of the flaws in the evidence purportedly supporting left hemisphere dysfunction.

REFERENCES

Benton, A.L. (1968). Differential behavioural effects of frontal lobe disease. *Neuropsychologia*, *6*, 53–60.

Bogousslavsky, J., & Regli, F. (1988). Response-to-next-patient-stimulation: A right hemisphere syndrome. *Neurology*, *38*, 1225–1227.

Brownell, H.H., Potter, H.H., Michelow, D., & Gardner, H. (1984). Sensitivity to lexical denotation and connotation in brain-damaged patients: a double dissociation? *Brain and Language*, *22*, 253–265.

Coslett, H.B., & Heilman, K.M. (1989). Hemihypokinesia after right hemisphere stroke. *Brain and Cognition*, *9*, 267–278.

Cutting, J. (1981). Judgement of emotional expression in schizophrenics. *British Journal of Psychiatry, 139,* 1–6.

Cutting, J. (1985). *The psychology of schizophrenia.* Edinburgh: Churchill Livingstone.

Cutting, J. (1990). *The right cerebral hemisphere and psychiatric disorders.* Oxford: Oxford University Press.

Cutting, J., & Murphy, D. (1990). Preference for denotative as opposed to connotative meanings in schizophrenics. *Brain and Language, 39,* 459–468.

De Renzi, E., Bonacini, M.H., & Faglioni, P. (1989). Right posterior brain-damaged patients are poor at assessing the age of a face. *Neuropsychologia, 27,* 839–848.

Feinberg, T.E., & Shapiro, R.M. (1989). Misidentification–reduplication and the other hemisphere. *Neuropsychiatry, Neuropsychology and Behavioral Neurology, 2,* 39–48.

Flor-Henry, P. (1969). Psychosis and temporal lobe epilepsy: A controlled investigation. *Epilepsia, 10,* 363–395.

Foldi, N.C. (1987). Appreciation of pragmatic interpretations of indirect commands: Comparison of right and left hemisphere brain-damaged patients. *Brain and Language, 31,* 88–108.

Gessler, S., Cutting, J., Frith, C.D., & Weinman, J. (1989). Schizophrenic inability to judge facial emotion: A controlled study. *British Journal of Clinical Psychology, 28,* 19–29.

Hoff, H., & Silbermann, M. (1933). Änderungen der akustischen Wahrnehmungswelt bei temporallappenläsionen. *Zeitschrift für die gesamte Neurologie und Psychiatrie, 152,* 433–447.

Joanette, Y., Goulet, P., Ska, B., & Nespoulous, J.-L. (1986). Informative content of narrative discourse in right-brain-damaged right-handers. *Brain and Language, 29,* 81–105.

Joseph, A.B. (1986). Focal central nervous abnormalities in patients with misidentification syndromes. *Bibliotheca Psychiatrica, 164,* 68–79.

Kimura, S. (1986). Review of 106 cases with the syndrome of Capgras. *Bibliotheca Psychiatrica, 164,* 121–130.

Ley, R.G., & Bryden, M.P. (1979). Hemisphere differences in processing emotions and faces. *Brain and Language, 7,* 127–138.

Mace, C.J., & Trimble, M.R. (1991). Psychosis following temporal lobe surgery: A report of 6 cases. *Journal of Neurology, Neurosurgery and Psychiatry, 54,* 639–644.

Murphy, D., & Cutting, J. (1990). Prosodic comprehension and expression in schizophrenia. *Journal of Neurology, Neurosurgery and Psychiatry, 53,* 727–730.

Oepen, G., Fünfgeld, M., Höll, T., Zimmermann, P., Landis, T., & Regard, M. (1987). Schizophrenia—an emotional hypersensitivity of the right cerebral hemisphere. *International Journal of Psychophysiology, 5,* 261–264.

Parnas, J., Korsgaard, S., Krautwald, O., & Jensen, P.S. (1982). Chronic psychosis in epilepsy. *Acta Psychiatrica Scandinavica, 66,* 282–293.

Penfield, W., & Perot, P. (1963). The brain's record of auditory and visual experience. *Brain, 86,* 595–696.

Perez, M.M., Trimble, M.R., Murray, N.M.F., & Reider, I. (1985). Epileptic psychosis: An evaluation of PSE profiles. *British Journal of Psychiatry, 146,* 155–163.

Roberts, G.W., Done, D.J., Bruton, C., & Crow, T.J. (1990). A "mock up" of schizophrenia: Temporal lobe epilepsy and schizophrenia-like psychosis. *Biological Psychiatry, 28,* 127–143.

Ross, E.D. (1981). The aprosodias: functional–anatomical organization of the affective components of language in the right hemisphere. *Archives of Neurology, 38,* 561–569.

Smith, M.L., & Milner, B. (1984). Differential effects of frontal-lobe lesions on cognitive estimation and spatial memory. *Neuropsychologia, 22,* 697–705.

Winner, E., & Gardener, H. (1977). The comprehension of metaphor in brain-damaged patients. *Brain, 100,* 717–729.

VI AUDITORY HALLUCINATIONS

15 Models of Hallucination: From Theory to Practice

Peter D. Slade
Liverpool University, Liverpool.

This paper will describe my attempt to understand the psychological mechanisms underlying hallucinatory experiences. Starting with some initial observations some twenty five years ago, I carried out a series of small scale studies which led to my propounding a provisional four-factor model of auditory hallucinations fifteen years ago. This model will be briefly described. During the last ten years a number of cognitive accounts of hallucinatory experience have appeared in the literature which share a common theme. Namely, they all suggest that hallucinations come about when individuals fail to recognise their own, internally-generated experience and attribute them to external causes. Several years ago I and Richard Bentall reviewed the scientific literature on hallucinations, including published papers on psychological treatments. We came to the conclusion that most psychological treatments work by encouraging patients to "focus" on their voices. We are currently conducting a controlled clinical study of "focusing treatment" versus "distraction therapy". This will be briefly described. Finally, it will be suggested that we now have a convergence between psychological theory and practice in the area of hallucinations, which has not been the case before.

INTRODUCTION

I first became interested in the subject of hallucination 25 years ago. At the time I was carrying out research into the information processing capacities of schizophrenic patients under varying conditions of external sensory input. This involved administering a card sorting task to patients under normal conditions, under conditions of reduced auditory input (i.e. while wearing a set of sound excluders), and under conditions of increased sensory input (i.e. while listening to either "white noise" or "distracting speech" being played through earphones). After testing one patient, who was diagnosed as schizophrenic on the sole basis of virtually continuous auditory hallucinations, I asked the patient what effect the various conditions were having. He reported that the sound excluders made his voices sound louder while the white noise and distracting speech made his voices sound fainter. This was an exciting discovery for me as it suggested that one of the core symptoms of schizophrenia may be amenable to psychological influence. This led me to conduct several single case studies (Slade, 1972, 1973) and several small group studies (Slade, 1974, 1976a), on patients presenting with auditory hallucinations. On the basis of these studies I published a provisional four-factor model of auditory hallucinations (Slade, 1976b).

THE SLADE FOUR-FACTOR MODEL (SLADE, 1976B)

In the four-factor model I suggested that stress events, either of the one-off traumatic kind or of a less severe but ongoing nature (factor 1), interact with the individual's hallucinatory predisposition level (factor 2). That, if the outcome of this interaction is sufficient to raise the hallucinatory tendency above a critical threshold level, then a hallucination may be experienced by the individual. Whether or not this happens is dependent on the prevailing level of external stimulation to which the individual is currently responding (factor 3). Finally, I suggested that if a hallucination is experienced, then, as a consequence of the mood-improvement that I had observed with a number of patients following the termination of their voices, a reinforcement effect was likely to operate (factor 4). This latter effect may serve to lower the individual's critical threshold level for subsequent hallucinatory experience. The first three factors were supported by the available literature at the time and have received further support from subsequent studies. The fourth factor is more questionable, although I still hold that many hallucinations serve a positive function for the individual and that this leads to their acquiring a habit status.

My four-factor model of 1976 (Slade, 1976b) was in effect a functional analysis of auditory hallucinations. It dealt with antecedent events (i.e. stress events and predisposition), behaviour (i.e. auditory hallucinations), and consequences (reinforcement). There was, however, one crucial missing aspect to the model: it did not have anything to say about the nature of hallucinatory experience, i.e. what a hallucination actually is (Bentall, 1990).

During the last 20 years, spurred on primarily by developments in Cognitive Psychology, a number of theoretical accounts of the nature of hallucinations have begun to appear in the literature. Interestingly enough, while using differing languages, these accounts have shown a remarkable convergence. I shall return to this point later.

RECENT THEORETICAL ACCOUNTS OF HALLUCINATION

Collicut and Hemsley (1981)

These authors began with the hypothesis that hallucinations may stem from an increased level of spontaneous neural activity in an individual's sensory system. They set out to test this hypothesis using a psychophysical detection task based on Weber's Law. In their study they found no differences between the three groups they tested, namely, auditorily hallucinated patients, elderly people, and neurotic patients.

Having found no clear support for their initial hypothesis they concluded that, if hallucinations were not due to an increased level of neural noise, they must be due to a bias problem whereby: "Unexpected, internally-generated experiences are attributed to external events".

Hoffman (1986)

One of the other contributors to this book, Ralph Hoffman (Chapter 16), put forward a very influential account of auditory hallucinations some years ago. Beginning with the assumption that schizophrenic patients have a basic disorder of "discourse planning", Hoffman argued that auditory hallucinations are: "Unintended verbal images that are experienced as alien to the self". Although he has subsequently moved on from this theoretical position, Hoffman's hypothesis concerning a failure of discourse planning has been well received and is consistent with the other cognitive accounts.

Frith and Done (1988)

Another contributor to this book, Chris Frith (Chapter 9) developed a related cognitive account of schizophrenic symptomatology, including auditory hallucinations, a few years ago. He and his co-worker used the general model of cognitive processing presented in Fig. 15.1. This model argues that there are two types of stimulus input. The first is external and has its impact via the appropriate sensory receptor. This leads to a perceptual response and a corresponding "stimulus intention", which generates an "action" that is monitored centrally and adjusted if necessary. The second kind of stimulus input is internally-generated, stemming from the individual's plans. This input leads to a "willed intention", which also generates appropriate action. Normally this internally-generated, "willed intention" will be monitored centrally.

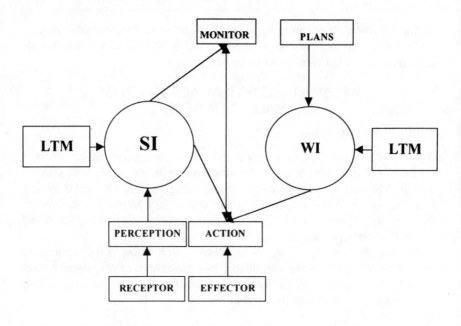

LTM = Long Term Memory

SI = Stimulus Intention

WI = Willed Intention

FIG. 15.1   Model of hallucination (Frith & Done, 1988). Reproduced with permission.

However, Frith and Done (1987) suggested that hallucinators have a "failure in the internal monitoring of willed thoughts", which leads to their experiencing internally generated thoughts as externally generated. Although Frith has moved on from this position (see Chapter 9) the essence of the argument remains.

Bentall (1990)

Another contributor to this book, Richard Bentall (Chapter 19) has recently proposed a cognitive theory of hallucination based on a series of experimental studies (Bentall, 1990). The major assumption underlying Bentall's theoretical account is that the ability to classify events as real or imaginary is a metacognitive skill (Fig. 15.2). That is, the task of the perceiver is to discriminate between external and internal sources of stimulation and to classify the source of the stimulation appropriately.

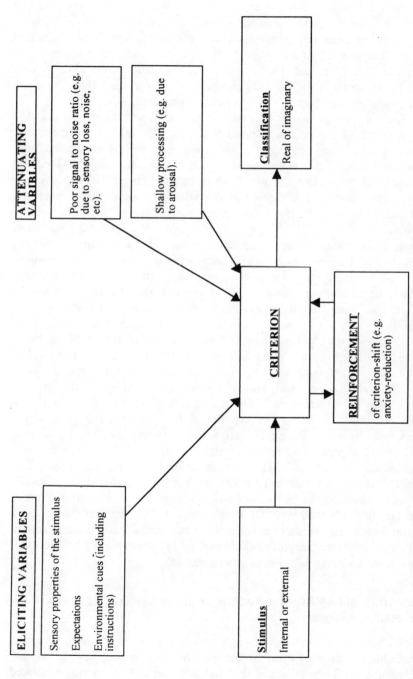

FIG. 15.2 Model of hallucination (Bentall, 1990, from Slade & Bentall, 1988). Reproduced with permission.

ATTENUATING VARIBLES

Poor signal to noise ratio (e.g. due to sensory loss, noise, etc).

Shallow processing (e.g. due to arousal).

ELICITING VARIABLES

Sensory properties of the stimulus

Expectations

Environmental cues (including instructions)

Stimulus
Internal or external

CRITERION

REINFORCEMENT
of criterion-shift (e.g. anxiety-reduction)

Classification
Real of imaginary

Bentall makes the further assumption that most of us have an optimum criterion for making this judgement, whereby we are likely to mistake real (external) for imaginary (internal) events as frequently as we are likely to make the opposite error, i.e. mistaking imaginary (internal) events for real ones. The central thesis of Bentall's theory is that hallucinators, and hallucination-prone individuals, experience a criterion-shift, whereby they are biased towards making only one type of error, namely that of judging internally-generated stimuli as emanating from external sources.

The crucial experiments that established the hypothesised criterion-shift used a signal-detection task (Bentall & Slade, 1985). In the first experiment, ten normal subjects scoring at a high level on a hallucination-prone scale (i.e. the Launay-Slade Hallucination Scale; Launay & Slade, 1981) and ten low scoring subjects were required to distinguish between 100 signal (voice) plus noise trials and 100 noise alone trials. In a second experiment, ten hallucinating and ten non-hallucinating schizophrenics were required to distinguish between 50 signal (voice) plus noise trials and 50 noise alone trials. In both experiments, no differences were found in terms of "sensory sensitivity". However, both hallucinating schizophrenics and hallucination-prone individuals differed from comparison subjects in showing a significant "bias" towards reporting more stimuli as signal rather than as noise only. That is, it appears that both those individuals who are actively hallucinating, and those who are strongly predisposed to hallucination, employ a biased criterion towards reporting imaginary events as real (Bentall & Slade, 1985).

Bentall suggests that other factors may affect the criterion shift (Fig. 15.2). For example, attenuating variables such as "poor signal to noise ratio" and high cortical arousal, which is associated with "shallow processing of information". However, the most important factor that is likely to have an impact on criterion-shift is suggestibility. In another experimental study (Young, Bentall, Slade, & Dewey, 1987) high- and low-hallucination-prone subjects, hallucinators and non-hallucinators, were compared on various tasks of suggestibility. The results showed that hallucinators and hallucination-prone subjects exhibited significantly stronger responses to hallucination-type suggestions than control subjects. So far, Bentall's theory (1990) is well supported by the available research data. The central thesis of this theory is that hallucinations stem from a: "Failure in the metacognitive skill involved in discriminating between self-generated and external sources of stimulation".

Commonalities Among Recent Cognitive Accounts of Hallucinations

The above four models, although couched in different languages and embedded in differing theoretic frameworks, do appear to have a common denominator. They all argue that hallucinations are internally-generated thoughts or images, which as a consequence of a failure in a central monitor or in the discrimination process, are mistaken for externally-generated events. Thus there appears to be some theoretical agreement, among at least four sets of psychopathological models, about the nature of hallucinatory experience.

PSYCHOLOGICAL TREATMENTS FOR PATIENTS WITH PERSISTENT AUDITORY HALLUCINATIONS

In a book published four years ago on the subject of hallucinations (Slade & Bentall, 1988) we reviewed, among other things, psychological treatment studies of persistent hallucinators. These treatment studies involved eight different treatment approaches, all of which appeared to have been at least partly successful. This led us to question the possible mechanism for the observed treatment effects. One possibility, although an unlikely one, is that they all work differently. Another is that they all share a common ingredient. The third possibility, and the one we favour, is that the eight treatments work through a smaller number of processes.

On the basis of a careful consideration of the eight treatments, we suggested that they might work through three treatment processes, namely:

1. Distraction. This includes counterstimulation/distraction treatments and operant procedures.
2. Anxiety procedures. This is represented only by systematic desensitisation at present.
3. Focusing. This includes the five remaining treatments, i.e. self-monitoring, aversion therapy, thought-stopping, first person singular therapy, and earplug therapy.

By the process of focusing we mean any psychological treatment that involves "... a powerful requirement on the patient to attend to and focus on hallucinatory experiences and the circumstances surrounding such experiences" (Slade & Bentall, 1988, p. 200).

The above theoretical analysis of treatment processes has led us to develop a "focusing therapy" for patients with auditory hallucinations. This therapy involves five stages, in which we help patients to focus on:

1. Physical characteristics of voices.
2. The content of their voices.
3. The meaning behind the content.
4. The relation of their voices to their thoughts.
5. Their beliefs about their voices.

Currently, we are carrying out a Medical Research Council-funded treatment study in which this "focusing therapy" is being compared with "distraction therapy" and with a "contact control" condition. On the basis of our early experiences of "focusing therapy" we are hypothesising that the therapeutic process will follow five stages as follows:

Stage 1: Voices experienced outside head.
Stage 2: Voices experienced inside head.
Stage 3: Difficulty in distinguishing between voices and thoughts.
Stage 4: Some voices accepted as thoughts but not others.
Stage 5: All voices accepted as own thoughts.

During therapy we are documenting changes in order to test the above hypothetical sequence.

CONVERGENCE OF THEORY AND PRACTICE

The above selected review demonstrates some convergence between theory and practice. On the one hand, four recent cognitive accounts of hallucination suggest that they occur because hallucinators fail to recognise self-generated events as self-generated. The therapeutic implication of these accounts is that hallucinators need to be given guided practice in the task of recognising the source of their "voices".

On the other hand, theoretical analysis of psychological treatments suggests that a process common to many of them is one of "focusing", in which patients are required to attend carefully to the nature and circumstances surrounding their voices. Both types of theoretical analysis point to the potential value of "focusing therapy", which we are now employing in an attempt to help our clients. Let us hope we can remain focused and not be distracted from our task!

REFERENCES

Bentall, R.P. (1990). The illusion of reality: A psychological model of hallucination. *Psychological Bulletin, 107*, 82–95.

Bentall, R.P., & Slade, P.D. (1985). Reality testing and auditory hallucinations: A signal detection analysis, *British Journal of Clinical Psychology, 24*, 159–171.

Collicut, J.R., & Hemsley, D.R. (1981). A psychophysical investigation of auditory functioning in schizophrenia. *British Journal of Clinical Psychology, 20*, 199–204.

Frith, C.D., & Done, D.J. (1988). Towards a neuropsychology of schizophrenia. *British Journal of Psychiatry, 153*, 437–443.

Launay, G., & Slade, P.D. (1981). The measurement of hallucinatory predisposition in male and female prisoners. *Personality and Individual Differences, 2*, 221–234.

Hoffman, R.E. (1986). Verbal hallucinations and language production processes in schizophrenia. *Behavioural and Brain Sciences, 9*, 503–548.

Slade, P.D. (1972). The effects of systematic desensitisation on auditory hallucinations. *Behavioural Research and Therapy, 10*, 85–91.

Slade, P.D. (1973). The psychological investigation and treatment of auditory hallucinations: A second case report. *British Journal of Medical Psychology, 46,* 293–296.

Slade, P.D. (1974). The external control of auditory hallucinations: An information theory analysis. *British Journal of Social and Clinical Psychology, 13,* 73–79.

Slade, P.D. (1976a). An investigation of psychological factors involved in the predisposition to auditory hallucinations. *Psychological Medicine, 6,* 123–132.

Slade, P.D. (1976b). Towards a theory of auditory hallucinations: Outline of an hypothetical four-factor model. *British Journal of Social and Clinical Psychology, 15,* 415–423.

Slade, P.D., & Bentall, R.P. (1988). *Sensory deception: A scientific analysis of hallucination.* London: Chapman & Hall.

Young, H.F., Bentall, R.P., Slade, P.D., & Dewey, M.E. (1987). The role of brief instructions and suggestibility in the elicitation of auditory hallucinations in normal and psychiatric subjects. *Journal of Nervous and Mental Disease, 175,* 41–48.

16 A Psycholinguistic Study of Auditory/verbal Hallucinations: Preliminary Findings

Ralph E. Hoffman and Jill Rapaport
Yale University School of Medicine, New Haven, Connecticut, U.S.A.

This study tests the hypothesis that verbal hallucinations derive from "parasitic memories" which disrupt language production processes and episodically co-opts these processes. The study assumed that speech perception also accesses language production processes when the acoustic clarity of speech is reduced because subjects need to produce linguistic hypotheses regarding the meaning and formal organisation of the text in order to "fill in the gaps". Subjects were requested to shadow prerecorded spoken texts whose phonetic clarity was reduced with multispeaker babbled. Patients with and without verbal hallucinations as well as a normal control group were studied. Hallucinators demonstrated much lower shadowing accuracy compared to the other two groups. Moreover, 4 out of 7 hallucinators "misheard" portions of target texts as verbalisations related to their voices. These data, although preliminary, point to specific language processing pathology underlying verbal hallucinations, and suggest the influence of parasitic verbal memories.

INTRODUCTION

Schizophrenia is aetiologically heterogeneous (Kennedy et al., 1988; Sherrington et al., 1988) with intrinsic diagnostic uncertainties—there are no "objective" laboratory tests for the disorder and the boundaries between schizophrenic and affective psychosis are frequently vague (Brockington & Leff, 1979; Procci, 1976). A reasonable research strategy, therefore, is to probe particular symptoms—including symptoms that seem to cut across diagnostic boundaries—to search for unitary pathophysiological processes.

Along these lines, the following is a preliminary report of a neuropsychological study of auditory/verbal hallucinations or "voices". Current estimates of the frequency of verbal hallucinations in schizophrenia range between 50 and 80% (Alpert, 1986; Sartorius, Shapiro, & Jablonsky, 1974). The high frequency of this symptom is not surprising given that it is one of the diagnostic criteria for schizophrenia, though not a necessary one. There is a fairly high prevalence in affective disorder as well (Chaturvedi & Sinha, 1990). In some patients, this symptom is limited to an acute decompensation, while, for others, voices can linger indefinitely as very disturbing and at times disabling, a kind of verbal plague.

The nature and causes of VHs are not known. One of us has hypothesised that this symptom reflects certain pathologically stored linguistic information in longer-term memory which disrupts language production processes and at times co-opts these processes by creating verbal messages that are consciously experienced as repeated, alien, unintended auditory images (Hoffman, 1986, 1991a; Hoffman & Dobscha, 1989). This model was suggested by computer simulations of cognitive pathology that can arise spontaneously in parallel, distributed processing information processing systems. These computer models are composed of large numbers of very simple computing units, generally referred to as "neurons", which are densely interconnected via "synapses". There is no single "command" unit; the effectiveness of the network as a whole reflects the co-operative interactions of its parts. Each neuron receives information simultaneously from a large number of other neurons, and computes its response to these inputs in parallel with the computations of the other neurons of the system. There is, moreover, no one-to-one correspondence between a memory and the activation of a particular neuron. Instead, a memory corresponds to a pattern of activation involving many neurons of the network; memories are stored by modifying functional connections between its neurons. Networks that store and retrieve information on the basis of distributed patterns of activation are referred to as parallel, distributed processing (PDP) systems. There is now increasing evidence that functional modules of the mammalian cerebral cortex are organised as parallel, distributed systems (Churchland & Sejnowski, 1989; Goldman-Rakic, 1988; Mesulam, 1990; Skarda & Freeman, 1987).

There are two conditions when memories stored in PDP systems become "parasitic:" (i) When too many memories are stored in the system (Crick & Mitchison, 1983; Hoffman, 1987); and (ii) when functional connections between neurons are excessively pruned away (Hoffman & Dobscha, 1989). Pruning of functional connections is of special interest insofar as it characterises a postnatal developmental process that occurs in the cerebral cortex of humans and other mammals. Parasitic memories function like computer viruses, where stereotyped messages are produced independent of current programs and disrupt information processing.

Parasitic memories could play a key role in inducing psychotic symptoms and cognitive deficits in schizophrenia (Crick & Mitchison 1983; Hoffman 1987; Hoffman & Dobscha 1989). For instance, parasitic memories might produce "messages" that are variants of ordinary "inner speech"; the term "inner speech" refers to the words that we use to talk to ourselves with verbal images during mentation. If inner speech is produced by a parasitic memory, the resulting verbal imagery would probably be experienced as alien and out of control of the subject; the unintendedness of verbal images seems to be a key component of the phenomonology of psychotic "voices" (Hoffman, 1986).

An objection to this hypothesis is that the "voices" of the schizophrenic are often not the person's own voice (unlike ordinary inner speech) and can be "heard" in some external space. These "non-self" acoustic features may, however, reflect expectations that mould the imagistic character of the "voice" (Hoffman, 1991b). Most verbal images that express content distinct from our wishes and current intentions derive from actual outside speakers; this is reaffirmed daily and reflects how we believe the world is constructed. A hallucinated voice expresses content that is also contrary to the conscious will of the person; therefore its imagistic characteristics are predicted to be moulded by the prevailing expectation—that an unwilled voice derives from another, external speaker.

Four types of empirical evidence support the model of voices just described:

1. VHs, like ordinary inner speech, seem to be accompanied by subtle activation of vocal musculature that is electromyographically detectable (Gould, 1948; Inouye & Shimizu, 1970); hence VHs seem to derive from language production processes.

2. The presence of VHs is a strong predictor of the presence of disruption of language production processes reflected as defects in multisentence language planning (Hoffman, 1986); this is additional evidence that there is a specific relationship between VHs and language production processes.

3. A positron emission tomography (PET) study of chronic schizophrenics with and without VHs suggests functional coupling of areas of the brain ordinarily involved in speech production in the former group (Cleghorn et al., 1990).

4. The content of voices tend to be repetitive and stereotypic over time (Chaturvedi & Sinha, 1990; Hoffman 1991; Kinsbourne 1990) and therefore act—if again one can think in "computer virus" terms—as if stored information is being slavishly reproduced.

In contrast to the model just proposed, other data have been presented that suggest a perceptual defect model of VHs, in particular, an impairment in "distinguishing signal from noise". This signal detection model has been supported by two empirical studies: (1) Mintz and Alpert (1972) requested subjects to shadow short word phrases whose intelligibility was obscured by white noise—schizophrenics with hallucinations tended to produce errors which were more elaborated and less constrained by the target text; and (2) Bentall and Slade (1985) requested subjects to listen to a single word, "who", embedded in white noise, and white noise alone. The task was to guess when the "who" actually occurred. As predicted, hallucinating schizophrenics tended (erroneously) to guess that the "who" was present with a greater frequency than non-hallucinating schizophrenics. Thus, under certain experimental conditions, hallucinating schizophrenics perceive meaning to a degree exceeding that which is intrinsic to the stimulus itself. This hypothesis is appealing insofar as: (i) VHs of schizophrenics can be triggered by meaningless sounds in the environment (Frith, 1979); and (ii) it is consonant with the view that schizophrenics fix inappropriately upon certain kinds of irrelevant sensory input and are distracted by them (Pogue-Geile & Oltmanns, 1980; Weilgus & Harvey, 1988).

The study described below attempts to test these two competing models of VHs. The key assumption of the study is that speech *perception* also activates neurocognitive processes central to speech *production*—especially when speech stimuli are unclear or ambiguous. This claim is substantiated by two kinds of findings.

1. *Intracortical electrical stimulation studies.* Direct electrical stimulation studies of the human brain demonstrate that in order for an externally generated auditory stream of phonetic information to be perceived as words and sentences, Broca's and other left frontal areas are activated (Ojemann, 1983). These brain areas, traditionally associated with speech generation, are activated in parallel with posterior speech perception systems.

2. *Computer programs for speech perception.* If a speaker produces speech very fluently, with pauses between each word in a totally quiet room, software programs for speech perception are relatively straightforward. The acoustic character of the stream of speech determines unambiguously, for the listener or computer, the intended string of words. These ideal conditions are never met, however. Speech is ordinarily produced less than perfectly as a steady, semi-uninterrupted stream of acoustic information with the background noise of modern life; consequently, the clarity of acoustic input of speech is ordinarily significantly obscured. To decode speech under these circumstances, the computer (and each of us as listeners) must elaborate hypotheses about what the speaker is saying (McClelland & Elman, 1986). These hypotheses are internally generated language representations based on prior speech, the apparent syntactic form of the speech input, and the gist of what the listener thinks the speech is about. These language hypotheses are then matched to acoustic information, fast

flowing and as ambiguous as they may be, to identify the "best fit". Thus, "higher-level" language representations are produced actively in parallel to, but partially independent from, acoustic input to "fill in the gaps" of missing or unclear phonetic information. Computers (and presumably people) that do not engage in this active language production process in parallel cannot interpret speech sounds under ordinary conditions.

Our study was designed to activate higher-order language representations by reducing phonetic clarity during speech perception. This was accomplished by masking speech with a background of multiperson babble, i.e. other electronically mixed voices. Speech perception research has demonstrated that babble is an optimally effective mask of phonetic features when combined with speech to be tracked by the listener (Kalikow & Stevens, 1977; Lewis et al., 1988).

A parasitic memory model of voices predicts two consequences:

1. The overall ability to accurately track speech will be impaired in patients with VHs. In computer simulations of Gestalt recognition afflicted with parasitic memories, the system often failed to converge upon any meaningful interpretation of input data when stimuli become ambiguous (Hoffman & Dobscha 1989).

2. In higher babble conditions, actual derivations of parasitic verbal messages productive of VHs will be elicited in patients with this symptom. In simulations of pathologically disturbed parallel processing systems, highly ambiguous stimuli were optimal in provoking the reproduction of a parasitic memory (Hoffman & Dobscha, 1989).

The signal detection model of VHs predicts that:

(i) Tracking accuracy would not be selectively impaired in hallucinating subjects, but rather would be expressed as a non-specific effect of distractibility among both hallucinating and non-hallucinating schizophrenics;

(ii) In high babble conditions (where even normal individuals cannot discern large segments of tax), hallucinating schizophrenics will make more guesses regarding what they think they hear.

METHOD

Subjects

Three research groups were recruited. The first was a group of eleven normal individuals; normal subjects were excluded if they had undergone psychiatric treatment or received medication that might impair concentration. The second group consisted of seven patients reporting VHs. The third group was a group of six patients who do not report hearing voices. All patients were recruited to participate in the study if they demonstrated significant positive symptoms within 1 week of the testing and met DSM-IIIR criteria for either schizophrenia, schizoaffective disorder, or mania. The sole criterion for placing a subject in the hallucinating versus non-hallucinating group was whether the following question was answered in the affirmative: "In the last week, have you heard one or more voices which, to the best of your knowledge, other people are not able to hear?" Subjects providing ambiguous answers to this question, or who had prior histories of significant substance abuse, were excluded from the study. Subjects were also excluded if they had histories of hearing loss or multiple ear infections.

Patient characteristics are described in Table 16.1. The three groups were well matched according to age and gender. Mean educational level in the non-hallucinating patient group was somewhat higher than the other two groups, however. Mean dose of neuroleptic medication was very similar in the two patient groups. DSM-III-R diagnoses for patients in the hallucinating group were: schizophrenia–paranoid type (5), schizophrenia—undifferentiated type (1), and mania (1). DSM-III-R diagnoses for patients in the non-hallucinating group were: schizophrenia–paranoid type (1), schizophrenia—undifferentiated type (1), schizoaffective disorder (1), and mania (3).

Testing Procedure

A total of eight passages taken from fiction with lengths ranging from 90 to 135 words were prerecorded, four by a female speaker and four by a male speaker. Each word in each passage had a familiarity score of at least 3 on the basis the word frequency study of the American English lexicon

TABLE 16.1
Subject Characteristics

	Age *		Gender*	Education level† (Grades Completed)		Neuroleptic* (CPZ Equivalents)	
	$\overline{X}$	SD	(M/F)	$\overline{X}$	SD	$\overline{X}$	SD
Normals (n = 11)	27.9	10.2	3/8	13.5	1.5		
Hall-positive (n = 7)	33.3	8.9	3/4	13.6	2.6	380	328
Hall-negative (n = 6)	31.2	7.0	2/4	15.2	.69	360	353

* Non-significant differences between groups.
† $F_{2,21} = 1.63$; $P < 0.20$

conducted by Francis and Kucera (1982); the four exceptions (out of a total of 939 words) were: "hangers", "wig", "booming", and "waltz". Thus, the words in the passages represented familiar American English, readily accessible to listeners educated at a high school level.

Babble was generated on the basis of the superimposed speech of six male and six female adult speakers reading different neutral scientific texts. The resulting combination rendered indecipherable all passages and individual words belonging to the twelve babble texts.

Two passages were mixed with babble with an amplitude that exceeded the latter by an average of 4.1 dB; this was the "low babble" condition. Three passages were selected for the "moderate babble" condition and were combined at a mean signal-to-babble difference of –4.86 dB. The remaining three passages comprised the "high babble" condition; the phonetic clarity of these target passages was markedly reduced with a mean signal-to-babble difference of –5.87 dB. Test stimuli were presented using a SONY digital audio tape (DAT) DTS-75ES recorder. Segments were presented as two separate blocks of four passages, each from the same speaker, with increasing babble levels over time within blocks; this allowed the listener to establish familiarity with the voice to be tracked prior to the more difficult high babble conditions. Order of presentation of male and female blocks was varied.

Subjects were requested to "shadow" each of the passages, i.e. simultaneously to verbally repeat what they hear while listening to the spoken text presented. Speech stimuli and babble were each presented binaurally. As indicated, the babble inputs alone were completely indecipherable and therefore were not intrinsically meaningful distractors during speech tracking, Tracking performance was tape recorded using a lapel-clip microphone.

The scoring categories and their reliabilities are described in Table 16.2. Transcription and scoring were conducted blind to group membership.

RESULTS

Accuracy

Figure 16.1 illustrates the accuracy data for the three tracking conditions and the three experimental groups. There is a very robust and expectable effect of babble level: increasing babble brings about decreases in tracking accuracy for all groups ($F_{2,42} = 657$; $P < 0.0001$). In addition, there was an overall significant difference between the three subject groups ($F_{2,21} = 8.13$; $P < 0.005$). Planned comparisons between groups revealed that the hallucinators demonstrated significant reductions in tracking accuracy compared to both non-hallucinators ($F_{1,21} = 12.35$; $P < 0.001$) and normal

TABLE 16.2
Scoring System

	Reliability (R_I)
Accuracy. Number of words correctly repeated	0.99
Semantically relevant. Number of words inserted into target text that are that are nonetheless related to the meaning of a word or phrase in the target text	0.76
Phonetically relevant. Number of words produced not belonging to the target text that nonetheless share a majority of phonemes with a word in the target text	0.83
Thematically plausible. Number of inserted words that are plausible when considered in context of target text but do are not semantically or phonetically relevant	0.86
Implausible/bizarre. Number of inserted words that do not belong to the above four categories	0.78
Non-words. Phonetic strings inserted into the text not belonging to the lexicon	0.51

controls ($F_{1,21} = 13.31$; $P < 0.001$). The interaction between group and condition achieved borderline significance ($F_{4,42} = 2.02$; $P < 0.10$).

The fact that mean education level was higher in the non-hallucinators than the hallucinators raises the question of whether the differences in tracking accuracies between these two groups could be secondary to these educational differences. Consequently, the correlation between education and tracking accuracy was computed for accuracy scores averaged across the three conditions for each subject in all three groups; this correlation was determined to be non-significant (Pearson $r = 0.04$).

"Guessing frequency"

To assess the signal detection model of hallucinations, the frequency of "guessing" was estimated using the number of implausible responses generated during each babble condition. The signal detection model predictors that increased amounts of spurious meaning would be perceived under higher babble conditions for patients with VHs compared to patients without VHs and normals. These misperceptions, insofar as they are not guided by the target text, would be expressed as implausible responses. As expected, there was general increase in implausible responses as babble increased for all three groups ($F_{2,42} = 12.58$; $P < 0.001$); however there were no detectable main effects for group ($F_{1,21} = 0.19$) nor was there a significant interaction effect between group and babble level ($F_{4,42} = 0.54$).

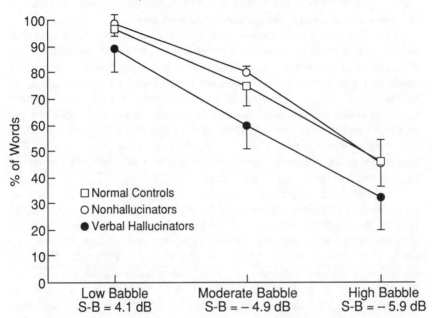

Speech Tracking Accuracy

□ Normal Controls
○ Nonhallucinators
● Verbal Hallucinators

Low Babble
S-B = 4.1 dB

Moderate Babble
S-B = – 4.9 dB

High Babble
S-B = – 5.9 dB

FIG. 16.1 Speech tracking accuracy. The *x*-axis reflects the three babble conditions. dB differences were computed by determining the average dB for the target texts and subtracting the mean dB level of the babble input; silent pauses in the target text were edited out prior to computation of dB level in order to eliminate the effects of pausing on dB computations. The *y*-axis refers to the total number of words successfully tracked for all the texts presented in each of the three stimulus conditions.

Content Analysis

A prediction of the "parasitic verbal memory" model of verbal hallucinations is that verbal material related to the content of hallucinations themselves may intrude into responses during higher babble conditions. There was some evidence that this might have occurred in some cases, though these findings are inconclusive.

A manic subject reported that he had heard frequent hallucinations of his lawyer and his housekeeper. During one high babble segment, he mistook the word "foyer" for "lawyer".

A patient with paranoid schizophrenia reported hearing two female voices urging her to undertake self-destructive acts, which she was reluctant to speak about. Under the high babble condition, the following transformation took place: "Phil's job in the restaurant was as ordinary as you can imagine—from making coffee in the morning to sweeping up at night" became "Phil's job in the restaurant was as ordinary as you can imagine—coffee and tea (long pause) was *beheaded*."

A third patient with paranoid schizophrenia noted prior to testing that his voices had become so soft and indistinct that he could no longer make out their content. While responding to the last high babble segment, he suddenly reported that he could no longer attend to the target text, but was listening to a "voice". When asked what the voice was saying, he reported that it was like his voices in general, i.e. that he could not make out the words, though he guessed that they were saying: "Don't worry about the test because these voices (i.e. the babble stimuli) are not 'real'." The experience of an indistinct alien vocal presence was reproduced when he later listened to the babble track alone.

The most striking example of possible intrusions of hallucinated material was provided by a fourth patient—a paranoid schizophrenic who reported hearing two types of voices, one from God and the second from the devil, who spoke of sexual matters that were "so bad I can't tell you what he says". During the moderate babble condition, he transformed, "There are no barges or colorful sailing boats", into "There are no barges *I feel savior*." Shortly thereafter, he transformed, "Just as I look back again, the young woman throws her bundle over the side of the bridge", into, "just as I look back (pause) young woman *close her buttocks*". He commented after this segment was over that "this is getting kind of scary".

Examples of an unanticipated type of error were demonstrated by two of the hallucinators; portions of earlier texts were reinserted into later responses. One patient (not inappropriately) transformed, "the car (referring to subway car) filled up quickly" to "train filled quickly". However, approximately 5 minutes later, another text stimulus, "Phil and their girlfriends would drive ten or fifteen miles to a roadhouse" was transformed to "... would drive ten or fifteen miles (pause) *filled the train*". A second hallucinator demonstrated three separate instances where words or portions of words from earlier portions of the same text were inappropriately reinserted into a later response to the same text. Errors of this sort were not seen in the normal and non-hallucinator groups.

CLOSING COMMENTS

Given the small subject size, these data must surely be considered to be preliminary. However, there is already a strong suggestion of speech tracking impairments specific to subjects with VHs; in fact there was no overlap in performance scores for hallucinating versus non-hallucinating patients in the moderate babble condition. One explanation for these differences is that the former group is in some general sense "sicker" than the latter and therefore more impaired cognitively overall. Although this explanation cannot be ruled out, it should be noted that two of the non-hallucinating schizophrenics were chronically disabled, while one of the hallucinating schizophrenics had completed graduate studies and worked full-time as a teacher prior to her decompensation. In addition, two of the hallucinating schizophrenics were tested as outpatients and held stable part-time jobs. Even if it turns out that hallucinations are in some quantifiable way "sicker" than non-hallucinators, this may be the result of the severity of the hallucinatory symptoms, and should not necessarily negate the significance of speech tracking findings.

It may be that a larger pool of experimental subjects will uncover a spurious misperception rate (as reflected by implausible responses) among hallucinators that is greater than that in the other two groups. At this point, implausible responses for hallucinators during the high babble condition was comparable to the other two groups ($\bar{x}$ = 1.4 ± 0.9 versus 1.1 ± 1.4 implausible words per 100 words of text). This is particularly surprising given that the accuracy of speech tracking was much lower among hallucinators, thereby giving these subjects more frequent opportunities to generate spurious responses. In any case, these preliminary data strongly suggest that the robustness of group differences in spurious responses is outweighed by the robustness of group differences in speech tracking accuracy. Therefore the data currently favour a language processing model of VHs compared to a signal detection model.

The relative paucity of intrusions of hallucinatory material into the speech tracking of hallucinations was noteworthy, though some responses were suggestive of this pathological process. One explanation is that the speech inputs were played at high volume—75 dB—this was to ensure that the speaker's own voice did not drown out the external speech input for those text presentations where signal was much reduced compared to babble. It may be that high volume auditory input in fact drowned out intrusive hallucinatory material. In the future, we plan to present speech stimuli at a much lower combined volume to attempt to elicit more frequent hallucinatory material. In addition to intrusions of hallucinatory material, intrusions of memories of prior responses were noted for two of the seven hallucinators, a finding not detected in the other two groups. This could reflect a novel pathology involving verbal working memory. However, more data needs to be collected before drawing any firm conclusions.

Other studies of hallucinating versus non-hallucinating schizophrenics have produced interesting data regarding cerebral laterality (Alpert, Rubenstein, & Kesselman, 1976) and allocation of attention (Heilburn, Diller, Fleming, & Slade, 1986). These studies, however, are not inconsistent with the parasitic verbal memory model of VHs presented earlier and therefore do not represent critical challenges to our model. Finally, a "pigeon-holing" deficit model of hallucinations has been proposed by Hemsley (1987). "Pigeon-holing" refers to one's ability to utilise regularities of previous experience to guide current response. A pigeon-hole deficit could account for the impaired speech tracking observed in hallucinators and, moreover, could result in an increased sense of unexpectedness of internally generated auditory images that could lead to alien or non-self qualities. However, to the best of our knowledge, pigeon-holing deficits have not been demonstrated to be specifically associated with VHs. Our current hypothesis is that parasitic verbal memories in fact induce secondary pigeon-hole-like deficits—deficits that are specific to the language processing domain.

In closing, it is hoped that these preliminary data will rekindle interest in the neuropsychological study of a bizarre, uncanny and all too common symptom of severe mental illness: auditory/verbal hallucinations. Most important at this time are studies that critically compare competing hypotheses regarding underlying pathophysiological mechanisms.

ACKNOWLEDGEMENTS

This research was supported by the Chrysalis Fund for Behavioral Research and NICHD contract NO1-HD-5-2910 to Haskins Laboratories.

REFERENCES

Alpert, M. (1986). Language process and hallucination phenomenology. *Behavioral and Brain Sciences, 9*, 618–519.

Alpert, M., Rubenstein, H., & Kesselman, M. (1976). Asymmetry of information processing in hallucinations and nonhallucinators. *Journal of Nervous and Mental Disease, 162*, 258–264.

Bentall, R.P., & Slade, P.D. (1985). Reality testing and auditory hallucinations. *British Journal of Clinical Psychology, 24*, 159–169.

Brockington, I.F., & Leff, J.P. (1979). Schizo-affective psychosis: Definitions and incidence. *Psychological Medicine, 9*, 91–99.

Chaturvedi, S.K., & Sinha, V.K. (1990). Recurrence of hallucinations in consecutive episodes of schizophrenia and affective disorder. *Schizophrenia Research, 3*, 103–106.

Churchland, P.S., & Sejnowski, T.J. (1989). Neural representation and neural computation. In L. Nadel, P. Culicover, & R.M. Harnish (Eds.), *Neural connections, mental computations* (pp. 16–48). Cambridge, MA: MIT Press.

Cleghorn, J.M., Garnett, E.S., Nahmias, G., Brown, G.M., Kaplan, R.D., Szechtman, H., Szechtman, B., Franco, S., Dermer, S.W., & Cook, P. (1990). Regional brain metabolism during auditory hallucinations in chronic schizophrenia. *British Journal of Psychiatry, 157*, 562–570.

Crick, F.H., & Mitchison, G. (1983). The function of dream sleep. *Nature, 304*, 111–114.

Francis, W.N., & Kucera, H. (1982). *Frequency analysis of English usage: Lexicon and grammar.* Boston: Houghton Mifflin.

Frith, C.D. (1979). Consciousness, information processing and schizophrenia. *British Journal of Psychiatry, 134*, 225–235.

Goldman-Rakic, P. (1988). Changing concepts of cortical connectivity: Parallel distributed cortical networks. *Annual Review of Neuroscience, 11*, 137–156.

Gould, L.N. (1948). Verbal hallucinations and the activity of vocal musculature: An electromyographic study. *American Journal of Psychiatry, 105,* 367–73.

Heilbrun, A.F., Diller, R., Fleming, R., & Slade, L. (1986). Strategies of disattention and auditory hallucinations in schizophrenics. *Journal of Nervous and Mental Disease, 174,* 265–273.

Hemsley, D.R. (1987). Hallucinations: Unintended or unexpected? *Behavioural and Brain Sciences, 10,* 532–533.

Hoffman, R.E. (1986). Verbal hallucinations and language production processes in schizophrenia. *Behavioral and Brain Sciences, 9,* 503–548.

Hoffman, R.E., & Dobscha, S. (1989). Cortical pruning and the development of schizophrenia: A computer model. *Schizophrenia Bulletin, 15,* 477–490.

Hoffman, R.E. (1991a). The mechanism of positive symptoms in schizophrenia. *Behavioral and Brain Sciences, 14,* 33–34.

Hoffman, R.E. (1991b). The Duphar Lecture: On the etiology of alien, nonself attributes of schizophrenic "voices". *Psychopathology, 24,* 335–343.

Inouye, T., & Shimizu, A. (1970). The electromyographic study of verbal hallucinations. *Journal of Nervous and Mental Diseases, 151,* 415–422.

Kalikow, D.N., & Stevens, K.N. (1977). Development of a test of speech intelligibility in noise using sentence materials with controlled word predictability. *Journal of the Acoustic Society of America, 5,* 1337–1351.

Kennedy, J.L., Giuffra, L.A., Moises, H.W., Cavalli-Sforza, L.L., Pakstis, A.J., Kidd, J.R., Castiglione, C.M., Sjogren, B., Wetterberg, L., & Kidd, K.K. (1988). Evidence against linkage of schizophrenia to markers on chromosome 5 in a northern Sweden pedigree. *Nature, 336,* 167–170.

Kinsbourne, M. (1990). Voiced images, imagined voices. *Biological Psychiatry, 27,* 811– 812.

Lewis, H.D., Benignus, V.A. Muller, K.E., Malott, C.M., & Barton, C.N. (1988). Babble and random-noise masking of speech in high and low context cue conditions. *Journal of Speech and Hearing Research, 31,* 108–114.

McClelland, J.L., & Elman, J.L. (1986). Interactive processes in speech perception: The TRACE model. In J.L. McClelland & D.E. Rumelhart (Eds.), *Parallel distributed processing: Explorations in the microstructure of cognition* (Vol. 2). Cambridge, MA: MIT Press.

Mesulam, M.-M. (1990). Large-scale neurocognitive networks and distributed processing for attention, language and memory. *Annals of Neurology, 28,* 597–613.

Mintz, S., & Alpert, M. (1972). Imagery vividness, reality testing and schizophrenic hallucinations. *Journal of Abnormal Psychology, 79,* 310–316.

Ojemann, G.A. (1983). Brain organization for language from the perspective of electrical stimulation mapping. *Behavioral and Brain Sciences, 2,* 189–230.

Pogue-Geile, M.F., & Oltmanns, T.F. (1980). Sentence perception and distractibility in schizophrenic, manic, and depressed patients. *Journal of Abnormal Psychology, 89,* 115–124.

Procci, W.R. (1976). Schizo-affective psychosis: Fact or fiction? *Archives of General Psychiatry, 33,* 1167–1177.

Sartorius, N., Shapiro, R., & Jablonsky, A. (1974). The international pilot study of schizophrenia. *Schizophrenia Bulletin, 1,* 21–35.

Sherrington, R., Brynjolfsson, J., Petursson, H., Potter, M., Dudleston, K., Barraclough, B., Wasmuth, J., Dobb, M., & Gurling, H. (1988). Localization of a susceptibility locus for schizophrenia on chromosome 5. *Nature, 336,* 164–166.

Skarda, C., & Freeman, W.J. (1987). How brains make chaos in order to make sense of the world. *Behavioral and Brain Sciences, 10,* 161–195.

Wielgus, M.S., & Harvey, P.D. (1988). Dichotic listening and recall in schizophrenia and mania. *Schizophrenia Bulletin, 14,* 689–700.

17 The Neuropsychological Origin of Auditory Hallucinations

Anthony S. David
King's College Hospital and the Institute of Psychiatry, London.

Auditory hallucinations, in particular those with a verbal content often referred to as "hearing voices", are commonly regarded as a characteristic symptom of psychosis. They are assumed to arise from the abnormal activity of the auditory-receptive areas of the cortex. The evidence for this is scanty both in terms of recorded instances of verbal hallucinations occurring as a direct consequence of coarse brain disease and in terms of the detection of functional disturbance coinciding with the hallucination, using electrophysiological and neuroimaging techniques. Other possible sites for the origin of hallucinations are considered such as language-production areas. The neuropsychological literature pertaining to this is reviewed and areas of overlap with studies in psychosis addressed, such as the detection of sub-vocal muscular activity during verbal hallucinations. The hypothesis that these might arise from the right cerebral hemisphere is discussed and subsidiary hypotheses put forward. Other views which point to a link between inner speech, auditory imagery and verbal hallucinations are also reviewed with emphasis on their cerebral bases. An argument is developed which supports the placement of verbal hallucinations and related phenomena within a functional model of language reception and production taken from cognitive neuropsychology. Examples illustrating these phenomena in relation to such a model are presented for their heuristic value. Several testable predictions and avenues for further research are proposed throughout the article which might form the basis of a new branch of neuropsychology, namely, cognitive neuropsychiatry.

INTRODUCTION

This article is written with a number of assumptions.

1. The position taken on the nature of psychology vis à vis neurology might be termed "Theory Dualism" (Churchland, 1988). This is the

assumption that "any particular mental state or process is a state or process in the nervous system, but ... that psychology is an autonomous level of explanation".

2. A second basic assumption is that abnormal mental states can only be understood in terms of a distortion or deviation in normal psychological processes. It is a position with which psychologists have always felt comfortable (Claridge, 1987; Bentall, 1990) but which some psychiatrists have eschewed in favour of a disease-orientated, categorical view of mental illness.

Auditory hallucinations (AHs), particularly where the person hears a voice, sometimes called verbal hallucinations (VHs), are among the most fundamental features of mental illness, especially schizophrenia (Goodwin, Alderton, & Rosenthal, 1971). The prevalence of auditory hallucinations in schizophrenia has been calculated by Slade and Bentall (1988), based on 16 published reports including 2924 cases, as occurring in 60.2%. In the International Pilot Study on Schizophrenia (Wing, Cooper, & Sartorius, 1974), 74% of 306 schizophrenics had this symptom.

The form of hallucination is an aspect emphasised by the clinical psychiatrist. Is it experienced as real or unreal, inside the head or outside? Does it consist of meaningful sounds or noises? Is it verbal, is the voice known? Is it male or female (Deiker & Chambers, 1978)? What of the grammatical form: does the voice refer to the subject in the second or third person (Schneider, 1959)? Such considerations are of considerable diagnostic significance. Less attention has been given to the content of a hallucination (Larkin, 1979), such as whether it is critical or supportive, whether the content is unpleasant, sexual, violent, neutral, etc. Freud (1926), who had little knowledge or experience of psychotic disorders, believed that hallucinations were the "projection" of unfulfilled wishes or unwanted desires. The themes that dominate many hallucinations in psychotic illnesses are to some extent consistent with this view (Hill, 1936). Freudian theory does not address the grammatical structure of VHs, but then neither do neurological theories.

There are numerous experiential phenomena that resemble VHs. These are usually placed under the rubric of auditory imagery, a specific variety of which is inner speech. This phenomenon is normal and, presumably, universal, although there is little empirical data on this. The resemblance between inner speech and VHs has been noted for at least a century (see Johnson, 1978; Hoffman, 1986, for a revival of this view). This chapter will put forward the contention that inquiry into the nature of VHs would profit from a brain-based functionalist approach common in cognitive neuropsychological research. First, the notion that cerebral insult is either necessary or sufficient to cause VHs will be examined. Next, inner speech is discussed from both psychological and neurological perspectives. Then, the relevance of cerebral abnormality or asymmetry, auditory imagery, and inner speech to psychosis will be scrutinised, making use of contemporary studies in neuroimaging. Finally, there will be an attempt to draw together this disparate body of work. The argument will be developed that VHs are not merely outpourings from an abnormal brain, but rather, they are based on the functioning of a delicate and complex normal mechanism underlying inner speech whose normal in-built control mechanisms have been distorted by the disease process. Ways of testing this framework and subsidiary hypotheses will be suggested as we proceed.

NEUROLOGICAL INPUT MODELS

Auditory Experiences During Electrical Brain Stimulation

Penfield and co-workers in Montreal carried out a series of famous experiments, summarised in a paper published in 1963 (Penfield & Perot, 1963). Early work showed that stimulation of the primary auditory areas resulted in crude "noises", while more complex sounds followed stimulation of "secondary" association areas. In all, there were 1132 stimulation studies, 520 of the temporal lobes (TLs), yet only 40 resulted in "experiential hallucinations" including complex auditory-visual experiences, "voices" and music. Auditory responses were produced in 24 patients from 66 stimulation points. Going through each of these in turn, it is striking how unlike the reports are of auditory hallucinations described by psychotic patients. The authors record vague voices muttering, shouting or whispering, not the distinct, repetitive statements schizophrenic patients experience. In two-thirds, the patient reported "a voice from the past", i.e. the memory of an actual phrase spoken to them—usually by a close relative. Having a dreamlike vision of a person speaking to the subject was a frequent occurrence, one that would not be regarded as a "true" hallucination by most psychopathologists but rather a "dissociative hallucination" (Wing et al., 1974).

Verbatim accounts of clear VHs are limited to five cases (see Table 17.1). These consisted of a voice calling the patient's name, one calling the patient's husband's name, and voices giving instructions or repeating single words. Penfield and Perot localised the auditory experiences to the lateral and superior surface of the first temporal convolution, more often on the right.

Bancaud et al. (1976) carried out 521 stimulations of the anterior cingulate gyrus upon 83 patients, only two of whom experienced auditory sensations. A careful study by Halgren, Walter, Cherlow, & Crandall (1978) of 3495 deep temporal lobe simulations in 36 psychomotor epileptics

TABLE 17.1
Verbal Hallucinations of Patients Following Brain Stimulation (from Penfield & Perot, 1963)

Case no.	Age	Sex	Content of hallucination	*Side of stimulation
8	26	Female	"Jimmy, Jimmy, Jimmy"	R
11	24	Female	"Bend down ..."	R
13	19	Male	"Yes, get out"	L
			"Tokyo, tokike"	
24	34	Male	"Vite, vite"	L
29	25	Male	"Sylvère, Sylvère"	R

evoked no formed verbal hallucinations. Memory-like episodes were elicited in three cases, after stronger stimulation and hence wider activations. All three were found to be predisposed to aberrant perceptual experiences as assessed by a personality inventory. The authors argue that their inability to produce experiential responses as readily as Penfield may be explained by the weaker and more precise application of current, and that such experiences are the indirect result of extensive electrical disruption of the TLs. This would fit with the frequency of hallucinatory experiences occurring post/interictally in epileptics rather than during the ictus (see pp. 273–276). More sophisticated studies have been conducted using stereotactically placed electrodes, both superficially and deep within limbic structures (Gloor et al., 1982). Unlike Halgren et al. (1978) these authors found that experiential phenomena could be elicted by limbic (e.g. amygdala) stimulation alone. Again, purely auditory as opposed to visual hallucinations were found in just two of 35 patients, perhaps because of the privileged access visual input has to the amygdala. Gloor (1990) has discussed mechanisms based on concepts of parallel distributed processes, which might explain experiential phenomena. Clearly, early notions that they represent a replay of the past experience are not consistent with current theories of cognition.

An interesting single case study (Mahl, Rothenberg, Delgado, & Hamlin, 1964) involved extensive psychiatric evaluations before and after stimulation with left temporal depth electrodes in a young woman with psychomotor epilepsy. Her auditory experiences were of two kinds. The first consisted of people coming to mind who seemed to be speaking; these were of varying vividness. The second were less common and consisted of disembodied words and expression, often obscene, and usually related to preceding conversations (see also Ferguson et al., 1969, for similar detailed observations). The latter may be more relevant to VHs seen in psychiatric settings.

In summary, brain stimulation experiments, despite their promise, have failed to provide a plausible model of functional auditory hallucinations.

Verbal Hallucinations During Seizures

The experience of a complex auditory hallucination during a seizure (or coinciding with an EEG record of seizure activity) appears to be extremely rare. This must be distinguished from hallucinations and other psychiatric phenomena occurring in the postictal period or, alternatively, associated with a long-standing diagnosis of epilepsy (Ferguson & Rayport, 1984; Trimble, 1990). For example, a detailed study by So et al. (1990) using continuous stereotactic depth and epidural EEG confirmed that a young man's hallucination of a voice accusing him of being homosexual was a postictal phenomenon. While such an association is of considerable importance in suggesting an aetiology for "functional psychosis", it does not help us understand the genesis of the hallucination itself.

A study of 90 patients with temporal lobe epilepsy (TLE) by Bingley (1958) showed 18% experienced "auditory illusions and hallucinations" at some time. A survey of 666 patients (Currie, Heathfield, Henson, & Scott, 1971) revealed that 16% had auditory–sensory components to the attack, which were five times more likely to be "crude" than "elaborate". The elaborate ones often included sensations in more than one modality, so these do not provide an ideal analogy for "functional" auditory hallucinations. Hécaen and Ropert (1959) collected 34 cases over more than a decade. In only two cases did the AHs occur in the absence of either sensory impairment or perceptual disturbances in other modalities. Complex verbal hallucinations occurred in six cases (see Table 17.2). The authors found an association between complex musical or verbal hallucinations and left temporal lesions.

TABLE 17.2
Verbal Hallucinations of Patients with Demonstrable Cerebral Lesions (from Hécean & Ropert, 1959)

Case No.	Mechanism	Contents and comments
6	Postictal	"Oui" and "Eva"
1	Postictal	"I'm coming back, I'm coming back ..."
7	Epileptic aura	A phrase in Latin and "écho de la pensée" "Not like hearing people speaking"
14	Epileptic aura	"Genevieve, you are going to vanish ..."
10	L temporal glioma	Palinacousis
27	L temporoparietal discharges on EEG	Sister's voice, e.g. "Tata Lène". Knew it was "in her brain"

A survey of 20 highly selected patients by Tucker and colleagues (1986), with electrophysiologically confirmed temporal lobe dysfunction recorded "spells" of atypical psychotic phenomena, including auditory hallucinations from simple noises, to music or angry voices, in 50%. Again, the association with TL abnormalities is not in question, but rather the extrapolation that "the voices" are the mental equivalent of a paroxysmal brain discharge. A rare example, which comes nearer to demonstrating the latter, was reported by Weiser (1980), who recorded epileptic discharges from a 22-year-old woman in her right gyrus of Heschl, accompanied by the hallucination of songs (but not speech; see also Keshavan et al., 1992). Finally, a case of epilepsy due to an arterio-venous malformation in whom unspecified hallucinations occurred as an aura was studied using positron emission tomography (PET) (De Reuck, Van Aken, Van Langdegem, & Vakaet, 1989). A decrease in blood flow and oxygen metabolism was demonstrated behind the L insular region malformation, 14 days after the seizure.

Verbal Hallucinations Due to Static Brain Lesions in the Absence of Seizures

Here again, there is an important distinction between brain lesions found in association with an entire clinical syndrome like schizophrenia of which AHs may be a part (69% of 150 cases reviewed by Davison & Bagley, 1969), and the isolated production of VHs; the latter is extremely rare. Courville (1928) examined the records of 412 verified cases of brain tumour. Of 99 TL lesions, four had AHs and of 98 frontal lesions, six had AHs, but these were combined with experiences in other modalities. A different collection of 110 cases of TL tumours contained only four cases with AHs, two of whom had complex experiences, one of which was of Irish folk songs and the other, "crude visual hallucinations and a dreamy state" (Keschner et al., 1936). Gal (1958) studied 61 patients with TL tumours and found no instances of AHs. Despite this paucity of findings, if a brain region were to be chosen as the seat of AHs from this data it would probably be the TLs, although the only significant though weak ($r = 0.29$) correlation found by Davison and Bagley for AHs was with diencephalic lesion sites (Davison and Bagley, 1969).

Lowe (1973) studied both qualitative and quantitative aspects of AHs in a comparison between "functional" and "organic" psychoses. He suggested that AHs in organic states were less frequent, of shorter duration, and more often felt to be a shared sensory experience. A recent study by Feinstein and Ron (1990), of patients seen at a specialist neurological hospital, failed to find an association between site of brain pathology and type of psychotic disorder. Some of the data on hallucinations (present in 49 of 62 cases (79%)), have kindly been made available to me (Feinstein, personal communication). On close inspection, there seems to be a tendency for third personal hallucinations (obviously of interest because of their specificity for schizophrenia) to be more associated with lateralised lesions (four left, two right) rather than diffuse lesions, compared with second person and non-verbal hallucinations (Table 17.3). One interpretation of this pattern is that the more "schizophrenic" hallucinations depend on there being "intact" cerebral tissue (see p. 290).

A category of AH that should be considered separately is unilateral hallucinations. This again is uncommon, although it may follow contralateral brain lesions. Bergman (1965) reported in brief 12 such cases of unilateral auditory hallucinations but states that "intelligible speech was not reported by any patient". Of interest is the patient described by Tanabe et al. (1986) who had left superior temporal gyrus infarction and experienced transient aphasia and the voice of a female TV announcer coming from the right ear, as well as hearing her own words inside her head during conversation to the extent that others could not be heard—analogous to *Gedankenlautverden* or thought echo.

To complicate matters, another cause of unilateral AHs is ear disease. This has long been recognised (Morel, 1936) and has been re-emphasised by Gordon (1987). The mechanism of peripheral sensory disruption leading to hallucinations is an important one in some cases (Corbin & Eastwood, 1986). It is particularly relevant in musical hallucinations (Berrios, 1990; Hécaen & Ropert, 1963) and was present in at least 38 out of 59 cases reviewed recently (Keshavan et al., 1992). In schizophrenia it may represent co-morbidity. However, Collicut and Hemsley (1981) have shown that auditory perception is neither better nor worse in schizophrenic hallucinators, and detection of tones may be performed with increased alacrity in hallucinating patients (Schneider & Wilson, 1983).

In conclusion, VHs as a direct and immediate consequence of brain lesions, both irritative and destructive, are rare. If such hallucinations occur, they may be unilateral. Unilateral VHs in functional psychosis will be

TABLE 17.3
Type of Hallucination According to Nature of Lesions (data from Feinstein & Ron, 1991)

	Type of Hallucination		
Site of Lesion	Non-verbal	2nd Person	3rd Person
Lateralised	2	7	6
Non-lateralised	8	19	7

Chi^2 test for trend $P < 0.001$.

discussed later, as will EEG and brain stimulation studies of psychotic patients (see pp. 286–287).

NEUROLOGICAL OUTPUT MODELS

Before considering the neurological origins of auditory–verbal hallucinations it is important to broaden the discussion to encompass speech production. A disturbance manifesting in hearing voices could arise from any point in an inner-voice–inner-ear circuit. Brain stimulation experiments assume that exogenous stimulation at the input stage (auditory association cortex or "inner ear" or "mind's ear") will mimic AH. Equally plausible is that abnormal production of speech, or at least a motor programme, which would normally precede speech (i.e. an "inner voice") might, if redirected, produce the experience of hearing a voice. This assumes that the inner voice uses, in part, the same mechanism as that for speech output (see Green & Preston, 1981). Indirect support for this position can be justified with reference to short-term memory (STM) research, which has shown the presence of functional inner speech in subjects with both acquired (Logie et al., 1989) and congenital anarthria (Bishop & Robson, 1989).

Following this reasoning, the origin of speech in the brain may be the origin of verbal hallucinations. The "seat of articular language", after Broca, is usually located around the third inferior frontal convolution of the left hemisphere, although other regions such as the supplementary motor area and more anterior frontal areas are implicated in the initiation of speech (Ojemann, 1983). Cerebral mechanisms of speech production can be studied from the perspectives of brain stimulation and epilepsy.

Brain Stimulation and Epilepsy

Penfield and Roberts (1959) were unable to produce anything other than "crude vocalization" during their brain stimulation experiments to either the right or left precentral cerebral areas. This was in contrast to speech arrest, which arose when several wide areas were stimulated. Work by Ojemann and colleagues (1990) on 117 patients undergoing left fronto–temporo–parietal craniotomies has aimed at mapping language areas by assessing picture naming during electrical stimulation. Although discrete areas underlying this function were located in most individuals, as a group, localisation was highly variable.

Turning to epileptic disturbances of speech, Serafetinides and Falconer (1963) surveyed 100 cases of TLE and found 34 with dysphasic disturbances and 38 with speech automatisms. This concurs with Bingley's figure (1958) of 39% for automatisms. Left hemisphere discharges occurred more often in the dysphasic group, while those with automatisms had more on the right.

Serafetinides and Falconer divided the utterances into five subtypes (Table 17.4). In bilinguals, some utterances were in the patient's mother tongue. Similar speech fragments occur in severe aphasics (Code, 1987). All of these examples would fit into Jackson's category of non-propositional speech (1874/1932). These utterances, single words, and inane often repetitive phrases in the patients first language (Hoffman, 1986; Jaspers, 1913/1963), are reminiscent of some types of AH. Obscenities are commonly reported, although data are not available on the relative proportion of AHs of different content.

Right Hemisphere Speech

The dichotomy between propositional and non-propositional carries an anatomical division between the left and right hemispheres, respectively. This begs the question: to what extent do speech automatisms and other recurrent utterances reflect right hemisphere (RH) speech? The evidence for this will be reviewed, as will relevant information from left hemispherectomy and commissurotomy cases and studies on intact subjects.

It has been mentioned already that ictal and electrically induced speech is more common with RH activity, and the implication from recurrent utterances in aphasics is that it is their intact RHs that are doing the talking. Support for this comes from a number of studies of aphasics who, following a second lesion to the RH, suffer dramatic deterioration in language output (Basso, Gardelli, Grassi, & Mariotti, 1989). Secondly, experiments by Kinsbourne (1971) using the Wada technique (intracarotid amytal injection) showed that temporary anaesthesia of the two aphasic patients' RHs showed similar, though reversible, effects.

The Wada test was devised to establish cerebral dominance prior to temporal lobe surgery. The inability to speak while the left hemisphere (LH) is temporarily out of action remains the most reliable index. Milner (1975) showed that only 15% of right-handers could speak under these circumstances, compared with 45% of left-handers. Despite the fact that

TABLE 17.4
Classification of Paroxysmal Disturbances of Speech (from Serafetinides & Falconer, 1963)

Type	Example
Warning	"I Feel funny"
Recurrent	"I must go, I must go"
Irrelevant	"conversational character" but "out of context"
Emotional	swear words and "I don't care what you do to me"
Perplexity	"Why not? Who are you? Where am I?"

these data are derived from epileptic subjects, they are consistent with the effects of stroke in previously well individuals in terms of aphasia in right and left-handers (see McCarthy & Warrington, 1990), that is, dextrals seldom become aphasic following RH damage, while sinistrals may do. There is some evidence that females are less vulnerable than males to the aphasiogenic effects of LH disease (McGlone, 1980). However, this may in part be explained by selection bias in hospital admissions and may not represent a fundamental gender-related difference in cerebral organisation (Kertesz & Sheppard, 1981).

Additional research by Milner's group (1975) has clarified the role of handedness and early brain injury in determining lateralisation for speech. In a study of 109 subjects who had sustained early LH damage, 19% of 31 right-handers had RH or bilateral language representation, while 70% of 78 non-right-handers had right or bilateral language. A possible intermediary factor is corpus callosum thickness. O'Kusky et al. (1988) performed a magnetic resonance imaging (MRI) study, which revealed that increased callosal thickness predicted RH speech independently of handedness in epileptic subjects. Some authors have found an association between left handedness and increased callosal dimensions while others have not; similar claims have been made for female gender (Habib et al., 1991). While no firm conclusions can be reached at present it would be fair to state that in all the circumstances where RH language is suspected to be more developed than "normal", such as in females and left-handers, some studies have found increased callosal size. This finding is important in the light of studies of the corpus callosum in psychosis.

Studies of commissurotomy—the "split-brain" operation—have revealed a wide range of comprehension abilities in the separated RH (Zaidal, 1985). However, after more than 30 years of testing, none of the original Bogen–Vogel West Coast series have demonstrated anything but the most rudimentary RH speech (Gazzaniga & Hillyard, 1971). By way of contrast, RH speech has emerged in two subjects from the East coast series, operated in two stages and sparing the anterior commissure (Gazzaniga et al., 1984; Sidtis et al., 1981). The output is simple, mainly content words without connections between them. The question of why these subjects should have this ability while the others do not is debated (Gazzaniga, 1983; Zaidel, 1983). One explanation is the influence of early LH damage, which forces the RH to develop a greater than usual language competence.

Support for this position comes from hemispherectomy. Early left hemispherectomy has been shown to be compatible with a full range of linguistic ability (Bishop, 1983). However, patients who have undergone the same operation after childhood language acquisition remain severely limited in verbal expression. Smith (1966) described an adult case: postoperatively he struggled to utter a few isolated words, often exclaiming "Goddamit!" in frustration. Over the ensuing weeks he occasionally managed brief phrases and by six months, replied to the question "Is it snowing outside?" with, "What do you think I am? A mind reader?" More recently, Patterson, Vargha-Khadem, & Polkey (1989) described in detail the linguistic ability of a girl operated upon in early adolescence because of Rassmusen's encephalitis. The following speech sample was given in answer to the question "What do you particularly like to eat?"—"I like ... er ... you know ... the ... I can't say it now ... well, I like ... I don't like chips a lot but ... I like Bolognaise."

Zaidel and others (Coltheart, Patterson, & Marshall, 1987; Zaidel, 1985) have formulated a profile of RH language: reduced auditory–verbal STM, better comprehension of speech than reading, and limited access to abstract words in the lexicon. Phonology in the RH is rudimentary so that rhyme judgements are poor, as are tasks requiring written word-to-sound (grapheme–phoneme) correspondence. This profile is derived from left hemispherectomy, split brain, and certain aphasic syndromes such as deep dyslexia. In all these respects, the LH has much greater facility. However, the RH is thought to be "dominant" in such aspects of language as prosody—the variations in pitch, intensity, and rhythm that lend speech its "musical" quality (Ross, 1981). Furthermore, there is some evidence that the pragmatics of language, the appreciation of humour, metaphor and intended meaning, are curtailed following RH damage (Gardner, Brownell, Wapner, & Michelow, 1983).

To summarise, there is convergence in the neuropsychological literature that the RH seldom has the ability to speak despite significant language comprehension capacity. This ceases to pertain so strongly when the LH has undergone early disruption and/or when the subject is left-handed. Females may not show such extreme lateralisation. This situation is important as it figures prominently in various psychiatric theories which nominate the RH as the origin of AHs (see p. 290).

NEUROPSYCHOLOGICAL MODELS—INNER SPEECH

To many, the relationship between inner speech and VH is self-evident (see Johnson 1978 for a review). Thanks to the recent, belated interest in phenomenal awareness as a legitimate area for scientific endeavour (Marcel & Bisiach, 1988), this intuitive correspondence has now led to testable hypotheses, which may use well understood and validated experimental paradigms.

Inner speech, endophasy, the preverbitum or the *language interieur* (Critchley, 1970), is a topic of much speculation, even contempt (Ryle,

1949). Part of the problem is one of terminology. Levine, Calvino, and Popovics (1982) propose two definitions: the first is the "subjective phenomenon of talking to oneself, of developing an auditory–articulatory image of speech without uttering a sound". The second is the "ability to appreciate the auditory–articulatory structure of speech irrespective of its meaning". Both versions are subjectively real and capable of quantitative research.

Developmental and Social Aspects

Piaget (1926) observed that children between the ages of 3 and 7 years engaged in what he called egocentric speech. He believed that other people are "expected neither to hear or understand" this private "dia"-logue. However, Piaget's own experiments showed that the child's private speech is responsive to those around him/her. Vygotsky (1962) argued that the child vocalises as a means of cognitive self-guidance. Contemporaries of Vygotsky in the Soviet Union, such as Bakhtin (see Emerson, 1983), extended Vygotsky's position and regarded the interplay between inner and outer speech as a means whereby man defines himself in relation to the social world. Empirical studies (Kohlberg, Yaeger, & Hjertholm, 1968) have shown a curvilinear relationship between "private speech" and development. Such activity was shown to increase with task difficulty, supporting Vygotsky's "cognitive" view and his belief in its functioning as the transition between outer speech and thought, rather than Piaget's view that private speech declines steadily as social maturity increases. Such work provides the necessary underpinning to inner speech as a normal cognitive process, which may deviate in cases of VHs. It also carries implications for the issue of why psychiatrically disturbed children seldom experience hallucinations (Garralda, 1984). Presumably, inner speech must first become internalised before a disturbance in the internalisation process can show itself.

Phenomenology, Reading and Memory

When we think, we often do so using an inner voice, usually experienced as our own (external) voice, although it may not quite accord with how it sounds to others. (I find my own real voice slightly higher and more nasal than I expected. This is presumably due to the resonance given to the voice as it leaves the mouth compared to its conduction through bone.) Reading is frequently accompanied by a vivid inner voice, which may be identified with the writer if he/she is known. We may become especially aware of the inner voice when reading a difficult passage that we do not understand immediately. Subvocal muscular activity is sometimes detected, especially in poor readers who tend to mouth the words more obviously (Dooley & George, 1988). Certain aspects of reading would seem to rely on an inner voice, such as deriving the correct meaning from the sentence containing the word *tear*: Her dress had a *tear* in it *versus* Her eye had a *tear* in it (Ellis & Young, 1988). Similarly, how do we know that *brane* (a pseudohomophone) sounds like a real word and rhymes with *tayne* and *reign*? And that T42 is the title of a popular song?

Evidence that might shed light on the relationship between inner speech and VHs comes from experiments that utilise *articulatory suppression*. This entails subjects repeating a meaningless phrase or word (e.g. the-the-the), so occupying inner speech, while reading words, letter strings or sentences (Baddeley & Lewis, 1991; Besner, 1987). While it is possible to understand even complex sentences under conditions of articulatory suppression, detecting rhyme is impaired (Richardson, 1987) as is the detection of anomalous sentences where a homophone replaces the correct word (e.g. The king sat in his *thrown* room [Coltheart et al., 1990]). Another relevant phenomenon is auditory transformation. This describes the apparent change in the sound of a word or phrase when repeated over and over (e.g. *life* → *fly*). The effect still occurs when words are repeated internally and is weakened by articulatory suppression (Reisberg et al., 1990).

Articulatory suppression affects STM in a number of predictable ways (Baddeley, 1986). This includes reducing serial recall span of short words, whether heard or read, and dissimilar sounding letters when read. The explanation is that recall of these stimuli may be improved over long words and similar sounding letters, by rehearsal, i.e. inner speech. This is believed to take place in a system named the phonological loop, conceived of as being analogous to a tape loop lasting a few seconds. Abolishing rehearsal by articulatory suppression abolishes this improvement. Hence auditory–verbal STM is intimately bound up with inner speech. This framework allows for the investigation of VHs in terms of the phonological loop. If VHs inhabit the loop in the same way as the inner speech used to retain a small number of items in memory, then hallucinating patients should show the same effects on STM tasks as normals during suppression. Some preliminary studies of this kind have been carried out and it appears that the presence of VHs is not synonymous with inner speech in any simplistic sense (David & Lucas, in press). On reflection this is not surprising because many normal subjects report hearing an inner voice while reading, despite ongoing articulatory suppression. For the present it can be assumed that the phonological loop is not the only mechanism involved in all forms of auditory imagery including VHs (Monsell, 1987).

Auditory Imagery

The feeling that the inner voice is not always entirely under control (Akins & Dennett, 1986) and may have a separate motivation was noted by William James (see Schwartz, 1986). This gives some weight to the idea that further loosening of control may lead to frank hallucinations, with obsessional ruminations being an intermediary stage. One factor that may play a role is the ability to image in another person's voice. This has been shown to lead to confusion as to whether the voice was imagined or heard (Johnson, Foley, & Leach, 1988).

Hitherto, we have discussed inner speech, but clearly this is but one element of auditory imagery. We can summon musical imagery as well as environmental sounds with ease (Baddeley & Logie, 1992). These aspects have not been well studied but it appears that they are separable from verbal auditory imagery, which may be abolished by left hemisphere damage (Shallice, 1988).

Neuroimaging

Early research measuring cerebral blood flow confirmed classical neurological expectations in showing left anterior increases during speech (Ingvar & Schwartz, 1974). However, automatic speech appears to coincide with much wider areas of activation in addition to speech centres and involving both hemispheres (Ryding, Brådvik, & Ingvar, 1987). Inner speech has not been specifically studied using PET but work by Petersen et al. (1988) on word recognition is of relevance here. Using multiple scans and the subtraction method it is possible to localise specific cognitive processes to changes in blood flow. They found that phonological recoding was not a necessary aspect of reading but that phonological coding activated temporal cortical regions bilaterally and temporal–parietal cortex on the left. Speech involved perisylvian areas bilaterally and the left prefrontal region. Work by Wise and colleagues (Wise et al., 1991) suggests that the supplementary motor area, in association with left auditory association cortex is crucially involved in a verb retrieval task which was presumed to involve subvocal rehearsal.

A recent single photon emission tomography (SPET) study has looked specifically at imagery (Goldenberg et al., 1991). Subjects had to imagine the sound of five items in turn (e.g. dog, telephone). This was associated with increased flow in both hippocampi and the right inferior and superior temporal regions. Unfortunately, such "environmental" sounds cannot be assumed to be produced by the same mechanism as inner speech. Mazziotta, Phelps, Carson, & Kuhl (1982) used PET to investigate receptive responses to auditory stimulation. They observed differences in regional brain activation according to the cognitive strategy used to remember musical tones. Musically sophisticated subjects who recalled tones by analytic means such as visualising notes on a scale, showed a different pattern of brain activation from those who "re-sang" the tone in their minds. The former subjects showed evidence of left-sided posterior TL activation while the latter showed diffuse right-sided activity.

Inner Speech in Patients with Brain Damage

So far we have looked at ways of studying forms of auditory imagery generally (Johnson et al., 1988; Reisberg et al., 1990) and in the context of working memory (Baddeley, 1986). Another method stems from traditional neuropsychology and is provided by the study of patients who have lost this faculty following brain damage. Levine et al. (1982) described just such a case who, following a presumed LH stroke, was unable to "speak to himself". When reading he would only " 'see' words as ideas not sounds". Among his many deficits, he could not detect whether words rhymed nor could he select homophones from an array.

The classical aphasiological view is that a two-way connection links input and output language centres. Damage to this interconnection results in the loss of ability to repeat verbal sequences (e.g. digit span). This has been called "conduction aphasia" although current views stress the impairment of STM (Vallar & Shallice, 1990). As well as having a characteristic pattern of performance on STM tests, some individuals with this deficit lack inner speech (Feinberg, Gonzalez, Rothi, & Heilman, 1986). A detailed case study by Howard and Franklin (1990) provides good evidence for a mechanism underpinning rehearsal of phonological items that can be disrupted following brain disease. This patient had a variety of language difficulties alongside a markedly reduce STM span. He was unable to evoke a phonologically-based representation of written language and so was unable to appreciate rhyme, homophony, etc. His performance on these and other tests was best explained by an inability to rehearse internally.

Another case that bears upon this issue is that described by Ellis, Young, and Critchley (1989). This patient experienced "natterings" or "persistent inner speech vocalizations" plus musical fragments, inside her head, due to bilateral cerebrovascular brain disease. She was noted to have reduced STM (three digits) following a left thalamic haematoma but the uncontrollable inner speech began after a subsequent lesion in the right basal ganglia. The authors suggest that their patient's damaged STM system not only lost some of its capacity but also the ability to regulate is contents—allowing entry to unwanted memories, possibly arising from the damaged RH (see p. 290). Unlike most schizophrenic patients, Ellis et al.'s case retained her ability to label the voices as her own; like them, she lost her hallucinations when speaking or listening to speech (see Margo, Hemsley, & Slade, 1981). This suggests the phonological store is open to inappropriate activation, perhaps from the RH, due to a gating failure at a subcortical level (Ojemann, 1978). When activity engages the system, for example when speaking, other inputs are inhibited. Normally, some control mechanism of the cognitive system can also prohibit internally derived information from entering STM.

Neurophysiology

The preceding discussion has assumed that inner speech or the phonological loop is a functionally isolable subsystem or module (Fodor, 1983). This does not necessarily imply that the system has a precise anatomical location. Indeed it may be the result of the combined output of a number of smaller subunits. However, as it is sensible to talk to a speech area in the brain, then why not an inner speech area? One postulate would be that this module would have close functional ties with speech, especially repetition, language comprehension, and verbal memory. In fact, patients with defective auditory–verbal STM are found consistently to have lesions around the inferior parietal lobule on the left (Vallar & Shallice, 1990), somewhat removed from speech areas (Wise et al., 1991).

Studies of brain stimulation during an STM task were reported by Ojemann (1978). The critical cortical areas were "separate but adjacent" to those involved in object naming. During input and storage these were the posterior temporo–parietal regions (only the left hemisphere was stimulated). However, the task deployed was of naming a picture, holding it in memory during a distractor task and then recalling. This is quite different from the span tasks commonly used, and may not have involved rehearsal.

To summarise this section: inner speech can be studied profitably from a number of angles ranging from social psychology to cognitive neuroscience. Any of these approaches, alone or in combination, are likely to forward understanding of VHs. However, it is necessary to specify precisely the phenomenon under study, be it music or memory, before such knowledge may be applied.

STUDIES IN PSYCHOTICS

Phenomenology

General. The phenomenological distinction between inner speech and VHs has drawn comment from psychopathologists (Jaspers, 1913/1963). Sedman (1966) attempted to distinguish inner speech from both auditory pseudohallucination and "true" AH. The criteria for this was based on ego-compatibility and inner subjective space, and the "insight" into the unreality of the experience. Kraupl-Taylor (1981) distinguishes two kinds of pseudohallucination: one where the percept is experienced as having an alien quality yet occurring within subjective space (non-self-generated, intrapersonal), and the other where the percept arises outside subjective space yet the subject retains a sense of agency (self-generated, extra-personal). The latter could be regarded as equivalent to vivid mental imagery. Current thinking is now inclined towards a less categorical view of psychotic phenomena (e.g. David, 1990) and regards them as lying on a continuum. Support for this comes from a survey of schizophrenic patients' self-ratings of AHs on a number of dimensions (Junginger & Frame, 1985). The majority of patients regarded their hallucinations as "inside the head" despite the classical view that these should be clearly outside, to be counted as hallucinations. Clinical experience shows that many patients struggle with notions of whether the "voices" are under their control or outside their head, and that the nature of the experience changes according to course of illness, mood, and the amount of willingness the patient has to discuss their AHs with staff.

From data currently being collected by workers from the Department of Psychological Medicine, Institute of Psychiatry, London (P. Jones, personal communication) of consecutive psychotic admissions meeting DSM-III criteria for schizophrenia, schizophreniform, schizoaffective, and affective disorders (American Psychiatric Association, 1980), the rates of various forms of AH are available. These were classified according to the Present State Examination (PSE) (Wing et al., 1974). Of 215 cases, 108 (50%) were experiencing AHs. Of these, 24% experienced purely pseudohallucinations ("within the mind") while 23% experienced true hallucinations ("through the ears"). Both types occurred together in 53%.

Lateralisation of Auditory Hallucinations.   Localisation in space is an aspect of the heterogeneity of AHs, which may bear upon the anatomical site of brain processes. Abnormal visual and somatic sensations affect the left side of the body more than the right (Cutting, 1989; Taylor & Fleminger, 1981). By way of contrast, VHs in schizophrenia are usually unlateralised and poorly localised (Bracha, Cabrera, Karson, & Bigelow, 1985). In a series of 54 subjects with a variety of diagnoses, localising of a voice to the right side of the subject was associated with higher scores on the Hamilton rating score for depression (Gruber, Mangat, Balminder, & Abou-taleb, 1984). Where AHs are clearly located to one hemispace, the neurological literature (Bergman, 1965; Hécaen & Ropert, 1959; Tanabe et al., 1986) suggests a contralateral temporal lobe lesion or, alternatively, ipsilateral ear disease (Gordon, 1987; Morel, 1936). Hence, study of these admittedly atypical patients using neuroimaging techniques would allow unambiguous testing of the neurological/audiological hypotheses, already confirmed once by Notardonato et al. (1989).

Form and Content.   Crude hallucinations, odd noises, sound fragments, and indistinct whispers, were frequently elicited by Penfield by brain stimulation (Penfield & Perot, 1963) and have been shown to be associated with (contralateral) cerebral lesions (Hécaen & Ropert, 1959; Morel, 1936). While these are not commonly reported in schizophrenia, they do occur. From the recent survey at the Institute of Psychiatry (P. Jones, personal communication), 33 (23.4%) out of 247 patients experienced "non-verbal" hallucinations; 19 (7.7%) music, tapping, engines, etc., and 14 (5.7%) were mutterings or whisperings (David & Lucas, 1992). Again, given the neurological work reviewed earlier, these phenomena would make a suitable target for separate neurophysiological study, particularly of the primary auditory areas of the brain.

Hearing one's own thought spoken aloud (PSE item 56, rating = 1), and the similar experience of thought echo (PSE item 57, rating = 1) were rarely reported in the Institute of Psychiatry survey: 9.8% and 4.2% respectively among DSM-III schizophrenics. In the sample as a whole, thought broadcast (arguably a form of AH) was more common, occurring in 23.6%. The most common type of hallucination, affecting 91 patients or 36.4% overall, was of a voice addressing the subject (PSE item 63), in either a pleasant/neutral (rating = 1, 16.4%) or hostile (rating = 2, 20%) tone.

It would be expected that different types of hallucination have different pathogeneses: thought echo is most plausibly connected to inner speech; non-verbal hallucinations may be the result of cortical irritation, perhaps right more than left; third person VHs, being less common than second person and pseudohallucinations would be expected to represent a more severe and specific disturbance of inner speech control.

EEG recordings in hallucinating patients

The notion that sporadic psychotic phenomena such as AHs are the products of seizure discharges remains compelling for psychiatric researchers, despite the lack of empirical support. Systematic observations have been undertaken by Stevens and her colleagues (Stevens et al., 1979), who concluded that while EEG abnormalities were found in around 40% of 40 patients, "The abnormal waveforms ... seldom coincided with episodes of blocking, stereotypy, or other abnormal behaviours" (which included AHs). Stevens and Livermore (1982) later described differences in power spectra derived from scalp EEGs. These patterns, which resembled "ramps" when charted graphically, were seen during a range of abnormal behaviours and "hallucinatory periods". However, Serafetinides, Coger, and Martin (1986) found that the results were altered substantially when patients' self-report rather than observer rating of hallucinations was used. It appears that the "ramps" were more likely to occur between periods of hallucination.

Studies using depth electrodes for recording and brain stimulation in schizophrenic subjects have seldom been carried out, presumably because their invasiveness. Sem-Jacobsen et al. (1955) published the intracerebral EEG traces from a chronic schizophrenic patient obtained during a period of hallucination during which he began to argue with General MacArthur and the King of Sweden (sic). Focal high-voltage activity as well as synchronous slow waves in frontal and temporal regions were detected but it is not clear whether these relate to the patient's "confusion" and "disturbed behaviour" or specifically to the AH. A Japanese study (Ishibashi, Hori, Endo, & Sato, 1964) was conducted on 17 patients. As in normal subjects, complex AHs were seldom evoked (three cases only) during electrical stimulation of the temporal cortex. The authors make the important observation that the hallucinations produced in this way, "Greatly differ from those of schizophrenic hallucinations". For example, one subject habitually heard a voice threatening to send him to a syphilis village; during stimulation he heard the word "splendid" repeated. Again, the brain stimulation/epilepsy model for VHs in functional disorders, fails to find support.

SPET and PET in the Study of Auditory Hallucinations

Both PET and SPET permit regional cerebral blood flow (rCBF) or regional metabolism to be determined by recording the origin of gamma rays emitted by radioactive compounds injected into the circulation. By means of computerised tomography, a three-dimensional image can be built up and regions of interest within the brain compared in different subjects or, in the same subject under different conditions.

David and Lucas (1992) have reviewed the functional neuroimaging studies applied to psychotic patients, which have focused on hallucinations. The studies are summarised in Tables 17.5 and 17.6. As can be seen, AHs do not seem to arise from any clear anatomical location. This may be explained by a number of methodological weaknesses present in the published reports. First, the confounding effects of anxiety and inattention, which are most liable to occur in patients enduring psychotic symptoms, was seldom controlled (Reiman, Fusselman, Fox, & Raichle, 1989). Studies that retest the same individuals, with and without their hallucinations (Hawton, Shepstone, Soper, & Rezaek, 1990), may partially offset this criticism but are still open to the charge that any flow or metabolic changes noted may be related to other clinical factors, not just AHs. Non-replications are therefore to be expected (Géraud, Arne-bes, Guell, & Bes, 1987). Recent work by McGuire and Murray (1991) used technetium-99m-HMPAO (hexamethyl–propyleneamineoxime) and SPET to scan schizophrenics first while hallucinated and again after treatment had alleviated these symptoms. Preliminary findings point to greater flow to the middle part of the left lateral TL during auditory hallucinatory activity.

A second methodological problem concerns the assessment of hallucinations, which was often crude and retrospective, relying on a single item in

TABLE 17.5
Single Case Studies Using SPET in Patients with Auditory Hallucinations

Author	Technique	Diagnosis	Results
Matsuda et al. (1988a)	I^{123} Iodoamphetamine	Schizophrenia	Accumulation in L superior and inferior temporal gyrus
Matsuda et al. (1988b)	I^{123} Iodoamphetamine	Alcoholic hallucinosis	Accumulation in L superior temporal lobe
Notardonato et al. (1989)	I^{123} Iodoamphetamine	Schizophrenia (L-sided hallucinations)	↑ uptake caudate nuclei bilaterally and R temporal lobe (normalised after treatment)
Hawton et al. (1990)	^{99}TC^m HMPAO	Schizophrenia (prominent hallucinations)	↓ Frontal blood flow during psychosis and relapse. Reperfusion during remission

the Brief Psychiatric Rating Scale (BPRS) (Overall & Gorham, 1962). Related to this is the difficulty in validating the patients' report of AHs and ensuring that the phenomena take place during the window of the scans' temporal resolution, for metabolic scans, or at the time of injection of the radioactive ligand, for rCBF.

Third, most authors, with a few exceptions (e.g. Musalek et al., 1989), have failed to distinguish between hallucinators and hallucinations. Studies of the former may reveal abnormalities that predispose to hallucinations regardless of diagnosis, while those of the latter would reveal something of the nature of the phenomena themselves, particularly the brain areas responsible. Walter et al. (1990), using SPET, found different patterns of rCBF in schizophrenics with spontaneous AHs and normals with hypnotically-induced hallucinations. Interpretation of this study is complicated by the fact that the hallucinations induced in the normal subjects were of music. Additionally, Weiler et al. (1990) found no evidence for postulated similarities between the hallucinatory dream-states of rapid eye-movement (REM) sleep and brain processes in schizophrenia.

Finally, the report by Cleghorn et al. (1990) deserves comment. The authors looked at the pattern of correlations between measures of glucose metabolism in different parts of the brain in hallucinating and non-hallucinating schizophrenic patients. Hallucinations, as scored on the Schedule for the Assessment of Positive Symptoms (Andreasen & Olsen, 1982) were related to anterior cingulate blood flow, perhaps indicating an attentional effect, either primary or secondary (Posner, Petersen, Fox, & Raichle, 1988). The analysis also showed strong associations between input–output language-related cortical regions as well as between these areas on the left and their homologues on the right. While this might be taken to offer some support for the hypothesis that AHs originate in the right hemisphere

TABLE 17.6
SPET and PET Studies in Patients with Auditory Hallucinations

Authors	Technique	Subjects	Results
Matthew et al. (1982)	^{133}Xe inhalation	23 schizophrenics 18 normal controls	Hallucinations-BPRS: negative correlations (0.34 < r < 0.45) with L temporal/parietal R temporo-parietal/occipital blood flow
Erbaş et al. (1990)	^{99}Tc^m HMPAO	20 schizophrenics (all with auditory hallucinations) 11 normal controls	Reduced frontal:occipital blood flow ratios
Kurachi et al. (1985)	^{133}Xe inhalation	16 schizophrenics (8 hallucinators) 20 normal controls	↑ L temporal blood flow in hallucinators ↓ bilateral frontal flow in patients
Volkow et al. (1987)	^{11}C-deoxy-glucose Resting and activation scans	18 schizophrenics 12 normal controls	Hallucinations-BPRS: positive correlation (r = 0.49) with R temporal metabolism Hypofrontality
DeLisi et al. (1989)	^{18}Fluorodeoxy-glucose	21 schizophrenics off medication 19 normal controls	Hallucinations-BPRS: positive correlation (r = 0.47) with R:L superior temporal flow ratio
Musalek et al. (1989)	^{99}Tc^m HMPAO	28 hallucinators: 17 auditory, 11 tactile 28 normal controls	Auditory: ↑ hippocampus amygdala, parahippocampus R & L. Tactile: ↓ inferior temporal bilaterally
Weiler et al. (1990)	^{18}Fluorodeoxy-glucose	Combined data on: 49 schizophrenics 30 awake normal and 12 REM-sleep controls	Hallucinations-BPRS: negative correlation (r = –0.45) with L caudate activity
Cleghorn et al. (1990)	^{18}Fluorodeoxy-glucose	19 schizophrenics: 9 with hallucinations 10 normal controls	Hallucinations-SAPS: positive correlation (r = 0.82) anterior cingulate activity High inter-correlations between frontal language areas L and R

(see p. 290), the data are consistent with the view that VHs are directly linked with the orchestrated activity of normal language production and reception systems.

Structural Brain Imaging

The huge number of CT scan studies of schizophrenic patients will not be reviewed here. In general, the only finding of relevance to the present discussion has been the negative correlation between ventriculo–brain ratio and AHs (Owens et al., 1985), supporting the idea that VHs depend on an intact cerebral substrate. One unreplicated finding was of reversed cerebral symmetry, which was associated with positive symptoms (hallucinations and delusions) (Luchins & Meltzer, 1983). This is of interest in relation to the RH hypothesis of AHs.

Magnetic resonance imaging (MRI) provides detailed information about brain structure rather than brain function, yet some MRI observations are relevant to the explanation of the nature of hallucinations. Barta et al. (1990) have reported a reduction in volume of the left superior temporal gyrus and amygdala in schizophrenic subjects which correlates highly with the extent of their hallucinatory experience ($r = 0.7$). However, when this correlation coefficient is recalculated with the one non-hallucinating subject excluded, the correlation is reduced ($r = 0.54$; $P < 0.05$).

The Right Cerebral Hemisphere and Auditory Hallucinations

We have established that the RH can swear and make non-propositional statements. VHs are often described as having a similar content (Hill, 1936). The RH's language output increases in the absence of the LH and, more commonly, when the LH is subject to insults in development and when the usual pattern of cerebral asymmetry is altered. With and without this knowledge base, various authors have proposed theories linking the RH with AHs particularly VHs. The first was anthropologist Jaynes (1979), who argued that in early civilisations, man frequently experienced "voices", which he then attributed to divine powers but that in fact arose from a relatively autonomous RH. With evolution, the separateness or "bicamerality" of the hemispheres has broken down, leading to a reduction in VHs in ordinary people. One group that is an exception to this view is, according to Jaynes, psychotics, whose RH language system remains unintegrated with the left's, save communication via the anterior commissure. Randall (1983) put forward a neurodevelopmental account in which misconnections between brain regions, including right and left language areas, lead to VHs and other schizophrenic symptoms, such as thought insertion and withdrawal. A related theory, advanced by Nasrallah (1985), explained the same cluster of symptoms in terms of "partial disconnection" of the hemispheres. All of these accounts invoke interhemispheric communication as a key element. The evidence for this will be discussed below.

Cutting (1990, p. 264) proposed a novel theory that comes out of his view that underactivity of the RH is fundamental to schizophrenia. He suggests that verbal thoughts, presumably arising from the LH, lack their "accustomed tone ... which stamps them as uniquely ours ... because of the loss of the right hemisphere's prosodic contribution". Hence they are given non-self status. So far, this attractive notion has not been subject to empirical verification. The indirect support would be provided by an account from a patient with RH damage reporting loss of prosody of their inner voice. Such an account is awaited. An intriguing case report by Hoff and Silberman (1933) of the effects of ethyl chloride application to the exposed auditory area in the right superior temporal convolution during neurosurgery may be relevant. Not only did this procedure produce the experience of thought echo but the "voices" were said to have a strange tonality.[1]

A number of testable hypotheses arise from these theories linking the RH and cerebral commissures with VHs:

1. On-line, measures (EEG, SPET, PET) would reflect RH activity during hallucination. There is some support for this (Cleghorn et al., 1990; Notardonata et al., 1989; Volkow et al., 1987).

2. VHs will be more common in left-handers (and left-handers with schizophrenia). The only available data on this question in normals comes from the study of 375 students who were given a questionnaire on their experience of "hearing voices" (Posey & Losch, 1983). Most questions asked whether their name was ever heard in a variety of settings, although included was an item on whether they could hear their thoughts spoken aloud (39% said yes). Overall as many as 71% claimed to have had some experience of VH. The authors stated that there was no effect of handedness but no information on how this was measured is given.

Regarding schizophrenics, there have been few studies looking a phenomenological differences between right- and left-handers. Nasrallah, McCalley-Whitters, and Kuperman (1982) found that out of 27 paranoid schizophrenics, nine were left-handed compared with six out of 53 non-paranoid cases ($P < 0.05$; chi^2). We might infer that the paranoid group would have more prominent AHs. This finding has been confirmed by Merrin (1984).

Handedness data on 228 consecutive admissions to hospital for functional psychosis have kindly been made available to me (P. Jones, personal communication). Classification according to Annett (1970) revealed 187 right-handers, 17 left-handers, and 24 with inconsistent or mixed handedness. The presence of AHs, thought broadcast or withdrawal, did not differ between the groups. However, thought insertion (41 cases; 25.4%) was more common in the non-right-handers (41% versus 28%, $\chi^2 = 5.8$; $P < 0.02$).

3. VH may be more common in females (and female schizophrenics). A study performed for the Society for Psychical Research on 1519 volunteers,

---

[1] I thank Dr Cutting for drawing my attention to this article.

found that 217 experienced some sort of hallucination. Of these 138 (64%) were female (West, 1948).

In a recent review of gender-related differences in psychosis (Bardenstein & McGlashan, 1990), the authors found that several indicators of severity, including negative symptoms, were loaded against males. However, no mention is made of a correspondingly increased incidence of positive symptoms such as VHs, in females.

4. Measures of interhemispheric connectivity, both functional and anatomical (such as corpus callosal thickness) will be greater (Randall, 1983; Jaynes, 1979) / less (Nasrallah, 1985) in hallucinators. There does seem to be an association between increased callosal thickness and schizophrenia, at least in some studies (Raine et al., 1990). David (1987) showed that a measure of interhemispheric disconnection was associated with first rank symptoms (supporting Nasrallah's hypothesis). AHs were not considered separately. A more recent study examining a functional measure of increased callosal connectivity, found an association with schizophrenia, although there was no correlation with clinical features including AHs (David, in press). Work by Günther et al. (1991) has shown an association between positive symptoms and increased callosal thickness on MRI.

5. Right intracarotid amytal should abolish VHs (RH structural damage may also do so). This experiment has yet to be carried out.

To conclude this subsection, the RH is a plausible site for the origin of AHs when the content is rudimentary and non-propositional. Further, where there has been early brain damage, an alteration in cerebral asymmetry and/ or an increase in interhemispheric communication, the RH may have the capacity to support more complex VHs.

Imagery in Psychotic Patients

Auditory imagery has been well studied in psychotic, particularly schizophrenic patients, with and without hallucinations. The hypothesis under test has most often been that hallucinations have an especially vivid imagery mechanism leading to reality confusion. This was indeed found by Mintz and Alpert (1972) in a task in which hallucinators and non-hallucinators were asked to report whether they heard the song *White Christmas* following suggestion. However, the majority of studies (Heilbrun, Blum, & Haas, 1983; Roman & Landis, 1945; Seitz & Molholm, 1947) have found hallucinators to report less vivid auditory images. Heilbrun et al. (1983) asked subjects to imagine various events (e.g. clapping hands) and to rate the accompanying sensory experience. They found that the auditory component was less vivid in schizophrenic patients in general. Inconsistencies among these studies abound but there is little support for an increase in auditory imagery being an important factor in the generation of AHS.

Inner Speech, Subvocal Activity, and Verbal Hallucinations

Gould (1948) must be credited with first noticing that VHs may be associated with some form of perioral or vocal musculature contraction. These observations have been subject to several replications and attempted replications (Table 17.7), which offer tantalising evidence for a direct relationship between subvocal processes and VHs. It is assumed that the activity recorded (somewhat crudely) is epiphenomenal to the hallucination, representing a kind of motor overflow from an inner speech command proximal to the motor output (see p. 276). This provokes at least two questions. First, is the perioral and laryngeal muscular activity a non-specific accompaniment of hallucinations—perhaps related to tension and anxiety (as hinted by Junginger & Rauscher, 1987)? And, even if it is localised to the articulatory apparatus, does this necessarily imply a direct link with VHs? The second question appears to have been addressed by Gould (1949) in a study of single subject in which subvocal, or more accurately, inaudible speech was amplified and recorded and compared with the patient's account of the hallucination. The transcribed recording bore a close relationship to the subject's report of what she heard and indeed conversed with. A similar experiment was carried out by Green and Preston (1981) who amplified the sound to audible levels. Interestingly, both sets of authors comment that such feedback had little effect on the patients' conviction in the non-self origin of the voice.

Following this work, several authors have looked into ways of alleviating AHs. Methods have ranged from systematic desensitisation to the use of ear plugs (reviewed in Slade & Bentall, 1988). Of interest to the present discussion are those techniques that could act, theoretically, by interrupting inner speech. A useful study was reported by Margo et al. (1981), in which varieties of auditory input, ranging from sensory restriction to white noise, were presented to seven hallucinating subjects. It was found that reading aloud and listening to prose reduced the loudness, clarity, and duration of AHs most significantly.

As mentioned earlier, reading may involve inner speech mechanisms, especially where it is effortful. Listening to speech has been found to have a rather specific effect on STM, which has been narrowed down to the obligatory access such input has to the phonological loop (Salamé & Baddeley, 1982). A series of experiments by Baddeley and colleagues (Baddeley, 1986) and Hanley and Broadbent (1987) have shown that this

TABLE 17.7
Studies of "Subvocal Activity" in Patients and Verbal Hallucinations

Author	No of Cases/Controls	Methods	Results	Comment
Gould (1948)	100 patients 64 hallucinator 36 non-hallucinators 100 normals	Surface EMG + recording of speech	82% ↑ EMG in hallucinators 14% ↑ in others	Control EMG from non-vocal region recorded but not reported
Roberts et al. (1952)	10 patients 6 hallucinators plus 3 normals	Surface EMG	43 hallucinations 19 instances of ↑ EMG, 4 were coincident	3 hallucinators had no detectable activity (low sensitivity)
McGuigan (1966)	Single case	Surface EMG	↑ EMG in reported hallucinations 2 s before onset	
Inouye & Shimizu (1970)	9 schizophrenic hallucinators	Intramuscular EMG + record of speech	286 reported hallucinations 47% ↑ EMG for duration of hallucination	Correlation of 0.79 duration of EMG versus hallucination (8.3% false +ve)
Junginger & Rauscher (1987)	19 hallucinators 22 non-hallucinators	Surface EMG + recording of speech	↑ vocal EMG 52.3 µV cases versus 32.9 controls ↑ forearm EMG 18.9 µV (versus 17.0 controls)	No subvocal speech Only 16 cases had hallucinations Borderline significance
Green & Kinsbourne (1990)	20 schizophrenics	Surface EMG oral and larynx	No ↑ EMG during or before hallucination	Humming ↓ hallucinations and ↑ EMG activity

294

"unattended speech effect" disrupts rehearsal. Methods aimed at interfering with subvocalisation have yielded promising though contradictory results. Bick and Kinsbourne (1987) found that 14 out of 18 schizophrenic patients who experienced "voices" found a reduction in them when they opened their mouths but not during other similar manoeuvres such as eye closure. Green and Kinsbourne (1989) attempted to replicate this under EMG-controlled conditions and found that humming was effective but that mouth opening and several control tasks were not. A study that compared listening to music through headphones, wearing an earplug, and subvocal counting found all methods to be moderately effective, although the music proved most popular (Nelson, Thrasher, & Barnes, 1991).

The results from these interventions are at least consistent with the hypothesis which connects the phonological loop with VHs.

THEORETICAL INTEGRATION

Monitoring and Verbal Hallucinations

Current theories that take "unintendedness" and the feeling of alien influence as their central focus are the monitoring and discourse planning theories of Frith (1987; Frith & Done, 1988) and Hoffman (1986), respectively. Frith takes an information processing approach and argues that the primary abnormality is a failure of feed-forward or "corollary discharge", by which a central "monitor" can anticipate, and so label correctly, intended acts. Hoffman, from a psycholinguistic perspective, links thought disorder, essentially disordered speech output, and VHs, to disordered inner speech that is "nonconcordant with cognitive goals". Both of these models have received some empirical support, albeit indirect. Hoffman found an association between VHs and thought disorder in a group of psychotic patients and Frith and Done (1988) found a lack of rapid error correction in a video-game task, which they took to indicate a failure of internal monitoring. Researchers have not tackled the intermittent nature of VHs by examining cognitive processes during the hallucination.

Monitoring theory provides a useful basis for further research but needs to be more specific in at least two respects. First, Frith and Done (1988) posit a common mechanism for AHs, thought broadcast, thought insertion and delusions of control. Although attractive, this may be unjustified. Neuropsychologists have emphasised the need to consider dissociations in order to make theoretical advances (David, 1993; Shallice, 1988). It may be that these phenomena, while associated in patients diagnosed as schizophrenic, may have different bases in the same way that different hallucinations are unlikely to have a common cause. Second, there is a need to specify the nature of the information being fed-forward and that of the processor.

Staying with VHs, it is necessary to map them to processors thought to underlie language production and perception. The monitoring of speech errors, both in normals and aphasics, has excited debate in the aphasiological literature (Butterworth & Howard, 1987; Levelt, 1983; Rubens & Garrett, 1991), and this may inform discussions on VHs. Extraordinary failures of self-monitoring—or anosognosia—have been recorded in patients described by Kinsbourne and Warrington (1963) with jargon aphasia who were apparently unaware of their incomprehensible speech, even when it was played back to them, but became aware when it was repeated in a different voice (or transcribed in an examiner's handwriting). Other patients can be alerted to their disordered speech when it is played back, while others are immediately aware of their errors yet seem unable to correct or prevent them (Lebrun, 1990; Rubens & Garrett, 1991).

Finally, as Frith and Done note, it is strikingly odd that one should need to label thoughts as one's own. While a system of reafferentation is clearly necessary for a movable organism to determine relative motion, it is not obvious what advantage there is in a similar system for "thoughts" unconnected with action. Frith and Done seem to argue that such a system must exist purely because its malfunction explains the disorder, without offering any independent support for its existence.

Cognitive neuropsychological models of psychopathology

The following scheme is an attempted integration of the neuropsychological evidence reviewed above and the kind of model provided by Frith. It is based in part on a cognitive neuropsychological model of language input and output processes as outlined by Ellis and Young (1988) (Fig. 17.1). Several psychopathological phenomena can be fitted into such a scheme. These include disorders of the possession of thought (Schneider, 1959) such as thought withdrawal and thought insertion; allied disorders that have an auditory–perceptual component, such as thought echo and broadcast; and finally the subtypes of auditory–verbal sensations, both true and pseudohallucinations.

From Fig. 17.1, and subsequent figures, the auditory analysis system is presumed to be analogous to the "mind's ear" while the phoneme output system is analogous to the "mind's voice". Information flows in the direction of the arrows. Flow can be interrupted, (indicated by =), or increased, (indicated by a bold arrow). Thoughts originate in, and are understood by, the semantic system. An intended thought leaves the semantic system along the output track where it assumes a linguistic form in the auditory output lexicon. The thought takes on a speech-like

External   Internal

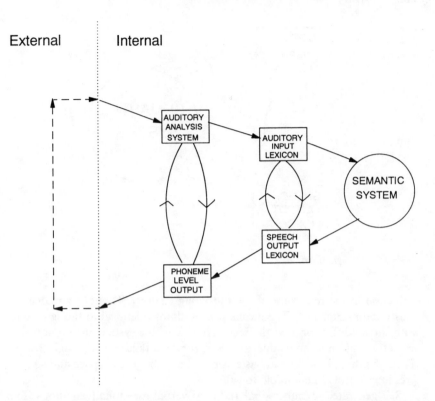

FIG. 17.1   A cognitive neuropsychological model of language perception and production (after Ellis & Young, 1988).

phonological representation in the phoneme output system and finally an articulatory structure prior to speech, with the possibility of some external "leakage" in the form of sub-vocal activity. Similarly, verbal input is captured by the auditory analysis system. Its lexical content is addressed in the auditory input lexicon, and the meaning derived by the semantic system. Hence this model proposes that a thought is experienced at the lexical level, while a voice is experienced at the phonological level.

Figures 17.2 and 17.3 illustrate mechanisms for thought insertion and withdrawal. These are along the same lines as Frith's model, except they are specific for language, or rather prelinguistic thought. Figure 17.4 illustrates thought echo. Here, there is no confusion as to the self-generated nature of the thought. The abnormal feature is that the thought as represented in the speech output lexicon, activates elements at the phoneme level so lending an auditory character to the experience. This could occur because of the high level of resting activation of certain elements in the output lexicon or a

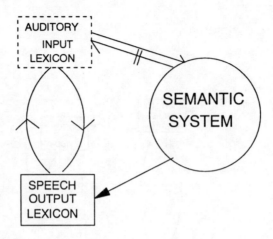

FIG. 17.2   Thought insertion.

reduction in the resistance of the out-going channel. Thought broadcast is illustrated in Fig. 17.5. The mechanism is almost identical to thought echo, with the modification that the receptive side of the system has no notice to expect an internal input, due to a feed-forward failure at the lexical level. Thus, the thought is "heard" as arising outside subjective space and so (it is presumed), it will be audible to others.

Self-generated, extrapersonal auditory–verbal pseudohallucinations (Fig. 17.6) can also be traced in this way. Again, like thought echo and broadcast,

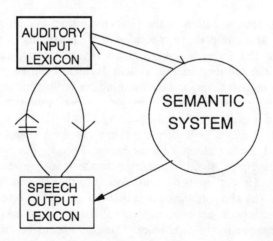

FIG. 17.3   Thought withdrawal.

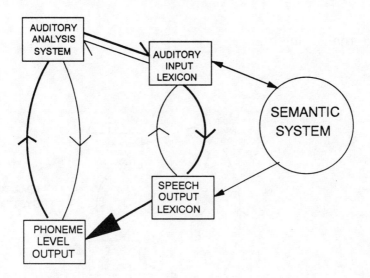

FIG. 17.4   Thought echo.

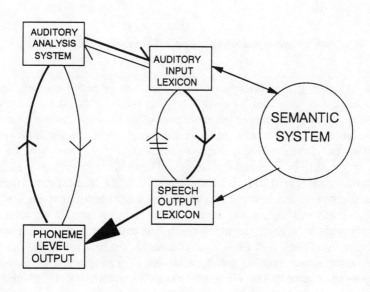

FIG. 17.5   Thought broadcast.

External ┊ Internal

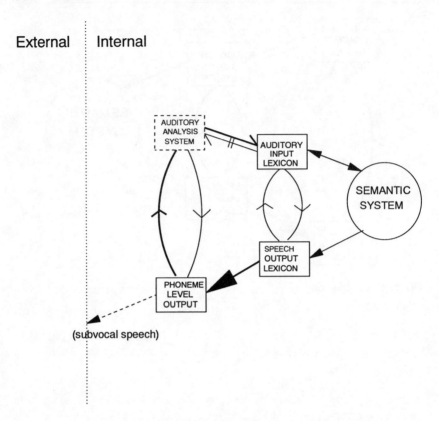

FIG. 17.6   Auditory–verbal pseudohallucination: self-generated, extrapersonal.

thought output overflows into the phoneme system. However, unlike broadcast, there is a feed-forward failure between the lexical and sublexical input modules. This leads to the experience of an actual voice being heard as opposed to an audible thought. If feed-forward from the semantic system itself is faulty, there will be no sense of ownership of the thought/voice, and this will result in a pseudohallucination, experienced within subjective, personal space (Fig. 17.7). If, on the other hand, the feed-forward from the semantic system and between lexical and sublexical input modules are both faulty, there will be neither a sense of ownership nor of an internally perceived thought/voice, so giving rise to the experience of a true auditory hallucination (Fig. 17.8). Finally, an alternative model is shown in Fig. 17.9. This obviates the need to specify a failure of feed-forward or feed-back because the source of the VH is an "ectopic" semantic system, which feeds into various input stages. If it does so at the auditory analysis level, a true AH will be produced, while entry at a deeper level would produce a non-self,

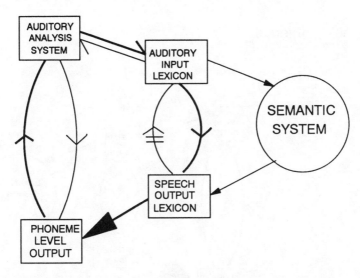

FIG. 17.7   Auditory–verbal pseudohallucination: non self-generated, intrapersonal.

pseudohallucination. Direct input to the LH semantic system might lead to thought insertion. The origin of this ectopic semantic system might be the RH.

All the models (with the exception of Fig. 17.9) postulate several abnormal loci. For example, why should the contents of the speech output lexicon "overflow" beyond its confines? One explanation would be that certain words or ideas may have higher resting levels of activation because their content is anxiety-provoking, as with sexual or violent thoughts. This is consistent with the content of many AHs. Equally, why should certain channels have raised "gain" or a lowered resistance (or threshold) for transmission? Again, this might be conceptualised in physiological terms as a generalised excitability because of say, a transmitter imbalance or poor electrical "tuning", or anatomically in terms of hyperconnection. The former might give rise to multimodal perceptual and cognitive abnormalities during an abnormal state (acute psychosis), while the latter would cause a predisposition or vulnerability trait, evident in "at risk" individuals.

Testability

To what extent are these models testable? To begin, the failure to demonstrate abnormally vivid auditory imagery in psychotic patients is consistent with normal output from the semantic system. The postulated increase in resting activation of items in the lexical, semantic or even phonological output systems could be tested psychophysiologically by

External   Internal

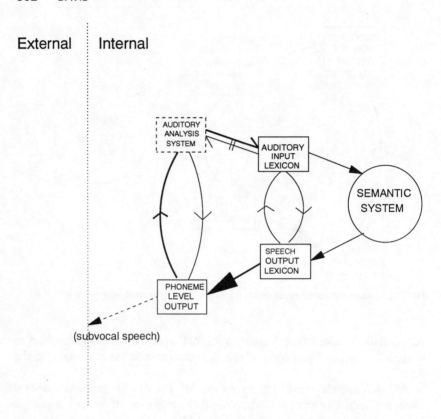

FIG. 17.8 Auditory–verbal (true) hallucination: non self-generated, extrapersonal.

showing increased reactance, using auditory evoked potentials (AEPs) or galvanic skin responses (GSR) to hallucinated words (see Ward et al., 1991; Cooklin, Strugeon, & Leff, 1983, for the relevant methodologies). A more cognitive strategy might be to measure reduced perceptual thresholds, increased priming, or increased interference in a selective attention paradigm (see Bentall & Kaney, 1990, for a related approach to delusions). It should be possible to distinguish between the site of overactivation by looking, for example, at lexical as opposed to semantic priming of words related to hallucinatory contents. Examining evoked responses to words in the visual modality would also do this. Reduced resistance within channels could also be tested using AEPs and behavioural measures. A generalised change in AEP latency and amplitude or in reaction time, not specific to hallucinatory items would favour a problem here rather than within the modules.

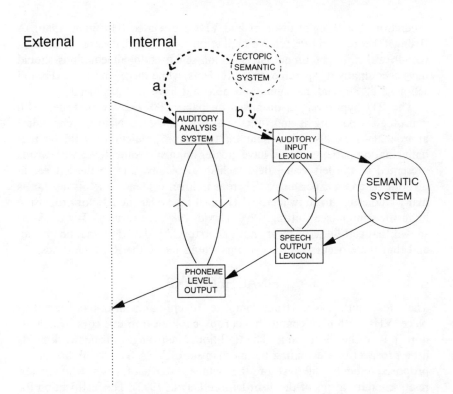

FIG. 17.9 Hallucinations from ectopic source (e.g. right hemisphere). (a) True hallucination; (b) pseudohallucination.

The integrity of the modules and connections shown in Fig. 17.1 can be tested within an aphasiological framework. This would entail the intact comprehension, spontaneous generation, and repetition of words and non-words. Neither phonological, morphological or semantic errors should occur (Ellis & Young, 1988). The presence of intact bidirectional flow of information between the semantic system and input lexicon can be demonstrated by intact comprehension and semantic priming of heard words. The two-way connection between auditory analysis and phoneme output systems can be tested by means of STM paradigms, as in David and Lucas (in press (b)) where it was found to be intact in a hallucinating patient. The connection linking the output lexicon with the input lexicon is the most difficult to test. One reason is the lack of clear understanding of the relationship between these modules and whether they are in fact distinct (Ellis & Young, 1988). At present such a link is entirely theoretical. It might, however, relate to monitoring of speech errors. This would give rise to the prediction that thought disorder and VHs are related (Hoffman, 1986). A stronger, more readily refutable prediction would be that cases of thought withdrawal, thought broadcast, and non-self pseudohallucinations should have accompanying speech output problems, while those with true AHs and self-generated pseudohallucinations need not have such problems.

The RH hypothesis as discussed on pages 290–292 can be tested with neurological paradigms and functional neuroimaging. Neuropsychological approaches may also shed light on this. One prediction would be that hallucinating patients should have greater linguistic competence with words presented to the left visual field tachistoscopically, and to the left ear in dichotic listening experiments. There is indirect evidence for this insofar as many studies fail to show a clear LH advantage over the RH for processing linguistic stimuli (see Cutting, 1990; David, 1989, for reviews). If it could be shown that certain words were not understood by the RH semantic system, and that these occurred in a VH, this would refute the RH hypothesis.

FINAL REMARKS

The above outline is far from complete. It represents an initial attempt to place VHs within a cognitive neuropsychological framework which is, hopefully, of heuristic value. The traditional neurological framework holds little prospect of elucidating the mechanism of VHs. The testability of the proposed models will rest on the detailed study of cases who exhibit relatively pure forms of the disorder (see David, 1993). The justification for presenting this approach in such a preliminary form is to "cast a wide net" so as to encourage researchers to "capture" suitable patients. Last of all it is an attempt to stimulate research into a new domain, which may be called cognitive neuropsychiatry.

REFERENCES

Akins, K.A., & Dennett, D.C. (1986). Who may I say is calling? *Behavioural and Brain Sciences*. *9*, 517–518.

American Psychiatric Association (1980). *Diagnostic and statistical manual of mental disorders (DSM III)* (3rd Ed.). Washington, APA.

Andreasen, N.C., & Olsen, S. (1982). Negative and positive schizophrenia: Definition and validation. *Archives of General Psychiatry, 39*, 789–793.

Annett, M. (1970). A classification of hand preference by association analysis. *British Journal of Psychology, 61*, 303–321.

Baddeley, A.D. (1986). *Working memory*. Oxford: Oxford University Press.

Baddeley, A.D., & Lewis, V.J. (1981). Inner active processing in reading: The inner voice, the inner ear and the inner eye. In A.M. Lesgold & C.A. Perfetti (Eds.), *Interactive processes in reading*. Hillside, N.J.: Lawrence Erlbaum Associates Inc.

Baddeley, A., & Logie, R. (1992). Auditory imagery and working memory. In D. Reisberg (Ed.). *Auditory imagery*, pp. 179–197. Hillsdale, N.J.: Lawrence Erlbaum Associates.

Bancaud, J., Talairach, J., Geier, S., Bonis, A., Trottier, S., & Marique, M. (1976).

Manifestations comportementales induites par la stimulation électrique due gyrus congulaire antérieur chez l'homme. *Revue Neurologique, 132,* 705–724.

Bardenstein, K.K., & McGlashan, T.H. (1990). Gender differences in affective, schizoaffective, and schizophrenic disorders: A review. *Schizophrenia Research, 3,* 159–172.

Barta, P.E., Pearlson, G.D., Powers, R.E., Richards, S.S., & Tune, L.E. (1990). Auditory hallucinations and smaller superior temporal gyral volume in schizophrenia. *American Journal of Psychiatry, 147,* 457–1462.

Basso, A., Gardelli, M., Grassi, M.P., & Mariotti, M. (1989). The role of the right hemisphere in recovery from aphasia. Two case studies. *Cortex, 25,* 555–566.

Bentall, R.P. (1990). The illusion of reality: A review and integration of psychological research on hallucinations. *Psychological Bulletin, 107,* 82–95.

Bentall, R.P., & Kaney, S. (1989). Content specific information processing and persecutory delusions: An investigation using the emotional Stroop test. *British Journal of Medical Psychology, 62,* 355–364.

Bergman, P.S. (1965). Unilateral auditory hallucinations. *Transactions of the American Neurological Association, 90,* 226–227.

Berrios, G.E. (1990). Musical hallucinations: A historical and clinical study. *British Journal of Psychiatry, 156,* 188–194.

Besner, D. (1987). Phonology, lexical access in reading, and articulatory suppression: A critical review. *Quarterly Journal of Experimental Psychology, 39A,* 467–478.

Bick, P.A., & Kinsbourne, M. (1987). Auditory hallucinations and subvocal speech in schizophrenia. *American Journal of Psychiatry, 144,* 222–225.

Bingley, T. (1958). Mental symptoms in temporal lobe epilepsy and temporal gliomas. *Acta Psychiatrica et Neurologica Scandinavica, 33,* (Suppl. 120), 1–151.

Bishop, D.V.M. (1983). Linguistic impairment after left hemidecortication for infantile hemiplegia? Reappraisal. *Quarterly Journal of Experimental Psychology, 35A,* 199–207.

Bishop, D.V.M., & Robson, J. (1989). Unimpaired short-term memory and rhyme judgment in congenitally speechless individuals. *Quarterly Journal of Experimental Psychology, 41A,* 123–140.

Bracha, H.S., Cabrera, F.J., Karson, C.N., & Bigelow, L.B. (1985). Lateralization of visual hallucinations in chronic schizophrenia. *Biological Psychiatry, 20,* 1132–1136.

Butterworth, B., & Howard, D. (1987). Paragrammatisms. *Cognition, 26,* 1–37.

Churchland, P.S. (1988). Reduction and neurobiological basis of consciousness. In A.J. Marcel & E. Bisiach (Eds.), *Consciousness in contemporary science.* Oxford: Oxford University Press.

Claridge, G. (1987). "The schizophrenias as nervous types" revisited. *British Journal of Psychiatry, 151,* 735–743.

Cleghorn, J.M., Garnett, E.S., Nahmias, C. et al. (1990). Regional brain metabolism during auditory hallucinations in chronic schizophrenia. *British Journal of Psychiatry, 157,* 562–570.

Code, C. (1987). *Language, aphasia and the right hemisphere.* Chichester: John Wiley & Sons.

Collicutt, J.R., & Hemsley, D.R. (1981). A psychophysical investigation of auditory functioning in schizophrenia. *British Journal of Clinical Psychology, 20,* 199–204.

Coltheart, M., Patterson, K., & Marshall, J.C. (1987). *Deep dyslexia* (2nd ed.). London: Routledge & Kegan Paul.

Coltheart, V., Arons, S.E., & Trollope, J. (1990). Articulatory suppression and phonological codes of reading for meaning. *Quarterly Journal of Experimental Psychology, 42A,* 375–399.

Cooklin, R., Strugeon, D., & Leff, J. (1983). The relationship between auditory hallucinations and spontaneous fluctuations of skin conductance in schizophrenia. *British Journal of Psychiatry, 142,* 47–52.

Corbin, S.L., & Eastwood, M.R. (1986). Sensory deficits and mental disorders of old age: Causal or coincidental associations? *Psychological Medicine, 16*, 251–256.

Courville, C.B. (1928). Auditory hallucinations provoked by intracranial tumors. *Journal of Nervous and Mental Disease, 67*, 265–272.

Critchley, M. (1970). *Aphasiology*. London: Edward Arnold.

Currie, S., Heathfield, K.W.G., Henson, R.A., & Scott, D.F. (1971). Clinical course and prognosis of temporal lobe epilepsy—a survey of 666 patients. *Brain, 92*, 173–190.

Cutting, J. (1989). Body image disorder: Comparison between unilateral hemisphere damage and schizophrenia. *Behavioural Neurology, 2*, 201–210.

Cutting, J. (1990). *The right cerebral hemisphere and psychiatric disorders*. Oxford: Oxford University Press.

David, A.S. (1987). Tachistoscopic tests of colour naming and matching in schizophrenia: Evidence for posterior callosum dysfunction? *Psychological Medicine, 17*, 621–630.

David, A.S. (1989). Divided visual field studies in schizophrenia. In J. Crawford & D. Parker (Eds.), *Developments in clinical and experimental neuropsychology*. New York: Plenum Press.

David, A.S. (1990). Insight and psychosis. *British Journal of Psychiatry, 156*, 798–808.

David, A.S. (1993). Cognitive neuropsychiatry? *Psychological Medicine, 23*, 1–5.

David, A.S. (in press). Callosal transfer in schizophrenia: too much or too little? *Journal of Abnormal Psychology*.

David, A.S., & Lucas, P.A. (1992). Neurological models of auditory hallucinations. In C. Katona & R. Levy (Eds.), *Delusions and hallucinations in old age*. London: Gaskell Publications.

David, A.S., & Lucas, P.A. (in press). Auditory–verbal hallucinations and the phonological loop: a cognitive neuropsychological study. *British Journal of Clinical Psychology*.

Davison, K., & Bagley, C.R. (1969). Schizophrenia-like psychoses associated with organic disorders of the central nervous system. In R.N. Herrington (Ed.), *Current problems in neuropsychiatry*. British Journal of Psychiatry Special Publication No 4, Ashford, Kent: Headley Brothers.

Deiker, T., & Chambers, H.E. (1978). Structure and content of hallucinations in alcohol withdrawal and functional psychosis. *Journal of Studies on Alcohol, 39*, 1831–1840.

De Lisi, L.E., Buchsbaum, M.S., Holcomb, H.H., Langston, K.C., King, A.C., Kessler, R., Pickar, D., Carpenter, W.T., Morihisa, J.M., Margolin, D., & Weinberger, D.R. (1989). Increased temporal lobe glucose use in chronic schizophrenic patients. *Biological Psychiatry, 25*, 835–851.

De Reuck, J., Van Aken, J., Van Langdegem, S., & Vakaet, A. (1989). Positron emission tomography studies of changes in cerebral blood flow and oxygen metabolism in arteriovenous malformation of the brain. *European Neurology, 29*, 294–297.

Dooley, C., & George, R.E. (1988). A single case study illustrating the reduction in subvocalisation and electromyography. *Behavioural Psychotherapy, 16*, 231–240.

Ellis, A.W., & Young, A.W. (1988). *Human cognitive neuropsychology*. Hove, Sussex: Lawrence Erlbaum Associates Ltd.

Ellis, A.W., Young, A.W., & Critchley, E.M.R. (1989). Intrusive automatic or nonpropositional inner speech following bilateral cerebral injury. *Aphasiology, 3*, 581–585.

Emerson, C. (1983). The outer word and inner speech: Bakhtin, Vygotsky and the internalization of language. *Critical Inquiry, 10*, 245–264.

Erbaş, B., Kumbasar, H., Erbengi, G., & Bekdik, C. (1990). Tc-99m HMPAO/SPECT determination of regional cerebral blood flow changes in schizophrenics. *Clinical Nuclear Medicine, 12*, 904–907.

Feinberg, F.E., Gonzalez Rothi, L.J., & Heilman, K.M. (1986). "Inner speech" in conduction aphasia. *Archives of Neurology, 43*, 591–593.

Feinstein, A., & Ron, M.A. (1990). Psychosis associated with demonstrable brain disease. *Psychological Medicine, 20*, 793–803.

Ferguson, S.M., & Rayport, M. (1984). Psychosis in epilepsy. In D. Blummer (Ed.), *Psychiatric aspects of epilepsy*, Washington D.C.: American Psychiatric Press Inc.

Ferguson, S.M., Rayport, M., Gardner, R., Bass, W., Weiner, H., & Reiser, M.F. (1969). Similarities in mental content of psychotic states, spontaneous seizures, dreams, and responses to electrical brain stimulation in patients with temporal lobe epilepsy. *Psychosomatics, 31*, 479–498.

Fodor, J.A. (1983). *The modularity of mind.* Cambridge MA: MIT Press.

Freud, S. (1926). Metapsychological supplement of theory of dreams. In *Collected Papers Vol. 4*. London: Hogarth Press.

Frith, C.D. (1987). The positive and negative symptoms of schizophrenia reflect impairments in the perception and initiation of action. *Psychological Medicine, 17*, 631–648.

Frith, C.D., & Done, C.J. (1988). Towards a neuropsychology of schizophrenia. *British Journal of Psychiatry, 153*, 437–443.

Gal, P. (1958). Mental symptoms in cases of tumor of the temporal lobe. *American Journal of Psychiatry, 115*, 157–160.

Gardner, H., Brownell, H.H., Wapner, W., & Michelow, D. (1983). Missing the point: The role of the right hemisphere in the processing of complex linguistic materials. In E. Perecman (Ed.), *Cognitive processing in the right cerebral hemisphere*. New York: Academic Press.

Garralda, M.E. (1984). Psychotic children with hallucinations. *British Journal of Psychiatry, 145*, 74–77.

Gazzaniga, M.S. (1983). Right hemisphere language following brain bisection: A 20 year perspective. *American Psychologist, 38*, 525–537.

Gazzaniga, M.S., & Hillyard, S.A. (1971). Language and speech capacity of the right hemisphere. *Neuropsychologia, 9*, 273–280.

Gazzaniga, M.S., Smylie, C.S., Baynes, K., Hirst, W., & McCleary, C. (1984). Profiles of right hemisphere language and speech following brain bisection. *Brain and Language, 22*, 206–220.

Géraud, G., Arne-Bes, M.C., Guell, A., & Bes, A. (1987). Reversibility of hemodynamic hypofrontality in schizophrenia. *Journal of Cerebral Blood Flow and Metabolism, 7*, 9–12.

Gloor, P. (1990). Experiential phenomena of temporal lobe epilepsy. *Brain, 133*, 1673–1694.

Gloor, P., Olivier, A., Quesney, L.F., Andermann, F., & Horowitz, S. (1982). The role of the limbic system in experiential phenomena of temporal lobe epilepsy. *Annals of Neurology, 12*, 129–144.

Goldenberg, G., Podreka, I., Steiner, M., Franzen, P., & Deeke, L. (1991). Contributions of occipital and temporal brain regions to visual and acoustic imagery—a SPECT study. *Neuropsychologia, 29*, 695–702.

Goodwin, D.W., Alderton, P., & Rosenthal, R. (1971). Clinical significance of hallucinations in psychiatric disorders. *Archives of General Psychiatry, 24*, 76–80.

Gordon, A.G. (1987). Letter to the editor. *Acta Psychiatrica Scandinavica, 75*, 664–668.

Gould, L.N. (1948). Verbal hallucinations and activity of vocal musculature, *American Journal of Psychiatry, 105*, 367–372.

Gould, L.N. (1949). Auditory hallucinations and subvocal speech. *Journal of Nervous and Mental Disease, 109*, 418–427.

Green, M.F., & Kinsbourne, M. (1989). Auditory hallucinations in schizophrenia: Does humming help? *Biological Psychiatry, 25*, 633–635.

Green, M.F., & Kinsbourne, M. (1990). Subvocal activity and auditory hallucinations: Clues for behavioral treatments? *Schizophrenia Bulletin, 16*, 617–625.

Green, P., & Preston, M. (1981). Reinforcement of vocal correlates of auditory hallucinations by auditory feedback: A case study. *British Journal of Psychiatry, 139*, 204–208.

Gruber, L.N., Mangat, B., Balminder, S., & Abou-taleb, H. (1984). Laterality of auditory hallucinations in psychiatric patients. *American Journal of Psychiatry, 141*, 586–588.

Günther, W., Petsch, R., Steinberg, R., Moser, E., Streck, P., Heller, H., Kurtz, G., & Hippius,

H. (1991). Brain dysfunction during motor activation and corpus callosum alterations in schizophrenia measured by cerebral blood flow and magnetic resonance imaging. *Biological Psychiatry*, *29*, 535–555.

Habib, M., Gayraud, D., Oliva, A., Regis, J., Salamon, G., & Khalil, R. (1991). Effects of handedness and sex on the morphology of the corpus callosum: a study with brain magnetic resonance imaging. *Brain and Cognition*, *16*, 41–61.

Halgren, E., Walter, R.D., Cherlow, D.G., & Crandall, P.H. (1978). Mental phenomena evoked by human electrical stimulation of the human hippocampal formation and amygdala. *Brain*, *101*, 83–117.

Hanley, J.R., & Broadbent, C. (1987). The effect of unattended speech on serial recall following auditory presentation. *British Journal of Psychology*, *78*, 287–297.

Hawton, K., Shepstone, B., Soper, N., & Rezaek, L. (1990). Single-photon emission computerised tomography (SPECT) in schizophrenia. *British Journal of Psychiatry*, *156*, 425–427.

Hécaen, H., & Ropert, R. (1959). Hallucinations auditives au cours de syndromes neurologiques. *Annales Médico-Psychologiques*, *1*, 257–306.

Hécaen, H., & Ropert, R. (1963). Les hallucinations auditives des otopaths. *Journal Psychologic Normale et Pathologique*, *117*, 257–306.

Heilbrun, A.B., Blum, N., & Haas, M. (1983). Cognitive vulnerability to auditory hallucination: Preferred imagery, mode and spatial location of sounds. *British Journal of Psychiatry*, *143*, 294–299.

Hill, J.M. (1936). Hallucinations in psychosis. *Journal of Nervous and Mental Disease*. *83*, 402–421.

Hoff, H., & Silberman, M. (1933). Änderungen der akusrischen Wahrnehmungswelt bei Temporallappenläsionen. *Zeitschrift für die Gesamte Neurologie und Psychiatrie*, *144*, 655–664.

Hoffman, R.E. (1986). Verbal hallucinations and language production processes in schizophrenia. *Behavioral and Brain Sciences*, *9*, 503–548.

Howard, D., & Franklin, S. (1990). Memory without rehearsal. In G. Vallar & T. Shallice (Eds.), *Neuropsychological impairments of short-term memory*. Cambridge: Cambridge University Press.

Ingvar, D.H., & Schwartz, M.S. (1974). Blood flow patterns induced in the dominant hemisphere by speech and reading. *Brain*, *96*, 274–288.

Inouye, T., & Shimizu, A. (1970). The electromyographic study of verbal hallucinations. *Journal of Nervous and Mental Disease*, *151*, 415–422.

Ishibashi, T., Hori, H., Endo, K., & Sato, T. (1964). Hallucinations produced by electrical stimulation of the temporal lobes in schizophrenic patients. *Tohuku Journal of Experimental Medicine*, *82*, 124–139.

Jackson, J.H. (1874/1932). In J. Taylor (Ed.), *Selected writings of John Hughlings Jackson* (Vol. 2). London: Hodder & Stoughton.

Jaspers, K. (1963). *General psychopathology* (Trans.). Manchester: Manchester University Press. (Original work published 1913.)

Jaynes, J. (1979). *The origins of consciousness in the breakdown of the bicamecal mind*. Boston: Houghton-Mifflin Co.

Johnson, F. (1978). *The anatomy of hallucinations*. Chicago: Melson Hall.

Johnson, M.K., Foley, M.A., & Leach, K. (1988). The consequence for memory of imagining in another person's voice. *Memory and Cognition*, *16*, 337–342.

Junginger, J., & Frame, C.L. (1985). Self-report of the frequency and phenomenology of verbal hallucinations. *Journal of Nervous and Mental Disease*, *173*, 149–155.

Junginger, J., & Rausher, F.P. (1987). Vocal activity in verbal hallucinations. *Journal of Psychiatric Research*, *21*, 101–109.

Kertesz, A., & Sheppard, A. (1981). The epidemiology of aphasic and cognitive impairment in stroke. *Brain*, *104*, 117–128.

Keschner, M., Bender, M.B., & Strauss, I. (1936). Mental symptoms in cases of tumour of the temporal lobe. *Archives of Neurology and Psychiatry*, *35*, 572–596.

Keshavan, M.S., David, A.S., Steingard, S., & Lishman, W.A. (1992). Musical Hallucinations: A review and synthesis. *Neuropsychiatry, Neuropsychology & Behavioral Neurology*, *5*, 211–223.

Kinsbourne, M. (1971). The minor cerebral hemisphere as a source of aphasic speech. *Archives of Neurology*, *25*, 302–306.

Kinsbourne, M., & Warrington, E.K. (1963). Jargon aphasia. *Neuropsychologia*, *1*, 27–37.

Kohlberg, L., Yaeger, J., & Hjertholm, E. (1968). Private speech: four studies and a review of theories. *Child Development*, *39*, 691–736.

Kraupl-Taylor, F. (1981). On pseudo-hallucinations. *Psychological Medicine*, *11*, 265–279.

Kurachi, M., Kobayashi, K., Matsubara, R., Hiramatsu, H., Yamaguchi, N., Matsuda, H., Maeda, T., & Hisada, K. (1985). Regional cerebral blood flow in schizophrenic disorders. *European Neurology*, *24*, 176–181.

Larkin, A.R. (1979). The form and content of schizophrenic hallucinations. *American Journal of Psychiatry*, *136*, 940–943.

Lebrun, Y. (1990). Anosognosia in aphasics. *Cortex*, *23*, 251–263.

Levelt, W.J.M. (1983). Monitoring and self-repair in speech. *Cognition*, *14*, 41–104.

Levine, D.N., Calvino, R., & Popovics, A. (1982). Language in the absence of inner speech. *Neuropsychologia*, *20*, 391–409.

Logie, R.H., Cubelli, R., Della Sala, S. et al. (1989). Anarthria and verbal short-term memory. In J. Crawford & D. Parker (Eds.), *Developments in clinical and experimental neuropsychology*. New York: Plenum Press.

Lowe, G.R. (1973). The phenomenology of hallucinations as an aid to differential diagnosis. *British Journal of Psychiatry*, *123*, 621–633.

Luchins, D.J., & Meltzer, H.Y. (1983). A blind, controlled study of occipital asymmetry in schizophrenia. *Psychiatry Research*, *10*, 87–95.

Mahl, G.F., Rothenberg, A., Delgado, J.M.R., & Hamlin, H. (1964). Psychological responses in the human to intracerebral electrical stimulation. *Psychosomatics*, *26*, 337–368.

Marcel, A.J., & Bisiach, E. (Eds.) (1988). *Consciousness in contemporary science*. Oxford: Oxford University Press.

Margo, A., Hemsley, D.R., & Slade, P.D. (1981). The effects of varying auditory input on schizophrenic hallucinations. *British Journal of Psychiatry*, *139*, 122–127.

Mathew, R.J., Duncan, G.C., Weinman, M.L., & Barr, D. (1982). Regional cerebral blood flow in schizophrenia. *Archives General Psychiatry*, *39*, 1121–1124.

Matsuda, H., Gyobu, T., Masayasu, I., & Hisada, K. (1988a). Increased accumulation of *N*-isopropyl-(I-123) *p*-iodamphetamine in the left auditory area in a schizophrenic patient with auditory hallucinations. *Clinical Nuclear Medicine*, *13*, 53–55.

Matsuda, H., Gyobu, T.M., & Hisada, K. (1988b). Iodine-123 iodoamphetamine brain scan in a patient with auditory hallucination. *Journal of Nuclear Medicine*, *29*, 558–560.

Mazziotta, J.C., Phelps, M.E., Carson, R.E., & Kuhl, D.E. (1982). Tomographic mapping of human cerebral metabolism: auditory stimulation. *Neurology*, *32*, 921–937.

McCarthy, R.A., & Warrington, E.K. (1990). *Cognitive neuropsychology: A clinical introduction*. London: Academic Press Inc.

McGlone, J. (1980). Sex differences in human brain asymmetry. *Behavioural and Brain Sciences*, *3*, 215–263.

McGuigan, F.J. (1971). Covert oral behaviour and auditory hallucinations. *Psychophysiology*, *3*, 73–80.

McGuire, P.K., & Murray, R. (1991). Auditory hallucinations and regional cerebral blood flow in schizophrenia. (Abstract.) *International Congress on Schizophrenia Research*, Tucson, Arizona.

Merrin, E.L. (1984). Motor and sighting dominance in schizophrenic and affective disorder. *British Journal of Psychiatry, 146*, 539–544.

Milner, B. (1975). Psychological aspects of focal epilepsy and its neurological management. *Advances of Neurology, 8*, 299–321.

Mintz, S., & Alpert, M. (1972). Imagery vividness, reality testing and schizophrenic hallucinations. *Journal of Abnormal Psychology, 79*, 310–316.

Monsell, S. (1987). On the relation between lexical input and output pathways for speech. In D.G. Allport, W. Mackay, W. Prinz, & E. Sheerer (Eds.), *Language perception and production: Relationships between listening, speaking, reading and writing*. London: Academic Press.

Morel, F. (1936). Des bruits d'oreille des bourdennements des hallucinations auditives élémentaires, communes et verbales. *Éncephale, 31*, 81–95.

Musalek, M., Podreka, I., Walter, H., Suess, E., Passweg, V., Nutzinger, D., Strobl, R., & Lesch, O.M. (1989). Regional brain function in hallucinations: A study of regional cerebral blood flow with 99M Tc HMPAO-SPECT in patients with auditory hallucinations, tactile hallucinations and normal controls. *Comprehensive Psychiatry, 30*, 99–108.

Nasrallah, H.A. (1985). The unintegrated right cerebral hemispheric consciousness as alien intruder. *Comprehensive Psychiatry, 26*, 273–282.

Nasrallah, H.A., McCalley-Whitters, M., & Kuperman, S. (1982). Neurological differences between paranoid and non-paranoid schizophrenia. *Journal of Clinical Psychiatry, 43*, 305–306.

Nelson, H.E., Thrasher, S., & Barnes, T.R.E. (1991). Practical ways of alleviating auditory hallucinations. *British Medical Journal, 302*, 327.

Notardonato, H., Gonzalez-Avilez, A., Van Heertum, R.L., O'Connell, R.A., & Yudd, A.P. (1989). The potential value of serial cerebral SPECT scanning in the evaluation of psychiatric illness. *Clinical Nuclear Medicine, 14*, 319–321.

Ojemann, G.A. (1978). Organization of short-term verbal memory in language areas of human cortex: evidence from electrical stimulation. *Brain and Language, 5*, 331–340.

Ojemann, G.A. (1983). Brain organization for language from the perspective of electrical stimulation mapping. *The Behavioural and Brain Sciences, 6*, 189–230.

Ojemann, G.A., Ojemann, J., Lettich, B.A., & Berger, M. (1990). Cortical language localization in left, dominant hemisphere. *Journal of Neurosurgery, 71*, 316–326.

O'Kusky, J., Strauss, E., Kosaka, B., Wada, J., Li, D., Druhan, M., & Petrie, J. (1988). The corpus callosum is larger with right-hemisphere cerebral dominance. *Annals of Neurology, 24*, 379–383.

Overall, J., & Gorham, D. (1962). The brief psychiatric rating scale. *Psychological Reports, 10*, 799–812.

Owens, D.G.C., Johnstone, E.C., Crow, T.J., Frith, C.D., Jagoe, J.R., & Kreel, L. (1985). Lateral ventricular size in schizophrenia: Relationship to the disease process and its clinical manifestations. *Psychological Medicine, 15*, 27–41.

Patterson, K., Vargha-Khadem, F., & Polkey, C.E. (1989). Reading with one hemisphere. *Brain, 112*, 39–63.

Penfield, W., & Perot, P. (1963). The brain's record of auditory and visual experience: A final summary and conclusion. *Brain, 86*, 595–696.

Penfield, W., & Roberts, L. (1959). *Speech and brain mechanisms*. Princeton, N.J.: Princeton University Press.

Petersen, S.E., Fox, P.T., Posner, M.I., Mintum, M., & Raichle, M.E. (1988). Positron emission tomographic studies of the cortical anatomy of single-word processing. *Nature, 331*, 585–589.

Piaget, J. (1926). *The language and thought of the child.* London: Routledge & Kegan Paul.

Posey, T.B., & Losch, M.E. (1983). Auditory hallucinations of hearing voices in 375 normal subjects. *Imagination, Cognition and Personality, 2,* 99–113.

Posner, M.I., Petersen, S.E., Fox, P.T., & Raichle, M.E. (1988). Localisation of cognitive operations in the human brain. *Science, 240,* 1627–1631.

Raine, A., Harrison, G.N., Reynolds, G.P., et al. (1990). Structural and functional characteristics of the corpus callosum in schizophrenics, psychiatric controls, and normal controls. *Archives of General Psychiatry, 47,* 1060–1064.

Randall, P.L. (1983). Schizophrenia, abnormal connection and brain evolution. *Medical Hypotheses, 10,* 247–280.

Reiman, E.M., Fusselman, M.J., Fox, P.T., & Raichle, M.E. (1989). Neuroanatomic correlates of anticipatory anxiety. *Science, 243,* 1071–1074.

Reisberg, D., Smith, D.J., Baxter, D.A., & Sonenshine, M. (1990). Enacted auditory images are ambiguous; pure auditory images are not. *Quarterly Journal of Experimental Psychology 41A,* 619–641.

Richardson, J.T.E. (1987). Phonology and reading: The effects of articulatory suppression on homophony and rhyme judgements. *Language and Cognitive Processes, 2,* 229–244.

Roberts, B.H., Greenblatt, M., & Solomon, H.C. (1952). Movements of the vocal apparatus during auditory hallucinations. *American Journal of Psychiatry, 108,* 912–914.

Roman, R., & Landis, C. (1945). Hallucinations and mental imagery. *Journal of Nervous and Mental Disease, 102,* 327–331.

Ross, E.D. (1981). The aprosodias: functional–anatomic organization of the affective components of language in the right hemisphere. *Archives of Neurology, 36,* 144–148.

Rubens, A.B., & M.F. Garrett. (1991). Anosognosia of linguistic deficits in patients with neurological deficits. In G.P. Progatano & D.L. Schacter (Eds.), *Awareness of deficit after brain injury.* New York: Oxford University Press.

Ryding, E., Brådvik, B., & Ingvar, D.H. (1987). Changes of regional cerebral blood flow measured simultaneously in the right and left hemisphere during automatic speech. *Brain, 110,* 1345–1358.

Ryle, G. (1949). *The concept of the mind* (pp. 36–40). Harmondsworth: Penguin Books.

Salamé, P., & Baddeley, A. (1982). Disruption of short-term memory by unattended speech: Implications for the structure of working memory. *Journal of Verbal Learning and Verbal Behavior, 21,* 150–164.

Salamé, P. & Baddeley, A. (1989). Effects of background music on phonological short-term memory. *Quarterly Journal of Experimental Psychology, 41A,* 107–122.

Schneider, K. (1959). *Clinical Psychopathology.* New York: Grune & Stratton.

Schneider, S.J., & Wilson, C.R. (1983). Perceptual discrimination and reaction time in hallucinatory schizophrenics. *Psychiatry Research, 9,* 143–253.

Schwartz, R.M. (1986). The internal dialogue: On the asymmetry between positive and negative coping thoughts. *Cognitive Therapy and Research, 10,* 591–605.

Sedman, G. (1966). Inner voices: Phenomenological and clinical aspects. *British Journal of Psychiatry, 112,* 485–490.

Seitz, P.F., & Molholm, H.B. (1974). Relation of mental imagery to hallucinations. *Archives of Neurology and Psychiatry, 57,* 469–480.

Sem-Jacobsen, C.W., Petersen, M.C., Lazarte, J.A., & Dodge, H.W. (1955). Intracerebral electrographic recordings from psychotic patients during hallucinations and agitation. *American Journal of Psychiatry, 112,* 278–288.

Serafetinides, E.A., & Falconer, M.A. (1963). Speech disturbances in temporal lobe seizures: A study of 100 epileptic patients submitted to temporal lobectomy. *Brain, 86,* 333–346.

Serafetinides, E.A., Coger, R.W., & Martin, J. (1986). Different methods of observation affect

EEG measurements associated with auditory hallucinations. *Journal of Psychiatric Research*, 7, 73–74.

Shallice, T. (1988). *From neuropsychology to mental structure*. Cambridge: Cambridge University Press.

Sidtis, J.J., Volpe, B.T., Wilson, D.H., Rayport, M., & Gazzaniga, M.S. (1981). Variability in right hemisphere language function after callosal section: Evidence for a continuum of generative capacity. *International Journal of Neuroscience*, 1, 323–331.

Slade, P.D., & Bentall, R.P. (1988). *Sensory deception: A scientific analysis of hallucinations*. London: Croom-Helm.

Smith, A. (1966). Speech and other functions after left (dominant) hemispherectomy. *Journal of Neurology, Neurosurgery and Psychiatry*, 49, 159–187.

So, N.K., Savard, G., Andermann, F., Olivier, A., & Quesney, L.F. (1990). Acute postictal psychosis: A stereo EEG study. *Epilepsia*, 31, 188–193.

Stevens, J.R., Bigelow, L., Denney, D., Lipkin, J., Livermore, A.H., Rauscher, F., & Wyatt, R.J. (1979). Telemetered EEG–EOG during psychotic behaviors of schizophrenia. *Archives of General Psychiatry*, 36, 251–262.

Stevens, J.R., & Livermore, A. (1982). Telemetered EEG in schizophrenia: Spectral analysis during abnormal behaviour episodes. *Journal of Neurology, Neurosurgery and Psychiatry*, 45, 385–395.

Tanabe, H., Sawada, T., Asai, H., Okuda, J., & Shiraishi, J. (1986). Lateralisation phenomenon of complex auditory hallucinations. *Acta Psychiatrica Scandinavica*, 74, 178–182.

Taylor, P., & Fleminger, J.J. (1981. The lateralization of symptoms of schizophrenia. *British Journal of Medical Psychology*, 54, 59–65.

Trimble, M.R. (1990). First-rank symptoms of Schneider: A new perspective? *British Journal of Psychiatry*, 156, 195–200.

Tucker, G.J., Price, T.R., Johnson, V.B., & McAllister, T. (1986). Phenomenology of temporal lobe dysfunction: A link to atypical psychosis—a series of cases. *Journal of Nervous and Mental Disease*, 174, 348–356.

Vallar, G., & Shallice, T. (1990). *Neuropsychological impairments of short-term memory*. Cambridge: Cambridge University Press.

Volkow, N.D., Wolf, A.P., Van Gelder, P., Brodie, J., Overall, J.E., Cancro, R., & Gomez-Mont, F. (1987). Phenomenological correlates of metabolic activity in 18 patients with chronic schizophrenia. *American Journal of Psychiatry*, 144, 151–158.

Vygotsky, L.S. (1962). *Thought and language*. Cambridge, MA: MIT Press.

Walter, H., Podreka, I., Steine, M. et al. (1990). A contribution to classification of hallucinations. *Psychopathology*, 23, 97–105.

Ward, P.B., Catts, S.V., Fox, A.M., Michie, P.T., & McConaghy, N. (1991). Auditory selective attention and event-related potentials in schizophrenia. *British Journal of Psychiatry*, 158, 534–539.

Weiler, M.A., Buchsbaum, M.S., Gillin, J.C., et al. (1990). Explorations in the relationship of dream sleep to schizophrenia using positron emission tomography. *Biological Psychiatry*, 23, 109–118.

Wieser, H.G. (1980. Temporal lobe or psychomotor status epilepticus. *Electroencephalography and Clinical Neurophysiology*, 48, 558–572.

West, D.J. (1948). A mass observation questionnaire on hallucinations. *Journal of the Society for Psychical Research*, 34, 187–196.

Wing, J.K., Cooper, J.E., & Sartorius, N. (1974). *Measurement and classification of psychiatric symptoms*. Cambridge: Cambridge University Press.

Wise, R., Chollet, F., Hadar, U., Friston, K., Hoofner, E., & Frackowiak, R. (1991). Distribution of cortical neural networks involved in word comprehension and word retrieval. *Brain*, 114, 1805–1817.

Zaidel, E. (1983). A response to Gazzaniga: Language in the right hemisphere, convergent perspectives. *American Psychologist, 38,* 542–546.
Zaidel, E. (1985). Language in the right hemisphere. In D.F. Benson & E. Zaidel (Eds.), *The dual brain.* New York: Guildford Press.

VII DELUSIONS AND DELUSIONAL MISIDENTIFICATION

18 The Cognitive Neuropsychiatric Origins of the Capgras Delusion

Hadyn D. Ellis
School of Psychology, University of Wales, College of Cardiff

Karel W. de Pauw
Department of Psychiatry, Doncaster Royal Infirmary

Following a brief description of the principal Delusional Misidentification Syndrome (DMS) we shall concentrate on Capgras Syndrome. This so-called syndrome involves patients, often but not exclusively, diagnosed as paranoid schizophrenic insisting that others have been replaced by dummies, robots, etc. Psychodynamic explanations will be reviewed before neuropsychiatric data are discussed. The advantages of a cognitive neuropsychiatric data are discussed. The advantages of a cognitive neuropsychiatric approach will be outlined and a variety of theoretical explanations for Capgras Syndrome will be detailed. Some of the predictions made by these hypotheses will be highlighted and the results of recent pilot work will be given. The tentative conclusion from the initial results point to a right hemisphere involvement, and their implications for the theoretical analyses of Joseph (1986) and Cutting (1990) will be discussed.

INTRODUCTION

In 1923, Capgras and Reboul-Lachaux published the most frequently-quoted, comprehensive account of what soon became known as Capgras Delusion, in which a patient typically believes that familiar persons, objects, or locations have been replaced by impersonating doubles. Although the origins of the phenomenon have been traced to classical myths (Christodoulou, 1986), the clinical features were, in fact, first delineated by Kahlbaum (1866) and similar observations were made by other psychiatrists, e.g. Kraepelin. The Capgras Delusion (CD) is the most common of several, phenomenologically-similar, forms of delusional misidentification and occurs in a variety of diagnostic settings, including

317

idiopathic ("functional") psychoses (Signer, 1987), toxic–metabolic disorders, and structural brain ("organic") disorders (Cummings, 1985). It also ranges across the boundaries of race, culture, and sex (Chawla, Buchan, & Galen, 1987; Maharajh & Lutchman, 1988; Signer, 1987); and cases have been reported in children as young as 8½ years (Kourany, 1983). A fascinating description, from the patient's point of view, can be found in the autobiography of Clifford Beers (1908), founder of the American mental hygiene movement. During an episode of psychotic depression, Beers became convinced that friends and relatives had been replaced by sinister impersonators. As the depressive symptoms resolved, so did the CD and the author gained insight into his delusional beliefs.

Although this chapter will concentrate upon the delusion described by Capgras, it is worthwhile noting that like other delusions, it shares many of the features delineated by Jaspers (1959), namely firmly sustained beliefs, despite what everyone else thinks. Many such commonalities are described elsewhere (e.g. Oltmanns & Maher, 1988). Others have expressed possible unifying mechanisms for all delusions, such as the idea that deluded individuals generally make risky probabilistic judgements and, therefore, may make hasty, overconfident decisions about all manner of doings (Huq, Garety, & Hemsley, 1988). Here we shall only emphasise the specific nature of the CD because, whatever characteristics exist common to those with delusions, the fact remains that the manifestations tend to be confined to one topic area. Thus those with the CD appear to have delusions restricted to people.

PSYCHODYNAMIC APPROACHES

Over the last seven decades, a plethora of mutually-incompatible psychodynamic explanations, reflecting the imagination and conceptual frameworks of individual authors, have been invoked to account for the CD (Koritar & Steiner, 1988; Todd, 1982). As early as 1923 Halberstadt mooted the notion that a phylogenetic regression to more primitive modes of cognitive and emotional functioning, in which archaic concepts of doubles and dualisms predominate, had a part to play in the development of delusional misidentification. Recently Koritar and Steiner (1988) resurrected this approach, albeit couched in terms of Kleinian developmental theory, a view severely criticised by Signer (1988).

In their original article, Capgras and Reboul-Lachaux (1923) drew attention to the probable importance of derealisation and morbid suspiciousness as factors facilitating the appearance of the delusion. Similar views were voiced by Derombies (1935) and Merrin and Silberfarb (1976); while Christodoulou (1977) and Todd, Dewhurst, and Wallis (1981) suggested that in some cases the CD may represent a delusional evolution of the phenomena of depersonalisation and derealisation. Earlier, Stern and MacNaughton (1945) had argued that because of altered self-perceptions, patients are confronted with an internal response to the environment that is novel and unusual. The changes are projected on to others in the environment, resulting in the delusion of doubles.

In a second paper Capgras and Carrette (1924) offered the first suggestion that the CD might arise as a result of a mental mechanism offering a solution to a patient's intrapsychic conflicts. They described a young woman with schizophrenia who believed that her parents had been replaced by doubles. The authors claimed that she had shown a strong erotic interest in her father and suggested that the delusion that her father was an imposter enabled her to solve her Electra complex and incestuous desires. However, Lévy-Valensi (1929) cast doubt on the credibility of this hypothesis by drawing attention to the fact that the patient also claimed that her brother, uncle, and aunt had likewise been replaced by doubles. Apparently unaware of the earlier German accounts of male patients with the CD, Coleman (1933) argued that the delusion was due to a mental mechanism peculiar to women—their distrust of all subsequent love objects, having been deceived during the preoedipal phase by the primary love object, the mother. When Murray (1936) subsequently did describe a man with the CD, he suggested that the patient was a latent homosexual whose infantile sexuality had developed along lines typical of women.

Although this ill-founded and convoluted theory did not prevail for very long, psychodynamic approaches continued to dominate many theoretical explanations of the CD. As early as 1936, Brochado contended that the delusion is used to solve the problem of conflicting or ambivalent emotions and to serve the needs of wish fulfilment. Despite trenchant criticism (Sinkman, 1983) this theory is still widely held and has been propagated enthusiastically by Berson (1983) and Enoch and Trethowan (1991). Initially Todd (1957) supported this view, but subsequently came to doubt whether ambivalence and projection could explain all cases of CD (Todd et al., 1981).

Berson (1983), in a comprehensive review of the CD literature, stressed the concepts of disturbance of the mother–child relationship. He focused upon pathological splitting of internalised object representations and emphasised the occurrence of a significant change in crucial interpersonal relationships, producing feelings of strangeness, in turn eliciting previously unconscious feelings that are both alien and intolerable. Utilisation of the primitive ego defence mechanisms—projection, denial, and splitting—provides a way for the patient to cope with these hostile impulses towards the love object by minimising the guilt experienced with anger and aggression directed at the real love object. The view of Enoch and Trethowan (1991) is very similar to that of Berson and will be discussed in detail below. According to these authors, the CD results from a love–hate conflict, which is resolved by directing ambivalent feelings towards the love object to its imagined double.

Such ambivalence has been reported by others. O'Reilly and Malhotra (1987), for example, described a 47-year-old female patient who at various times believed that her father, sisters, husband, and children, as well as nursing staff and fellow patients, had all been substituted. She openly expressed ambivalent feelings towards members of her family, which, coupled with depersonalisation, led the authors to suggest that these underlay the CD. Why the patient should have had such intense ambivalence for people outside her family, however, was not explained.

Chawla et al. (1987) reported a case of the CD from Zimbabwe in which the patient, a 27-year-old man suffering from schizophrenia, claimed that his father and the neighbourhood had been duplicated. The authors' explanation rests upon the idea that in traditional Zimbabwean culture respect for the father is important. If a son feels hostile towards his father conflict is created and this ambivalence may manifest itself as the CD. Again, however, no explanation was offered for the reduplicative paramnesia for place, which occurred alongside the misidentification of person. We shall return to the relationship between the CD and other reduplicative phenomena in a later section.

The psychodynamic approach to explaining the CD rests upon one fundamental observation: namely, that in the majority of cases the person or persons thought to have been substituted are intimately associated with the patient. The apparent selectivity of the phenomenon convinced Berson (1983) and Enoch and Trethowan (1991) that only a psychodynamic interpretation was possible. As Berson (1983, p. 971) put it, "cerebral lesions, traumas or atrophies ought not to discriminate among individuals". We shall unpack this assertion later but for now let us examine the premise. Clearly the CD does involve the belief that some individuals have been replaced by doubles or robots. But these are not necessarily people in close relationship with the patient. Often neighbours, nursing staff, doctors, and other patients are the objects of what some have termed hypoidentification (Christodoulou, 1976; Joseph, 1986). Silva, Leong, Weinstock, and Ferrari (1991), for example, reported the case of a 37-year-old male with delusions related to the identities of not only his father, sister, nephew, brother, and brother-in-law but also prominent political figures, including ex-President and Mrs Carter and ex-President Reagan. This does not invalidate the assertion that the CD is a selective delusion; it does indicate, however, that potentially anyone may be the object of the delusion—particularly, perhaps, those with whom the patients interact during their illness.

Although psychodynamic approaches to the CD should not be dismissed out of hand, the fact remains that, as Guze (1988) has succinctly pointed out, the psychotherapeutic process is intrinsically incapable of establishing the causal basis of psychopathology. Aetiological hypotheses generated during therapy are therefore of doubtful validity unless tested critically outside of the therapeutic situation. Psychodynamic accounts of patients with the CD invariably fail to provide such corroborating evidence and make no allowance for the possibility that the content of the delusion might have been a clinical manifestation of the psychotic illness itself rather than a special clue to its aetiology. Of course, this does not imply that psychosocial factors do not play a part in the development of such delusions—what remains to be proved is that such factors are necessary and sufficient. In addition, the psychodynamic explanations are generally *post hoc* and teleological in nature, postulating motives that are not introspectable and defence mechanisms that can neither be observed, measured, nor refuted. As a result, virtually no predictions can be made. The latter point is crucial to our own analysis in reviewing the theories of the CD that have been published. According to Popper (1959) the essence of a good theory is its falsifiability. Theories that do not make predictions cannot be falsified. Moreover, the psychodynamic approach lacks precision in defining the mechanism whereby the CD may occur. True, Todd (1957), for example, was quite clear about how patients might split their ambivalent feelings for certain people but why this should occur and, more importantly, why it should manifest itself in the form of believing there to be two separate entities—the original person and his or her double—is not explained, other than by vague reference to archaic modes of thought. This is to compound vagueness with mysticism and, though it may make a pleasing literary analysis, the approach is based on a hermeneutic–finalistic (teleological) ideology (Lunn, 1988), which essentially lacks scientific credibility (Horner, 1985; Peterfreund, 1978). There are important ethical and therapeutic implications too: an uncritical acceptance of Enoch and Trethowan's (1991) dictum that the CD is basically a love–hate conflict would require that successful treatment includes helping the person implicated to change his or her attitudes towards the patient.

Enoch and Trethowan's views, recently restated in a new edition of their popular book *Uncommon psychiatric syndromes* (1991), have been highly influential, particularly upon the Anglophone literature. Nevertheless, their position involves contradictory, sometimes unstated and inevitably untested assumptions that even they would find difficult to support; as well as questionable factual material. It is worthwhile quoting some of their statements verbatim to illustrate these points:

... the patient believes that a person, usually closely related to him has been replaced by an exact double. (p. 1)

The delusion ... assumes a *central dominating* role in the symptomatology even in the presence of other psychotic features. It certainly is a *highly specific* condition having a *characteristic constant* pattern ... (p. 1)

... fragmentary forms of the Capgras phenomenon are *rare*. (p. 4)

... before the onset of the delusion of doubles the patient exhibits increased affection and sexual craving towards the object. (p. 11)

... the paranoid component ... is *always* present. (p. 12)

A deterioration [occurs before the onset of the delusion] in the relationship with the object and a "new" hate appears which is in conflict with the love that is already present. (p. 13)

An important feature ... is the considerable personal *specificity* of the double. (p. 10) (emphasises ours)

These assertions are simply not supported either by our own clinical observations or by the reports of others (Alexander, Stuss, & Benson, 1979; Christodoulou, 1977; Todd et al., 1981). Patients often claim to discern minor physical differences distinguishing the original individual (or object) from the impostor. The delusion may be transient or overshadowed by other psychotic phenomena—in fact, fragmentary forms of the CD may prove to be the rule rather than the exception. Although the relationship of the patient to the misidentified person is often, though not invariably, emotionally charged, it is not necessarily negative, hostile, or ambivalent. The issue of the specificity of the doubt will be commented on in the next section.

Enoch and Trethowan's aetiological formulations reflect the psychodynamic/organic dichotomy that continues to bedevil the clarification of the psychosocial and neurological correlates of psychiatric disorders. Much is made of the face that "... cases which have no organic involvement whatsoever are consistently being reported, including some which have had neuroimaging studies. Such reports emphasize how the majority of cases ... occur in the setting of a functional psychosis, mainly schizophrenia" (Enoch & Trethowan, 1991, p. 6). However, it should be pointed out that many of these reports either date from several decades ago or—including those of Enoch and Trethowan—make no mention of sophisticated investigations, even when these had become available. In view of the evidence, discussed elsewhere in this book, in favour of at least a subtype of schizophrenia being a neurodevelopmental disorder, their argument that the CD is "... a functional illness and as such is understandable on a psychodynamic basis" (p. 11), becomes increasingly unconvincing. It is perhaps not surprising that they failed to mention the seminal findings of Joseph and his colleagues (1990) that schizophrenic patients with the CD had significantly more bilateral frontal and temporal lobe atrophy on CT scanning than a matched group of control patients.

It is clear that Enoch and Trethowan arrive at their psychodynamic position via an essentially negative route, i.e. the dismissal of the major alternative avenue of explanation for CD in terms of organic factors. Apart from ignoring inconvenient evidence, their arguments contain the following curious *non sequitur*:

> It is important to note that the Capgras Syndrome usually occurs in a setting of clear consciousness. This would be expected when ... the patients suffer from a functional psychosis [and] helps to explain the personal specificity of the misidentification ..., where the ... delusion occurs in the setting of an organic syndrome, a toxic, metabolic or structural brain disorder and especially degenerative dementia, confusion will occur and cognitive deficits such as disorientation and memory loss will be elicited on clinical examination and psychometric testing (Enoch & Trethowan, 1991, p. 10).

However, as Förstl (1990) has pointed out, a clear sensorium cannot exclude an organic cause, because this understanding would restrict the organic psychoses to obvious delirious states. In fact, there are several reports, discussed in the next section, of such cases where the results of psychometric testing were normal. Misidentifications often occur in people with perfectly clear sensoriums—we all make such errors almost on a daily basis (Young, Hay, & Ellis, 1985). Brain damage that produces profound inability to recognise faces, i.e. prosopagnosia, does not usually impair other cognitive/ emotional functioning (Bodamer, 1947, translated by Ellis & Florence, 1990). The CD is commonly reported as a symptom of dementia *without* accompanying delirium (Lipkin, 1988; Molchan et al., 1990) and Cummings, Miller, Hill, and Neshkes (1987) have suggested that the delusion and the declining cognitive functions stem from a common pathophysiology, attributable to the degenerative process itself. Having argued that "... the basic mechanism of misidentification [in the CD] is ... fundamentally different from the misidentification which occurs in organic confusional states..." (Enoch & Trethowan, 1991, p. 10), it is astonishing to find Enoch and Trethowan none the less insisting that "[when] the Capgras delusion occurs in an organic setting ... an understanding of the psychodynamic processes is still necessary for a full explanation of the ... phenomenon." (p. 11)

ORGANIC APPROACHES

Recently the organic approach to an understanding of the CD was forcefully stated by Anderson (1988, p. 623):

> An organic basis for the Capgras phenomenon is becoming increasingly likely ... and the continued preoccupation with psychodynamic formulations which have not furthered our understanding of these interesting conditions over the last 60 years is unhelpful and unrewarding.

Although two out of the three cases published by Capgras and his colleagues had an organic aetiology (Capgras and Carrette, 1924; Capgras, Lucchini, & Schiff, 1924), this aspect was generally neglected until the reports by Gluckman (1968) and Weston and Whitlock (1971). Another significant paper to signal the organic approach was that of MacCallum (1973, p. 639), who described five cases of the CD associated with medical conditions that were felt to be either causative or contributory to the patients' delusions and concluded that "an organic cause should always be sought at least as a precipitant". Christodoulou (1977) subsequently published 11 cases where evidence of cerebral dysfunction was present and suggested that the CD would probably not have become manifest if this component had not existed. A landmark paper was that by Joseph (1986), in which he reported 29 cases of delusional misidentification, of whom 23 were examined with CT scanning. Of these 16 had signs of cortical atrophy and a further six, in addition, had posterior fossa and subcortical abnormalities. Most patients had either bifrontal and/or bitemporal and/or biparietal damage.

More recently, Joseph et al. (1990) described 12 cases of the CD that, compared with 12 controls matched for age, sex, and psychiatric diagnosis (other than the CD), had greater signs of bilateral frontal and temporal lobe atrophy. Precise location of any underlying brain pathology in the CD is difficult, in part, perhaps, because of the difficulties in making accurate brain images (Damasio & Damasio, 1989). An example of this problem is given by the study of the three CD patients reported by Collins, Hawthorne, Gribbin, & Jacobson (1990). One patient was found to have a right cerebral infarction; the second to have nephrotic syndrome secondary to severe pre-eclampsia in the puerperium; and the third to have uncontrolled diabetes mellitus with dementia.

The finding that the CD may arise from systematic and transient causes provide further reasons for doubting that psychodynamic factors alone precipitate it. Crichton and Lewis (1990) found the CD in a 30-year-old, HIV-positive, male homosexual with pneumocystis pneumonia. The mildly delirious patient claimed that two of his colleagues were impostors and that the hospital ward was really a garage workshop. These and other delusions resolved after seven days treatment with haloperidol. A CT scan revealed widened sulci over the vertex and right parietal abnormalities. An area of low density disappeared after treatment. The authors suggested that the delusional misidentification, for persons and place, was mediated by transient right-sided parietal dysfunction causing a subtle visuospatial deficit.

Other cases of transient CD, without delirium, have been reported. Bhatia (1990) described a 35-year-old woman who regarded her husband as an impostor during a migraine attack which lasted for 48 hours. No other evidence of psychopathology was elicited and she remained fully orientated throughout the episode, which resolved fully after treatment with aspirin and haloperidol. Similarly, a 28-year-old woman who developed the CD associated with a seizure and transient EEG abnormalities two weeks after she had commenced on a therapeutic dose of disulfiram, maintained a clear sensorium (Daniel, Swallows, & Wolff, 1987). The CD as part of an interictal psychosis of epilepsy has also been documented on several occasions (Chawla & Virmani, 1977; Drake, 1987; Lewis, 1987).

It is difficult to see how such cases of transient CD can all possibly be accounted for fully by psychodynamic factors. Their onset and resolution are each far too abrupt for us to entertain such an approach as the sole aetiology. But it must also be recognised that the organic approach is itself somewhat limited. The fact that not all cases of CD that have been studied with neuroimaging techniques reveal lesions is not a particular problem: as mentioned earlier, not all scans are technically well conducted and analysed (Damasio & Damasio, 1989). More significantly, perhaps, it is not essential for organic explanations that there be brain damage that is detectable by conventional scanning. The transient cases themselves forcefully inform us that the CD does not always require structural brain lesions. It is likely that, as with other manifestations of psychotic states, alterations in normal neurotransmitter functioning, for example, may precipitate the delusion (Gray et al., 1991).

The presence of brain pathology, either permanent or transient, does not itself explain the CD. Rather, it may simply indicate likely breakdown in the way sensory information is perceived or stored. This is also true of those cases traditionally classified as neurological as opposed to psychiatric. Indeed, as some have observed, the CD is not unlike the reduplicative paramnesias, which have always been viewed as neurological (Alexander et al., 1979).

Pick (1903) first described and named reduplicative paramnesia (RP). He reported a patient who asserted that there were two clinics exactly alike: each contained a director who had the same name. Another patient, a 67-year-old woman, diagnosed as demented, declared that she was in another town where the entire hospital and its patients were duplicated and staffed by the same people. On being confronted with the absurdity of this belief she replied, "Why, good God! Everything can go round about and back again."

Pick at first wondered whether RP originated from a disturbance in a sense of familiarity. However, he decided against this view, favouring instead the idea that it was produced when patients, through memory disturbance, cannot discriminate one situation from another. These ideas were *post hoc* attempts to make sense of patterns of cognitive deficit in patients suffering from degenerative brain diseases. Since then RP, which at least bears some superficial resemblance to the CD, has been classified as a neurological disorder and efforts have always been made to relate it to brain pathology.

Some commentators have noted the resemblance between the CD and RP. Alexander et al. (1979), for example, conceptualised the CD as a reduplicative phenomenon. They described a 44-year-old man who, following general brain damage, particularly right frontal, thought his family had changed: they were identical to his "first" family and lived in a house like theirs. He showed positive feelings for both wives. The authors noted the clear parallel between the behaviour of their patient, whom they diagnosed as displaying the CD, and those cases of RP described by Pick (1903). They suggested that a common aetiology exists for the CD and RP.

It is interesting, of course, that both the CD and RP involve reduplication and, that both often seem to be the result of organic disorders. But neither this parallel, nor the fact that brain pathology may be necessary, themselves explain how the two conditions arise. In other words the presence of brain lesions gives us only limited information—however consistently it is observed. What is needed in addition to such findings is an appropriate cognitive theory of the mechanisms underlying the phenomenon.

A COGNITIVE NEUROPSYCHIATRIC APPROACH

Here we introduce a new term to describe the detailed analysis of sometimes single cases where cognitive theory informs the questions being addressed. Cognitive neuropsychiatry takes as its model the cognitive neuropsychology approach to the study of brain damaged individuals. We first applied this term to parallel work in the field of neuropsychiatry at a recent symposium on the neuropsychology of schizophrenia (Ellis, 1991) to emphasise distinctions between it and cognitive neuropsychology, which we believe important. These include the fact that patients under study are normally diagnosed as having psychiatric disorders and that, even if these proved to be fundamentally cognitive in origin and brought about as a result of neuropathology, there may well be associated psychological problems. The term "cognitive neuropsychiatry" has also been used and justified more elaborately by David (1993).

In a particularly thoughtful discussion of the CD, Anderson (1988) showed that it is not confined to beliefs about people. He reported the case of a 74-year-old man who believed that, over a 10-year period, his wife and her nephew had stolen more than 300 of his personal belongings. Moreover, he insisted that some of the items had been replaced by inferior doubles that were older, more worn, etc. When a policeman called upon him, the patient thought him to be the nephew's son. A CT scan demonstrated a pituitary tumour and visual field testing revealed bilateral upper quadrant visual field defect. Anderson (1988) suggested that the CD may be the result of a dysfunction at some stage of the neurological processes underlying object recognition. As such it may be seen as similar though not identical with prosopagnosia, which is the profound, usually acquired inability to recognise previously familiar faces (Bodamer, 1947; Bornstein, 1963; Damasio, Damasio, & Van Hoesen, 1982; Ellis, 1975; Meadows, 1974). Shraberg and Weitzel (1979) actually claimed that the CD and prosopagnosia were more closely related. They examined two CD patients using a modified Benton Face Matching Test (Benton & Van Allen, 1968), which requires the testee to spot target faces among a set of alternative faces. Finding that the patients showed some errors on this test, the authors suggested that the CD may arise from a combination of prosopagnosia-like neurological impairment and a psychotic state.

One problem with this explanation is that, despite their inability to recognise familiar faces, prosopagnostic patients can usually manage to perform normally on the Benton Face Matching Test—albeit by adopting abnormally slow strategies (Bauer, 1984; Young & Ellis, 1989). More recently Young, Ellis, Szulecka, and de Pauw (1990), using a battery of face-processing tests with patients with various forms of delusional misidentification, found significant signs of impairment; and Young (personal communication) has found the CD patients to be poor at a particular test of face recognition—the Warrington Recognition Memory Test (Warrington, 1984). Other findings by Bidault, Luauté, and Tzavaras (1986) are consistent with the notion that the CD patients may be impaired on face processing tasks. However, Ellis et al. (in press) found that poor performance on the Warrington test is not confined to the CD. Psychotic patients without the CD were also found to score low on it while gaining a normal score on the equivalent word recognition test. They argue that the observations are superficially consistent with Cutting's (1990) items linking psychoses in general to right hemisphere dysfunction.

Thus there may be some merit in pursuing parallels between the CD and prosopagnosia. Indeed, Lewis (1987) described a case of transient CD in a 19-year-old woman following phenytoin overdose. As a child she had shown signs of prosopagnosia that were consistent with the results from CT scanning, which revealed bilateral occipito-temporal areas of low density; smaller bilateral frontal lesions were revealed by MRI scanning.

Ellis and Young (1990) put forward a more complex proposal relating the CD and prosopagnosia. To understand their argument it is necessary first to consider what is now termed covert face recognition in prosopagnosia. Bauer (1984, 1986) described two prosopagnosia patients, each of whom, when shown a previously familiar face they could not recognise overtly, none the less displayed larger skin conductance responses (SCRs) to the correct spoken name when it occurred randomly mixed in sequence with four other names. This response usually accompanies an increase in arousal or an orienting response to a significant stimulus. Tranel and Damasio (1985), using a different paradigm, found that some prosopagnosic patients reveal high SCRs to previously familiar faces mixed with unfamiliar faces. Young and his colleagues have also discovered a whole range of normal face processing patterns in PH, a prosopagnostic patient, who, for example, while unable to identify faces, can learn face-naming pairings more easily than incorrect pairings (Young et al., 1990).

Young and de Haan, 1992 have argued that these and other data indicate that some prosopagnosics may have an intact face recognition mechanism that is somehow disconnected from conscious awareness. An alternative explanation was offered by Bauer (1986). He suggested that there are two routes to recognition: a ventral route from visual cortex to limbic system, which is the principal pathway to facial identification; and a dorsal route, which has the same start and end points but passes through the inferior parietal lobe. He argued that covert recognition occurs because in some prosopagnosic patients, while the ventral route is damaged, the dorsal route conveys some information concerning the emotional significance of the face. This aspect of the face may not be consciously detected but can manifest itself in increased autonomic activity.

Ellis and Young (1990) suggested that the CD may well be related to prosopagnosia but as its mirror image (Fig. 18.1). That is, the CD may involve an intact ventral route together with a damaged or disconnected dorsal route. According to this model the CD patients fail to register the emotional significance of a face and, consequently, infer that it is that of an impostor. Interestingly, Derombies had argued along similar lines in 1935, suggesting that the CD resulted from simultaneous intellectual recognition and affectively engendered non-recognition of faces. Ellis and Young (1990) further proposed that such discrepancies are more likely to be noticed for faces of those emotionally close to the patient. Tranel and Damasio (1985) have found that normal subjects show higher SCRs to familiar compared with unfamiliar faces. It is not yet known, but it seems a plausible prediction, that the greater the degree of personal involvement with the familiar person, the greater will be the SCR. As mentioned earlier, CD patients usually insist that close family members have been replaced by impostors but some reveal similar beliefs about fellow patients, hospital staff, and even political figures. All of this is consistent with the cognitive neuropsychiatric explanation offered by Ellis and Young (1990).

One very obvious advantage of the explanation offered by Ellis and Young (1990) is that it makes specific, testable predictions. The first is that CD patients ought not to manifest increased SCRs to familiar faces. The second is that they should not necessarily have delusional misidentification for voices (unless this is secondary to dysfunctional face processing). Neither of these predictions has yet been tested but each should prove amenable to experimental analysis and clearly it is imperative that appropriate studies be carried out.

Prosopagnosia

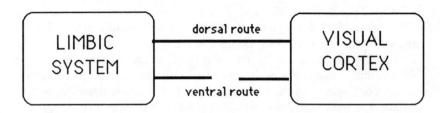

The Capgras Delusion

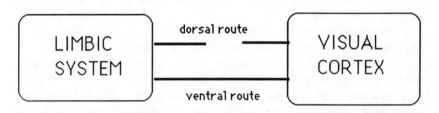

FIG. 18.1   Schematic illustration of Ellis and Young's (1990) suggestion that the CD and prosopagnosia may be mirror images. In prosopagnosia the ventral route to face recognition may be impaired or disconnected, whereas for the CD it is claimed that the problem lies along the dorsal route.

At this point it is timely to mention again Pick's (1903) original idea that RP may occur as a result of a disruption in familiarity feelings. Mandler (1980) has suggested that the appreciation of stimulus identification and its familiarity are two parallel and independent processes that normally combine to give rise to recognition. Ellis and Shepherd (1992) have argued that the CD may arise if the familiarity-detecting mechanism in face recognition is impaired. This idea is not necessarily so different from the analysis offered by Ellis and Young (1990): it is feasible that the dorsal route identified by Bauer (1984) may serve the function of signalling both significance and familiarity. Moreover, we are aware that there exists in the psychiatric literature a body of evidence to support the idea if an independent sense of familiarity that may occur at inappropriate times (déjà vu) or fail to be triggered by events or objects that have been experienced (jamais vu). These have been reviewed recently by Sno and Linszen (1990).

The predictions from Ellis and Young's (1990) theoretical position are quite obvious, but theirs is by no means the only candidate for further empirical work. Joseph (1986) outlined an interesting explanation for the CD that also has yet to be formally tested. He suggested that the left and right cerebral hemispheres each possess its own representations of known faces. According to Joseph, when a familiar face is encountered, these two separate representations may be activated but are subsequently integrated. In patients with the CD, however, there is a failure to integrate the information and, as a result, some sort of split percept occurs which manifests itself in the symptoms of delusional belief in doubles, etc.

No-one has yet published a study of interhemispheric communication and cerebral asymmetry in CD patients. This is a relatively easy exercise and is long overdue. There is, of course, a history of theory and research, starting with Wigan (1844), to link mental illness with abnormalities in cerebral interaction. Efforts to examine the CD within this framework are long overdue.

Cutting (1990) has made a tentative attempt to associate the CD with right hemisphere dysfunction. His ideas are firmly predicted on the assumption that the CD and RP are related phenomena and that both conditions require right hemisphere damage. His specific hypothesis regarding the CD is based upon the assumption that an intact right hemisphere is necessary for recognising the uniqueness of objects, faces, and places. Therefore, the CD may ensue when a patient loses the ability to individualise faces and confabulates to cover the perceptual deficiency.

Interesting though Cutting's (1990) views undoubtedly are, they fall far short of explaining the CD. First, he unquestionably accepts the theory that the left hemisphere responds to categories and the right hemisphere to individual or within-category discriminations. This view does not find much empirical support in the neuropsychological literature, where bilateral involvement in face processing has been shown to be important, but not in the way Cutting believes (Ellis, 1983; Meadows, 1974). Moreover, Cutting's (1990) explanation of the CD ignores its double specificity, i.e. it is usually confined to faces, and only a subset of these. His model would predict some forms of agnosia or, if adapted appropriately, even prosopagnosia, but not the CD. It is probably worthwhile submitting his ideas to empirical test in order to examine whether the distinction he draws between categorical-based and exemplar-based information processing has any relevance for explaining any of the manifestations of the CD.

Yet another theoretical position to explain the CD is based upon considerations of it alongside RP. Staton, Brumback, and Wilson (1982) reported the case of a male patient who, 8 years after injury to his right hemisphere, developed the belief that family and friends looked different. He also showed RP for the hospital, the family farm, his cat, and even himself. The authors were impressed by the patient's attempts to explain the discrepancies between the duplicates and the originals. Often the "differences" seemed due to ageing. The "new" people, places, and objects were sometimes perceived as being older than the true ones.

Staton et al. (1982) explained these phenomena in terms of a disconnection syndrome of memory. According to their analysis the patient, while able to register new information, failed to integrate it with past memories. Essentially this dysfunction caused the patient to be in some sense disorientated. He was basing his judgements of his present orientation upon recollections from the past. Our own interpretation of the view of Staton et al. (1982) is that memory representations of people, objects, places, etc. normally must undergo continuous change—an on-going update of the items in memory that means we often fail to appreciate how the objects or people alter over time unless there is a significant interruption in experience of them. If this process breaks down it is possible that changes subsequent to the damage may not be integrated and, therefore, the kinds of "discrepancies" noted by their patient may occur. This is an attractive approach; it is consistent with many observations of the CD where patients insist that the impostor is older than the true person; and fits perfectly with the remarks made by Anderson's (1988) patient that his belongings were older or more worn-looking.

One very simple way of testing the arguments of Staton et al. (1982) would be to present patients not with the people whom they now believe to be impostors but with photographs of them taken before the onset of their delusion belief. According to Staton et al. (1982), the patients ought to perceive these as being of the original people. As yet, this technique has not been tried in any systematic manner. Todd et al. (1981) reported one patient who thought that her husband had been substituted and was uncertain about whether a photograph was of him or his double. No details were provided regarding the age of the photograph, however, which limits the relevance of this chance observation to the arguments of Staton et al. (1982).

Finally, it is worth repeating a recent comment by Frith (1991, p. 28) on the symptoms of schizophrenia. He states that "it is not symptoms themselves that we should be examining ... but the cognitive abnormalities that underlie them...". What we have here termed the cognitive neuropsychiatric approach to understanding the CD, patently, is neither uniform nor complete. Our own belief, however, is that this avenue is likely to be more productive than either the psychodynamic one, which focuses on symptoms and presents *post hoc* and untestable explanations, or the organic one, which is simply incomplete. But, as we indicated earlier, it would be foolish at this stage to throw out both baby and bath water. There may well be tensions, ambivalence, and other psychological factors occurring between patients and the people whom they believed to have been substituted (Fleminger, 1992). At this stage such possible predisposing factors should not be ruled out, for conceivably they could determine the specific shape and course of the disorder. The apparent psychodynamic characteristics of the CD, however, may arise solely from organic causes that require there to be no interaction with the patients' experiences, particularly those within the family. It is almost 70 years since the study of the CD began in earnest: let us hope that the phenomenon will be fully understood well before the centenary of Capgras and Reboul-Lachaux's seminal paper.

REFERENCES

Alexander, M.P., Stuss, D.T., & Benson, D.F. (1979). Capgras syndrome: A reduplicative phenomenon. *Neurology*, *29*, 334–339.

Anderson, D.N. (1988). The delusion of inanimate doubles: Implications for understanding the Capgras phenomenon. *British Journal of Psychiatry*, *153*, 694–699.

Bauer, R.M. (1984). Autonomic recognition of names and faces in prosopagnosia: A neurological application of the Guilty Knowledge Test. *Neuropsychologia*, *22*, 457–465.

Bauer, R.M. (1986). The cognitive psychophysiology of prosopagnosia. In H.D. Ellis, M.A. Jeeves, F. Newcombe, & A. Young (Eds.), *Aspects of face processing*. Dordrecht: Nijhoff.

Beers, C.W. (1908). *A mind that found itself*. New York: Longman's Green.

Benton, A.L., & Van Allen, M.W. (1968). Impairment in facial recognition. *Cortex*, *4*, 344–358.

Berson, R.J. (1983). Capgras' syndrome. *American Journal of Psychiatry*, *140*, 969–978.

Bhatia, M.S. (1990). Capgras syndrome in a patient with migraine. *British Journal of Psychiatry*, *157*, 917–918.

Bidault, E., Luauté, J.-P., & Tzavaras, A. (1986). Prosopagnosia and the delusional misidentification syndromes. *Bibliotheca Psychiatrica*, *164*, 80–91.

Bodamer, J. (1947). Die Prosop-Agnosie. *Archiv für Psychiatrie und Nervenkrankheiten*, *179*, 6–54.

Bornstein, B. (1963). Prosopagnosia. In L. Halpern (Ed.), *Problems of dynamic neurology*. Jerusalem: Hadassah Medical Organization.

Brochado, A. (1936). Le syndrome de Capgras. *Annales Médico-Psychologiques*, *15*, 706–717.

Capgras, J., & Carrette, P. (1924). Illusion de sosies et complexe d'Oedipe. *Annales Médico-Psychologiques*, *82*, 48–68.

Capgras, J., & Reboul-Lachaux, J. (1923). L'illusion des "sosies", dans un délire systématisé chronique. *Bulletin de la Sociéeté Clinique de Médecine Mentale*, *11*, 6–16.

Capgras, J., Lucchini, P., & Schiff, P. (1924). Du sentiment d'étrangeté à l'illusion des sosies. *Bulletin de la Société Clinique de Médecine Mentale*, *12*, 210–217.

Chawla, H.M., & Virmani, V. (1977). Capgras phenomenon in a case of temporal lobe epilepsy. *Folia Psychiatrica et Neurologica Japonica*, *31*, 615–617.

Chawla, S., Buchan, T., & Galen, N. (1987). Capgras syndrome: A case report from Zimbabwe. *British Journal of Psychiatry*, *151*, 254–256.

Christodoulou, G.N. (1976). Delusional hyper-identifications of the Frégoli type. *Acta Psychiatrica Scandinavica*, *54*, 305–314.

Christodoulou, G.N. (1977). The syndrome of Capgras. *British Journal of Psychiatry*, *130*, 556–564.

Christodoulou, G.N. (1986). The origin of the concept of "doubles". *Bibliotheca Psychiatrica*, *164*, 1–8.

Coleman, S.M. (1933). Misidentification and non-recognition. *Journal of Mental Science, 79*, 42–51.

Collins, M.N., Hawthorne, M.E., Gribbin, N., & Jacobson, R. (1990). Capgras' syndrome with organic disorders. *Postgraduate Medical Journal, 66*, 1064–1067.

Crichton, P., & Lewis, S. (1990). Delusional misidentifications, AIDS and the right hemisphere. *British Journal of Psychiatry, 157*, 608–610.

Cummings, J.L. (1985). Organic delusions: Phenomenology, anatomical correlations, and review. *British Journal of Psychiatry, 146*, 184–197.

Cummings, J.L., Miller, B., Hill, M.A., & Neshkes, R. (1987). Neuropsychiatric aspects of multi-infarct dementia and dementia of the Alzheimer type. *Archives of Neurology, 44*, 389–393.

Cutting, J. (1990). *The right cerebral hemisphere and psychiatric disorders.* Oxford: Oxford University Press.

Damasio, H., & Damasio, A.R. (1989). *Lesion analysis in neuropsychology.* New York: Oxford University Press.

Damasio, A.R., Damasio, H., & Van Hoesen, G.W. (1982). Prosopagnosia: Anatomical basis and behavioural mechanisms. *Neurology, 32*, 331–341.

Daniel, D.G., Swallows, A., & Wolff, F. (1987). Capgras delusion and seizures in association with therapeutic dosages of disulfiram. *Southern Medical Journal, 80*, 1577–1579.

David, A.S. (1993). Cognitive neuropsychiatry? Editorial. *Psychological Medicine, 23*, 1–5.

Derombies, M. (1935). L'illusion de sosie, forme particuliére de la méconnaissance systématique. In *Thèse de Paris.* Paris: Jouve and Co.

Drake, M.E. (1987). Postictal Capgras syndrome. *Clinical Neurology and Neurosurgery, 89*, 271–274.

Ellis, H.D. (1975). Recognising faces. *British Journal of Psychology, 66*, 409–426.

Ellis, H.D. (1983). The role of the right hemisphere in face perception. In A.W. Young (Ed.), *Functions of the Right Cerebral Hemisphere.* London: Academic Press.

Ellis, H.D. (1991). *Delusional misidentification syndromes—a cognitive neuropsychiatric approach.* Paper presented at the international symposium on The Neuropsychology of Schizophrenia, Institute of Psychiatry, London. October 1991. (Unpublished.)

Ellis, H.D., de Pauw, K.W., Christodoulou, G.N., Luauté, J.-P., Bidault, E., & Szulecka, T.K. (1992). Recognition memory in psychotic patients. *Behavioural Neurology, 5*, 23–26.

Ellis, H.D., & Florence, M. (1990). Bodamer's (1947) paper on prosopagnosia. *Cognitive Neuropsychology, 7*, 81–105.

Ellis, H.D., & Shepherd, J.W. (1992). Face memory—theory and practice. In M. Gruneberg et al. (Eds.) *Aspects of Memory.* London: Routledge.

Ellis, H.D., & Young, A.W. (1990). Accounting for delusional misidentifications. *British Journal of Psychiatry, 157*, 239–248.

Enoch, M.D., & Trethowan, W. (1991). *Uncommon psychiatric syndromes* (3rd Ed.). Oxford: Butterworth–Heinemann.

Fleminger, S. (1992). Seeing is believing: The role of "preconscious" perceptual processing in delusional misidentifications. *British Journal of Psychiatry, 160*, 293–303.

Förstl, H. (1990). Capgras' delusion: An example of coalescent psychodynamic and organic factors. *Comprehensive Psychiatry, 31*, 447–449.

Frith, C.D. (1991). In what context is latent inhibition relevant to the symptoms of schizophrenia? *Behavioral and Brain Sciences, 14*, 28–29.

Gluckman, L.K. (1968). A case of Capgras syndrome. *Australian and New Zealand Journal of Psychiatry, 2*, 39–43.

Gray, J.A., Feldon, J., Rawlins, J.N.P., Hemsley, D.R., & Smith, A.D. (1991). The neuropsychology of schizophrenia. *Behavioral and Brain Sciences, 14*, 1–84.

Guze, S.B. (1988). Psychotherapy and the etiology of psychiatric disorders. *Psychiatric Developments*, *3*, 183–193.

Horner, T.M. (1985). The psychic life of the young infant: Review and critique of the psychoanalytic concepts of symbiosis and omnipotence. *American Journal of Orthopsychiatry*, *55*, 324–344.

Huq, S.F., Garety, P.A., & Hemsley, D.R. (1988). Probabilistic judgements in deluded and non-deluded subjects. *The Quarterly Journal of Experimental Psychology*, *4*, 801–812.

Jaspers, K. (1959). *General psychopathology* (7th ed.). Manchester: Manchester University Press.

Joseph, A.B. (1986). Focal central nervous system abnormalities in patients with misidentification syndromes. *Bibliotheca Psychiatrica*, *164*, 68–79.

Joseph, A.B., O'Leary, D.H., & Wheeler, H.G. (1990). Bilateral atrophy of the frontal and temporal lobes in schizophrenic patients with Capgras syndrome: A case-control study using computed tomography. *Journal of Clinical Psychiatry*, *51*, 322–325.

Kahlbaum, K.L. (1866). Die Sinnesdelirien. C. Die Illusion. *Allgemeine Zeitschrift für Psychiatrie*, *23*, 56–78.

Koritar, E., & Steiner, W. (1988). Capgras' syndrome: A synthesis of various viewpoints. *Canadian Journal of Psychiatry*, *33*, 62–66.

Kourany, R.F.C. (1983). Capgras syndrome variant in an 8½-year-old boy. *Journal of the American Academy of Child Psychiatry*, *22*, 571–572.

Lévy-Valensie, J. (1929). L'illusion des sosies. *Gazette des Hôpitaux Civils et Militaires*, *55*, 1001–1003.

Lewis, S. (1987). Brain imaging in a case of Capgras' syndrome. *British Journal of Psychiatry*, *150*, 117–121.

Lipkin, B. (1988). Capgras syndrome heralding the development of dementia. *British Journal of Psychiatry*, *153*, 117–118.

Lunn, V. (1988). Biological psychiatry and ethics. *Acta Psychiatrica Scandinavica*, *78* (Suppl. 345), 11–14.

MacCallum, W.A.G. (1973). Capgras syndrome with an organic basis. *British Journal of Psychiatry*, *123*, 639–642.

Maharajh, H.D., & Lutchman, R.D. (1988). Capgras syndrome and organic disease. (C) *British Journal of Psychiatry*, *153*, 715.

Mandler, G. (1980). Recognizing: The judgment of previous occurrence. *Psychological Review*, *87*, 252–271.

Meadows, J.C. (1974). The anatomical basis of prosopagnosia. *Journal of Neurology, Neurosurgery and Psychiatry*, *37*, 489–501.

Merrin, E.L., & Silberfarb, P.M. (1976). The Capgras phenomenon. *Archives of General Psychiatry*, *33*, 965–968.

Molchan, S.E., Martinez, R.A., Lawlor, B.A., Grafman, J.H., & Sunderland, T. (1990). Reflections of the self: Atypical misidentification and delusional syndromes in two patients with Alzheimer's disease. *British Journal of Psychiatry*, *157*, 605–608.

Murray, J.R. (1936). A case of Capgras' syndrome in the male. *Journal of Mental Science*, *82*, 63–66.

Oltmanns, T., & Maher, B.A. (Eds.). (1988). *Delusional beliefs*. Chichester: John Wiley.

O'Reilly, R., & Malhotra, L. (1987). Capgras Syndrome—an unusual case and discussion of psychodynamic factors. *British Journal of Psychiatry*, *151*, 263–265.

Peterfreund, E. (1978). Some critical comments on psychoanalytic conceptualizations of infancy. *International Journal of Psycho-Analysis*. *59*, 427–441.

Pick, A. (1903). On reduplicative paramnesia. *Brain*, *26*, 344–383.

Popper, K. (1959). *The logic of scientific discovery*. London: Hutchinson.

Shraberg, D., & Weitzel, W.D. (1979). Prosopagnosia and the Capgras syndrome. *Journal of Clinical Psychiatry, 40,* 313–316.

Signer, S.F. (1987). Capgras' syndrome: The delusion of substitution. *Journal of Clinical Psychiatry, 48,* 147–150.

Signer, S.F. (1988). Capgras' syndrome: A synthesis of viewpoints. *Canadian Journal of Psychiatry, 33,* 574–575.

Silva, J.A., Leong, G.B., Weinstock, R., & Ferrari, M.M. (1991). *Misidentified political figures: An underappreciated danger.* Paper presented at the 43rd Annual Meeting of the American Academy of Forensic Sciences, Anaheim, CA.

Sinkman, A.M. (1983). The Capgras delusion: A critique of its psychodynamic theories. *American Journal of Psychotherapy, 37,* 428–438.

Sno, H.N., & Linszen, D.H. (1990). The déjà vu experience: Remembrance of things past? *American Journal of Psychiatry, 147,* 1587–1595.

Staton, R.D., Brumback, R.A., & Wilson, H. (1982). Reduplicative paramnesia: A disconnection syndrome of memory. *Cortex, 18,* 23–36.

Stern, K., & MacNaughton, D. (1945). Capgras syndrome, a peculiar illusionary phenomenon, considered with special reference to the Rorschach findings. *Psychiatric Quarterly, 19,* 139–163.

Todd, J. (1957). The syndrome of Capgras. *Psychiatric Quarterly, 31,* 250–265.

Todd, J. (1982). The history of the syndrome of Capgras. In F.C. Rose & W.F. Bynum (Eds.), *Historical aspects of the neurosciences.* New York: Raven Press.

Todd, J., Dewhurst, K., & Wallis, G. (1981). The syndrome of Capgras. *British Journal of Psychiatry, 139,* 319–327.

Tranel, D., & Damasio, A.R. (1985). Knowledge without awareness: An automatic index of facial recognition by prosopagnosics. *Science, 228,* 1453–1454.

Warrington, E.K. (1984). *Recognition memory test.* Windsor: NFER–Nelson.

Weston, M.J., & Whitlock, F.A. (1971). The Capgras syndrome following head injury. *British Journal of Psychiatry, 119,* 25–31.

Wigan, A.L. (1844). *The duality of the mind.* London: Longman.

Young, A.W., & de Haan, E.H.F. (1992). Face recognition and awareness after brain injury. In A.D. Milner and M.D. Rugg (Eds.). *The Neuropsychology of Consciousness.* London: Academic Press.

Young, A.W., & Ellis, H.D. (1989). Childhood prosopagnosia. *Brain and Cognition, 9,* 16–47.

Young, A.W., Ellis, H.D., Szulecka, T.K., & de Pauw, K.W. (1990). Face processing impairments and delusional misidentification. *Behavioural Neurology, 3,* 153–168.

Young, A.W., Hay, D.C., & Ellis, A.W. (1985). The faces that launched a thousand slips: Everyday difficulties and errors in recognizing people. *British Journal of Psychology, 76,* 495–523.

19 Cognitive Biases and Abnormal Beliefs: Towards a Model of Persecutory Delusions

Richard P. Bentall
Liverpool University, Liverpool.

Despite the existence of substantial literature on the social and cognitive determinants of normal beliefs and attitudes, there has until recently been a dearth of experimental data on the topic of delusional beliefs. Psychological explanations of abnormal beliefs have tended to be of two sorts. First, some authors following Maher have argued that delusions are almost always rational interpretations of anomalous experiences, and that the reasoning of deluded patients is almost always normal. Although there are grounds for believing that some delusions are driven by abnormal experiences, the evidence that this is generally the case is almost entirely negative and unconvincing. The second type of explanation of delusions focuses on the role of cognitive biases in the aetiology and maintenance of abnormal beliefs. Studies carried out by other authors have suggested that delusional beliefs are associated with abnormal hypothesis testing in some individuals. In our own research, however, we have focused on the social reasoning of patients suffering from persecutory delusions. In a series of studies we have shown that: (a) persecuted patients show an abnormal attributional style, generally attributing negative outcomes to causes external to themselves; (b) attributional biases are also evident in deluded patients' judgements about the causes of the behaviour of other people; (c) patients with persecutory delusions show an abnormal "self-serving bias" on contingency judgement tasks; and (d) that these biases reflect selective information processing for threat-related information as shown on attention and memory tasks. Taken together, this evidence suggests that persecuted patients have much in common with depressives, and that their abnormal beliefs serve a function of preventing low self-esteem thoughts from entering consciousness. In our most recent study we have tested this hypothesis using an opaque attributional measure and other tests. As predicted, patients with persecutory delusions reported high depression and high self-esteem, but like depressives attributed negative outcomes to self on the opaque test.

337

INTRODUCTION

Despite the existence of a considerable body of research into normal reasoning, delusions have until recently received little attention from experimental psychopathologists (Oltmanns & Maher, 1988; Winters & Neale, 1983). This failure to apply models derived from normal psychology to the problem of abnormal beliefs may be the consequence of a general failure of communication between psychologists and psychopathologists. Alternatively, it may reflect the psychopathologist's long-held preference for studying broadly defined syndromes rather than particular manifestations of madness. A third possibility is that this dearth of research reflects the paradoxical attitude of those psychopathologists who, while assuming that delusions and normal beliefs have little in common, at the same time admit to a certain difficulty in stating exactly why some beliefs and not others should be thought of as delusional.

Jaspers (1963) argued that abnormal beliefs are held with extraordinary conviction, are impervious to other experiences or counterargument, and have bizarre or impossible content. However, he went on to distinguish between those overvalued or delusion-like ideas, which arise understandably from the individual's personality, mood, or other experiences (including abnormal experiences) and those primary delusions that are not understandable, and that result from a more fundamental change of personality (see Walker, 1991 for a detailed account of Jaspers' analysis). Jaspers' concept of "understandability" is difficult to operationalise in practice, which may be why most contemporary definitions of delusions lean on some combination of his three more general criteria. DSM-IIIR (American Psychiatric Association, 1987), for example, suggests that delusions are false personal beliefs "based on incorrect inference about external reality and firmly sustained in spite of what almost everyone else believes and in spite of what constitutes incontrovertible and obvious proof or evidence to the contrary".

An obvious objection to such definitions is that they do not discriminate between the kinds of abnormal beliefs observed in the psychiatric clinic and other non-empirical but subjectively important beliefs, for example religious and political convictions. Such criteria have the further drawback of excluding many of those beliefs expressed by psychiatric patients that are regarded as delusional. Clinical studies, for example, have shown that patients' delusions vary over time in terms of fixity and conviction (Garety, 1985; Hole, Rush, & Beck, 1979). Moreover, the success of cognitive psychotherapy with some deluded patients indicates that their beliefs are not always resistant to counterarguments expressed in the right way (Chadwick & Lowe, 1990; Hartman & Cashman, 1983; Watts, Powell, & Austin, 1973).

Not surprisingly, some authors have argued that delusions should therefore be regarded as existing at the extreme end of a continuum running from normal to pathological belief (Strauss, 1969) although there have been a number of different proposals about the most appropriate criteria for locating the position of any particular belief along this continuum (Harrow, Rattenbury, & Stoll, 1988; Kendler, Glazer, & Morgenstern, 1983). This commonsensical proposal has been rejected by Berrios (1991) on the grounds that it has not led to clinical or neurobiological advances. Berrios (1991, p. 12) instead argues that delusions are not beliefs at all but "empty speech acts, whose informational content refers to neither world or self. They are not the symbolic expression of anything". However, it is not obvious that this claim should be accepted in the absence of clear evidence that delusions are a function of psychological and neurobiological processes different to those that regulate the acquisition and maintenance of normal beliefs and attitudes. Indeed, the apparent existence of a continuum between normal and delusional beliefs provides a strong argument for psychological research into delusions.

In this chapter I will outline some recent research findings that help to clarify the relationship between normal and abnormal beliefs, and that may pave the way towards an understanding of the relative contributions of psychological and neurobiological processes to delusion formation. Before describing this work in detail, however, I wish to preface my account with a few remarks about some pertinent problems of explanation in psychopathology.

SOME PROBLEMS OF EXPLANATION IN PSYCHOPATHOLOGY

Although recent decades have seen substantial advances in the neurological and psychological sciences, two fundamental issues must be resolved before these advances can be applied to the study of madness (Bentall, 1991). First, we must be certain that we chose adequately described and scientifically valid targets for research and, second, we must be sure that the explanations we construct are consistent with an adequate philosophical account of human mental processes. I have discussed the first of these problems in detail elsewhere and therefore will not dwell on it at length here. It is sufficient to note that traditional psychopathologists have usually targeted for research broad diagnoses such as those defined in DSM-IIIR, despite a general lack of evidence that such diagnoses have any scientific validity (Bentall, 1990a; Bentall, Jackson, & Pilgrim, 1988). As a result, the value of studying more narrowly defined classes of abnormal behaviour (such as delusions) has not been widely recognised.

The problem of constructing philosophically adequate explanations of abnormal behaviour, once appropriately defined, is more complex, particularly when we are concerned about the relative contributions of biological and psychological determinants. In recent years, there has been something of a paradigm shift towards more biological explanations of abnormal behaviour (Klerman, 1991). Whereas biological findings are clearly of interest in their own right, extreme advocates of this approach have tended to overestimate the achievements of biological psychiatry (Charlton, 1990) while at the same time ignoring some serious philosophical objections to biological research conducted in the absence of psychological theory. Three objections are particularly important in the present context.

First, an exclusive emphasis on biological determinants of abnormal behaviour is dualistic if it presumes that psychological phenomena are somehow epiphenominal to biological phenomena (Rose, 1984). Although there continues to be vigorous debate in the philosophical literature about various accounts of mind–brain relations it seems clear, on any account, that interactions between the brain and the environment are not one-way. Just as events in the brain determine subjective experience, so too environmental stimuli help to determine brain functioning.

The second and related point follows from the claim that the main function of the brain is information processing. On this view, the discovery of a correlation between an event in the brain and a certain type of abnormal behaviour must remain little more than sophisticated phrenology in the absence of an understanding of the information-processing functions of the relevant part of the brain. Marr (1982) offered an influential account of the relationship between psychological and biological explanations of behaviour, which, although proposed in the context of vision research, provides a suitable framework for guiding neuropsychological studies of psychiatric disorders. Marr argued that, to understand how the brain works, it is first necessary to define its functions (what it is capable of; the kinds of ecological problems it is the solution to). Second, the algorithms or rules by which it executes these functions can be studied; this is analogous to studying the software of a computer and is the proper task of cognitive psychology. Third, once this second step has been achieved it is then possible to ask how the brain as a physical machine implements these algorithms? An obvious implication of this analysis is that biological research into madness is most likely to yield useful results if conducted in the context of adequate psychological accounts.

A final related problem, which has not been addressed adequately by most biological researchers, and which is of particular relevance to the study of delusions, concerns what philosophers term "intentionality" (Tallis, 1991): the *aboutness* that links mental events to the world that they represent. Intentionality (which is a feature not only of what are ordinarily called "intentions" but also of beliefs, desires, and all other kinds of mental events) carries the implication that information processing in the brain is content-specific. That is, how the brain processes information depends on what the information is.

As Dennett (1971) observes, it is precisely when we are unable to give an intentional account of behaviour in terms of the beliefs and goals we believe an individual to hold that we instead tend to look for a disorder of biological mechanism. It is therefore interesting to note the similarity between the concept of "intentionality" and Jaspers' concept of "understandability"; ununderstandable behaviour is precisely that kind of behaviour for which intentional explanations appear to fail. The choice faced when encountering such behaviour is whether, with Berrios, to dismiss it as epistemologically empty or, alternatively to search for meanings that are not immediately apparent.

The fact that delusions tend to concern certain themes (for example, persecution or grandiosity), most of which reflect the patient's position in the social universe, should caution us against dismissing them as completely meaningless. Put another way, although we might think of delusions as reflecting a disorder of intentionality it is probably wrong to think of them as non-intentional altogether. If we are right to follow this intuition (which I hope will prove justified in the light of the evidence to be outlined below) it follows that an adequate understanding of the mind of the deluded person must make reference not only to the state of the person's brain but also to the individual's personal history and relationship with the social environment.

TOWARDS A COGNITIVE ACCOUNT OF DELUSIONAL BELIEFS

A very crude outline of some of the factors that might be implicated in the acquisition and maintenance of any kind of belief is shown in Fig. 19.1. Beliefs are presumably influenced by events in the world (the requirement for intentionality). These events must be perceived and attended to before various inferential algorithms can be applied to that portion of the data set that has been perceived adequately. It is these heuristic strategies (which take the form of non-logical and highly efficient rules of thumb), which give rise to beliefs and that have been of most interest to social and cognitive psychologists. Finally, the individual may or may not seek further information to either corroborate or refute these beliefs; Karl Popper's famous injunctions to scientists notwithstanding, the available evidence suggests that in most circumstances people attempt to corroborate their theories rather than refute them (Gilhooly, 1982).

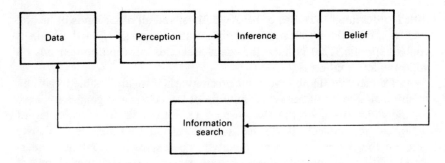

FIG. 19.1   A crude model of processes involved in the acquisition of normal and abnormal beliefs. From Bentall (1990a). Reproduced with permission.

This model should not be considered a definitive account of belief acquisition. None the less, we can ask how abnormalities at each stage in the model might contribute to the formation of the kinds of abnormal beliefs observed in the psychiatric clinic. Most of the remarks that follow will concern persecutory delusions (delusion-like ideas in Jasper's terminology), which have been the focus of our own research in Liverpool. However, in passing, some observations will be made about other kinds of abnormal beliefs.

The Environment

The possibility that patients who complain of being persecuted really are being persecuted is not often taken seriously. However, Mayerhoff, Pelta, Valentino, and Chakos (1991) describe a case in which a woman initially diagnosed as deluded on the basis of her report that threats had been made against her subsequently proved to be the victim of genuine threats. Cases such as this raise additional problems for definitions of delusions (such as that found in DSM-IIIR), which rely on the obviousness of proof or evidence to the contrary. As the old joke goes: just because you are paranoid does not mean they are not out to get you. Whether this is true of all persecutory delusions remains a moot point.

Lemert (1962) conducted detailed interviews with paranoid patients and concluded that most, if not all, had been victims of genuine conspiracies. However, in the absence of objective criteria for conspiracy it is difficult to know how to evaluate this claim, which is based on deliberately adopting the patient's perspective (see Lidz, 1975, for a critique). Some observers (Heilbrun & Norbert, 1972; Kaffman, 1983) have suggested that paranoid constructions emerge in the context of family atmospheres characterised by aversive control, inflexible rules, irrational beliefs, distrust, and apprehensiveness. Other researchers have looked to the broader social environment for the origins of delusions. Mirowsky and Ross (1983), for example, have argued that paranoia is generally associated with social positions characterised by powerlessness and the threat of victimisation. In this context it is worth considering the impact of delusional systems on those closest to the patient; the appearance of flagrant madness often elicits controlling responses, which, it might be argued, provide further data to fuel the patient's delusional system.

Perceptual Abnormalities

Jaspers' noted that delusion-like ideas are sometimes understandable in the context of other kinds of psychopathology experienced by the patient, for example hallucinations. More recently, the idea that delusions are primarily driven by perceptual abnormalities has been vigorously promoted by Maher (1974), who has argued that abnormal beliefs are almost always rational interpretations of anomalous experiences, and that cognitive abnormalities are therefore not implicated in their genesis.

Consistent with the first of these propositions, some psychopathologists have noted that delusional episodes are often preceded by periods of "delusional mood", a vague feeling that the world has been subtly altered so that it has become sinister in some peculiar yet undefinable way (Sims, 1988). This experience is usually distressing and it is possible that attempts to explain it sometimes generate to delusional ideas. Case-study evidence points to other kinds of abnormal experiences that might fuel delusional beliefs, for example, unusual or unexpected bodily sensations (Johnson, Ross, & Mastria, 1977; Maher & Ross, 1984).

It is possible that not only anomalous experiences but perceptual deficits can leave the individual vulnerable to developing abnormal beliefs. For example, it has been suggested that persecutory delusions are associated with deafness (Kay, Cooper, Garside, & Roth, 1976); although the evidence for this is less than consistent (Watt, 1985) it might be expected that individuals with hearing difficulties will be especially vulnerable to believing that others are expressing negative views about them. The same logic can be used to implicate disorders of facial recognition in the genesis of delusions of misidentification (Ellis & Young, 1990). Again, it is easy to see how the failure to recognise a loved one might encourage the erroneous conclusion that he or she has been replaced by an alien imposter.

These claims notwithstanding, it is clear that delusions often develop in the absence of either abnormal experiences or perceptual impairments (Chapman & Chapman, 1988). Moreover, as hallucinations appear to be partially driven by top-down processes (Bentall, 1990b) it is possible that some hallucinations are secondary to abnormal beliefs rather than vice versa. These observations count against Maher's second proposition that the reasoning of deluded individuals is almost always normal.

In fact the only quantitative evidence cited by Maher in favour of this proposition is a study by Williams (1964), in which it was observed that DSM-II diagnosed schizophrenics perform normally on syllogistic reasoning tasks. Because these patients were selected on the basis of a very broad definition of schizophrenia, there is no reason to suppose that more than a minority were deluded. Moreover, syllogistic reasoning has been rejected by modern cognitive psychologists as an inadequate measure or model of normal reasoning processes (Johnson-Laird, 1987). The human brain is not good at these kinds of tasks because they require computational skills that are not required in everyday life. Clearly, when assessing the role of reasoning in delusions it is important to use tests that sample relevant cognitive domains. As we will see, when such tests are used ample evidence of abnormal reasoning has been found with deluded patients.

Selective Information Processing

A number of investigators have attempted to demonstrate general differences in information processing between paranoid and nonparanoid schizophrenics. Neufeld (1990), in a review of this literature, has argued that paranoid schizophrenics, in comparison with non-paranoids, take longer to encode stimuli prior to subsequent information processing, are more vulnerable to interference on short-term memory tasks, and, despite intact semantic organisation, make less efficient use semantic dimensions when making judgements about stimuli. At present it is not clear how these findings relate to the genesis and maintenance of delusional beliefs. A further limitation of this kind of research is that it has generally failed to take into account the content-specific aspect of information processing, which, as we have seen, is a necessary feature of intentional systems. Given that the brain responds to different kinds of information in different ways it seems likely that delusions and other disorders of intentionality reflect processing biases rather than deficits.

An early theory that did point to the role of information processing biases in abnormal beliefs was proposed by Ullmann and Krasner (1969) who suggested that persecutory delusions might be caused by selective attention to threatening events. Although there is no clear evidence that selective biases in attention are responsible for the onset of persecutory delusions (Locascio & Snyder, 1975) there is consistent evidence that they are present once delusions have become established (Shannon, 1962). In our own attempt to demonstrate this we used the emotional Stroop test (Bentall & Kaney, 1989). Subjects were required to name the print colours of paranoid words, depressive words, neutral words and meaningless strings of

0s. The deluded subjects took significantly longer to colour name the paranoid words in comparison with the controls, indicating that they were unable to avoid attending to the meanings of these words (see Fig. 19.2). It is of some interest that similar processing biases towards negative-affect laden words have been found in depressed and anxious subjects (Williams, Watts, MacLeod, & Mathews, 1988).

In a subsequent study using a story recall task, we found some (although not conclusive) evidence that patients with persecutory delusions preferentially recall threat-related propositions (Kaney, Wolfenden, Dewey, & Bentall, 1992). More recently we have tested deluded, depressed, and normal subjects for free-recall of a mixed list of paranoia-related, depression-related, and neutral words. The deluded subjects showed significantly greater recall of the paranoia-related words compared with the two control groups. Again, these findings parallel observations of similar memory biases in depressed patients (Williams et al., 1988).

It is interesting to note that at least one study has found that patients suffering from persecutory delusions show a heightened ability to discriminate expressions of emotion (LaRusso, 1978). Whether this apparent heightened attentiveness to non-verbal cues is best regarded a consequence of the kind of persecutory experiences alluded to above or, rather, is involved in the onset of persecutory delusions must, at present, remain a matter of speculation. Whatever the role of information processing biases in the origins of abnormal beliefs it seems clear that they can only serve to maintain such beliefs once established.

Reasoning and Attributional Processes

I have already observed that, when studying the role of reasoning in abnormal beliefs, it is important to focus on those aspects of reasoning most likely to be implicated in the kinds of beliefs observed in the psychiatric clinic. Hemsley and Garety (1986) argued that deficits in the ability to evaluate probabilistic evidence may be implicated in some kinds of delusions and suggested that Bayes' decision-theorem may provide an appropriate framework for investigating this possibility. Consistent with this hypothesis, Brennan and Hemsley (1984) found that, compared to non-paranoids, paranoid schizophrenics were more likely to perceive illusory correlations between repeatedly presented but randomly correlated pairs of words, particularly when the words were of paranoid content. Subsequently, Huq, Garety, and Hemsley (1988) studied the performance of deluded and non-deluded patients on a probabilistic reasoning task and found that the deluded patients in comparison with the controls requested less information before reaching a judgement while expressing higher levels of confidence in

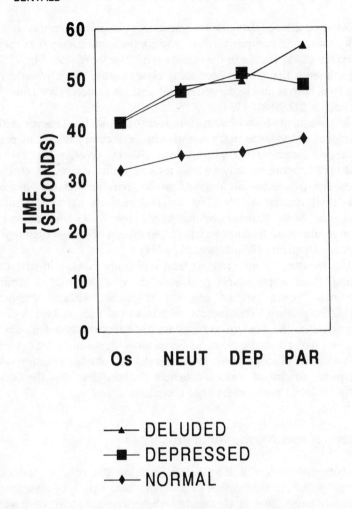

FIG. 19.2 Times taken by deluded, depressed and normal subjects to colour–name meaningless strings of zeros (0s), neutral words (NEUT), depression-related words (DEP) and paranoia-related words (PAR). Adapted from Bentall and Kaney (1989).

their judgements. This result was substantially replicated in a later study (Garety, Hemsley, & Wessely, 1991). Ironically, the deluded subjects performed better, on average, than the controls when compared to the normative criteria of Bayes' theorem. This is not a reason for discounting these findings. Because normal subjects typically perform conservatively compared to Bayes' theorem, the superior performance of the deluded subjects nonetheless represents a relative tendency towards jumping to conclusions. Similarly, the cognitive biases of depressed patients have often been interpreted as evidence of "depressive realism" because they result in a more realistic appraisal of the world's more negative features (see Ackermann & De Rubeis, 1991).

An alternative but not incompatible approach to studying the reasoning of deluded individuals is offered by attribution theory, which provides a framework for understanding the explanations that individuals give for their own behaviour and the behaviour of other people. This approach is particularly relevant to the problem of delusions because of the social nature of many of the abnormal beliefs encountered in clinical practice. Attributional accounts have already been offered for those types of depression marked by low self-esteem. Thus, Abramson, Seligman, and Teasdale (1978) argued that depressed people make relatively internal, stable, and global attributions for negative events. That is, if something unpleasant happens the depressed person is more likely to explain it in terms of a cause internal to him or herself, which is unlikely to change and that will effect all areas of life (for example, explaining exam failure in terms of lack of intelligence). While the evidence that this cognitive style is causal in depression is at best equivocal, there is modest evidence that depression characterised by low self-esteem is indeed associated with this style of reasoning (Brewin, 1988). The specific difference in internality between depressed and non-depressed people in fact seems to reflect a certain evenhandedness on behalf of the depressed, who tend not to share the non-depressed's "self-serving bias" towards attributing only good outcomes to internal causes (Musson & Alloy, 1988).

In a preliminary attempt to explore the role of attributional processes in delusions, we gave Petersen et al.'s (1982) Attributional Style Questionnaire (ASQ) to patients suffering from persecutory delusions, psychiatric controls and normal subjects (Kaney & Bentall, 1989). This questionnaire requires subjects to generate possible causes for hypothetical positive and negative events (e.g. "You go on a date and it turns out badly"; "You win a prize"). The subjects then rate their own causes on bipolar scales of internality, stability, and globalness. Because the persecuted patients in our study all showed substantial depressive symptomatology, we matched them with psychiatric controls on the basis of scores on the Beck Depression Inventory, as well as for education and gender. As we had anticipated, the deluded patients were found to make excessively external, stable, and global attributions for negative events. They were also observed to make excessively internal, global and stable attributions for positive events (Fig. 19.3). In other words, if something went wrong they showed a systematic tendency to blame other people, whereas if something went right they showed an equally systematic and excessive tendency to credit themselves. This result has the interesting implication that persecutory and grandiose delusions may be different manifestations of the same cognitive bias,

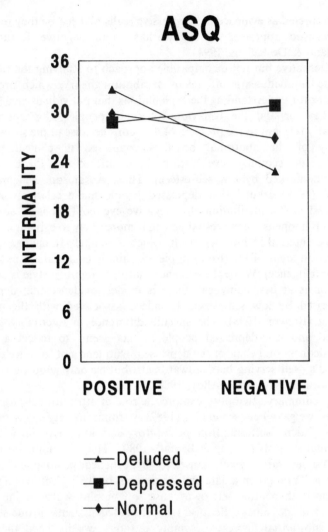

FIG. 19.3 Deluded, depressed, and normal subjects' internality ratings for positive and negative events on the Attributional Style Questionnaire. Adapted from Kaney and Bentall (1989).

suggesting that the traditional grouping of these two types of delusions under the term "paranoid" may well be justified. Candido and Romney (1990), who studied non-depressed paranoids, depressed paranoids, and depressed controls subsequently added to these findings. In their study depressed paranoids were found not to differ from non-depressed paranoids on attributions for negative events, but were less inclined to make extreme internal attributions for positive events.

The observation that patients with persecutory delusions have precisely the opposite attributional bias to that found in depressives can be accounted for by assuming that they have an exaggerated "self-serving bias", the general tendency to attribute positive outcomes to self and negative outcomes to external causes alluded to above. This bias, usually regarded as a mechanism for maintaining self-esteem, has been demonstrated with normal subjects in numerous experiments (Hewstone, 1989; Zuckerman, 1979).

The hypothesis that persecutory delusions have the function of maintaining self-esteem is hardly new; indeed Colby, Weber, and Hill (1971) constructed a computer simulation of paranoia along these lines. Two recent findings by other authors are consistent with this hypothesis. First, Fenigstein and Vanable (1992) found that a manipulation designed to increase attention to self led to an increase in paranoid thinking in student subjects. Second, Roberts (1991) has reported that deluded patients (in common with Anglican ordinands) score highly on tests designed to measure perceived meaning and purpose in life. As recovered deluded controls scored low on these scales this finding suggests that delusions occur during periods of life in which the individual has a great need for order, purpose, and (presumably) positive self-regard.

In a further demonstration that the self-serving bias is relatively absent in depressives Alloy and Abramson (1989) used a contingency judgement task. We tried a version of this experimental procedure with patients with persecutory delusions (Kaney & Bentall, 1992). Subjects were asked to play two computer games in which they had to make choices between stimuli presented on a screen. Starting with 20 points, incorrect choices led to the loss of one point and correct choices led to a gain of one point. Unbeknown to the subjects, the games were preprogrammed so that the outcome was predetermined, with one game (the "lose game") leading to a net loss of points and the other game (the "win game") leading to a gain of points. After each game the subjects were asked to estimate their degree of control over outcomes. As we had predicted, the deluded patients exhibited a strong self-serving bias (Fig. 19.4) compared to both normal and depressed controls. The latter group were sadder but wiser, and claimed very little control over the outcome of either game as had been found by Alloy and Abramson.

We have attempted to extend this analysis of the attributions made by patients with persecutory delusions in various ways. An attributional phenomenon much studied by social psychologists is the "false consensus effect", the almost ubiquitous tendency to assume that others see the world exactly as we do. Although the mechanisms responsible for this bias are

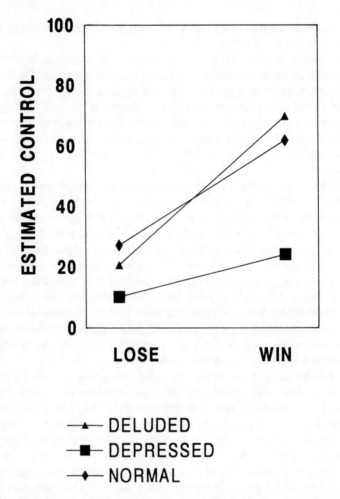

FIG. 19.4   Deluded, depressed and normal subjects' judgements of control over a computer game with two conditions, "lose" and "win". From Kaney and Bentall (1992). © Williams & Wilkins. Reproduced with permission.

much debated in the social psychology literature (Marks & Miller, 1987) two likely causes are worth considering here. First, the effect may reflect attempts at self-esteem maintenance (we like to believe that most other people are similar to ourselves). Second, the phenomenon is linked to attributional style in the following way: if we perceive an event as internally caused (for example, if we assume that we have failed an exam as a consequence of our innate stupidity) we are likely to assume a lack of consensus (others will not fail the exam because not everyone is quite so stupid). On the other hand, if we perceive an event as externally caused (for example, we believe that we failed the exam because the examiner set some particularly difficult questions) we are likely to perceive a great deal of consensus for this event (everyone should find the exam difficult). Crocker, Kayne, and Alloy (1988) were able to demonstrate differences in consensus judgements between depressed and nondepressed students.

These observations suggest an apparently paradoxical prediction in the case of persecuted patients. Contrary to what might be expected on clinical grounds, because they see negative events as externally caused they should perceive a great deal of consensus for those events (in other words, they should believe that everyone and not only themselves is hard done to). In a recent study (Bentall & Kaney, unpublished data) we attempted to test this prediction by asking persecuted, depressed, and normal subjects to rate the frequency with which selected negative, neutral, and positive events had happened to them and to other people in the past, and the frequency with which they expected these events would happen to themselves and others in the future. Both the deluded patients and the depressed controls estimated that negative events occur relatively more frequently and neutral events occur relatively less frequently in comparison to the normal subjects (Fig. 19.5). Also as expected, the deluded patients, in comparison with both groups of controls, gave very similar ratings of the frequency of negative events for themselves and for others, whereas depressed subjects rated negative events as occurring more often to themselves than to others, and the normal controls rated negative events as occurring less often to themselves. However, the deluded subjects also showed a high false consensus effect for positive events. This latter finding suggests that, rather than being a consequence of the attributional biases previously described, the consensus judgements of the deluded subjects reflect a general need for self-esteem maintenance.

Another way in which we have attempted to extend our attributional analysis is by studying the explanations made by deluded patients for the behaviour of others (Bentall, Kaney, & Dewey, 1991). Kelley (1967) has argued that our attributions for observed social interactions, for example, whether Jim's observed assault on Bill is believed to be caused mainly by some characteristic of Jim (technically termed a "person" attribution) or mainly by some characteristic of Bill (termed a "stimulus" attribution), are influenced by three kinds of data: (1) whether the behaviour is distinctive with respect to the target (for example, if we know that Jim has only hit Bill and no-one else); (2) whether the behaviour is consistent with the actor's previous conduct towards the target person (for example, Jim has hit Bill in the past); and (3) whether there is a consensus about actions towards the target (for example, if other people have been observed to hit Bill). Adapting a method first used by McArthur (1972), we studied the influence of these types of information on the attributions made by deluded, depressed, and

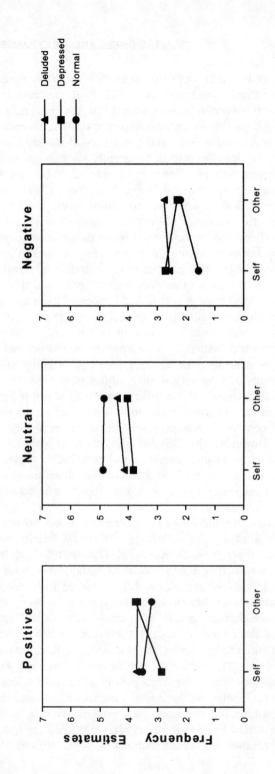

FIG. 19.5   Deluded, depressed and normal subjects' estimates of the frequency of positive, neutral, and negative events occurring to "self" and "others" adapted from Bentall and Kaney, (unpublished data). The estimates given here are averages of those made for past and future events.

normal subjects for positively and negatively valued conduct described in brief vignettes. The results indicated that the attributions of subjects with persecutory delusions were influenced by distinctiveness, consistency, and consensus information in the expected manner (i.e. that they were using the same "attributional algorithm" as the controls) but that they had a significant bias towards making person attributions for negatively valued actions, such as assaults or insults. In other words, when observing such actions the deluded patients were more likely to reason like trait psychologists and were less likely to reason like behaviourists than the two groups of control subjects. These findings parallel the previously obtained attributional style data obtained by Kaney and Bentall (1988) and Candido and Romney (1990); just as deluded subjects are unwilling to make internal attributions about their own negative experiences they are equally unwilling to blame other victims of negatively valued social interactions.

A PARANOID DEFENCE?

The evidence presented so far indicates that, contrary to Maher's (1974) theory, paranoid patients show a tendency to "jump to conclusions" in situations requiring probabilistic reasoning, attend selectively to threatening events, and exhibit a characteristic pattern of attributions, most marked when they make external attributions for negative events. It is worth repeating that these are cognitive biases rather than deficits. There is no evidence that deluded patients are incapable of reasoning; rather, they tend to weigh evidence relevant to their beliefs in a different way than normal individuals. The biases observed indicate that persecutory delusions may have the function of protecting the individual against chronic feelings of low self-esteem. This hypothesis is consistent with the observation that beliefs in external control are associated with low social status (Mirowsky & Ross, 1983), with the observed correlation between self-consciousness and paranoia (Fenigstein and Vanable, 1991), and with the more general suggestion that paranoia is a form of camouflaged depression (Zigler & Glick, 1988).

Past attempts to test hypotheses about defence mechanisms are not a source of great encouragement. However, Winters and Neale (1985) were able to design a method of accessing defended feelings of low self-esteem using a variant of the ASQ. In their pragmatic inference test (PIT), subjects were told brief stories and then answered simple multiple-choice questions about them. Some of the questions were factual, some required a non-attributional inference, and some required an attributional inference. For example, in a story about setting up a successful and expanding dry-cleaning business, subjects were required to infer in which of two US states the business was located from the information that it was "close to the border" (a non-attributional inference), to answer simple factual questions (for example, about where the loan to fund the expansion came from), and to make an attributional inference about the cause of the business's success (hard work or lack of competition). Winters and Neale found that remitted manics, like depressives and unlike normal controls, made more internal attributional inferences about negative events, a finding consistent with the view that mania is a defence against chronic feelings of low-self esteem.

In our most recent study (Lyon, Kaney, & Bentall, in press) we have tested patients with persecutory delusions, depressed and normal controls using an Anglicised version of Winters and Neale's test. We also gave subjects the BDI, a self-esteem scale, and a parallel version of the ASQ developed by ourselves (we were unable to administer the original ASQ because its items are too similar to those in the PIT). On the psychometric tests the deluded subjects reported the expected paradoxical combination of high self-esteem and high depression. The results on the parallel form of the ASQ (despite its limited psychometric adequacy) were broadly consistent with our previous findings and those of Candido and Romney (1990). However, the deluded subjects' scores on the PIT were particularly remarkable: like the depressed controls, and in marked contrast to their scores on the parallel ASQ, they inferred internal attributions for negative events and external attributions for positive events (Fig. 19.6). These findings suggest that persecutory delusions indeed serve the hypothesised function of defending the patient against deeply held feelings of low self-esteem or, to put the matter another way, that delusions of this sort are motivated by a strong need to avoid the presence of negatively self-referent thoughts in consciousness.

IMPLICATIONS

The results of the studies I have described in this chapter compel us to reject Berrios' (1991) claim that delusions are empty speech acts, symbolic of nothing. The hypothesis that, on the contrary, persecutory delusions have a motivational basis is consistent with clinical experience with paranoid patients, who vigorously resist direct challenges to their beliefs. For this reason the most effective psychological strategies for treating delusions require the therapist to avoid directly confronting the patient with evidence inconsistent with the delusional content (Chadwick & Lowe, 1990; Hartman & Cashman, 1983; Watts et al., 1973).

One implication of the account I have outlined is that delusional beliefs may reflect abnormalities at any or all of the stages in the crude model of belief acquisition shown in Fig. 19.1. Events in the deluded person's world; perceptual abnormalities; attentional, memory, and inferential biases are all likely to increase the probability that a particular person will express bizarre convictions that are resistant to counterargument. Moreover, these

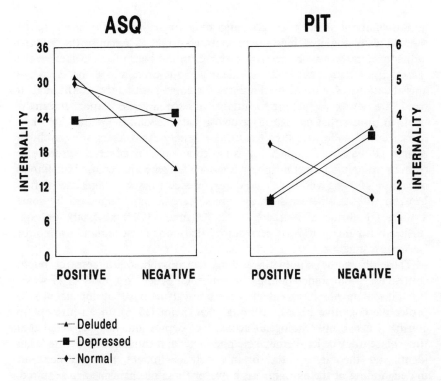

—▲— Deluded
—■— Depressed
—◆— Normal

FIG. 19.6 Deluded, depressed and normal subjects' internality ratings on a modified version of the Attributional Style Questionnaire and on the Pragmatic Inference Test. Adapted from Lyon et al., in press.

contributing factors may be functionally interconnected in quite complex ways. For example, the deluded person's behaviour may provoke others to persecutory acts, which in turn may lead the deluded person to be highly attentive to threat-related stimuli. Persistent attention to threats may lead to ever more desperate attempts at coping, thus biasing still further an already defensive cognitive style.

A further implication concerns the aetiology of abnormal beliefs. Given the intentionality of persecutory delusions and the apparent functional nature of the attributional biases that underlie them, we should not harbour high expectations of finding specific neurological lesions that directly and solely cause paranoid behaviour. Rather, we must look to the history and social environment of the deluded person for at least some of the determinants of these kinds of beliefs. Taylor (1983) has observed that normal individuals, when faced with threatening events, tend to search for some meaning to their experiences, struggle to gain mastery over the threats in particular and in life in general, and maintain self-esteem by means of the same kinds of cognitive biases demonstrated, to the extreme, by the deluded individuals in the studies described above. In the light of this evidence, the reasoning biases exhibited by deluded subjects might be seen as amplifications of normal mechanisms for coping with threat. Although it would be unwise at present to indulge in excessive speculation about the kinds of threats that might trigger delusional episodes, theoretical links can obviously be made with the literature on family atmosphere and psychotic relapse. It has been known for some time that an adversely critical or overcontrolling family atmosphere is associated with an increased likelihood of relapse in those who have already experience a psychotic episode (Leff & Vaughn, 1985). Whether such an atmosphere is, as is supposed by some authors (Heilbrum & Norbert, 1972; Kaffman, 1983) necessary or even sufficient for the genesis of persecutory delusions must remain a topic for future investigation.

These observations notwithstanding, neuropsychological research might contribute to our understanding of abnormal beliefs in a number of ways. First, it may be possible to identify the brain structures that implement self-protective cognitive biases. Although Sackheim (1986), in an attempt to construct a neuropsychological account of depression, has suggested that these biases may be left-hemisphere phenomena, it should be recognised that identifying the site of the brain's defences might not advance our understanding of their origins as, however these mechanisms are acquired, they must be implemented somewhere in the brain. Second, it may be possible to identify specific neuropsychological deficits that generate the anomalous experiences that appear to drive some types of abnormal beliefs. The limitations of exclusively perceptual accounts of delusions (Maher, 1974) have already been discussed, but it does seem that some delusions reflect at least semirational attempts to explain unpleasant and unexpected experiences. Third, it is possible that some neuropsychological deficits (perhaps affecting general intellectual and problem-solving skills or the regulation of arousal) contribute to the formation of delusions either by magnifying the impact of stressors or by depriving the individual of abilities that are essential for coping with them. Such deficits would create a strong need for the kinds of self-protective cognitive biases evident in paranoid patients. The wide range of neuropsychological abnormalities associated with psychotic disorders (Berquier & Ashton, 1991; Seidman, 1984) is consistent with this hypothesis.

Earlier in this chapter I discussed a number of problems of explanation in psychopathology. I particularly highlighted the difficulty of accounting for intentional phenomena. The tendency, observed by Dennett (1971), to look for exclusively neurobiological accounts of behaviour when intentional accounts fail, is undoubtedly justified but the correct application of this principle depends on our ability to determine when intentional accounts are no longer adequate. It is in fact difficult to think of any kind of brain damage (even dementia) in which intentionality is entirely compromised, and in which psychological and motivational factors therefore play no role. In the case of delusions at least (and I suspect also in the case of most other psychotic experiences), careful study reveals an intentionality that is not apparent on first inspection. What appeared to be ununderstandable becomes understandable on closer examination. A psychopathology that adequately explains these experiences must therefore find a way to make reference to neuropsychological processes, to the social environment and personal histories of the persons affected, and to the complex and mutually influencing interactions between these two domains of events.

ACKNOWLEDGEMENTS

Much of the research described in this chapter has been funded by a grant to the author from the Wellcome Trust. I would like to thank Peter Kinderman, Helen Lyon, Heather Young, David Harper, and, of course, Sue Kaney for numerous discussions which have helped to shape my ideas about delusional beliefs.

REFERENCES

Abramson, L.Y., Seligman, M.E.P., & Teasdale, J.D. (1978). Learned helplessness in humans: Critique and reformulation. *Journal of Abnormal Psychology, 78*, 40–74.

Ackermann, R., & DeRubeis, R.J. (1991). Is depressive realism real? *Clinical Psychology Review, 11*, 565–584.

Alloy, L.B., & Abramson, L.Y. (1979). Judgement of contingency in depressed and non-depressed students: Sadder but wiser? *Journal of Experimental Psychology: General, 108*, 441–485.

American Psychiatric Association (1987). *Diagnostic and statistical manual of mental disorders.* (3rd edn.), revised. Washington: APA.

Bentall, R.P. (1990a). The syndromes and symptoms of psychosis: Or why you can't play 20 questions with the concept of schizophrenia and hope to win. In R.P. Bentall (Ed.), *Reconstructing schizophrenia.* London: Routledge.

Bentall, R.P. (1990b). The illusion of reality: A review and integration of psychological research on hallucinations. *Psychological Bulletin, 107*, 82–95.

Bentall, R.P. (1991). Explaining and explaining away insanity. In R. Tallis & H. Robinson (Eds.), *Pursuit of mind.* London: Carcanet.

Bentall, R.P., Jackson, H.F., & Pilgrim, D. (1988). Abandoning the concept of "schizophrenia": Some implications of validity arguments for psychological research into psychotic phenomena. *British Journal of Clinical Psychology, 27*, 156–69.

Bentall, R.P., & Kaney, S. (1989). Content specific processing and persecutory delusions: An investigation using the emotional Stroop test. *British Journal of Medical Psychology, 62*, 355–64.

Bentall, R.P., Kaney, S., & Dewey, M.E. (1991). Paranoia and social reasoning: An attribution theory analysis. *British Journal of Clinical Psychology, 30*, 13–23.

Berquier, A., & Ashton, R. (1991). A selective review of possible neurological etiologies of schizophrenia. *Clinical Psychology Review, 11*, 645–661.

Berrios, G. (1991). Delusions as "wrong beliefs": A conceptual history. *British Journal of Psychiatry, 159, Suppl. 14,* 6–13.

Brennan, J.H., & Hemsley, D.R. (1984). Illusory correlations in paranoid and non-paranoid schizophrenia. *British Journal of Clinical Psychology, 23,* 225–226.

Brewin, C. (1988). *Cognitive foundations of clinical psychology.* Hove, Sussex: Lawrence Erlbaum Associates Ltd.

Candido, C., & Romney, D.M. (1990). Attributional style in paranoid vs depressed patients. *British Journal of Medical Psychology, 63,* 355–363.

Chadwick, P., & Lowe C.F. (1990. The measurement and modification of delusional beliefs. *Journal of Consulting and Clinical Psychology, 58,* 225–232.

Chapman, L.J., & Chapman, J.P. (1988). The genesis of delusions. In T.F. Oltmanns & B.A. Maher (Eds.), *Delusional beliefs.* New York: Wiley.

Charlton, B.G. (1990). A critique of biological psychiatry. *Psychological Medicine, 20,* 3–6.

Colby, K.M., Weber, S., & Hilf, F.D. (1971). Artificial paranoia. *Artificial Intelligence, 2,* 1–25.

Crocker, J., Kayne, N.T., & Alloy, L.B. (1988). Attributional style, depression and perceptions of consensus for events. *Journal of Personality and Social Psychology, 54,* 840–846.

Dennett, D. (1971). Intentional systems. *Journal of Philosophy, 68,* 87–106.

Ellis, H.D., & Young, A.W. (1990). Accounting for delusional misidentification. *British Journal of Psychiatry, 157,* 239–248.

Fenigstein, A., & Vanable, P.A. (1991). Paranoia and self-consciousness. *Journal of Personality and Social Psychology, 62,* 129–138.

Garety, P. (1985). Delusions: Problems of definition and measurement. *British Journal of Medical Psychology, 58,* 25–34.

Garety, P., Hemsley, D., & Wessely, S. (1991). Reasoning in deluded schizophrenic and paranoid patients. *Journal of Nervous and Mental disease, 179,* 194–201.

Gilhooly, K.J. (1982). *Thinking: Directed, Undirected and Creative.* London: Academic Press.

Harrow, M., Rattenbury, F., & Stoll, F. (1988). Schizophrenic delusions: An analysis of their persistence, of related premorbid ideas and three major dimensions. In T.F. Oltmanns & B.A. Maher (Eds.), *Delusional beliefs,* New York: Wiley.

Hartman, L.M., & Cashman, F.E. (1983). Cognitive-behavioural and psychopharmocological treatment of delusional symptoms: A preliminary report. *Behavioural Psychotherapy, 11,* 50–61.

Heilbrun, A.B., & Norbert, N. (1972). Style of adaption to aversive maternal control and paranoid behaviour. *Journal of Genetic Psychology, 121,* 145–153.

Hemsley, D.R., & Garety, P.A. (1986). The formation and maintenance of delusions: A Bayesian analysis. *British Journal of Psychiatry, 149,* 51–56.

Hewstone, M. (1989). *Causal attribution: From cognitive processes to collective beliefs.* Oxford: Blackwell.

Hole, R.W., Rush, A.J., & Beck, A.T. (1979). A cognitive investigation of schizophrenic delusions. *Psychiatry, 41,* 312–319.

Huq, S.F., Garety, P.A., & Hemsley, D.R. (1988). Probabilistic judgements in deluded and non-deluded subjects. *Quarterly Journal of Experimental Psychology: Human Learning and Memory, 40A,* 801–812.

Jaspers, K. (1963). *General Psychopathology* (J. Hoenig & M.W. Hamilton, Trans.). Manchester: Manchester University Press.

Johnson, W.G., Ross, J.M., & Mastria, M.A. (1977). Delusional behaviour: An attribution analysis of development and modification. *Journal of Abnormal Psychology, 89,* 421–426.

Johnson-Laird, P.N. (1987). *The computer and the mind.* London: Fontana.

Kaffman (1983). Paranoid disorders: Family sources of the delusional system. *Journal of Family Therapy, 5,* 107–116.

Kaney, S., & Bentall, R.P. (1989). Persecutory delusions and attributional style. *British Journal of Medical Psychology*, *62*, 191–198.

Kaney, S., & Bentall, R.P. (1992). Persecutory delusions and the self-serving bias: Evidence from a contingency judgement task. *Journal of Nervous and Mental Disease*, *180*, 773–780.

Kaney, S., Wolfenden, M., Dewey, M.E., & Bentall, R.P. (1992). Persecutory delusions and the recall of threatening and non-threatening propositions. *British Journal of Clinical Psychology*, *31*, 85–87.

Kay, D.W., Cooper, A.S., Garside, R.F., & Roth, M. (1976). The differentiation of paranoid from affective psychoses by patients' premorbid characteristics. *British Journal of Psychiatry*, *129*, 207–215.

Kelley, H.H. (1967). Attribution theory in social psychology. In D. Levine (Ed.), *Nebraska symposium on motivation, Vol. 15*. Lincoln: University of Nebraska.

Kendler, K.S., Glazer, W.M., & Morgenstern, H. (1983). Dimensions of delusional experience. *American Journal of Psychiatry*, *140*, 466–469.

Klerman, G.L. (1991). An American perspective on the conceptual approaches to psychopathology. In A. Kerr & H. McClelland (Eds.), *Concepts of mental disorder: A continuing debate*. London: Gaskell.

LaRusso, I. (1978). Sensitivity of paranoid patients to non-verbal cues. *Journal of Abnormal Psychology*, *87*, 463–471.

Leff, J.P., & Vaughn, C. (1985). *Expressed emotion in families: Its significance for mental illness*. New York: Guildford Press.

Lemert, E.M. (1962). Paranoia and dynamics of exclusion. *Sociometry*, *25*, 2–20.

Lidz, C.W. (1975). Conspiracy, paranoia and the dynamics of exclusion. *Qualitative Sociology*, *1*, 3–20.

Locasio, J.J., & Snyder, C.R. (1975). Selective attention to threatening stimuli and field independence as factors in the etiology of paranoid behaviour. *Journal of Abnormal Psychology*, *84*, 637–643.

Lyon, H., Kaney, S., & Bentall, R.P. (in press). The defensive function of persecutory delusions: Evidence from attribution tasks. *British Journal of Psychiatry*.

Maher, B.A. (1974). Delusional thinking and perceptual disorder. *Journal of Individual Psychology*, *30*, 98–113.

Maher, B.A., & Ross, J.S. (1984). Delusions. In H.E. Adams & P. Suther (Eds.), *Comprehensive handbook of psychopathology*. New York: Plenum.

Marks, G., & Miller, N. (1987). Ten years of research on the false consensus effect: An empirical and theoretical review. *Psychological Bulletin*, *102*, 72–90.

Marr. D. (1982). *Vision*. San Francisco: Freeman.

Mayerhoff, D., Pelta, D., Valentino, C., & Chakos, M. (1991). Real-life basis for a patient's paranoia. *American Journal of Psychiatry*, *148*, 682–683.

McArthur (1972). The how and what of why: Some determinants and consequences of causal attribution. *Journal of Personality and Social Psychology*, *22*, 171–193.

Mirowsky, J., & Ross, C.E. (1983). Paranoia and the structure of powerlessness. *American Sociological Review*, *48*, 228–239.

Musson, R.F., & Alloy, L.B. (1988). Depression and self-directed attention. In L.B. Alloy (Ed.), *Cognitive processes in depression*. New York: Guilford Press.

Neufeld, R.W. (1990). Memory in paranoid schizophrenia. In P. Magaro (Ed.), *Cognitive bases of mental disorders: Annual review of psychopathology, 1*, Newbury Park, CA: Sage.

Oltmanns, T.F., & Maher, B.A. (Eds.) (1988). *Delusional beliefs*. New York: Wiley.

Peterson, C., Semmel, A., Von Baeyer, C., Abramson, L.Y., Metlasky, G.I., & Seligman, M.P.E. (1982). The attributed style questionnaire. *Cognitive Therapy and Research*, *6*, 287–300.

Roberts, G. (1991). Delusional belief systems and meaning in life: A preferred reality? *British Journal of Psychiatry, 159, Suppl. 14,* 19–28.

Rose, S. (1984). Disordered molecules and diseased minds. *Journal of Psychiatric Research, 18,* 351–359.

Sackheim, H.A. (1986). A neurodynamic perspective on the self. In L.M. Hartman & K. Blankstein (Eds.), *Perception of self in emotional disorders and psychotherapy.* New York: Plenum, 51–83.

Seidman, L.J. (1984). Schizophrenia and brain dysfunction: An integration of recent neurodiagnostic findings. *Psychological Bulletin, 94,* 195–238.

Shannon, D.T. (1962). Clinical patterns of defence as revealed in visual recognition thresholds. *Journal of Abnormal and Social Psychology, 64,* 370–377.

Sims, A. (1988). *Symptoms in the mind.* London: Bailliere Tindall.

Strauss, J.S. (1969). Hallucinations and delusions as points on continua function. *Archives of General Psychiatry, 21* 581–586.

Tallis, R. (1991). A critique of neuromythology. In R. Tallis & H. Robinson (Eds.), *Pursuit of mind.* London: Carcanet.

Taylor, S.E. (1983). Adjustment to threatening events. *American Psychologist,* 1161–1173.

Ullmann, L.P., & Krasner, L. (1969). *A psychological approach to abnormal behaviour.* Englewood Cliffs, N.J.: Prentice-Hall.

Walker, C. (1991). Delusion: What did Jaspers really say? *British Journal of Psychiatry, 159, Suppl. 14,* 94–103.

Watt, J.A. (1983). Hearing and premorbid personality in paranoid states. *American Journal of Psychiatry, 142,* 1453–1455.

Watts, F.N., Powell, E.G., & Austin, S.V. (1973). The modification of abnormal beliefs. *British Journal of Medical Psychology, 46,* 356–363.

Williams, E.B. (1964). Deductive reasoning in schizophrenia. *Journal of Abnormal and Social Psychology, 69,* 47–61.

Williams, J.M.G., Watts, F.N., MacLeod, C., & Mathews, A. (1988). *Cognitive psychology and emotional disorders.* London: Wiley.

Winters, K.C., & Neale, J.M. (1983). Delusions and delusional thinking: A review of the literature. *Clinical Psychology Review, 3,* 227–53.

Winters, K.C., & Neale, J.M. (1985). Mania and low self-esteem. *Journal of Abnormal Psychology, 94,* 282–290.

Zigler, E., & Glick, M. (1988). Is paranoid schizophrenia really camouflaged depression? *American Psychologist, 43,* 284–290.

Zimbardo, P.G., Andersen, S.M., & Kabat, L.G. (1981). Induced hearing deficit generates experimental paranoia. *Science, 212,* 1529–1531.

Zuckerman, M. (1979). Attribution of success and failure revisited, or the motivational bias is alive and well in attribution theory. *Journal of Personality, 47,* 245–287.

20 Top-down Preconscious Perceptual Processing and Delusional Misidentification in Neuropsychiatric Disorder

Simon Fleminger
Senior Lecturer, London Hospital Medical College, London

Observations on a man with dementia who presented with episodes of delusional misidentification of short duration that could be terminated by a specific psychological event, lead to the development of a model of delusional misidentification which attempts to explain how organic cerebral disorder and psychological forces may interact with one another to produce the symptom. The model relies on the susceptibility of preconscious perceptual processes to the "top-down" influence of expectations and preconceptions. A positive feedback loop therefore exists which may enable abnormal beliefs to distort perceptions in such a way as to reinforce the abnormal belief: this may result in a delusional misidentification. Good perceptual and mnemonic processing, unimpaired by organic cerebral disorder, will reduce the likelihood of this happening. Therefore either powerful psychic forces, particularly paranoia, and/or organic cerebral disorder may produce a delusional misidentification. The model predicts that, across a population of patients with this symptom, there will be an inverse relationship between the strength of organic cerebral disorder evident within an individual, and the likelihood that they will have paranoid delusions preceding the onset of the delusional misidentification. The model also draws attention to the possibility that the reasoning strategies which may be involved in normal belief formation are similar to those that take place, preconsciously, during perceptual processing. It is therefore possible that patients with delusions who tend to "jump to conclusions" may also be liable to "jump to perceptions", and thereby be prone to delusional misidentification.

INTRODUCTION

Joseph (1986) brought together all the delusional misidentification syndromes and showed convincingly that they were to be found in both neurological and functional psychiatric disorder. In this chapter I will discuss a model of the interaction between expectancies and perceptual processing that may be able to bring together neuropsychological and psychic explanations for delusional misidentification (Fleminger, 1992). The analysis also demonstrates that the decision and judgement processes that underpin belief formation may be very similar to those that result in percept formation; attempts to demonstrate that disordered reasoning (Hemsley & Garety, 1986) or disordered perceptions (Maher, 1974) are the primary process in delusion formation may fail to acknowledge this. The fundamental impairment responsible for the psychosis may result in both disordered reasoning and disordered perception (Maher, 1988).

The model relies on the fact that there is considerable preconscious processing of sensory information. Preconscious processing occurs "... in the brief but measurable interval between arrival of a stimulus at the peripheral receptor and its representation in consciousness..." (Dixon, 1984). Preconscious processing has a surprising authority over perception; under certain conditions much of the information arriving at the visual cortex may never gain access to consciousness (binocular suppression: Breese, 1899; Cobb et al., 1967). Because a person can have no conscious knowledge of these processes, and because people are not inclined to doubt the evidence of their perceptions, particularly what they see, any distortion of perception that occurs during preconscious processing may be particularly invidious.

PERCEPTIONS AS HYPOTHESES THAT HAVE BEEN TESTED

Helmholtz (quoted in Gregory, 1987a) considered that perceptions "are the conclusions of unconscious inductive inferences." The inductive quality of the inferences means that they have to be tested to ensure that the conclusions are correct. The senses both suggest the hypotheses to be tested and provide the evidence to check them against. Perceptions are therefore the best bet given the sensory information. Marcel (1983) has elaborated the concept of perceptual hypotheses in his theoretical model of conscious perception, "A conscious percept is a constructive act of fitting a perceptual hypothesis to its sensory source." Good sense data will improve the accuracy of this task. In addition, Marcel suggests that consequent on the selection of one perceptual hypothesis other competing hypotheses receive inhibition.

The selection of the perceptual hypothesis is a probabilistic process, which depends on selecting the most likely perceptual hypothesis that reasonably matches the sense data, from likely representations held in memory. However, with ambiguous figures (the Necker cube drawing, the

Rubin vase; Gregory, 1987b) there is no best bet, and the two alternative perceptual hypotheses, and therefore perceptions, alternate.

The advantage of such a system is its speed. The visual system, rather than having to undergo a large labour of "bottom-up" processing, is quickly able to produce a percept by a process of "trial and check" (Woodworth, 1947).

However, this method of perceptual processing does depend on previous experience and consequent expectation. Such a system therefore allows top-down effects to bias the selection and testing of hypotheses. "Top-down" processing of perceptions is said to occur when "context or general world knowledge" (Anderson, 1980) or belief, expectation or emotion, guides perception. An example of this, found in normal subjects, is "effort after meaning" (Bartlett, 1932), which describes the active unconscious attempts to match meaningless percepts to familiar objects. Expectancy effects hinder the perception of incongruity in a picture (Bruner & Postman, 1950), particularly when subjects are under stress (Smock, 1955).

Gregory (1987a) notes the power of top-down processing in facial perception. When a hollow mask of a face is seen with its internal aspect facing the observer, it will almost invariably be seen as a solid face looking towards the observer. Subtle but incompatible clues (the direction of the shadows, depth perception) have been suppressed by top-down processes that attempt to match the image to that of a solid face.

Cross-modal interactions demonstrate the breadth of influence that top-down processes may have. As we will see, this is important when considering the many sensory modalities in which concurrent misidentifications occur in the syndromes of delusional misidentification. In a situation of conflict the visual modality tends to dominate over the auditory (Jackson, 1953).

Retrieval of Memories

Bartlett (1932) noted that distortions occur when an image is retrieved from memory, these distortions are similar to those that occur at perception (see above).

Affective (Lishman, 1972) and cognitive (Fisher & Craik, 1977) effects on retrieval of memories have been observed.

Memories are enhanced if the context that is associated with the encoding of the event is present at the time of retrieval. A colourful example of this effect is the experiment by Emmerson (1986), which found that scuba divers have better recall of information learnt underwater when subsequently tested underwater, than when tested on dry land.

Therefore the concordance of states of mind and surroundings between the time an image is originally perceived and encoded, and the time when it is subsequently presented for recognition, will facilitate recognition. On the other hand discordant states of mind and surroundings, between the two presentations, will tend to hinder recognition.

PERCEPTIONS AS INTERPRETATIONS

Hochberg (1956) was aware of the difficulty of defining perceptions, falling as they do between sensations and judgements. "Usage has ranged from a narrowing almost to previous connotations of sensation, to a widening that includes almost all of cognition". Preconscious processing of perceptions not only allows distortions of perceptions but also enables sophisticated interpretation of the sense data, before conscious cognitive processes have access to it.

Studies on subliminal perception have demonstrated the possibility for sophisticated perceptual processing despite the subject remaining unaware of the stimulus. Words, presented in a dichotic listening task (Groeger, 1984) or briefly presented visually (Marcel, 1983), which are not identified may nevertheless have cognitive effects, e.g. on subsequent semantic judgements.

Several lines of evidence indicate the ability of stimuli to influence affect directly, without having to be consciously perceived. Tyrer, Lewis, and Lee (1978) were able to demonstrate that emotive cine film, shown at a subliminal intensity, was able to increase subjects' self-rating of anxiety. Zajonc (1980), in a paper subtitled *Preferences need no inferences*, argues convincingly that stimuli may produce an affective response without impinging on conscious cognitive processes (see also Seaman, Brody, & Kauff, 1983).

Preconscious processing may also influence the processing of affective material. Highly emotive words, e.g. raped, presented tachistoscopically, have a higher threshold for conscious recognition than do neutral words (perceptual defence; McGinnies, 1949).

Marcel (1983) suggested that conscious percepts result from the synthetic recovery of information from several perceptual analysers, e.g. line, colour, and face analysers. These are then integrated, preconsciously, to form an internally consistent conscious percept. The perception itself is generally regarded as a unitary experience. This unitary nature of perceptions is important. If preconscious processing allows considerable affective interpretation of the scene, then the affective colouring of the perception, including the sense of familiarity of the scene (see below), may be an integral part of it. Affective and interpretive characteristics of perceptions may be attributes of the perception, rather than something added, at a later stage, by conscious cognitive processing.

The murky border that separates perceptions from cognitions means that attempts to distinguish illusions (misperceptions of external stimuli) from delusional misinterpretations or misidentifications are likely to fail. Kraupl-Taylor (1983) distinguishes between "attribute" and "interpretive" illusions. With interpretive illusions, he suggests, the subject is very much aware of the meaning of the percept; the illusory characteristic is one that is meaningful. Attribute illusions, on the other hand, are those in which some emotionally neutral perceptual characteristic of the object is altered. He considers delusional misidentification to be an example of a morbid misinterpretive illusion.

Kraupl-Taylor acknowledges that the distinction between "attribute" and "interpretive" illusions is a practical, rather than a theoretical one. As noted above, characteristics of percepts, that may intuitively be regarded as conscious interpretations of the percept, may in fact be processed preconsciously and presented to consciousness as attributes of the percept.

To illustrate this, let us take the example of a delusional misidentification of the bang of a door by a man in a delirious state. He believes a gun has been fired. However, he did not hear a bang and consciously *interpret* it as gunfire; he *heard* a gun being fired. The quality of the perception has been altered by the interpretation (preconscious) that has been made.

TESTING THE VALIDITY OF PERCEPTIONS

It is possible to dissect out three stages on the path to conscious acceptance of the validity of a perceptual attribute (Fig. 20.1). The first two stages are regarded as preconscious, while the third is conscious:

1. Look and select. A perceptual hypothesis regarding the attribute is put forward. This may be regarded as a probabilistic decision. The suggested hypothesis is usually determined by links between the sensory data and likely perceptual representations in memory. Healthy links with memory stores are necessary if the correct hypothesis is to be selected. Incorrect hypotheses will be proposed when the sensory data is incongruous. Expectancies may influence which hypothesis is selected.

2. See and perceive no mismatch. The hypothesis is matched to sensory data and the result is the basis for the experience of the perceptual attribute. A clear mismatch of the proposed hypothesis to sensory data will normally result in it being rejected. Powerful top-down effects, e.g. as seen in facial processing (see above), may overcome this mismatch. Testing of the hypothesis will be more difficult if the sensory data is poor. Expectancies, conscious and unconscious, will facilitate matching of congruent hypotheses.

3. Judge and accept validity. The validity of the perceptual attribute is then tested consciously in relation to its context. Again, expectancies will determine the degree to which it is tested; if the percept fulfils expectancies it

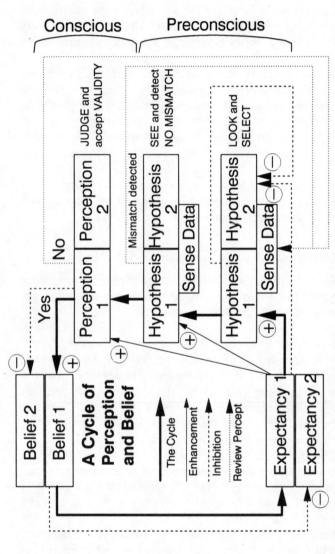

FIG. 20.1 The interaction between two incompatible mental states, 1 and 2, and their associated cycles of belief and perception. The cycle of State 1 is illustrated with the heavy line and large arrows, and might be the delusional misidentification of the object, e.g. Mr L., believing (Belief 1), incorrectly, that he is not in his own house, and seeing the house as different from his own and unfamiliar (Perception 1, generated by Perceptual Hypothesis 1). State 2 is the correct belief (Belief 2) that he is at home, associated with the correct perception (Perception 2) of his house as familiar.

State 1 is sustained by the positive feedforward effects of expectancy 1, both on preconscious perceptual processing and on the conscious judgement as to whether to accept Perception 1 as valid. In addition State 1 is sustained by the suppression of the rival Perception 2 (dashed arrow).

No attempt has been made in this figure to identify the beginning of the cycle of perception and belief. Undoubtedly alterations in sense data may be able to shift the cycle from one state to the other. However, in Mr L.'s case it was noteworthy that attempts to shift him from a state of delusional misidentification (State 1) by asking him to examine in detail the house and its contents, failed. He reverted to the normal state (Belief 2 and Perception 2) only when Belief 1 was challenged by his alighting from the bus.

366

will be more readily accepted as valid. In addition, in patients with delusions and/or schizophrenia, impairments in reality testing (Johnson, 1988; Mintz & Albert, 1972) real-world knowledge (Cutting & Murphy, 1988), the monitoring of willed intentions (Frith, 1987), or a tendency to jump to conclusions (Huq, Garety, & Hemsley, 1988) will tend to make them more likely to accept the validity of incorrect perceptual attributes. The impaired judgement of patients with dementia or frontal lobe disease will do likewise.

The distinction between these three stages is hazy, and possibly somewhat artificial. However, this description does serve to clarify the various components of the system, and their vulnerability to disruption. At all three stages of the operation expectancies, and consequently beliefs, tend to foster perceptions that are complementary to themselves, and hinder those that are not.

SIMILARITIES BETWEEN PRECONSCIOUS PERCEPTUAL PROCESSING AND COGNITIVE REASONING

In both perceptual processing and in cognitive reasoning, subjects are inclined to go "beyond the information given" (Bartlett, 1932; Bruner, Goodnow, & Austin, 1956). Many of the reasoning biases that are observed in normal subjects, and are possibly exaggerated in deluded subjects, may occur also during perceptual processing.

The selection of perceptual hypotheses, as discussed above, is influenced by expectation and the quality of sensory information. These processes are, then, rather similar to those by which humans assess covariation between two events, which plays an important part in reaching judgements about meaning and causation (Alloy & Tabachnik, 1984); there is trade-off between prior expectation and the quality of current situational information (see Alloy & Tabachnik, 1984's Table 1).

If deluded subjects are abnormal in their assessment of probabilistic judgements (see Hemsley, Chapter 6; Huq et al., 1988) and use a similar reasoning style in their selection of perceptual hypotheses then some deluded subjects who are inclined to "jump to conclusions" (Huq et al., 1988), may also be inclined to "jump to perceptions" (McReynolds, Collins, & Acker, 1964).

We are all inclined to use more lax criteria for accepting observations that fit our beliefs or expectations than for those that do not. If we also use lax criteria for matching sense data to a selected perceptual hypothesis that is incorrect, but congruent with our expectations, this will facilitate perception of congruent perceptions. If deluded subjects use inappropriately lax criteria to facilitate delusion formation (Johnson, 1988), then they may also be inclined to use inappropriately lax criteria for their perceptions, and therefore be inclined to misperceptions, including misidentifications.

A FEEDBACK MODEL OF DELUSIONAL MISIDENTIFICATION

Lishman (1987), attempting to understand the delusions commonly observed in acute organic reactions, suggests: "Chance noises may similarly be misinterpreted, and often ·in a manner which contributes towards delusion formation. The latter in turn reinforces the direction which misinterpretations may take...". He does not comment on the level at which such misinterpretations may be taking place. The studies on preconscious processing of perceptions, described above, indicate that they may take place during perceptual processing.

People are inclined to accept the evidence of their perceptions as incontrovertible, particularly for the visual modality, as illustrated by the expression "I saw it with my own eyes!" They are not conscious of the powerful effects that preconscious processes may have had on what they see (see above), and consequently not aware of the possibility that their expectations may have prejudiced their perceptions. An expectation will do this by asserting itself on preconscious processes to foster perceptions that are congruent with the expectation (Fig. 20.1). It will facilitate the selection of perceptual hypotheses that conform to the expectation, and then facilitate the match of this conforming hypothesis to the sense data by inhibiting the detection of any mismatch that may exist. In addition, it is likely that the expectation will influence judgement, and enhance the prospect of the congruent percept being accepted as valid.

Therefore expectancies, driven by beliefs, facilitate the perception of attributes that reinforce those beliefs. This is a system with positive feedback. If the system goes wrong, false beliefs may result in misperceptions that reinforce those false beliefs. This cycle is central to the delusional misidentification syndromes; the cycle may start with either an erroneous expectancy or a misperception. In its fully developed form it consists of a perceptual misidentification reinforcing a delusion that then serves to reinforce the misperception. This cycle is quite incompatible with the normal cycle: correct perceptual recognition reinforces the conscious acceptance of the correct identity, which in turn serves to facilitate correct perception.

All sensory modalities are subject to top-down effects. Not only are visual percepts distorted, but auditory, somatic, and olfactory senses will all be distorted in such a way as to reinforce the belief. This helps to explain how all modalities of perception may be involved in delusional misidentification syndromes. For example, in some patients with Capgras' syndrome it is not just the face of the "alter" that is different, but their voice and sometimes their gestures.

In addition, distortions of recognition memory may help to reinforce a state of delusional misidentification. States of delusional misidentification may be associated with high arousal or suspiciousness. The mental state of the subject may therefore be quite different from the occasion when the object was last perceived correctly. This difference between the mental state at the time of the antecedent perception on the one hand and retrieval on the other, will hinder recognition (see above). Distortions will also occur in the retrieval from memory of the stored representation of the object when last correctly perceived. When the person recalls this object, for comparison with the selfsame object that they are now confronted with and misidentifying, the recollected image will have been exposed to exactly the opposite perceptual distortion as the object they are faced with. The recollection will be influenced by delusional beliefs which seek to maximise the differences between the two images.

The cycle, involving as it does positive feedforward, is intrinsically unstable. Relatively trivial changes in the objects that are perceived, or in the attitudes of the person, may result in their flipping from one state to another. Many of the factors that demand the rejection of invalid perceptual attributes are also those that maintain the stability of the system. Poor sensory data, weak links between sensory data and memory stores, poor judgement, or a tendency to jump to conclusions will all facilitate acceptance of the validity of misperceptions, whilst also impairing the stability of the system.

It therefore helps to understand the dramatically variable delusional misidentification of his surroundings observed in a man with dementia:

Mr L., a 71-year-old man with a moderate dementia presented with episodes, lasting from minutes to a few hours, during which he became convinced that his house was not his house. Everywhere he looked served only to reinforce this belief. The belief had coloured, preconsciously, his perception. It served to remove all sense of familiarity in the perception. However, during the episodes he showed unimpaired recognition of faces and places when asked to describe the details of old photograph albums.

He would demand to leave the house and "go home". Attempts to walk him round the block and back to his house would invariably fail to break the conviction that it was not his home. However, walking with him some two or three hundred yards up the road to a bus stop, and then getting a bus back to his house would be successful. He would alight from his brief bus journey with some comment like "Ah, here we are; back home now"! Alighting from the bus outside his house was indivisibly associated, in his mind, with coming home (he had no car). The sense of familiarity aroused on alighting from the bus restored the normal affective colouring of the perception of his home. This restored the belief that it was his home, which served to reinforce the hue of familiarity. It was this, relatively trivial, change of attitude and affect that enabled Mr L.'s beliefs and perceptions to flip back into place.

It is valuable to compare the sudden and complete shifts between two rival perceptions experienced by Mr L. with those that take place during perception of a Necker cube. A three-dimensional wire cube, when observed with binocular vision, in close up, in a light that casts clear shadows, will be seen in its correct depth-perspective and this percept will be stable. If the cube is now moved away from the observer, the perceptible depth cues will be reduced in strength. Suddenly the rival perception will appear; the depth-reversed illusion with the cube appearing back to front (the cube will also appear to change shape as it does so (Gregory, 1987c, p. 508); this is an attribute illusion—see above. Moving the cube away from the observer has reduced the strength of the depth cues contained in the sense data. This allows the incorrect hypothesis to be selected and successfully matched to the sense data. The system is now unstable and will flip between the two rival states.

DELUSIONAL MISIDENTIFICATION: THE SYNDROMES

There is little doubt that in the majority of cases of delusional misidentification reported in the literature no organic lesion is identified (see, for example, Berson, 1983). However, any neuropsychological model that purports to explain delusional misidentification must be able to embrace all the syndromes found in functional and organic disorders (Joseph, 1986), and their many associations. What is of particular interest is how the various processes involved may play upon one another.

Cerebral Disorder and Delusional Misidentification

Dementia may result in delusional misidentification, which is commonly confined to discrete episodes (Burns & Philpot, 1987; Kumar, 1987; Lipkin, 1988) similar to those observed in Mr L. Patients with bilateral frontal lobe involvement, describing not dissimilar phenomena, may be described as confabulating (Stuss, Alexander, Lieberman, & Levine, 1978). Most recent studies indicate the greater propensity for lesions of the right hemisphere to produce these syndromes, particularly if associated with bilateral frontal abnormalities (Alexander, Stuss, & Benson, 1979; Cutting, 1990; Feinberg & Shapiro, 1989; Hakim, Verma, & Greiffenstein, 1988; Morrison & Tarter, 1984; Staton et al., 1982). This is probably a result of the right hemisphere being more concerned with Gestalt analysis of perceptions and tagging objects with the label "familiar" (Mullan & Penfield, 1959). The site of damage may be reflected in the area of misidentification; parietal lesions result in misidentifications of spatial orientation (Fisher, 1982); temporo–occipital lesions are associated more with misidentifications of persons (Lewis, 1987). However, because of cross-modal, top-down effects, the misidentification will often spill over into sensory modalities that are analysed some distance from the site of injury.

Delusional misidentification syndromes have been interpreted as resulting from disconnection of the visual system from limbic structures involved in memory and affective responses (Anderson, 1988; Lewis, 1987; Staton, Brumback, & Wilson, 1982; Wilcox, 1986). Ellis and Young (1990) have produced a convincing neuropsychological model of delusional misidentifications of persons based on dysfunction of the information processing involved in recognition of familiar people. For example, they suggest that in patients with Capgras' syndrome the dysfunction is the "mirror image of prosopagnosia".

Psychological influences

Intense suspiciousness and vigilance, or a persecutory psychosis, may often occur before the emergence of the delusional misidentification (Chawla, Buchan, & Galen, 1987; Christodoulou, 1986; Enoch & Trethowan, 1979; Merrin & Silberfarb, 1976; Todd et al., 1981) even in cases in whom the syndrome has arisen in the context of an organic disorder (Burns, 1985; Staton, Brumback, & Wilson, 1982; Thompson, Silk, & Hover, 1980).

In Capgras' syndrome the person who is misidentified is almost always very familiar to the patient and of personal significance; spouses are particularly susceptible to being the object of a delusional misidentification (Wallis, 1986). It seems likely that two characteristics of preconscious processing may explain this. First, familiarity with an object results in changes in the perceptual quality of the object; the percept becomes coloured with a sense of familiarity, and indeed, as noted by Proust (see Fleminger, 1992), some of the more fundamental attributes of the percept may be altered. Alterations in perceptual processing associated with familiarity with the object have been demonstrated (Barret, Rugg, & Perrett, 1988; Wittreich, 1952). As noted above (Gregory, 1987a), perception of faces seems particularly vulnerable to top-down effects, and might therefore be expected to be sensitive to the effects of familiarity. Second, powerful emotional forces are particularly likely to involve objects of personal significance. These forces may be able to disrupt the usual effects of familiarity on preconscious processing, resulting in a distinct alteration in the quality of the perception, which may in turn reinforce, or trigger, the belief that it is unfamiliar. Again, facial processing may be particularly vulnerable; Bartlett (1932) noted how perception of faces is peculiarly liable to be influenced by affect. Ellis and Young (1990) comment on the importance of the affective state of patients with delusional misidentification. Hostile or ambivalent feelings towards the "alter" are commonly expressed before the misidentification. Often there has been a period of absence from the object (Stern & MacNaughton, 1945), during which time there may have been small, but real, changes in the object (Haslam, 1973).

In many patients it is difficult to ignore a psychodynamic explanation for the delusional misidentification of a spouse as "colourful way of solving the love–hate problem" (Enoch, 1986). It is likely that unconscious defence mechanisms, in particular splitting, do, in some patients, play a large part in determining the content and form of the misidentification (Lansky, 1986; O'Reilly & Malhotra, 1987). Perceptions could be influenced by the effects of such unconscious processes on "preconscious processing".

Colouring of the misidentification with events of personal significance is not only observed in functional psychiatric disorder. In reduplicative paramnesias, observed in the presence of organic cerebral disorder, the place in which the patient mistakenly believes themselves to have been is often endowed with special personal meaning (Benson, Gardner, & Meadows, 1976; Fisher, 1982).

DELUSIONAL MISIDENTIFICATION: A MULTIFACTORIAL SYNDROME

I have proposed that delusional misidentification syndromes result from a cycle of perceptual misidentification and false belief reinforcing one another. I would suggest that this cycle is the final common pathway that draws together the multifactorial pathogenesis of the syndrome.

In organic disorder, weakening of the normal checks in the system will occur when there is impairment of intellect, memory, or perceptual processing. For example, Capgras' syndrome may be associated with dysfunction of those processes that are involved in the generation of a sense of familiarity by familiar faces (Ellis & Young, 1990), or in the correct identification of an object's individuality or uniqueness (Cutting, 1990). In either case, one of the links in the perceptual system that ensure that familiar people are perceived correctly as such will have been weakened. This will therefore facilitate the development of a morbid cycle of misperception and delusion, though this may only take place under the stress of an assertive affective state.

In schizophrenia some of the checks in the perceptual system may be disturbed (Abroms, Taintor, & Lhamon, 1966; McCormick & Broekema, 1978; McReynolds et al., 1964). These perturbations will tend to produce a system that is unstable, and thereby facilitate the development of a delusional misidentification. It is likely that the effects are small. Delusional misidentification will therefore only arise in a patient with schizophrenia when powerful top-down effects are able to disrupt their perceptual system. Suspiciousness, or persecutory paranoia, seem to be particularly domineering. Capgras' syndrome is the most common delusional misidentification found in schizophrenic patients; their tendency to misidentify people will be facilitated by impaired facial perceptual processing (Frith et al., 1983; Griffith, Frith, & Eysenck, 1980).

Interaction Between Cerebral Disease and Psychological Disorder

The model of delusional misidentification that has been proposed therefore predicts that there will be an interaction between organic disease and psychological state. Psychological forces resulting in top-down forces on perceptual processes, e.g. suspiciousness associated with persecutory delusions, will be more frequently observed when the syndrome appears in patients with functional psychoses, than in patients with well defined organic disease. A systematic study of case reports of patients with delusional misidentification, organic, or functional mental disorder, has been undertaken (Fleminger & Burns, 1993) and confirms this conclusion. Fifty cases of delusional misidentification reported in the literature were chosen for study, half in patients with undoubted cerebral disease, the other half in patients with a diagnosis of functional psychiatric disorder and with no evidence of cerebral disease (Table 20.1). Paranoid psychosis was very much more common in those patients with functional psychiatric disorder, and in most of these patients the psychosis antedated the onset of the delusional misidentification. It is interesting to note that the only patient in whom the delusional misidentification appeared before the onset of persecutory delusions was a patient with cerebral disease.

TABLE 20.1
Persecutory Delusions

Organic brain disease?	Preceding	Simultaneous	Following	None	Total
Yes	2	1	1	20	24
No	17	4	–	5	26

Fifty cases with a delusional misidentification, reported in the literature and in approximately half of whom there was clinical evidence of organic mental disease, were taken at random from the literature. The case reports were scrutinised for descriptions of persecutory delusions, and these were assessed as being present before, simultaneously with, or after the onset of the delusional misidentification.

PRECONSCIOUS PROCESSING IN THE
DELUSIONAL DISORDERS

Delusional misidentification may be seen in association with disorders that fall within the Delusional (Paranoid) Disorders (297.10; American Psychiatric Association, 1987). Capgras' syndrome has been described in association with erotomania (Barton & Barton, 1986; Signer & Ibister, 1987; Sims & White, 1973), and with somatic delusions (McLaughlin & Sims, 1984; Signer & Ibister, 1987; Stern & MacNaughton, 1945). Perhaps the delusional disorders may be induced by a cycle of misperceptions and delusions similar to that proposed for the delusional misidentification syndromes?

The development of many of the delusional disorders relies heavily on evidence adduced from perceptions, such as the expression on the face of the deluded person's "lover", the threats heard on the bus, specks of dust that are seen to be little parasites. Other patients with these disorders may rely on the false testimony of their memories. Kraepelin (1921) has described the pseudomemories of paranoia. Both perceptions and memories will be subject to top-down effects. The model of positive feedback that has been described in this chapter may therefore contribute to our understanding of how such disorders can arise and be maintained. Recently Tarrier, Beckett, Harwood, and Bishay (1990) have highlighted the possible role of misperceptions in morbid jealousy.

It is likely that perceptual and mnemonic processing in the delusional disorders is relatively intact. On the other hand, in patients with schizophrenia the perceptual system is disrupted such that it is more unstable than normal (see above). The model therefore helps to explain three characteristics of the delusional disorders:

1. Large top-down effects will be necessary to cause misinterpretations. These may, for example, result from a period of intense suspicion or love; or if a new sensory symptom develops, e.g. itch, and demands explanation. Once the delusional state has been achieved the cycle will be fairly stable. They therefore tend to run a chronic course.

2. The focus of the delusion will tend to remain unchanged. However, the delusion will exert its mischievous effects on new observations that may be considered pertinent to its case. There will therefore be a tendency for the delusion to become systematised to form a complex and related set of misinterpretations and false beliefs.

3. There may be relatively little disturbance of other areas of mental life. The abnormal cycle may turn without any disturbance of entirely neutral perceptions and beliefs.

Poor sense data, as for example results from disease of the sense organs, will facilitate the development of delusional disorders. Cooper (1976) has suggested that chronic deafness is an important aetiological factor in the development of chronic paranoid hallucinatory states of middle and late life.

The delusional infestations tend to be disorders of the elderly (Gelder, Gath, & Mayou, 1983), and often arise in the context of sensory symptoms in the skin, for example itching due to senile eczema. The parasites are felt to be crawling under the skin, but may also be seen in clothes or around the house. The delusion and the misperceptions go hand in hand. Of interest is the finding that perceptual closure, i.e. identifying a picture in which most of the elements have been removed, is performed badly in the elderly (Salthouse, 1988). It seems not unlikely that this impairment facilitates expectancies making what they will out of specks of dust, etc. The misperception reinforces the belief, and the cycle begins to turn.

CONCLUSIONS

We are inclined to believe what we see. We have no introspective knowledge of the effects of preconscious processing on our perceptions. We are therefore not aware that our expectancies may have prejudiced our perceptions. Expectancies are able to do this by asserting themselves on preconscious perceptual processing, tending to foster perceptions with which they are consonant. Therefore false expectations, driven by false beliefs, may result in misperceptions that reinforce those false beliefs. It is proposed that this morbid cycle is central to the delusional misidentification syndromes, whether caused by organic or functional mental disorder.

Good sensory data, strong links between sense data and likely perceptual representations in memory, and good judgement will all help to prevent misperceptions being perceived and accepted as valid. In general, the less these constraints are disrupted, by for example organic disease, the stronger will be the psychological forces needed to generate a delusional misidentification. Of all the psychological states, it is likely that suspiciousness generates particularly assertive effects on preconscious processing of perceptions. A review of cases of delusional misidentification in patients with or without evidence of cerebral disease, reported in the literature, has confirmed this conclusion; paranoid psychosis antedating the onset of the delusional misidentification was observed very much more commonly in patients without cerebral disease.

Several of the abnormalities of perceptual processing in patients with schizophrenia explain their proclivity to developing delusional misidentification. The invidious effects on preconscious processing of delusions may occur in other disorders, in particular the delusional disorders.

The model also indicates that the reasoning strategies that may be involved in normal belief formation are similar to those that take place, preconsciously, during perceptual processing. It is therefore possible that patients with delusions who tend to "jump to conclusions" may also be liable to "jump to perceptions", and thereby be prone to delusional misidentification.

ACKNOWLEDGEMENTS

Drs Derek Bolton, Alistair Burns, John Cutting, Tony David, and Phillipa Garety provided stimulating discussions. The work was supported by the Mental Health Foundation.

REFERENCES

Abroms, G.M., Taintor, Z.C., & Lhamon, W.T. (1966). Percept assimilation and paranoid severity. *Archives of General Psychiatry*, *14*, 491–496.

Alexander, M., Stuss, D.T., & Benson, D.F. (1979). Capgras' syndrome: A reduplicative phenomenon. *Neurology*, *29*, 334–339.

Alloy, L.B., & Tabachnik, N. (1984). Assessment of covariation by humans and animals: The joint influence of prior expectations and current situational information. *Psychological Review*, *91*, 112–149.

American Psychiatric Association, (1987). *Diagnostic and Statistical Manual of Mental Disorders* (3rd ed.), revised [DSM- III-R]. Washington: American Psychiatric Association.

Anderson, D.N. (1988). The delusion of inanimate doubles: Implications for understanding the Capgras phenomenon. *British Journal of Psychiatry*, *153*, 694–699.

Anderson, J.R. (1980). *Cognitive psychology and its implications*. San Francisco: W.H. Freeman & Co.

Barrett, S.E., Rugg, M.D., & Perrett, D.I. (1988). Event-related potentials and the matching of familiar and unfamiliar faces. *Neuropsychologia*, *26*, 105–117.

Bartlett, F.C. (1932). *Remembering*. London: Cambridge University Press.

Barton, J.L., & Barton, E.S. (1986). Misidentification syndromes and sexuality. *Bibliotheca Psychiatrica*, *164*, 105–120.

Benson, D.F., Gardner, H., & Meadows, J.C. (1976). Reduplicative paramnesia. *Neurology*, *26*, 147–151.

Berson, R.J. (1983). Capgras' syndrome. *American Journal of Psychiatry*, *140*, 969–978.

Breese, B.B. (1899). On inhibition. *Psychological Review Monographs*, *3*, (1 Whole No. 2).

Bruner, J.S., & Postman, L. (1950). On the perception of incongruity: A paradigm. In J.S. Bruner and H. Krech (Eds.) *Perception and personality* (pp. 206–223). Durham, NC: Duke University Press.

Bruner, J.S., Goodnow, J.J., & Austin, G.A. (1956). *A study of thinking*. New York: Wiley.

Burns, A. (1985). The oldest patient with Capgras' syndrome? *British Journal of Psychiatry*, *147*, 719–720.

Burns, A., & Philpot, M. (1987). Capgras' syndrome in a patient with dementia. *British Journal of Psychiatry*, *150*, 876–877.

Chawla, S., Buchan, T., & Galen, G. (1987). Capgras syndrome: A case report from Zimbabwe. *British Journal of Psychiatry*, *151*, 254–256.

Christodoulou, G.N. (1986). Course and outcome of the Delusional Misidentification Syndromes. *Bibliotheca Psychiatrica*, *164*, 143–148.

Cobb, W.A., Morton, H.B., & Ettlinger, G. (1967). Cerebral evoked potentials evoked by pattern reversal and their suppression in visual rivalry. *Nature*, *216*, 1123–1125.

Cooper, A.F. (1976). Deafness and psychiatric illness. *British Journal of Psychiatry*, *129*, 216–226.

Cutting, J. (1985). *The psychology of schizophrenia*. Edinburgh: Churchill Livingstone.

Cutting, J. (1990). *The right cerebral hemisphere and psychiatric disorders*, p. 143. Oxford: Oxford University Press.

Cutting, J., & Murphy, D. (1988). Schizophrenic thought disorder: A psychological and organic perspective. *British Journal of Psychiatry*, *152*, 310–319.

Dixon, N.F. (1984). Subliminal perception and microgenesis. In W.D. Froelich, G. Smith, J. Draguns, & U. Hentschel (Eds.), *Psychological processes in cognition and personality*, pp. 225–230. Washington: Hemisphere Publishing Corporation.

Ellis, H.D., & Young, A.W. (1990). Accounting for delusional misidentifications. *British Journal of Psychiatry*, *157*, 239–248.

Emmerson, P.G. (1986). Effects of environmental context on recognition memory in an unusual environment. *Perceptual and Motor Skill*, *63*, 1047–1050.

Enoch, D.M. (1986). Whose double? The psychopathology of the delusional misidentification syndromes, especially the Capgras syndrome. *Biblioteca Psychiatrica*, *164*, 22–29.

Enoch, M.D., & Trethowan, W.H. (1979). *Uncommon Psychiatric Syndromes*. Bristol: Wright.

Feinberg, T.E., & Shapiro, R.M. (1989). Misidentification–Reduplication and the Right Hemisphere. *Neuropsychiatry, Neuropsychology and Behavioural Neurology*, *2*, 39–48.

Fisher, C.M. (1982). Disorientation for place. *Archives of Neurology*, *39*, 33–36.

Fisher, R.P., & Craik, F.I.M. (1977). Interaction between encoding and retrieval operations in cued recall. *Journal of Experimental Psychology: Human Learning and Memory*, *6*, 701–711.

Fleminger, S. (1992). Seeing and believing: The role of preconscious perceptual processing in delusional misidentification. *British Journal of Psychiatry*, *160*, 293–303.

Fleminger, S., & Burns, A. (1993). The delusional misidentification syndromes in patients with and without evidence of organic cerebral disorder: A structural review of case reports. *Biological Psychiatry*, *33*, 22–32.

Frith, C.D. (1987). The positive and negative symptoms of schizophrenia reflect impairments in the perception and initiation of action. *Psychological Medicine*, *17*, 631–648.

Frith, C.D., Stevens, M., Johnstone, E.C., Owens, D.G.C., & Crow, T.J. (1983). The integration of schematic faces and other complex objects in schizophrenia. *Journal of Nervous and Mental Diseases*, *171*, 34–39.

Gelder, M., Gath, D., & Mayou, R. (1983). *Oxford Textbook of Psychiatry*. Oxford: Oxford University Press.

Gregory, R.L. (1987a). Perception as hypotheses. In R.L. Gregory (Ed.). *The Oxford companion to the mind* (pp. 608–611). Oxford: Oxford University Press.

Gregory, R.L. (1987b). Illusions. In R.L. Gregory (Ed.), *The Oxford companion to the mind* (pp. 337–343). Oxford: Oxford University Press.

Gregory, R.L. (1987c). *The Oxford companion to the mind*. Oxford: Oxford University Press.

Griffith, J.H., Frith, C.D., & Eysenck, S.B.G. (1980). Psychoticism and thought disorder in psychiatric patients. *British Journal of Social and Clinical Psychology*, *19*, 65–71.

Groeger, J.A. (1984). Evidence of unconscious semantic processing from a forced error situation. *British Journal of Psychology*, *75*, 305–314.

Hakim, H., Verma, N.P., & Greiffenstein, M.F. (1988). Pathogenesis of reduplicative paramnesia. *Journal of Neurology, Neurosurgery and Psychiatry*, *51*, 839–841.

Haslam, M. (1973). A case of Capgras' syndrome. *American Journal of Psychiatry*, *130*, 493–494.

Hemsley, D.R., & Garety, P.A. (1986). The formation and maintenance of delusions: A Bayesian analysis. *British Journal of Psychiatry*, *149*, 51–56.

Hochberg, J.E. (1956). Perception: Toward the recovery of a definition. *Psychological Reviews*, *63*, 400–405.

Huq, S.F., Garety, P.A., & Hemsley, D.R. (1988). Probabilistic judgements in deluded and non-deluded subjects. *Quarterly Journal of Experimental Psychology*, *40A*, 801–812.

Jackson, C.V. (1953). Visual factors in auditory localisation. *Quarterly Journal of Experimental Psychology*, *5*, 52–65.

Johnson, M.K. (1988). Discriminating the origin of Information. In T.F. Oltmanns & B.A. Maher (Eds.), *Delusional beliefs*. New York: John Wiley & Sons.

Joseph, A.B. (1986). Focal CNS abnormalities in delusional misidentification syndromes. *Biblioteca Psychiatrica*, *164*, 68–79.

Kraepelin, E. (1921). *Manic depressive insanity and paranoia*. (R.M. Barclay (Trans.)). Edinburgh: E. & S. Livingstone.

Kraupl-Taylor, F. (1983). Descriptive and developmental phenomena. In M. Shepherd & O.L.Zangwill (Eds.), *Handbook of Psychiatry, vol. 1, general psychopathology* (pp. 59–94). Cambridge: Cambridge University Press.

Kumar, V. (1987). Capgras' syndrome in a patient with dementia. *British Journal of Psychiatry*, *150*, 251.

Lansky, M.R. (1986). Capgras syndrome and the significance of delusions. *Biblioteca Psychiatrica*, *164*, 49–58.

Lewis, S.W. (1987). Brain imaging in a case of Capgras' syndrome. *British Journal of Psychiatry*, *150*, 117–120.

Lipkin, B. (1988). Capgras' syndrome heralding the development of dementia. *British Journal of Psychiatry*, *153*, 117–118.

Lishman, W.A. (1972). Selective factors in memory. Part 2: Affective disorder. *Psychological Medicine*, *2*, 248–253.

Lishman, W.A. (1987). *Organic psychiatry: The psychological consequences of cerebral disorder* (2nd ed.). Oxford: Blackwell Scientific.

Maher, B.A. (1974). Delusional thinking and perceptual disorder. *Journal of Individual Psychology*, *30*, 98–113.

Maher, B.A. (1988). Anomalous experience and delusional thinking: The logic of explanations. In T.F. Oltmanns & B.A. Maher (Eds.), *Delusional Beliefs*. New York: John Wiley & Sons.

Marcel, A.J. (1983). Conscious and unconscious perception: An approach to the relations between phenomenal experience and perceptual processes. *Cognitive Psychology*, *15*, 238–300.

McCormick, D.J., & Broekema, V.J. (1978). Size estimation, perceptual recognition and cardiac rate response in acute paranoid and non-paranoid schizophrenics. *Journal of Abnormal Psychology*, *87*, 385–398.

McGinnies, E. (1949). Emotionality and perceptual defense. *Psychological Review*, *56*, 244–251.

McLaughlin, J.A., & Sims, A. (1984). Co-existence of the Capgras' and Ekbom syndromes. *British Journal of Psychiatry*, *145*, 439–444.

McReynolds, P., Collins, B., & Acker, M. (1964). Delusional thinking and cognitive organisation in schizophrenia. *Journal of Abnormal and Social Psychology*, *69*, 210–212.

Merrin, E.L., & Silberfarb, P.M. (1976). The Capgras' phenomenon. *Archives of General Psychiatry*, *33*, 965–968.

Mintz, S., & Albert, M. (1972). Imagery vividness, reality-testing and schizophrenic hallucinations. *Journal of Abnormal Psychology*, *79*, 310–316.

Morrison, R., & Tarter, R.E. (1984). Neuropsychological findings related to Capgras' syndrome. *Biological Psychiatry*, *19*, 1119–1128.

Mullan, S., & Penfield, W. (1959). Illusions of comparative interpretation and emotion. *Archives of Neurology and Psychiatry*, *81*, 269–284.

O'Reilly, R., & Malhotra, L. (1987). Capgras' syndrome—an unusual case and discussion of psychodynamic factors. *British Journal of Psychiatry, 151,* 263–265.

Salthouse, T.A. (1988). Effects of aging on perceptual closure. *American Journal of Psychology, 101,* 217–238.

Seaman, J.G., Brody, N., & Kauff, D.M. (1983). Affective discrimination of stimuli that are not recognised: Effects of shadowing, masking, and cerebral laterality. *Journal of Experimental Psychology: Learning Memory and Cognition, 9,* 544–555.

Signer, S.F., & Ibister, S.R. (1987). Capgras' syndrome, de Clerambault's syndrome and folie a deux. *British Journal of Psychiatry, 151,* 402–404.

Sims, A.C.P., & White, A.C. (1973). Co-existence of the Capgras' and de Clerambault's syndrome—a case history. *British Journal of Psychiatry, 123,* 635–638.

Smock, C. (1955). The influence of stress on the perception of incongruity. *Journal of Abnormal and Social Psychology, 50,* 354–356.

Staton, R.D., Brumback, R.A., & Wilson, H. (1982). Reduplicative Paramnesia: A disconnection syndrome of memory. *Cortex, 18,* 23–36.

Stern, K., & MacNaughton, D. (1945). Capgras' syndrome, a peculiar illusory phenomena, considered with special reference to the Rorschach findings. *Psychiatric Quarterly, 19,* 139–163.

Stuss, D.T., Alexander, M.P., Lieberman, A., & Levine, H. (1978). An extraordinary form of confabulation. *Neurology, 28,* 1166–1172.

Tarrier, N., Beckett, R., Harwood, S., & Bishay, N. (1990). Morbid jealousy: A review and cognitive-behavioural formulation. *British Journal of Psychiatry, 157,* 319–326.

Thompson, M.I., Silk, K.R., & Hover, G.L. (1980). Misidentification of a city: Delimiting criteria for Capgras' syndrome. *American Journal of Psychiatry, 137,* 1270–1272.

Todd, J., Dewhurst, K., & Wallis, G. (1981). The syndrome of Capgras. *British Journal of Psychiatry, 139,* 319–327.

Tyrer, P., Lewis, P., & Lee, I. (1978). Effects of subliminal and supraliminal stress on symptoms of anxiety. *Journal of Nervous and Mental Disease, 166,* 88–93.

Wallis, G. (1986). Nature of the misidentified in the Capgras syndrome. *Biblioteca Psychiatrica, 164,* 40–48.

Wilcox, J.A. (1986). The anatomical basis of misidentification. *Biblioteca Psychiatrica, 164,* 59–67.

Wittreich, W.J. (1952). The Honi phenomenon: A case of selective personal distortion. *Journal of Abnormal and Social Psychology, 47,* 705–712.

Woodworth, R.S. (1947). Re-enforcement of perception. *American Journal of Psychology, 66,* 119–124.

Zajonc, R.B. (1980). Feeling and thinking: preferences need no inferences. *American Psychologist, 35,* 151–175.

Author Index

Subject Index

Caudate nucleus, 43, 46, 157
Causal relationship (delusional),
110–11
Central executive (working
memory), 198, 199–200, 201
Cerebral blood flow
PET studies, 15–19, 21, 29, 31, 287–8
volition and, 41–2, 43–5, 46–7
Cerebral disease/disorder, 370–1, 373
Cerebro-spinal fluid (CSF), 184
Children
CPT deficits, 63–5
intelligence, 137–40
precursors of schizophrenia, 119–28
theory of mind in, 148, 149
Choice reaction time paradigm, 107–8
Clifton Assessment Procedures for the
Elderly, 183–4, 189, 191, 194
Clinical neuropsychology
cognitive functioning, 215–24
cognitive impairment, 181–94
right hemisphere dysfunction,
231–41
working memory and cognitive
impairment, 198–209
CNS abnormalities, 120, 121, 127–8
Cognition and metacognition
semantic memory, 163–77
theory of mind, 147–59
Cognitive abnormalities
experimental studies, 102–8
information processing
disturbances, 108–12
introduction, 97–102
potential links with biological
models, 112–13
Cognitive accounts (of
hallucinations), 250–1
Cognitive biases, 337–57
Cognitive defects as working memory
deficits, 204–7
Cognitive deterioration, 190
Cognitive functioning and
symptomatology (frontal-subcortical
systems), 215–24
Cognitive impairment, 100, 108–9, 112
working memory and, 197–209

Cognitive impairment scale, 184,
190–1
Cognitive impairment of severe
psychiatric illness (clinical study)
discussion, 191–4
introduction, 181–2
method, 182–4
results, 185–91
Cognitive loop, 21–2
Cognitive model of working
memory, 198–201
Cognitive neuropsychiatric approach
(Capgras delusion), 326–32
Cognitive neuropsychological models
(of psychopathology), 296–301
Cognitive psychology, 246–7
Cognitive reasoning, 367–8
Cognitive theory of
hallucinations, 246–50
Colour-naming task, 345, 346
Commissurotomy, 278
Computer games, 349–50
Computer programs for speech
perception, 258–9
Computerised brain tomography, 184
Conduction aphasia, 283
Confabulation, 370
Conscious acceptance
(perceptions), 365–7
Consciousness, disorder of (theory of
mind), 155–6
"Contact control" condition, 252
Content analysis (psycholinguistic
study), 263–4
Continuous performance tests, 205,
208
anomalies, 58–63
deficits (among children), 63–5
degraded-stimulus CPT, 70–4
PET studies of performance, 65–70
vigilance and, 53, 57–8, 208
"Corollary discharge", 295
Corpus callosum (size), 278, 292
Corsi Block Tapping Test, 223
Cortical activity (CPT
performance), 65–70
"cortical sparing", 193

THE NEUROPSYCHOLOGY OF DEGENERATIVE BRAIN DISEASES

ROBERT G. KNIGHT (University of Otago)

This volume utilizes the various neurological diseases as its organizing principle, focusing specifically on their personal, social, and cognitive consequences. The book is designed to provide neuropsychologists, clinical psychologists, and those in related disciplines with an accessible survey of the available research on the psychological functioning of patients with various disorders. Each chapter consists of a background review of the major features of one of the diseases including: symptom pattern, neuroanatomical bases, neuropathology, genetic factors, and epidemiology. Finally, the psychological and cognitive deficits established by research are reviewed, and their practical implications discussed.

> *"I would recommend this book to interested clinicians, and particularly students coming to the area for the first time."* **Tony Ward** *in Neuropsychological Rehabilitation.*

Contents: Preface. Part I: *Assessment*. Dementia Scales. Neuropsychological Assessment. Part II: *Neuropsychological Research*. Korsakoff's Disease. Alzheimer's Disease. Multiple Sclerosis. Parkinson's Disease. Huntington's Disease. Progressive Supranuclear Palsy, Subcortical Dementia, and Other Degenerative Diseases. Part III: *Psychological Aspects*. Caregiver Burden. Conclusions: A Neuropsychosocial Model.

ISBN 0-8058-0927-9 1992 360pp. $71.95 £39.95 hbk

PUBLISHED BY LAWRENCE ERLBAUM ASSOCIATES INC.

European Orders:
LEA Ltd., 27 Church Road, Hove, East Sussex, BN3 2FA, UK
Orders from the USA & Canada:
LEA Inc., 365 Broadway, Hillsdale, NJ07642, USA

THE COGNITIVE NEUROPSYCHOLOGY OF SCHIZOPHRENIA

CHRISTOPHER DONALD FRITH (University College London & MRC Cyclotron Unit, Hammersmith Hospital)

Schizophrenic patients have bizarre experiences which reflect a disorder in the contents of consciousness. For example, patients hear voices talking about them or they are convinced that alien forces are controlling their actions. Their abnormal behaviour includes incoherence and lack of will. In this book an explanation of these baffling signs and symptoms is provided using the framework of cognitive neuropsychology.

The cognitive abnormalities that underlie these signs and symptoms suggest impairment in a system which constructs and monitors representations of certain abstract (especially mental) events in consciousness. For example, schizophrenic patients can no longer construct representations of their intentions to act. Thus, if actions occur, these will be experienced as coming out of the blue and hence can seem alien. The patient who lacks awareness of his own intentions will stop acting spontaneously and hence will show a lack of will.

The psychological processes that are abnormal in schizophrenia can be related to underlying brain systems using evidence from human and animal neuropsychology. Interactions between prefrontal cortex and other parts of the brain, especially temporal cortex appear critical for constructing the contents of consciousness. It is these interactions that are likely to be impaired in schizophrenia.

Contents: The Nature of Schizophrenia. Brain Abnormalities in Schizophrenia. Linking the Mind and the Brain. Abnormalities of Behaviour (Negative Signs). Abnormalities of Experience (Positive Symptoms). Language and Speech in Schizophrenia. Psychosis, Meta-Representation and the brain.

ISBN 0-86377-224-2 184pp. $28.50 £14.95 hbk Essays in Cognitive Psychology Series

PUBLISHED BY LAWRENCE ERLBAUM ASSOCIATES LTD
European Orders:
LEA Ltd., 27 Church Road, Hove, East Sussex BN3 2FA
Orders from the USA & Canada:
LEA Inc., 365 Broadway, Hillsdale, NJ07642, USA